IMMORTAL RAIN

VOLUME 7

BY
KAORI OZAKI

HAMBURG // LONDON // LOS ANGELES // TOKYO

Immortal Rain Vol. 7
Created by Kaori Ozaki

Translation - Bret Mayer
English Adaptation - Sam Stormcrow Hayes
Copy Editor - Sarah Morgan
Retouch and Lettering - ANDWORLD DESIGN
Production Artist - Lucas Rivera and Corey Whitfield
Cover Design - Christopher Tjalsma

Editor - Bryce P. Coleman
Digital Imaging Manager - Chris Buford
Pre-Production Supervisor - Erika Terriquez
Production Manager - Elisabeth Brizzi
Art Director - Anne Marie Horne
Managing Editor - Vy Nguyen
VP of Production - Ron Klamert
Editor-in-Chief - Rob Tokar
Publisher - Mike Kiley
President and C.O.O. - John Parker
C.E.O. and Chief Creative Officer - Stuart Levy

A **TOKYOPOP** Manga

TOKYOPOP Inc.
5900 Wilshire Blvd. Suite 2000
Los Angeles, CA 90036

E-mail: info@TOKYOPOP.com
Come visit us online at www.TOKYOPOP.com

ISBN: 1-59816-798-7

First TOKYOPOP printing: November 2006
10 9 8 7 6 5 4 3 2 1
Printed in the USA

OUR STORY SO FAR...

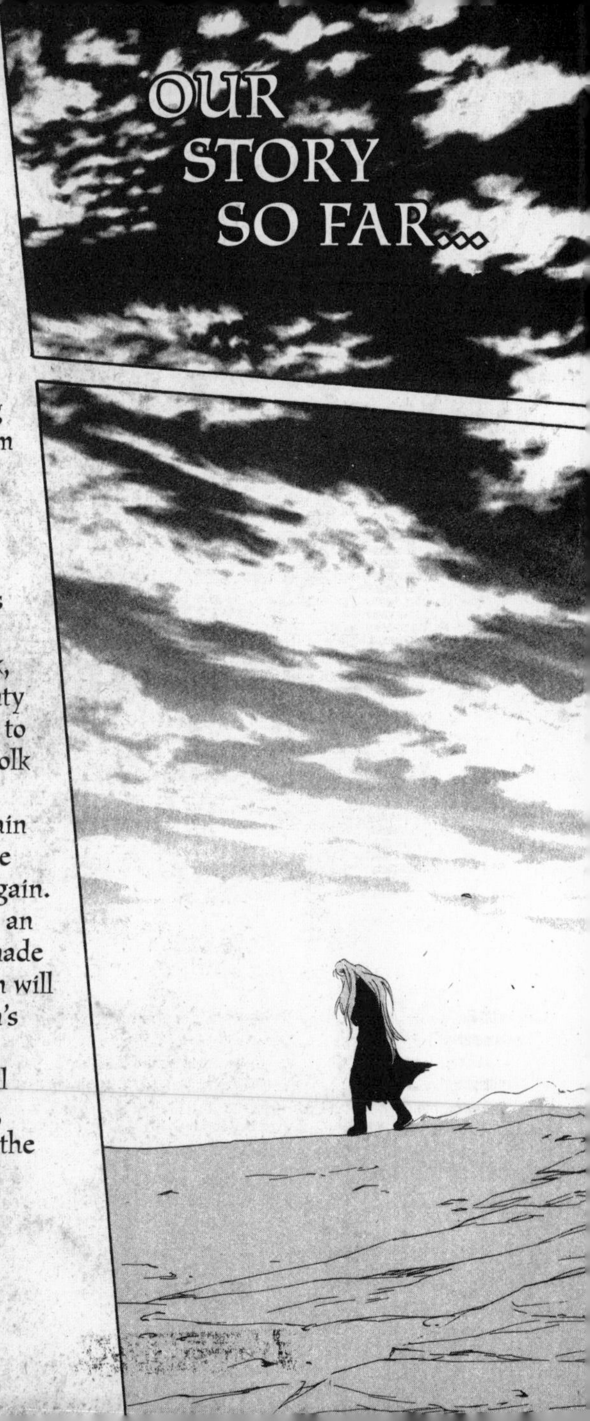

After a daring escape from the Calvaria headquarters, Rain and Machika once again find themselves separated. Having thrown himself from the tower, Rain makes a painful recovery at Eury Evan's hideout. Soon the pair finds themselves on the run from Dora Folk, the enigmatic bounty hunter hired by Ys to track Rain down. Folk nearly succeeds in killing Eury, but Rain rescues him and the pair escape once again. Then, inexplicably, an announcement is made on television—Rain will appear at the Siren's Castle amusement park and take on all comers. Desperate, Machika rushes to the park just in time to see Rain appear...

IMMORTAL RAIN

CONTENTS

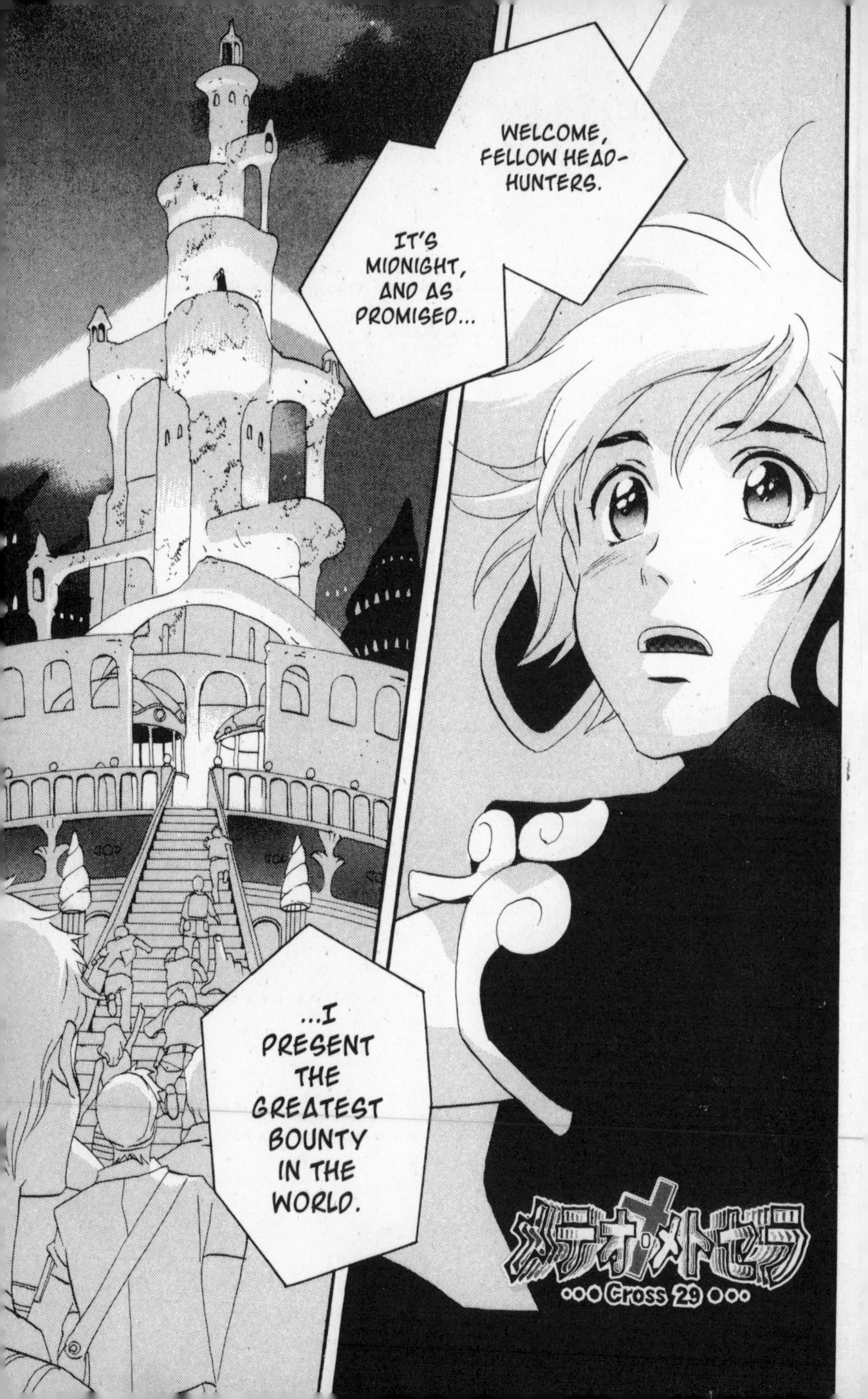
WELCOME, FELLOW HEAD-HUNTERS.
IT'S MIDNIGHT, AND AS PROMISED...
...I PRESENT THE GREATEST BOUNTY IN THE WORLD.
Cross 29

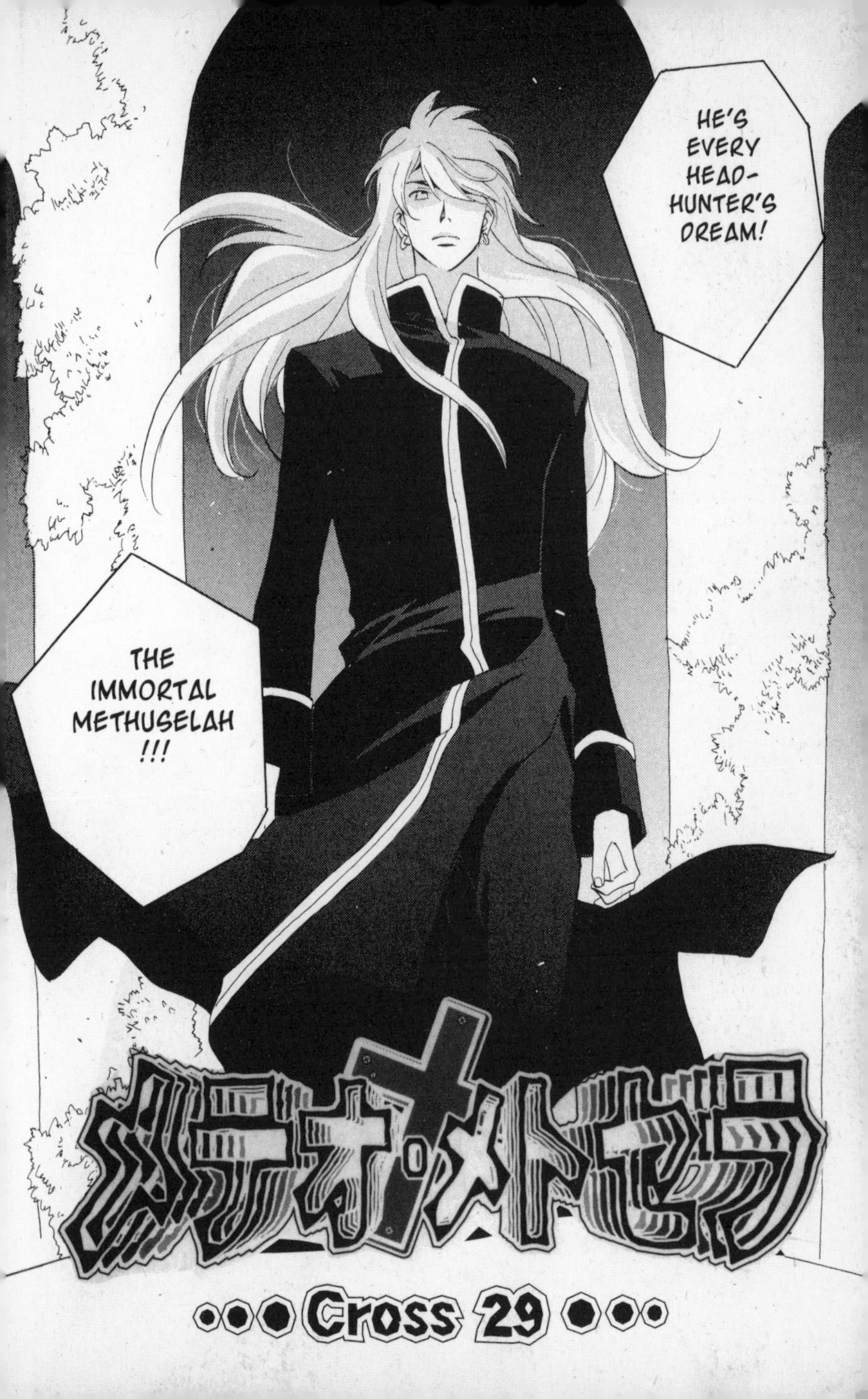
HE'S EVERY HEAD-HUNTER'S DREAM!
THE IMMORTAL METHUSELAH !!!
Cross 29

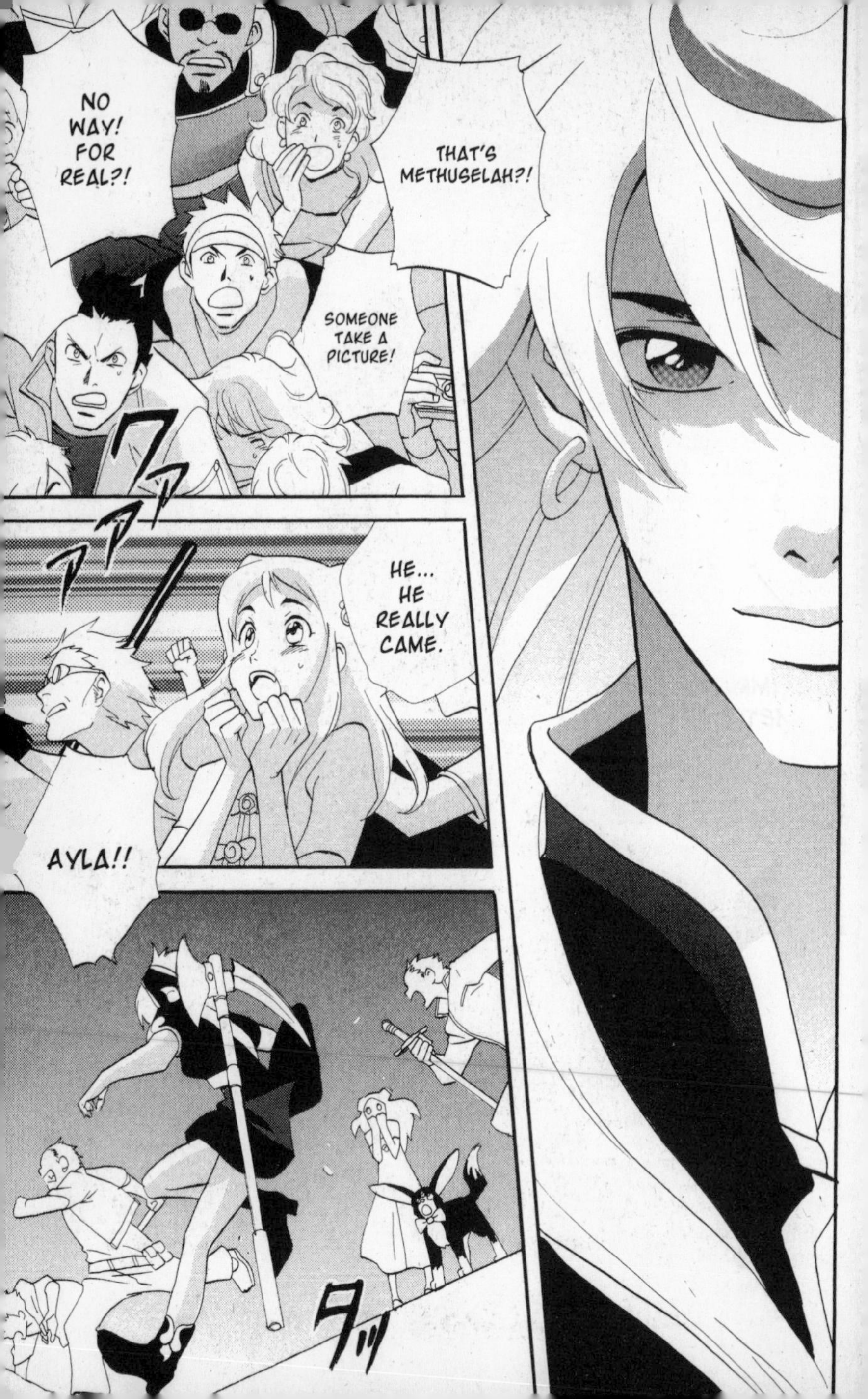
THAT'S METHUSELAH?!
NO WAY! FOR REAL?!
SOMEONE TAKE A PICTURE!
HE... HE REALLY CAME.
AYLA!!

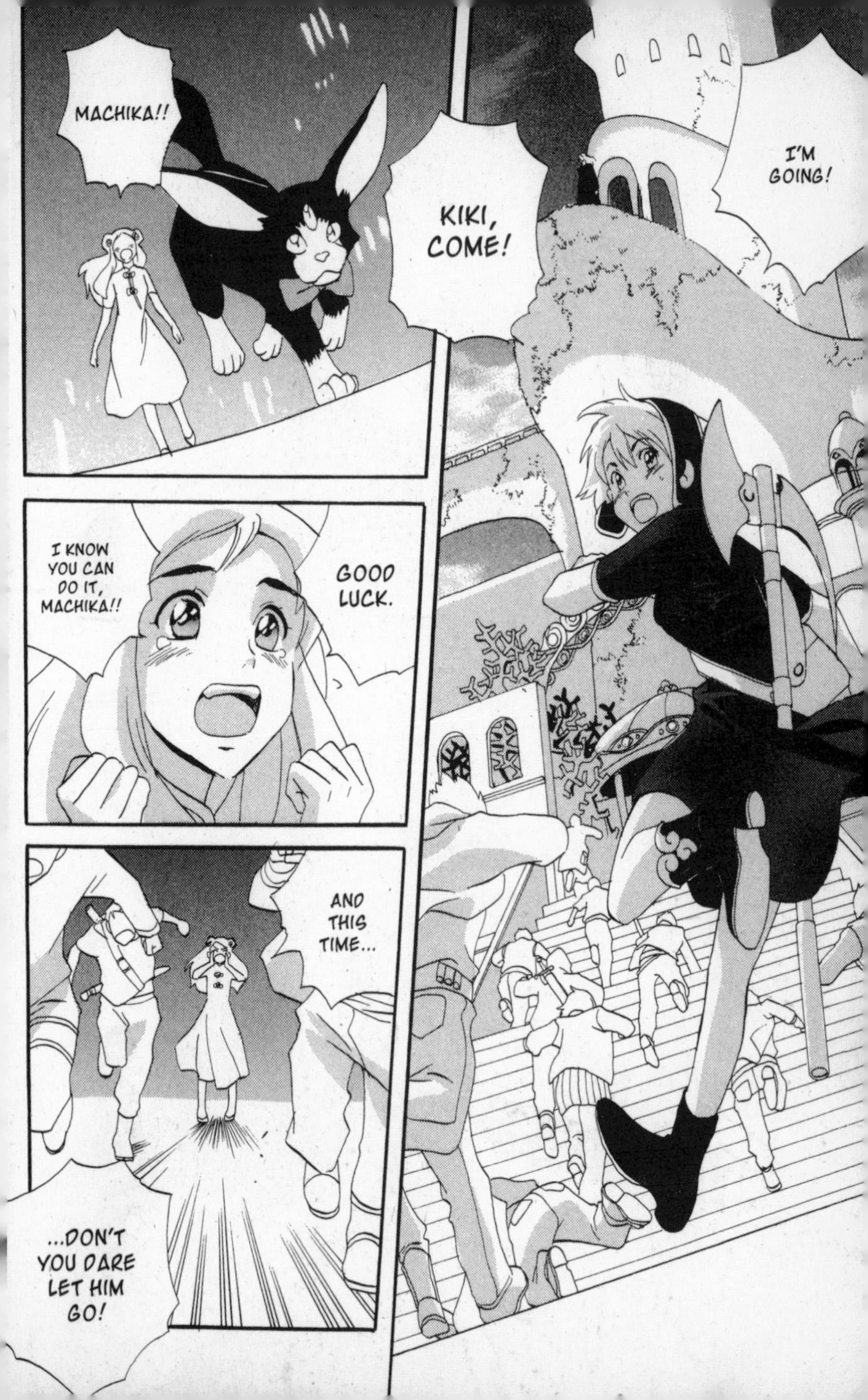
I'M GOING!
KIKI, COME!
MACHIKA!!
GOOD LUCK.
I KNOW YOU CAN DO IT, MACHIKA!!
AND THIS TIME...
...DON'T YOU DARE LET HIM GO!

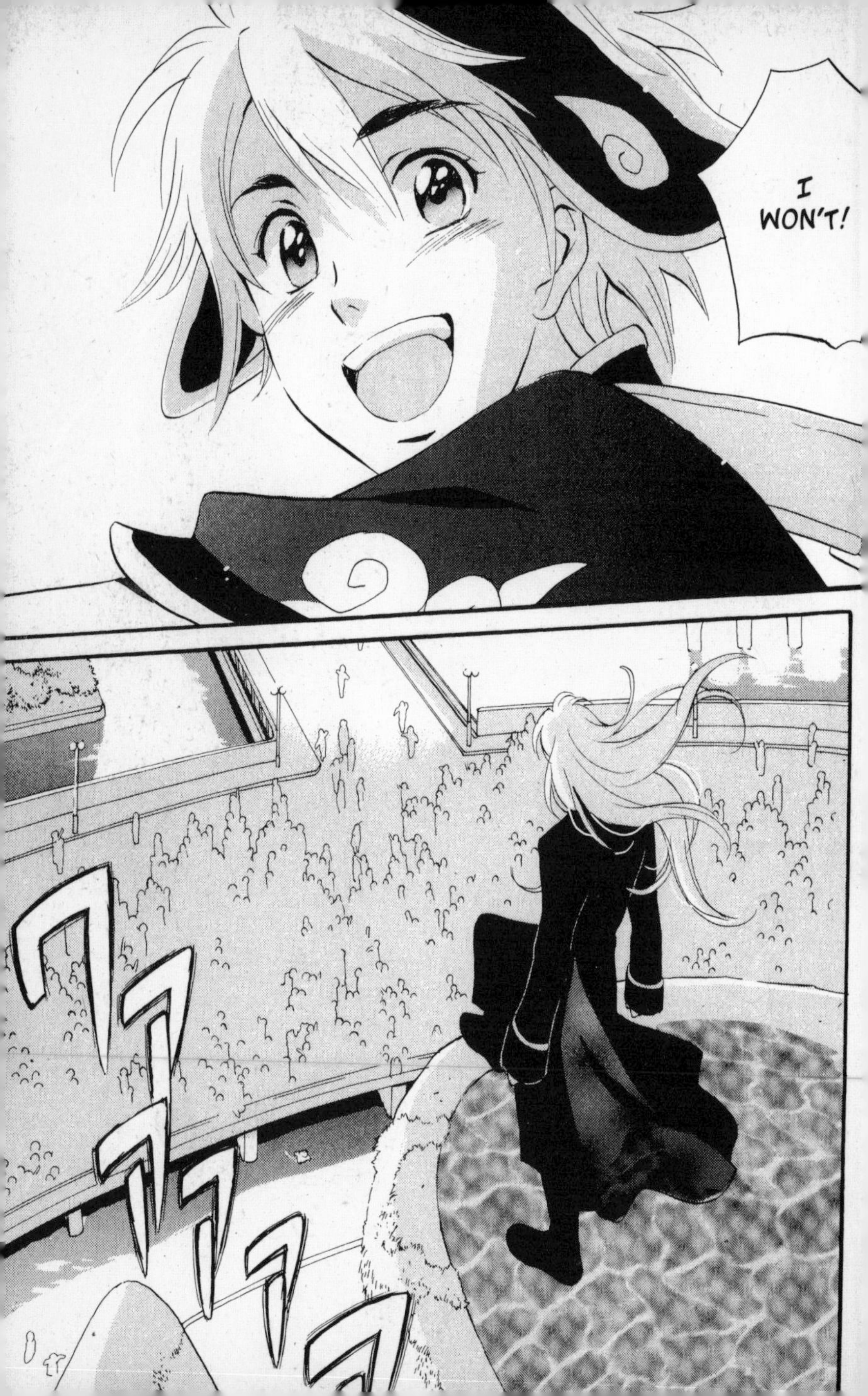
I WON'T!

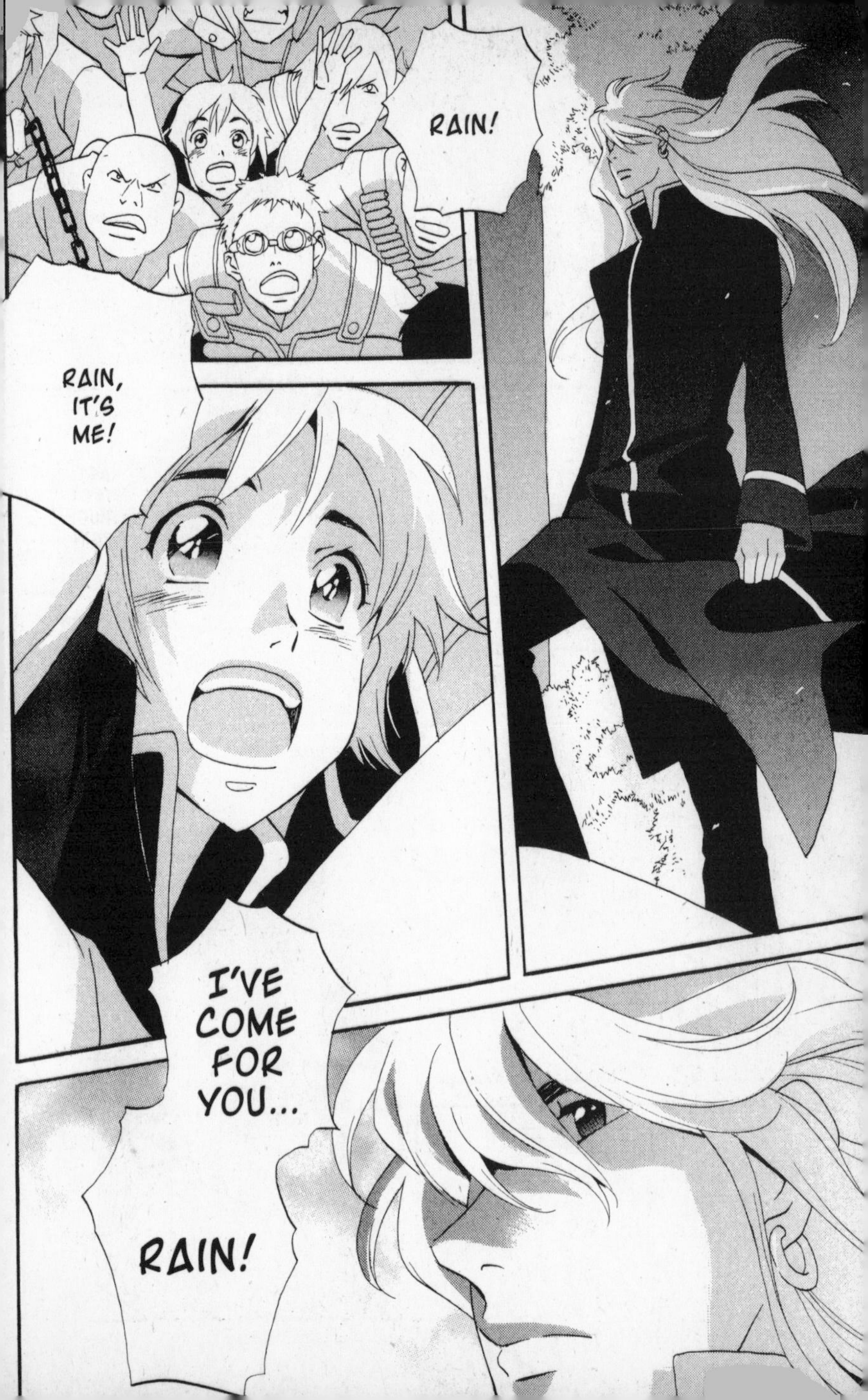
RAIN!
RAIN, IT'S ME!
I'VE COME FOR YOU...
RAIN!

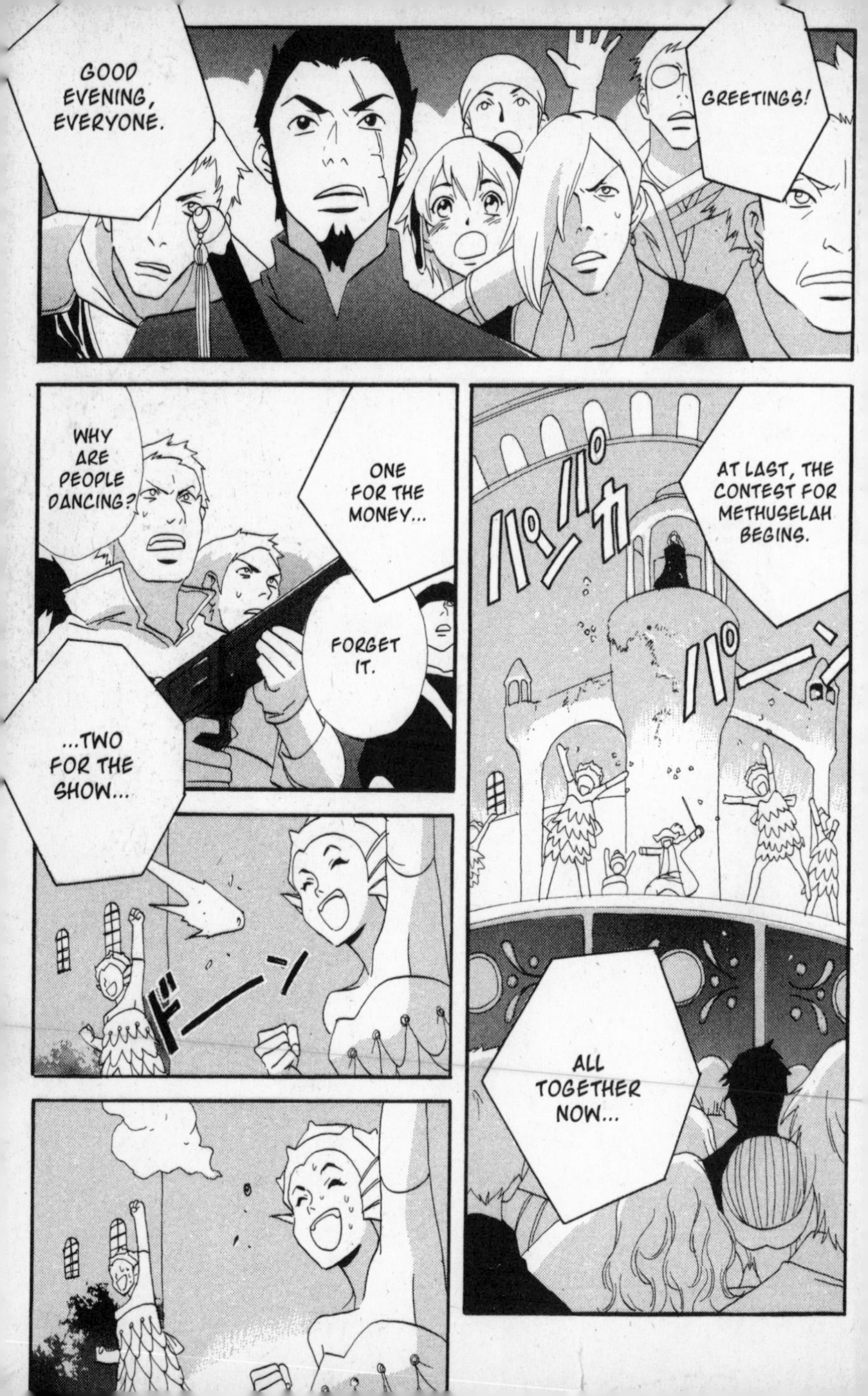
GREETINGS!
GOOD EVENING, EVERYONE.
AT LAST, THE CONTEST FOR METHUSELAH BEGINS.
パンパカ
パーン
ALL TOGETHER NOW...
ONE FOR THE MONEY...
WHY ARE PEOPLE DANCING?
FORGET IT.
...TWO FOR THE SHOW...
ドーン

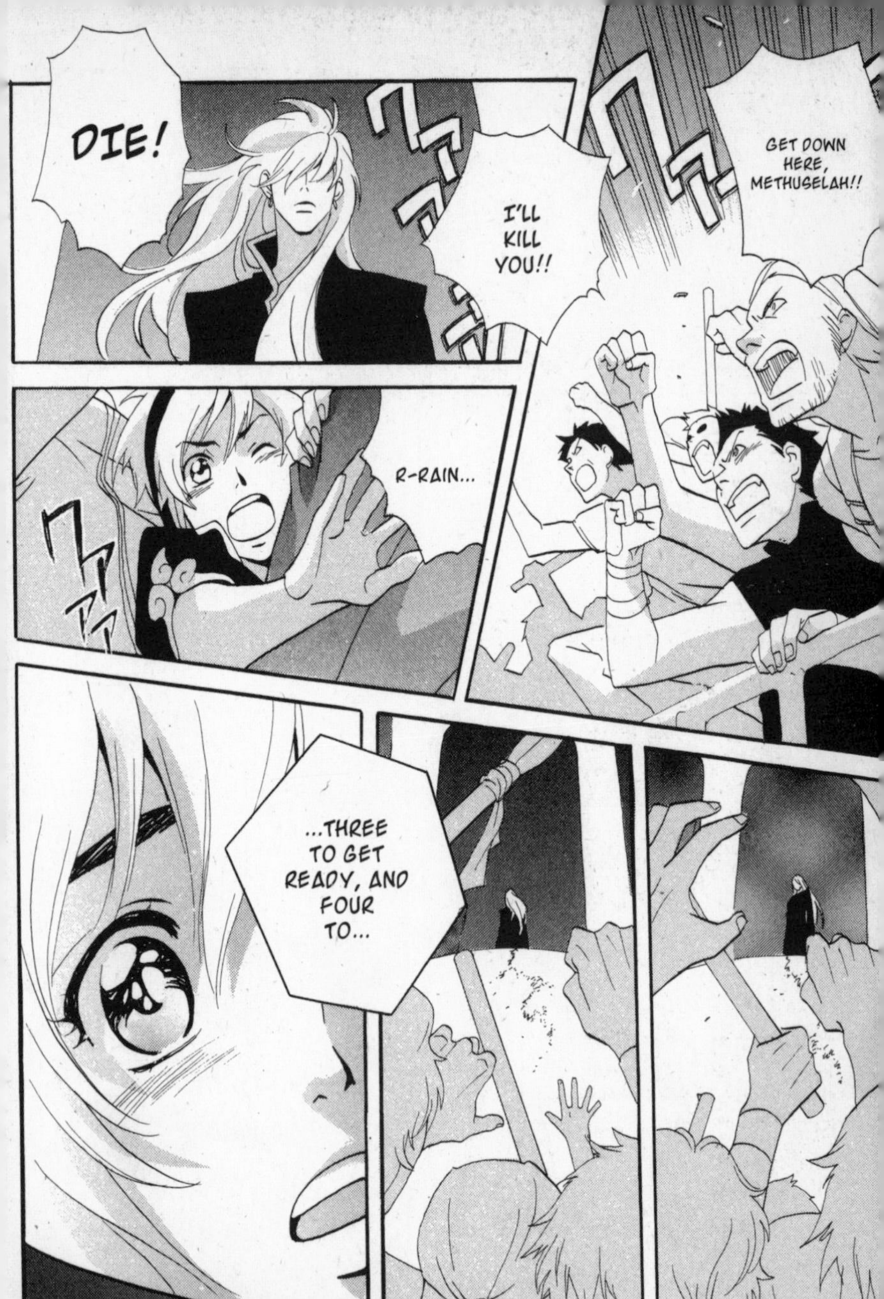
GET DOWN HERE, METHUSELAH!!
I'LL KILL YOU!!
DIE!
R-RAIN...
...THREE TO GET READY, AND FOUR TO...

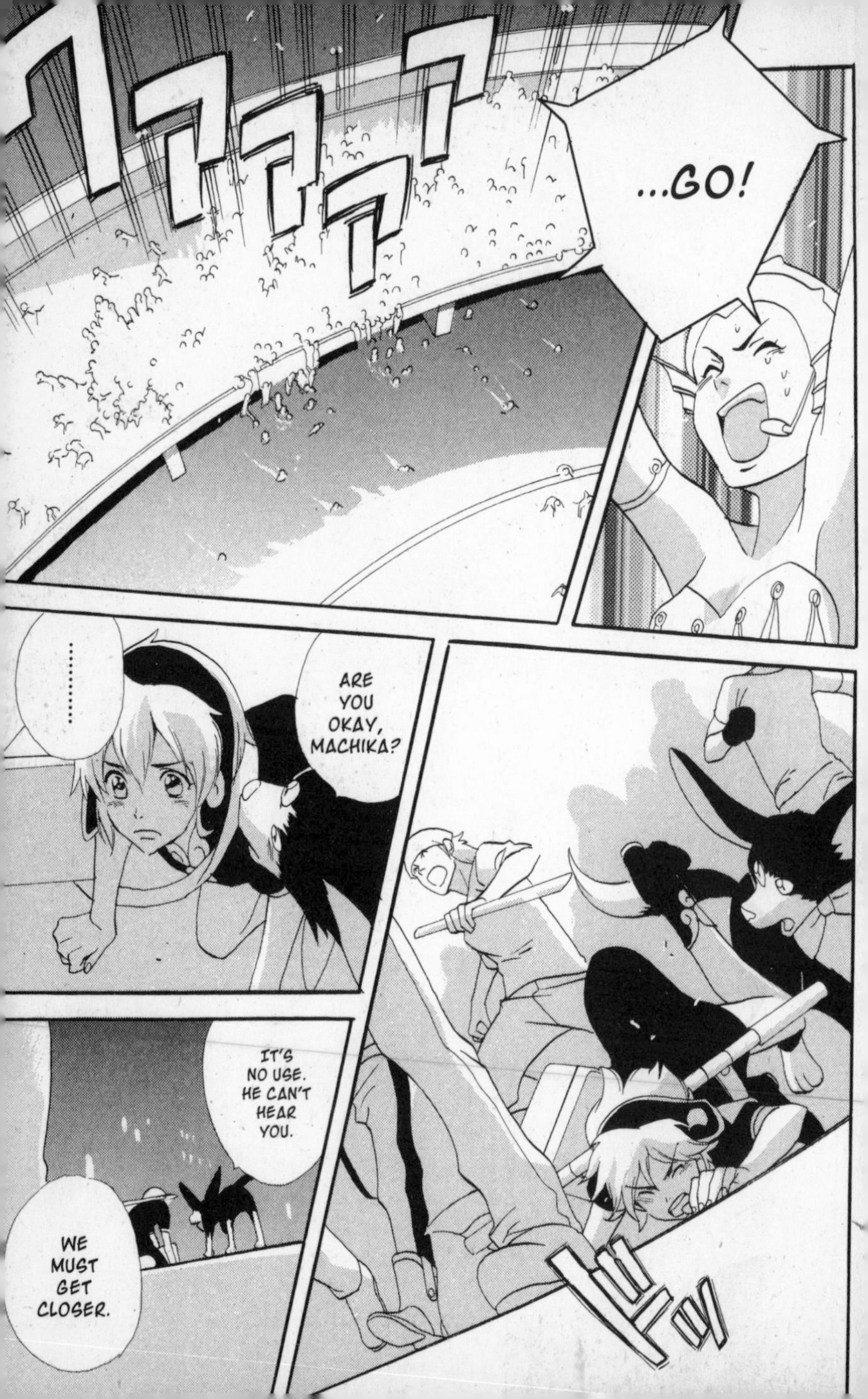
...GO!
ARE YOU OKAY, MACHIKA?
......
IT'S NO USE. HE CAN'T HEAR YOU.
WE MUST GET CLOSER.

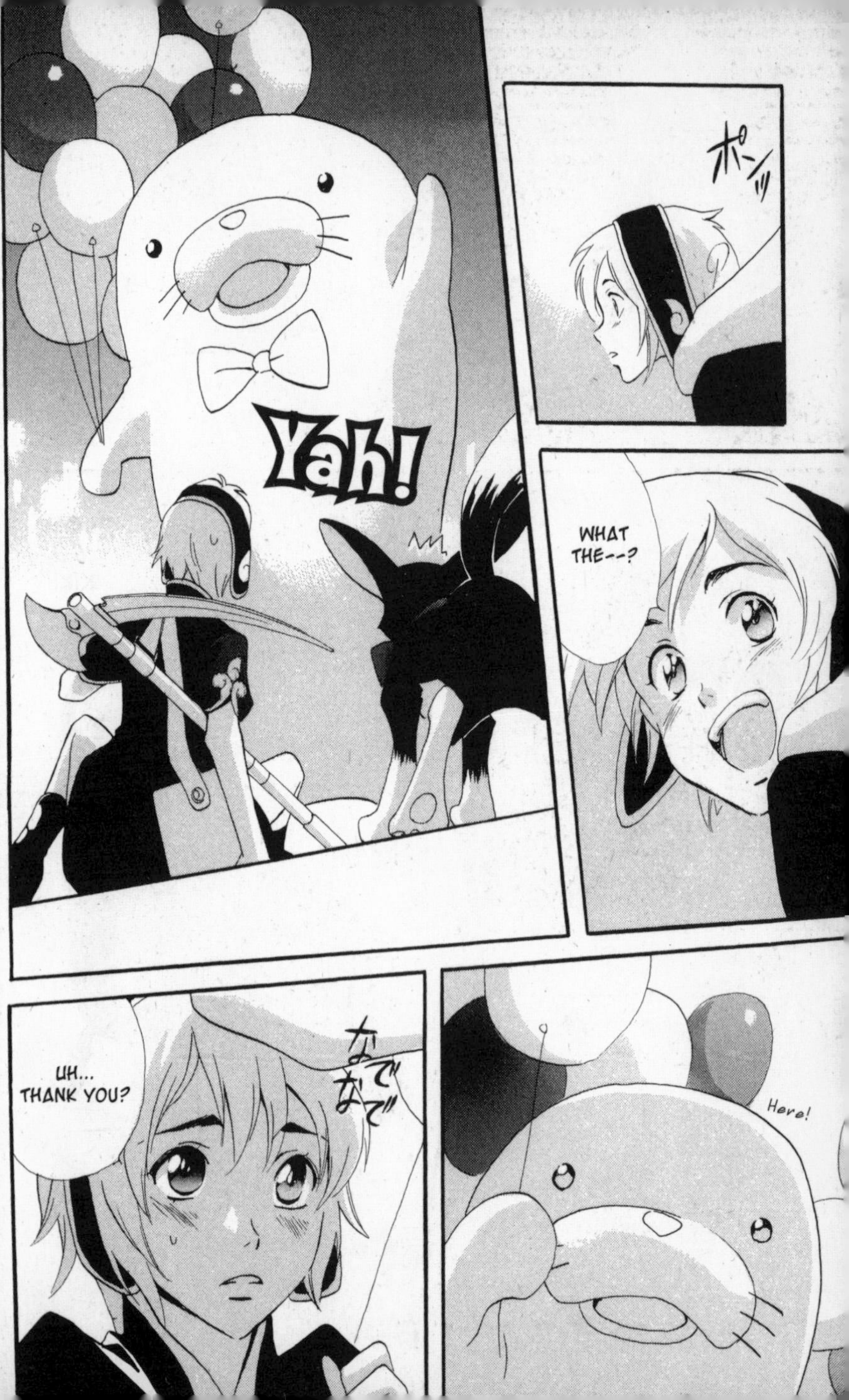
ポーンッ
WHAT THE--?
Yah!
Here!
UH... THANK YOU?
なでなで

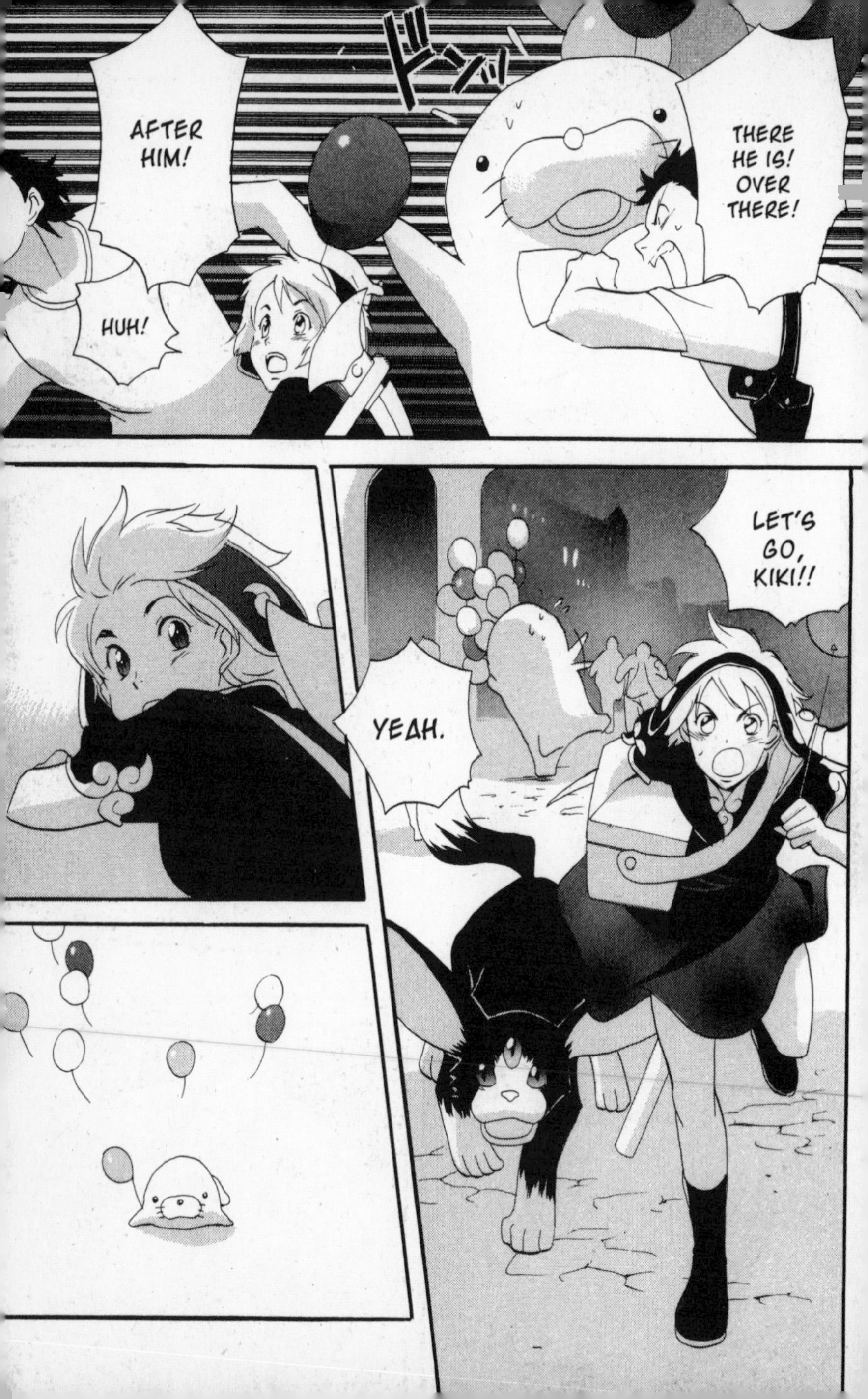
THERE HE IS! OVER THERE!
ドンッ
AFTER HIM!
HUH!
LET'S GO, KIKI!!
YEAH.

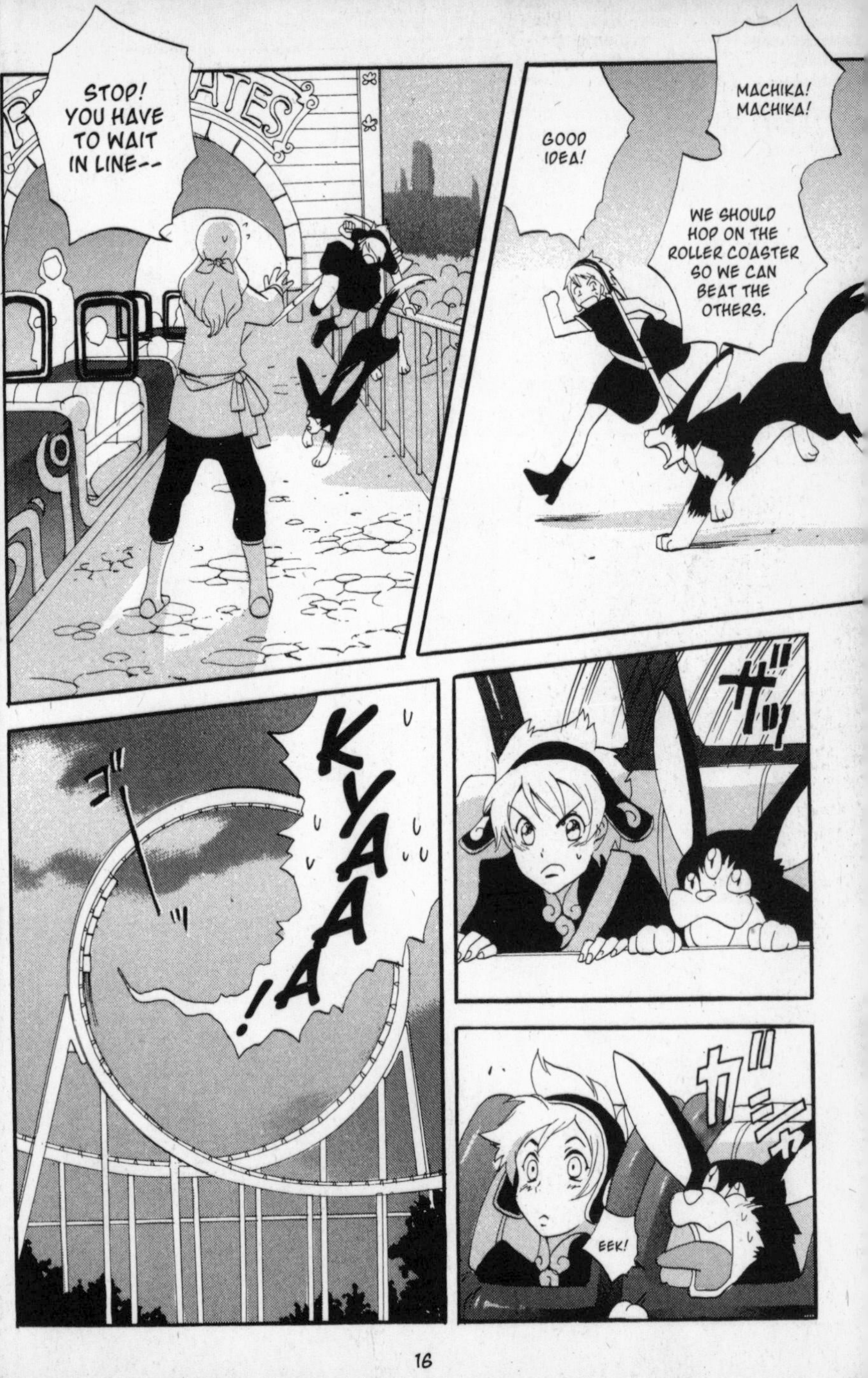
MACHIKA! MACHIKA!
WE SHOULD HOP ON THE ROLLER COASTER SO WE CAN BEAT THE OTHERS.
GOOD IDEA!
STOP! YOU HAVE TO WAIT IN LINE--
ザッ
ガシャ
EEK!
KYAAAA!
ゴーッ

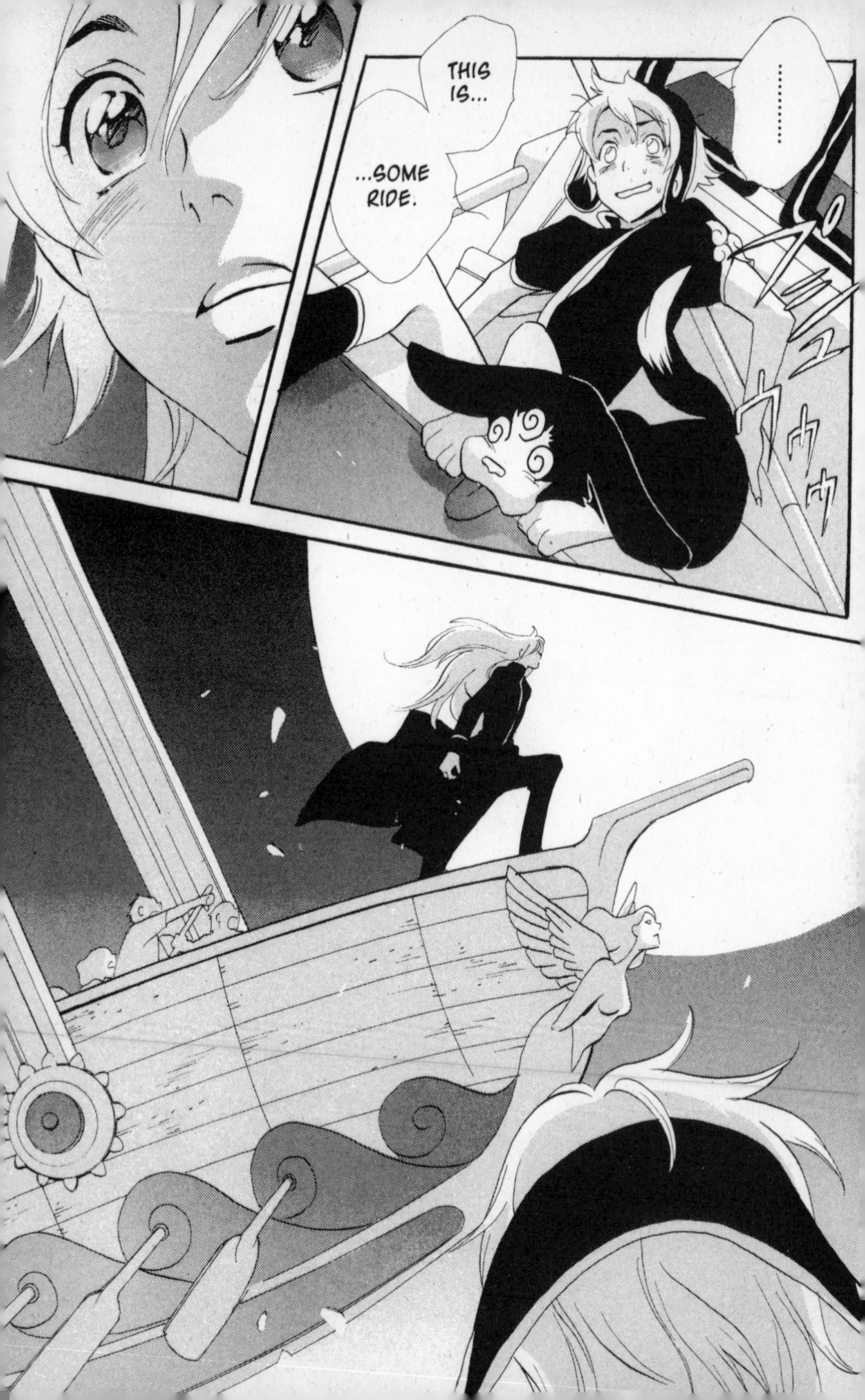
......
THIS IS...
...SOME RIDE.

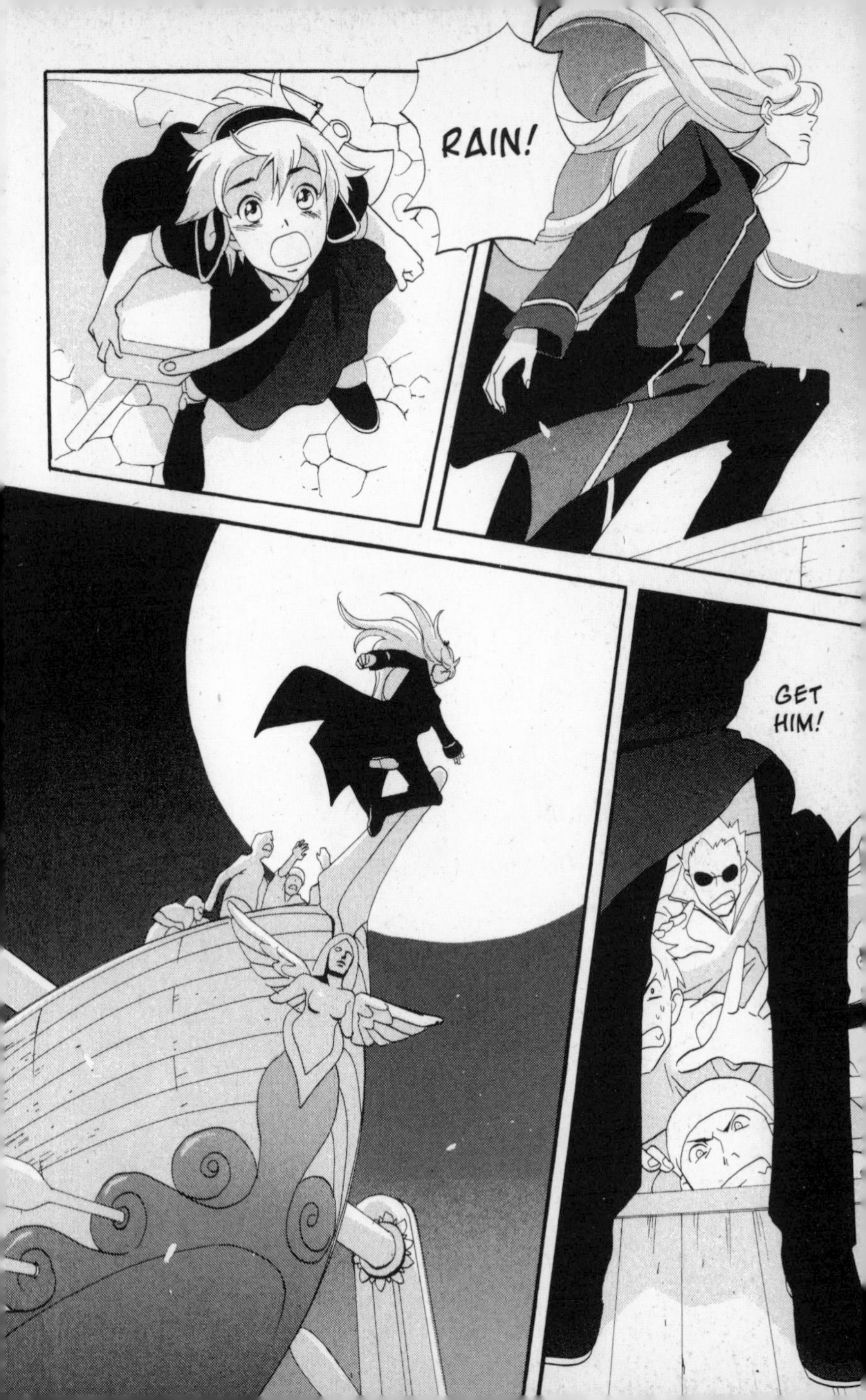
RAIN!
GET HIM!

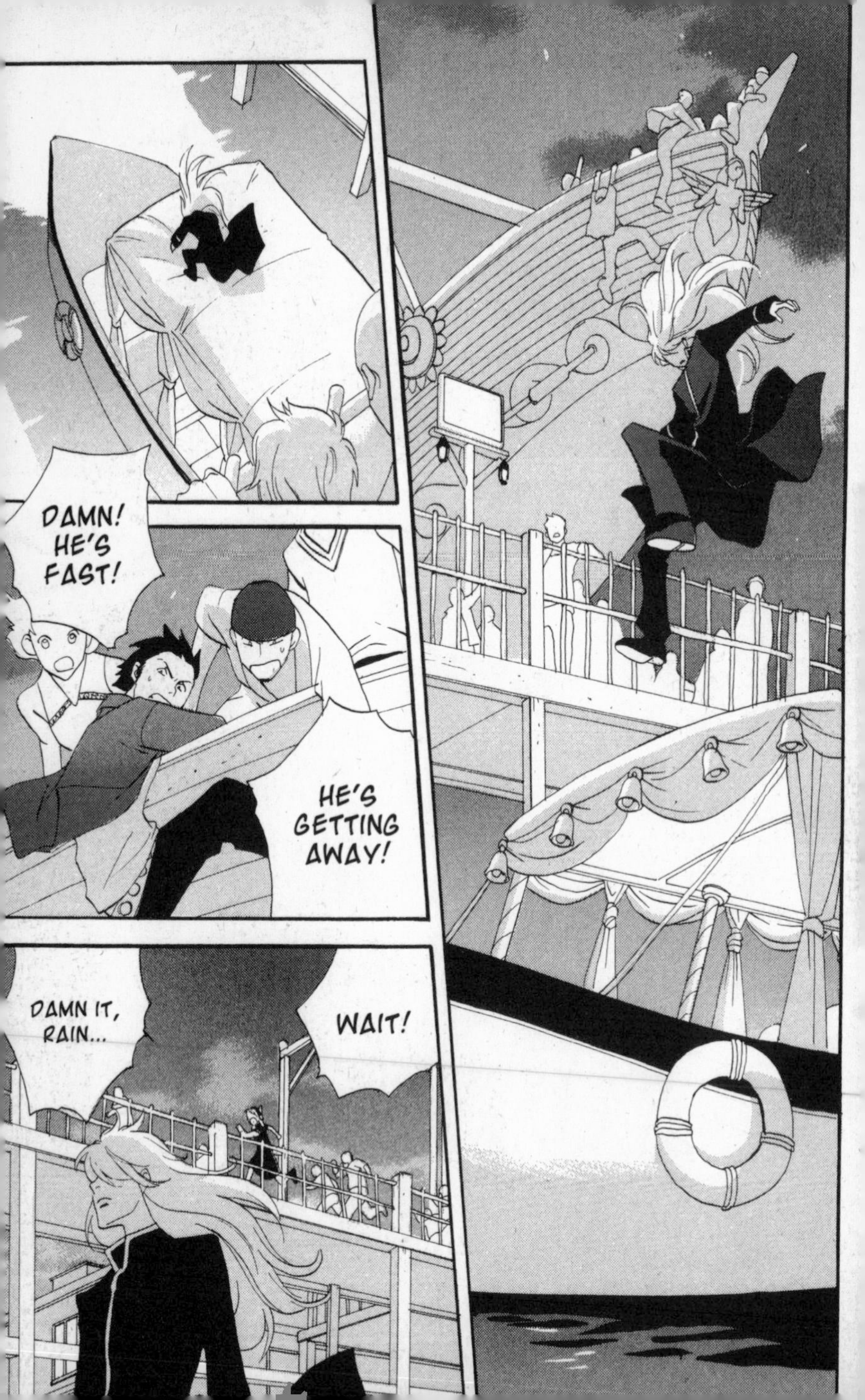
DAMN! HE'S FAST!
HE'S GETTING AWAY!
WAIT!
DAMN IT, RAIN...

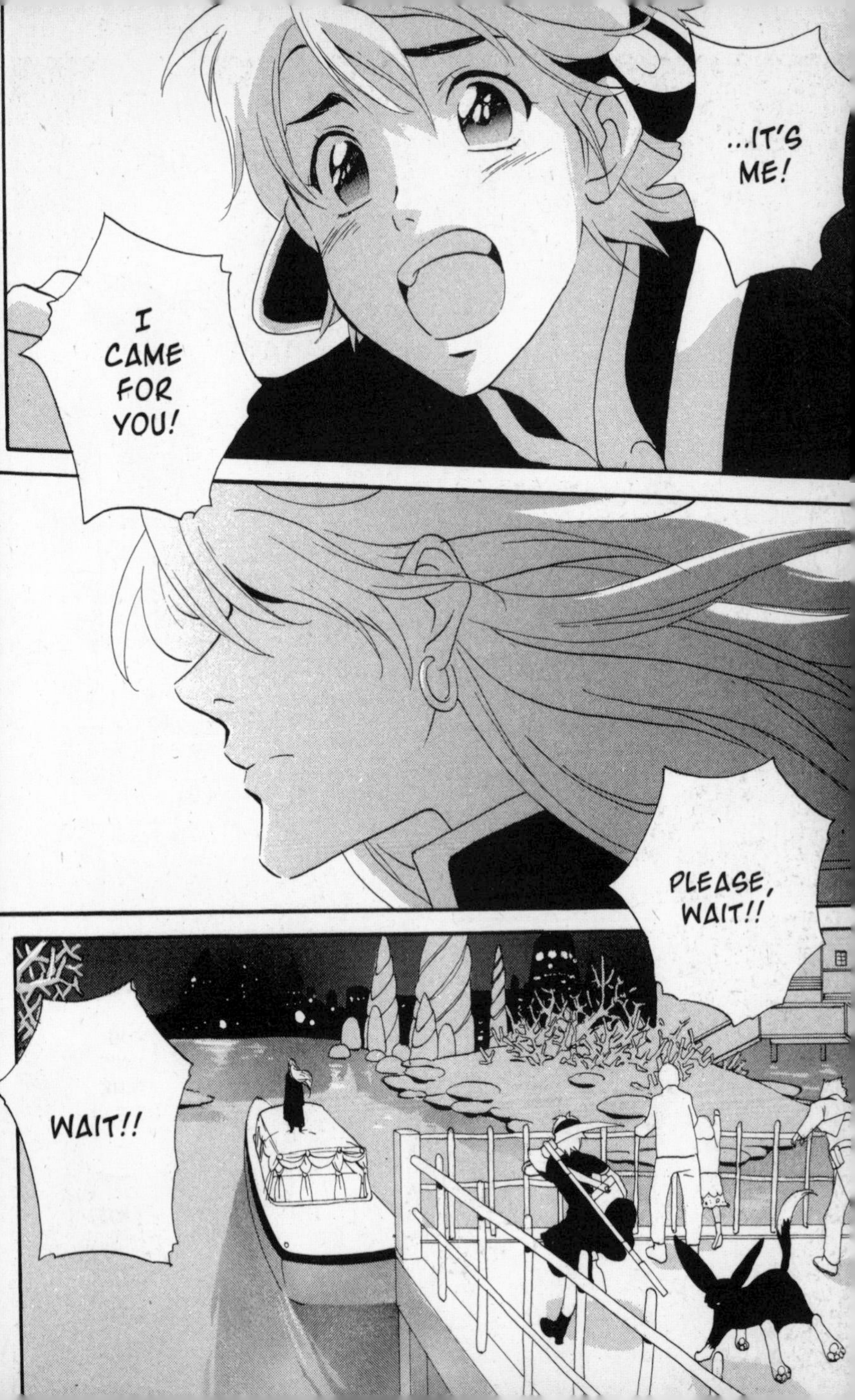
...IT'S ME!
I CAME FOR YOU!
PLEASE, WAIT!!
WAIT!!

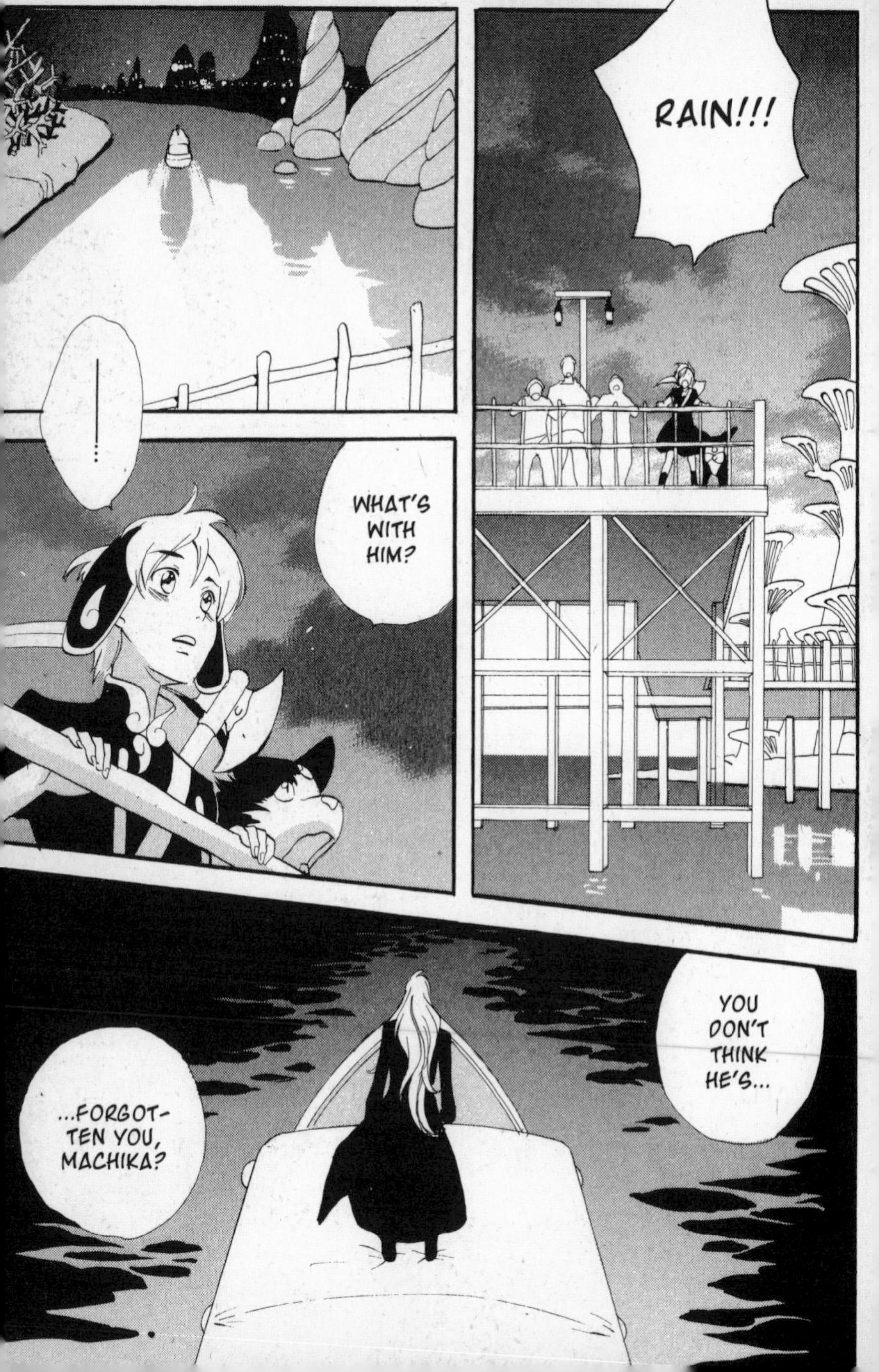
RAIN!!!
...!
WHAT'S WITH HIM?
YOU DON'T THINK HE'S...
...FORGOT-TEN YOU, MACHIKA?

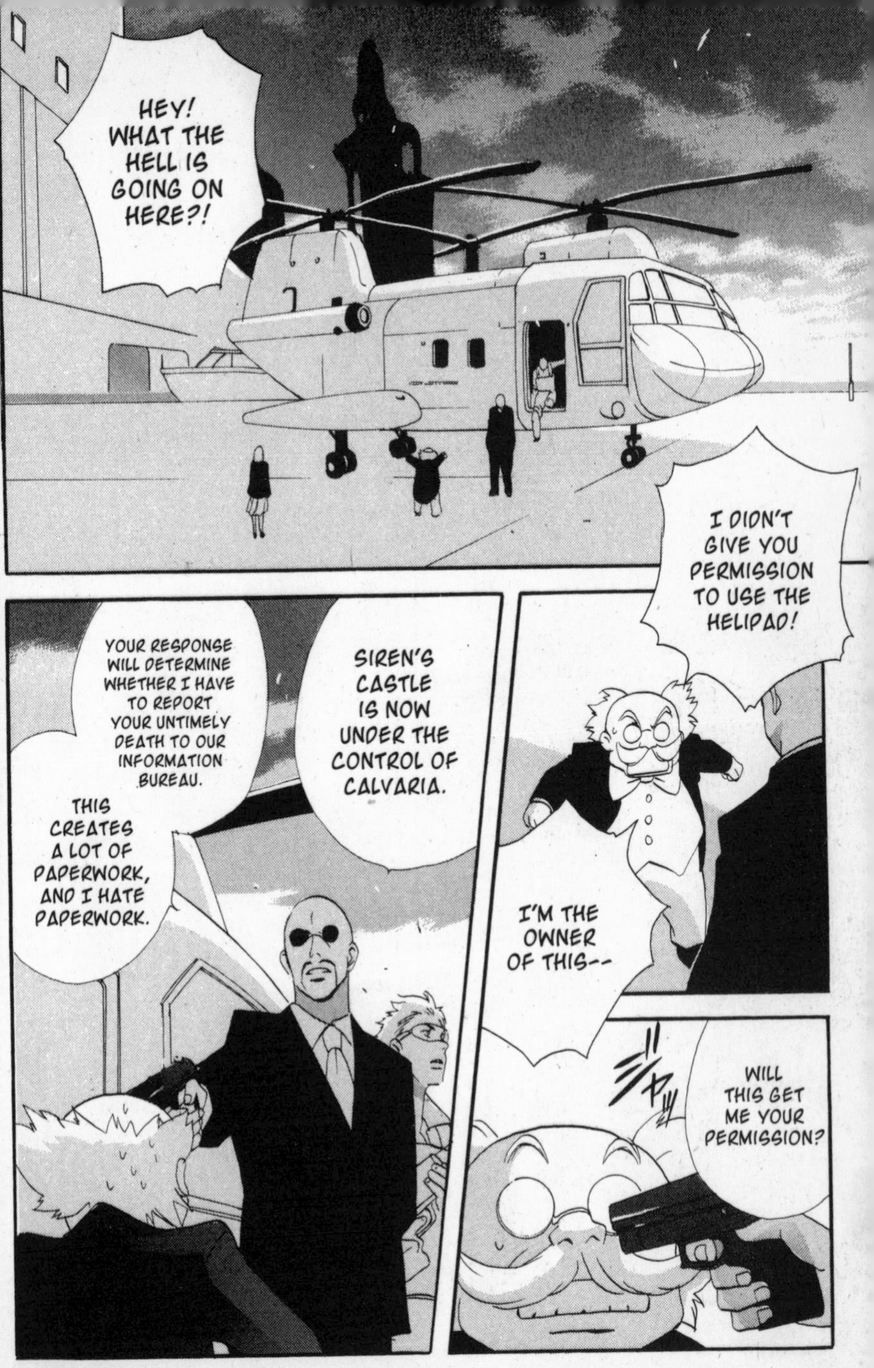
HEY! WHAT THE HELL IS GOING ON HERE?!
I DIDN'T GIVE YOU PERMISSION TO USE THE HELIPAD!
I'M THE OWNER OF THIS--
WILL THIS GET ME YOUR PERMISSION?
SIREN'S CASTLE IS NOW UNDER THE CONTROL OF CALVARIA.
YOUR RESPONSE WILL DETERMINE WHETHER I HAVE TO REPORT YOUR UNTIMELY DEATH TO OUR INFORMATION BUREAU.
THIS CREATES A LOT OF PAPERWORK, AND I HATE PAPERWORK.

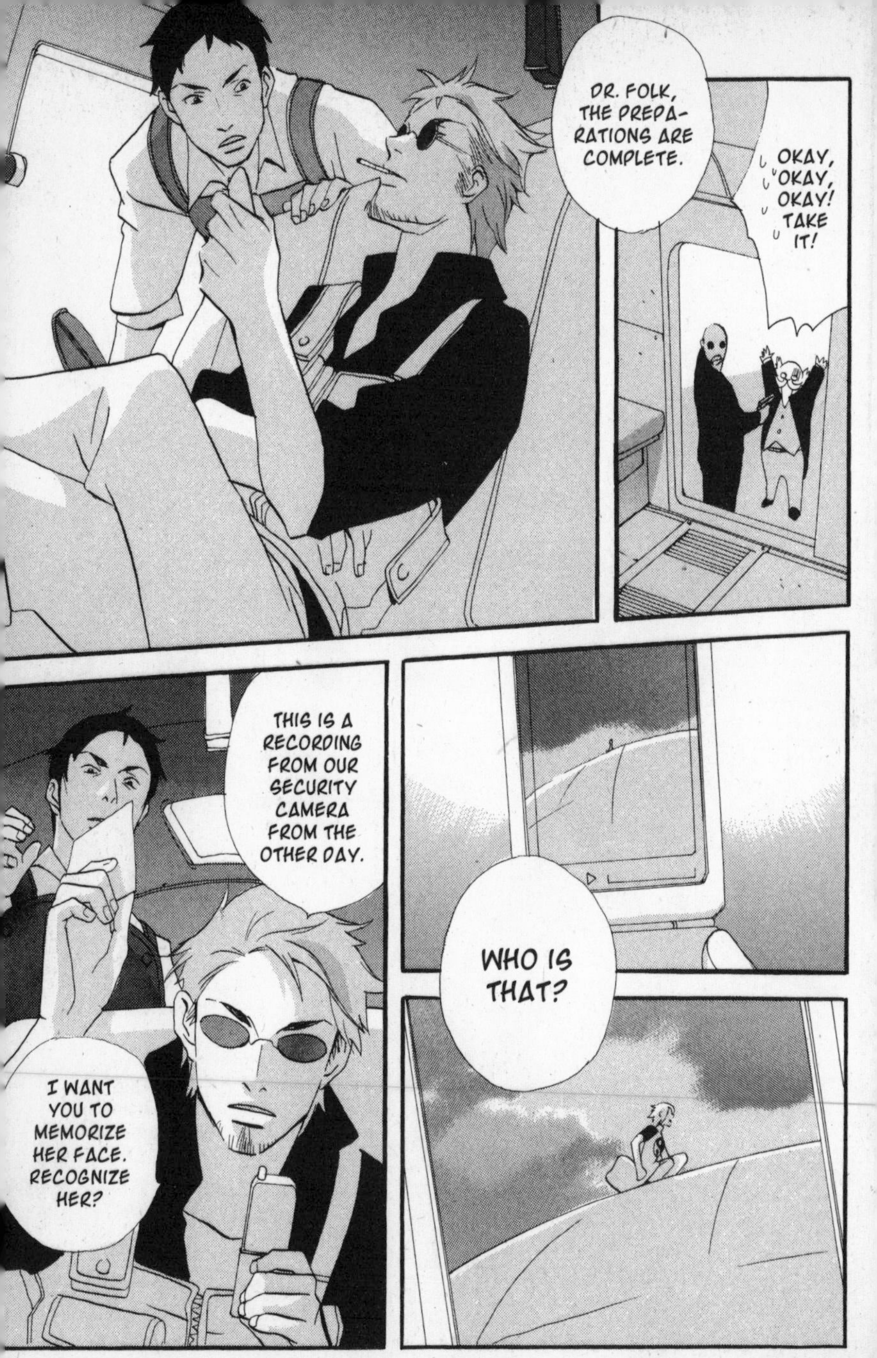
DR. FOLK, THE PREPARATIONS ARE COMPLETE.
OKAY, OKAY, OKAY! TAKE IT!
WHO IS THAT?
THIS IS A RECORDING FROM OUR SECURITY CAMERA FROM THE OTHER DAY.
I WANT YOU TO MEMORIZE HER FACE. RECOGNIZE HER?

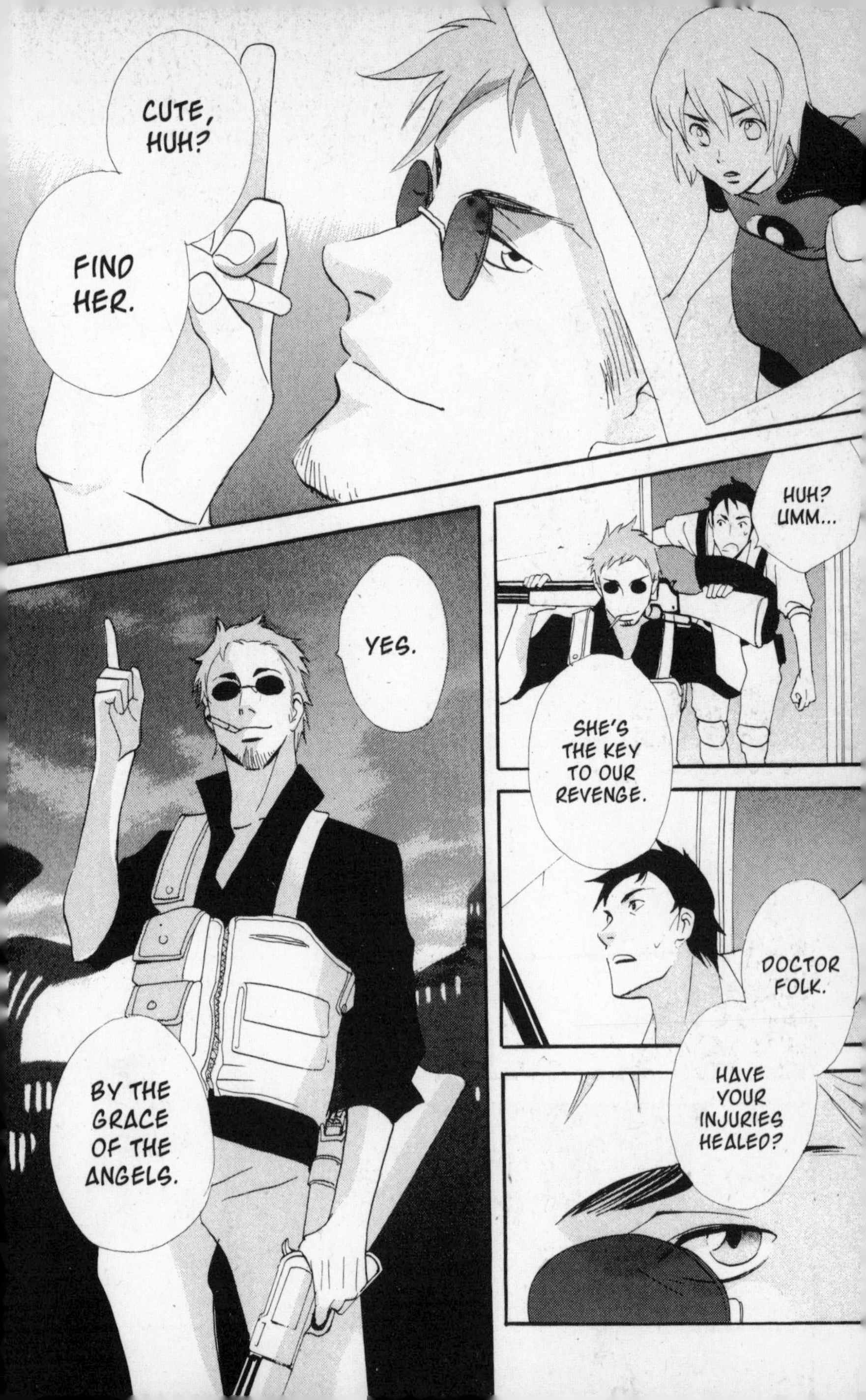
CUTE, HUH?
FIND HER.
HUH? UMM...
SHE'S THE KEY TO OUR REVENGE.
DOCTOR FOLK.
HAVE YOUR INJURIES HEALED?
YES.
BY THE GRACE OF THE ANGELS.

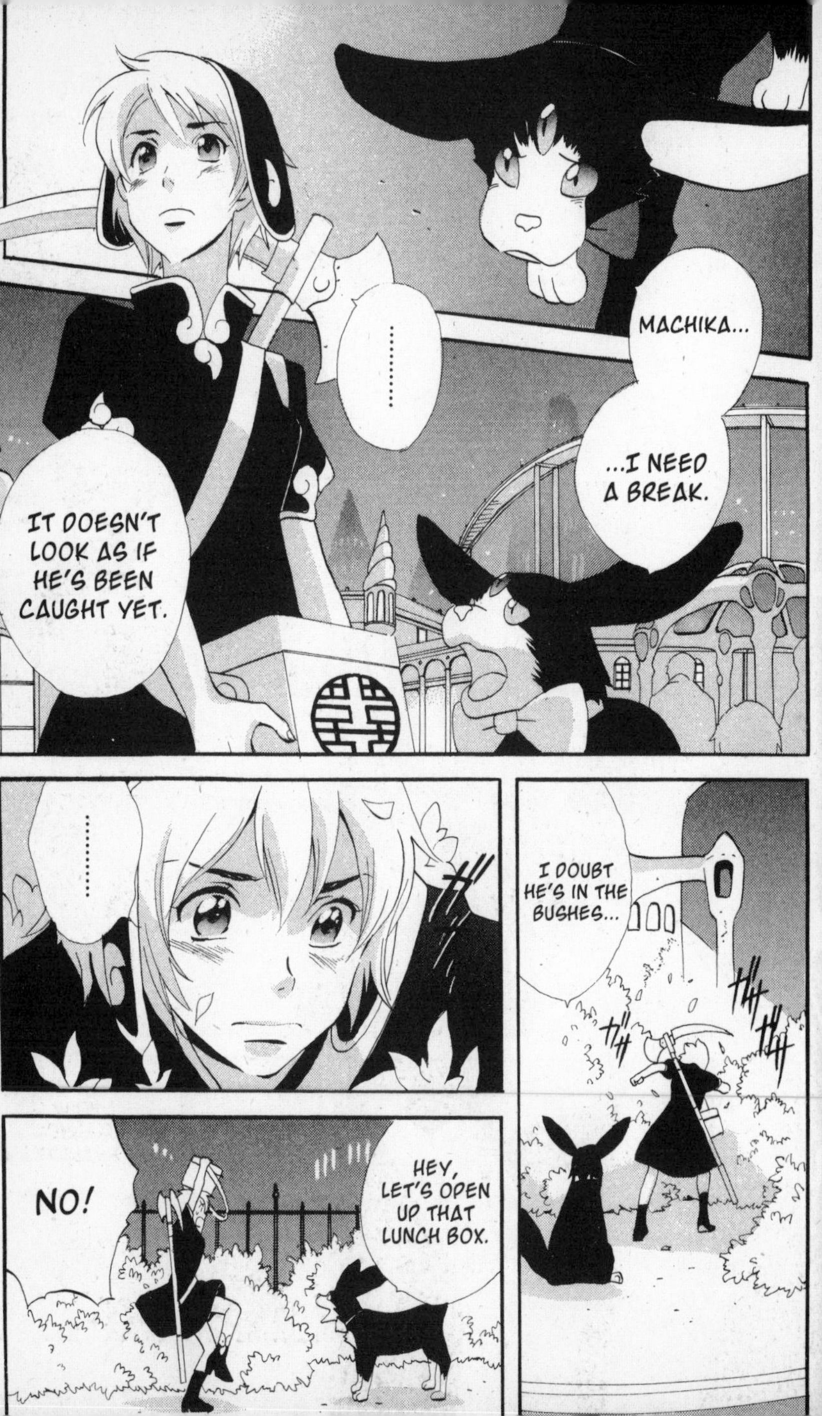
MACHIKA...
...I NEED A BREAK.
......
IT DOESN'T LOOK AS IF HE'S BEEN CAUGHT YET.
I DOUBT HE'S IN THE BUSHES...
......
HEY, LET'S OPEN UP THAT LUNCH BOX.
NO!

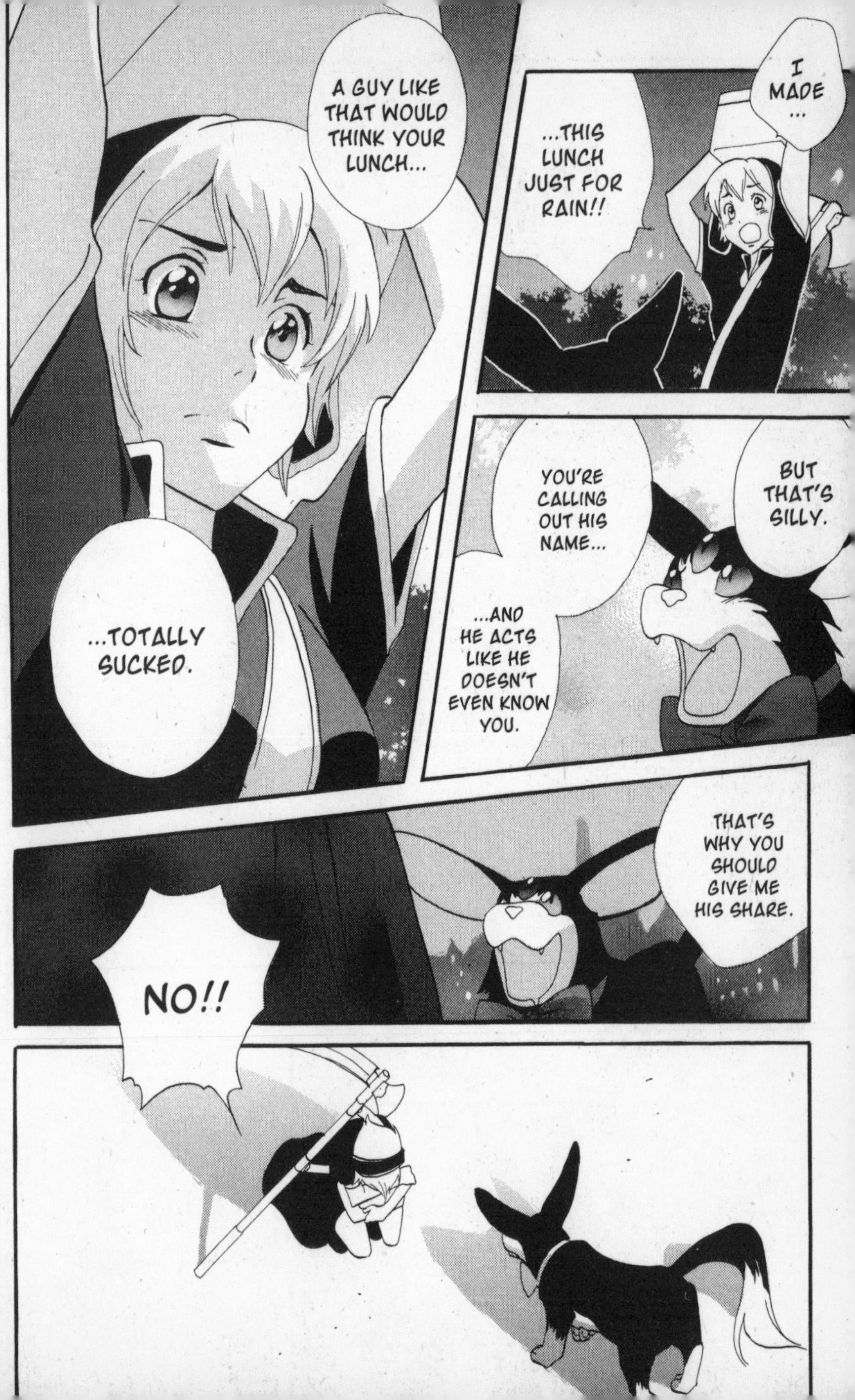
I MADE ...
...THIS LUNCH JUST FOR RAIN!!
BUT THAT'S SILLY.
YOU'RE CALLING OUT HIS NAME...
...AND HE ACTS LIKE HE DOESN'T EVEN KNOW YOU.
A GUY LIKE THAT WOULD THINK YOUR LUNCH...
...TOTALLY SUCKED.
THAT'S WHY YOU SHOULD GIVE ME HIS SHARE.
NO!!

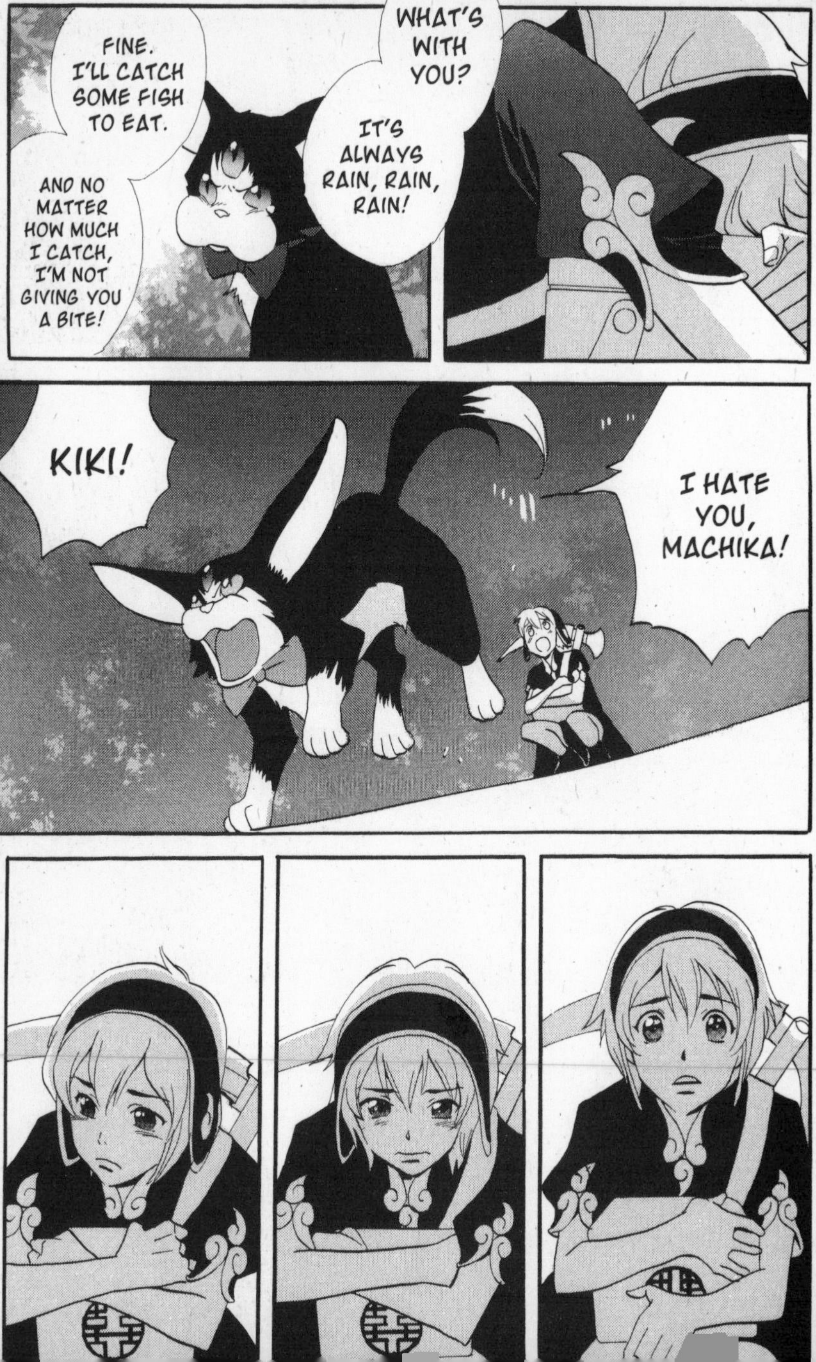
WHAT'S WITH YOU?
IT'S ALWAYS RAIN, RAIN, RAIN!
FINE. I'LL CATCH SOME FISH TO EAT.
AND NO MATTER HOW MUCH I CATCH, I'M NOT GIVING YOU A BITE!
I HATE YOU, MACHIKA!
KIKI!

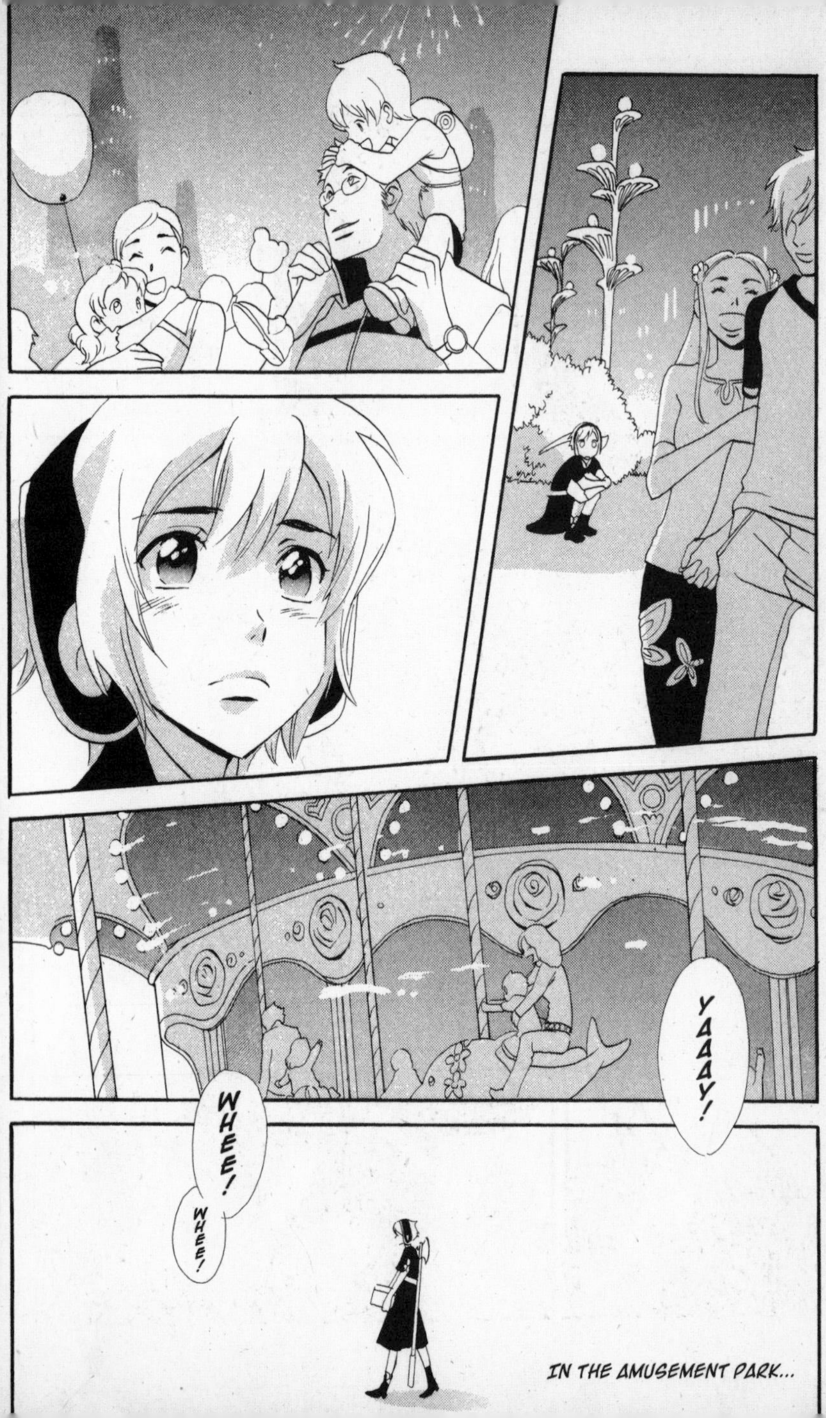
YAAAY!
WHEE!
WHEE!
IN THE AMUSEMENT PARK...

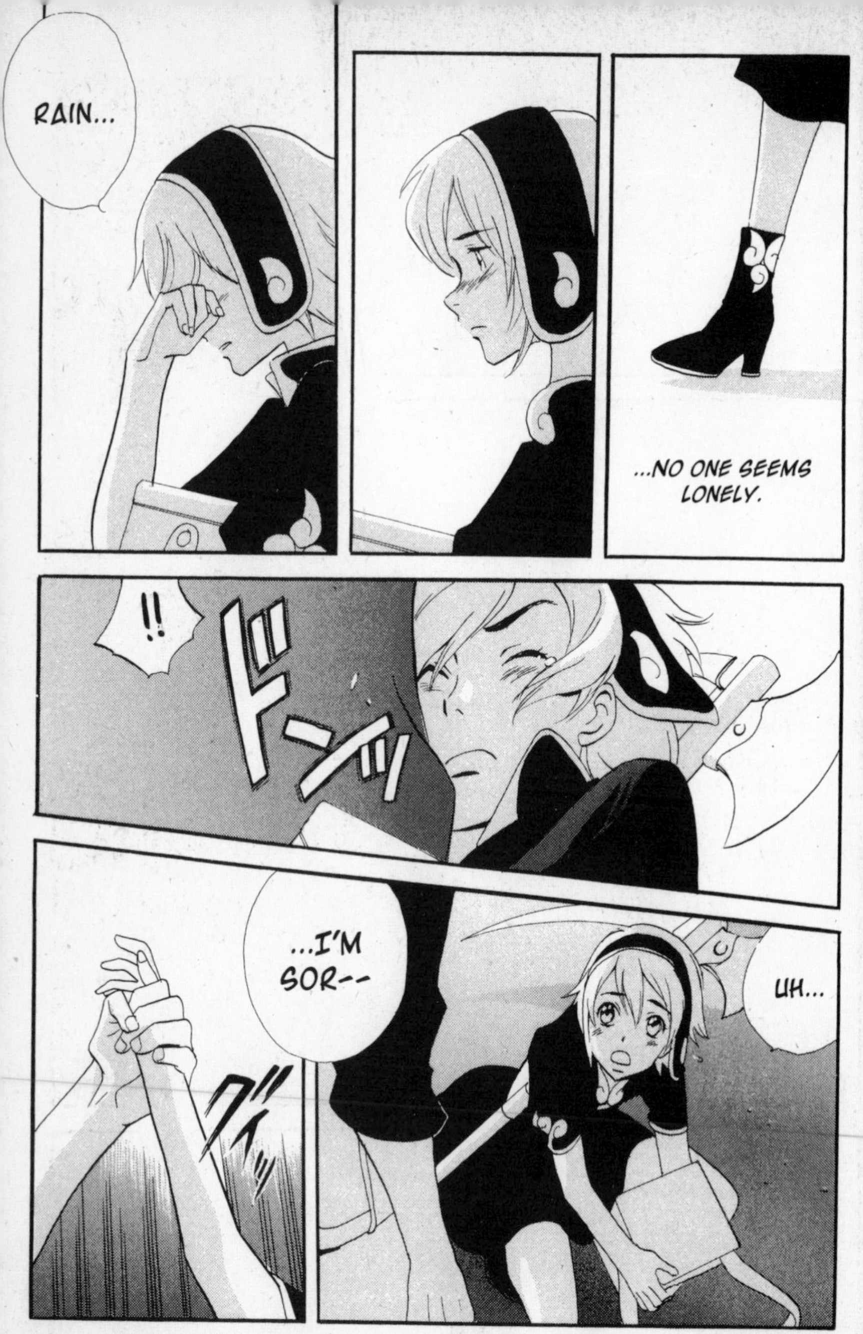
...NO ONE SEEMS LONELY.
RAIN...
!!
ドーン
UH...
...I'M SOR--
グイッ

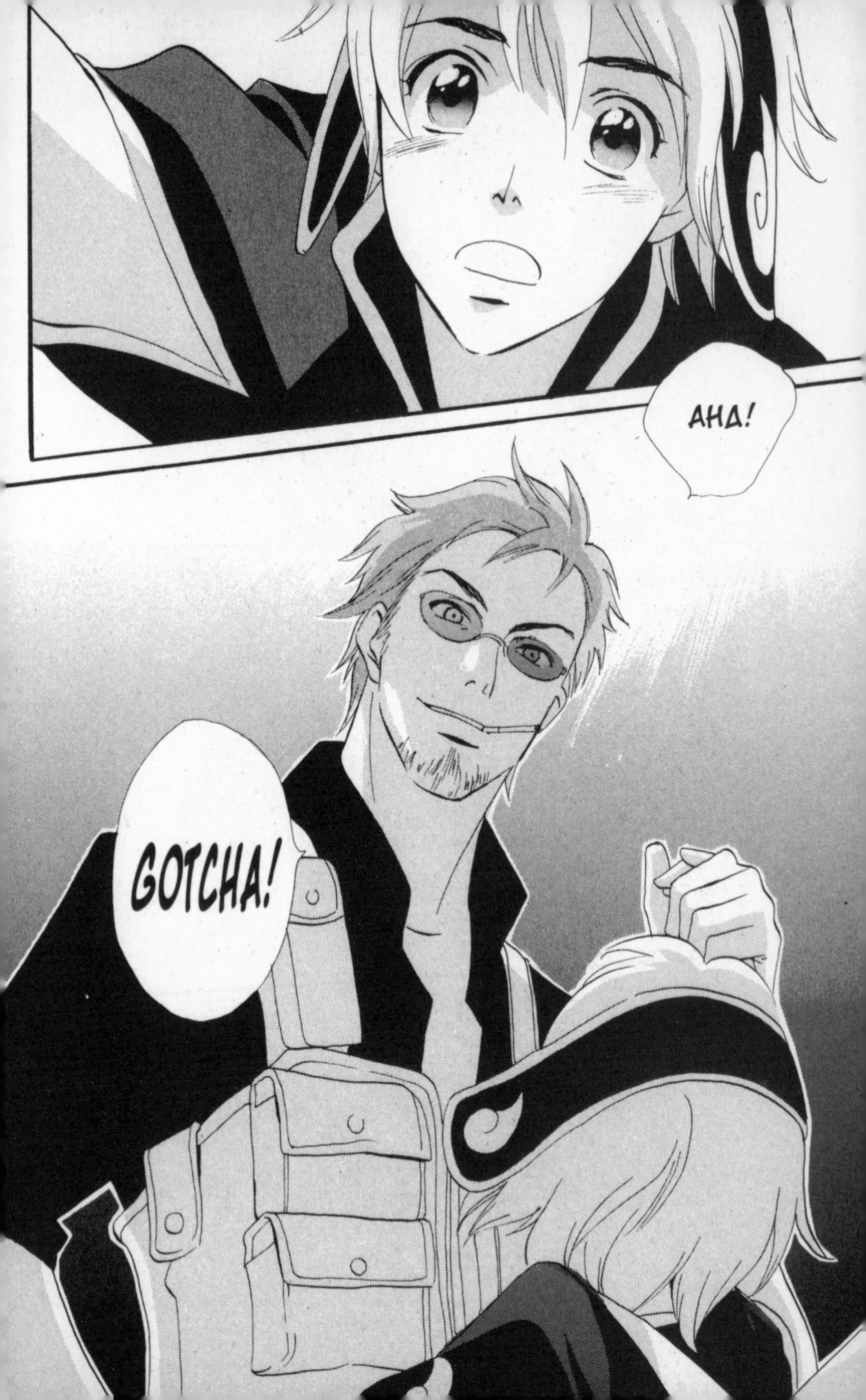
AHA!
GOTCHA!

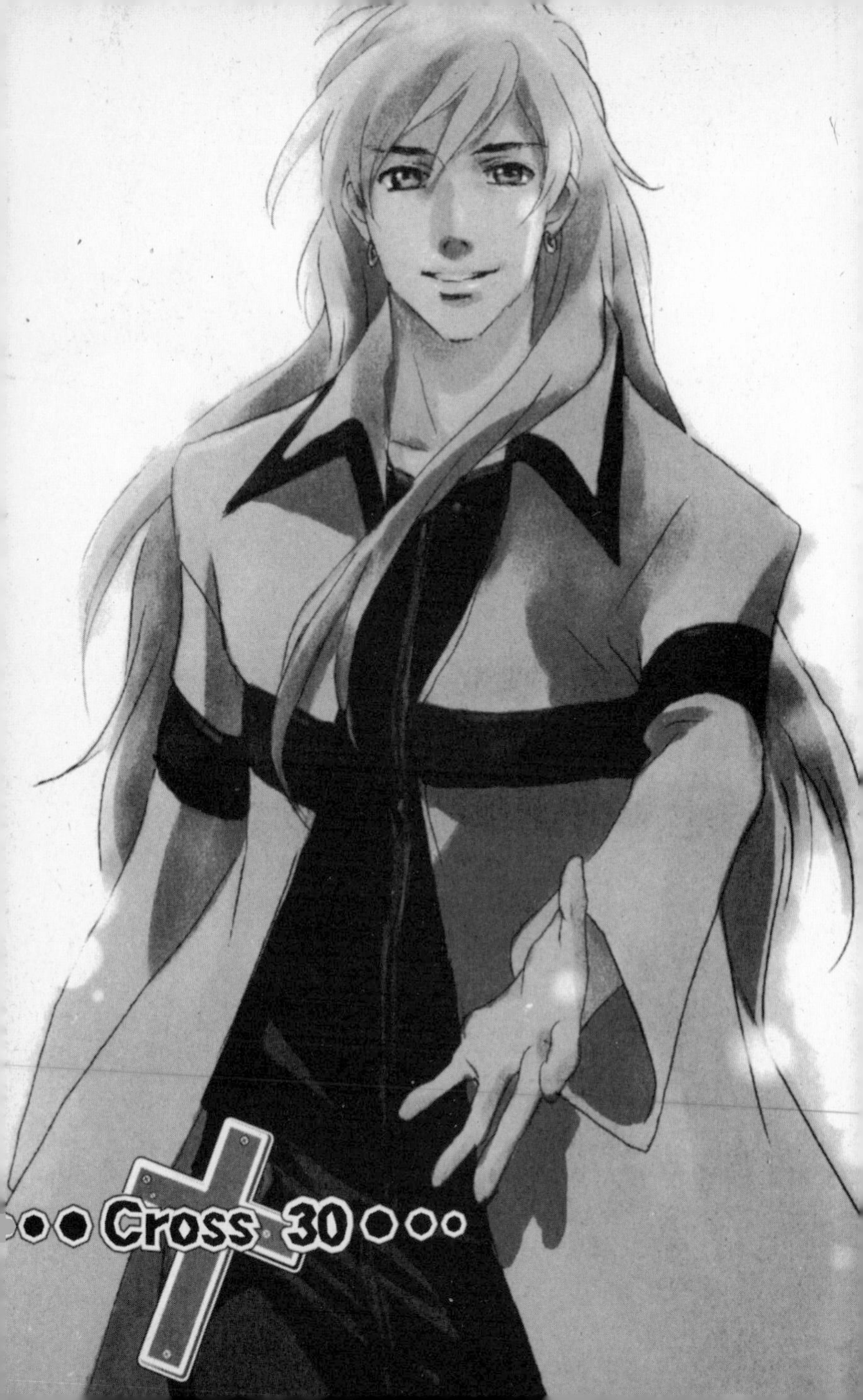
Cross 30

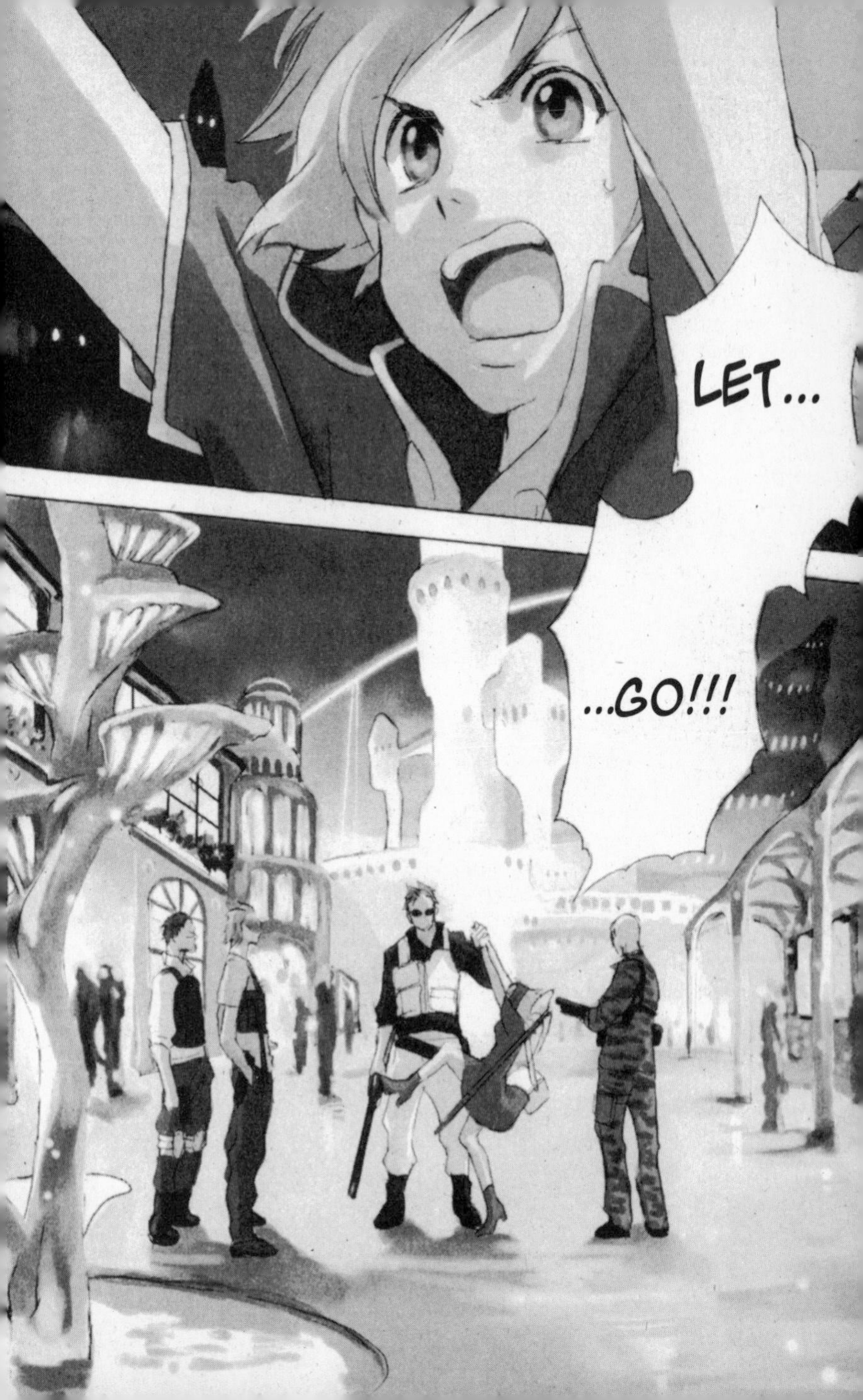
LET...
...GO!!!

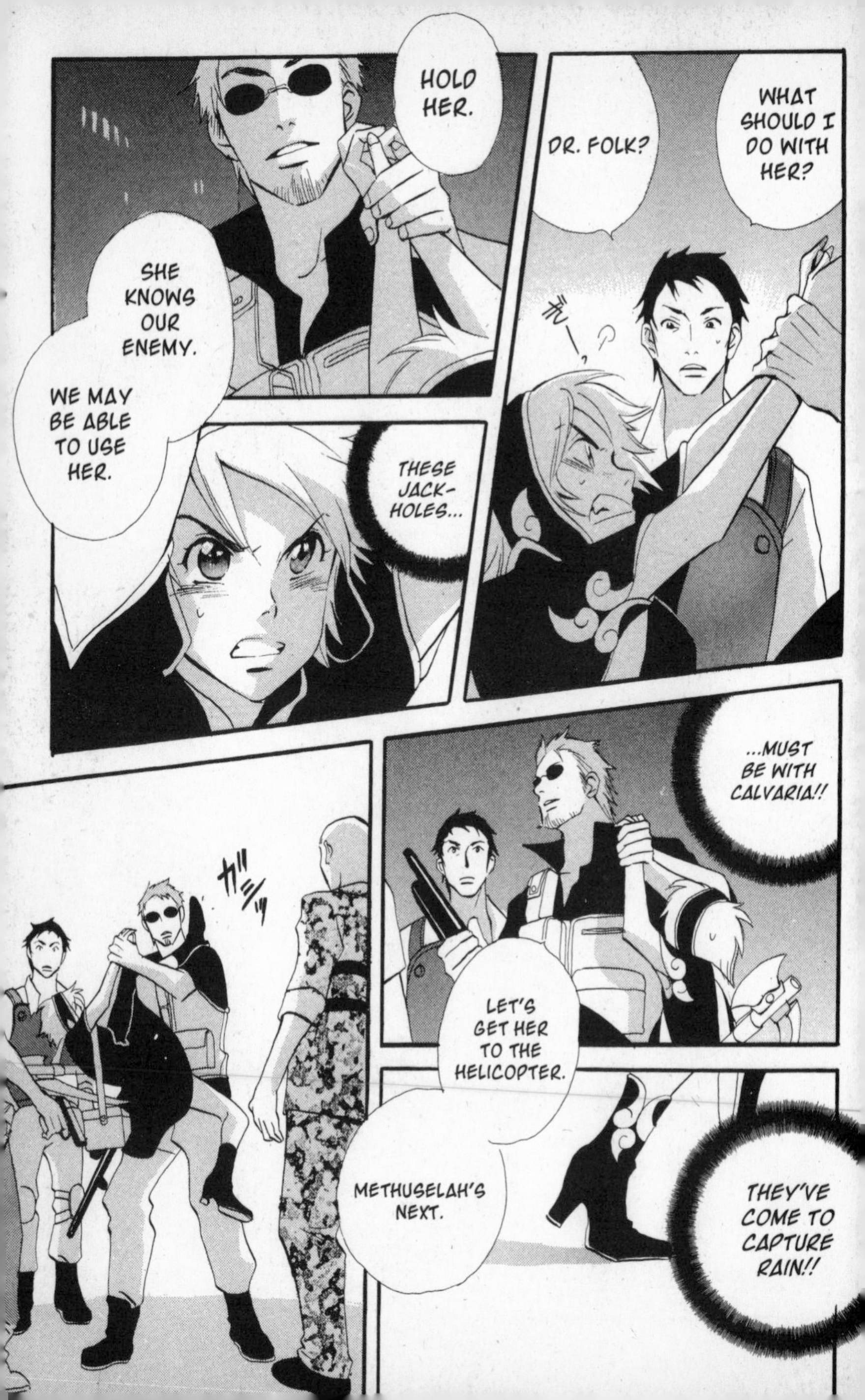
WHAT SHOULD I DO WITH HER?
DR. FOLK?
HOLD HER.
SHE KNOWS OUR ENEMY.
WE MAY BE ABLE TO USE HER.
THESE JACK-HOLES...
...MUST BE WITH CALVARIA!!
LET'S GET HER TO THE HELICOPTER.
THEY'VE COME TO CAPTURE RAIN!!
METHUSELAH'S NEXT.

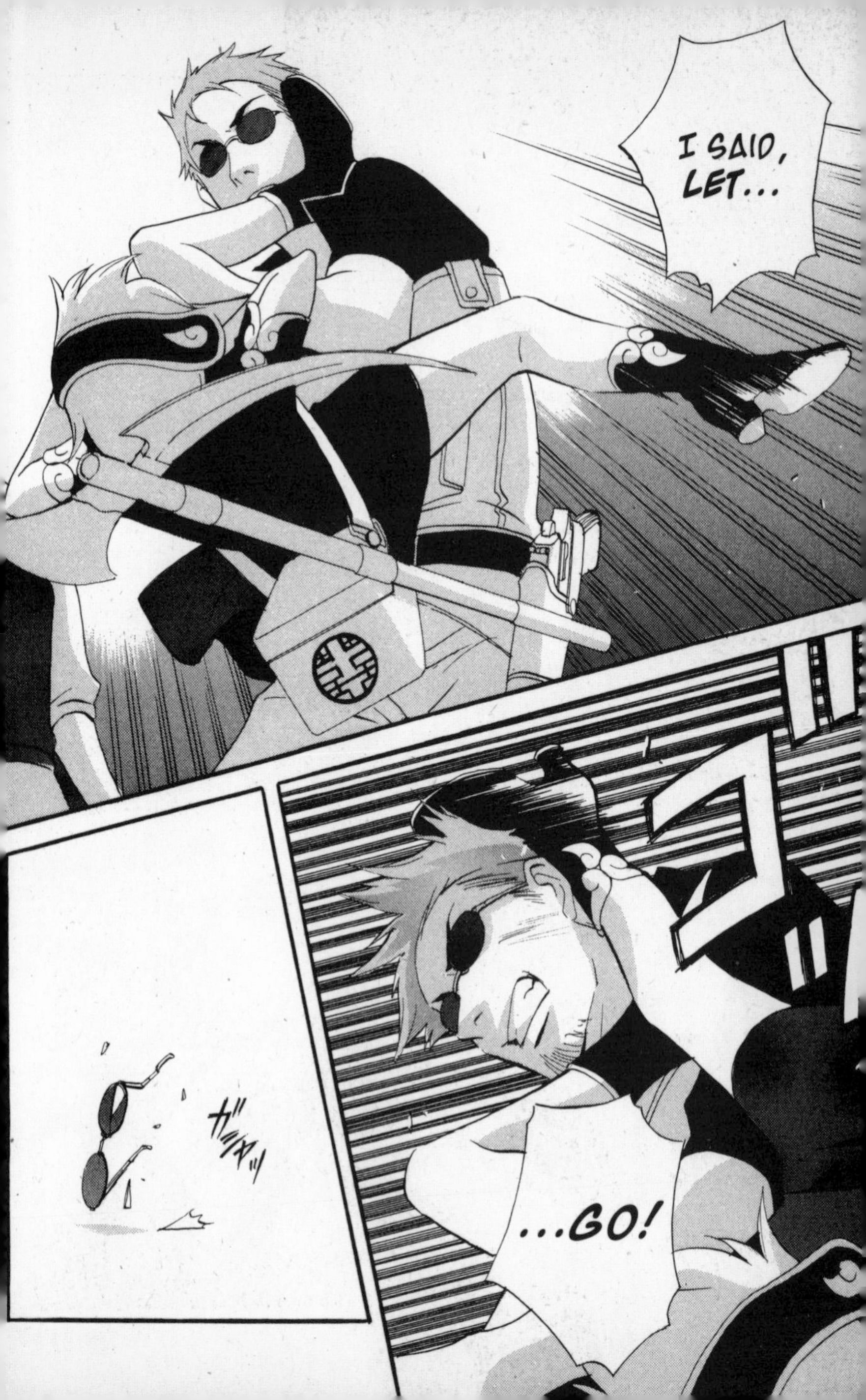
I SAID, LET...
...GO!
ガシャッ

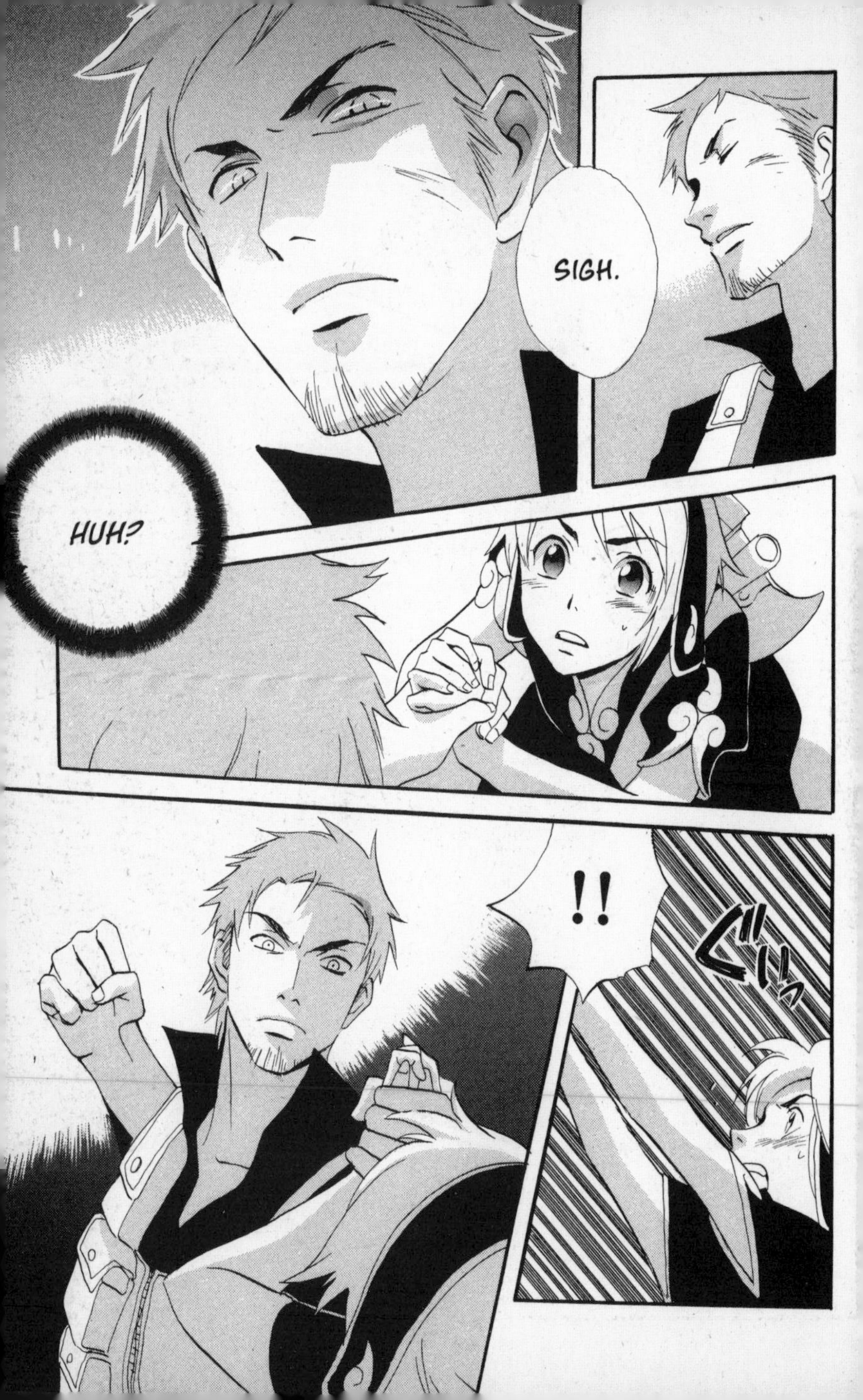
SIGH.
HUH?
!!

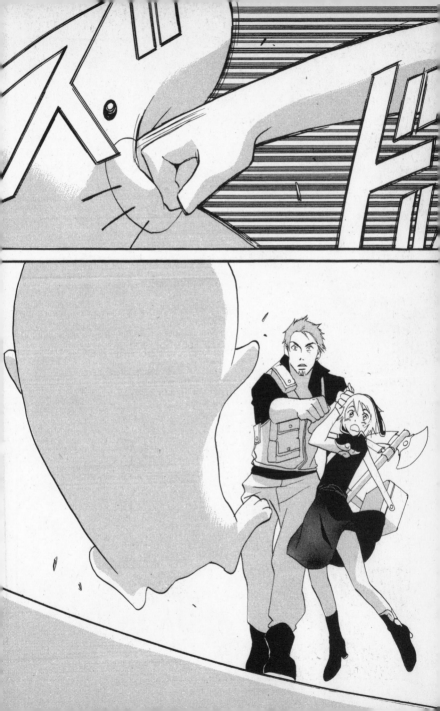

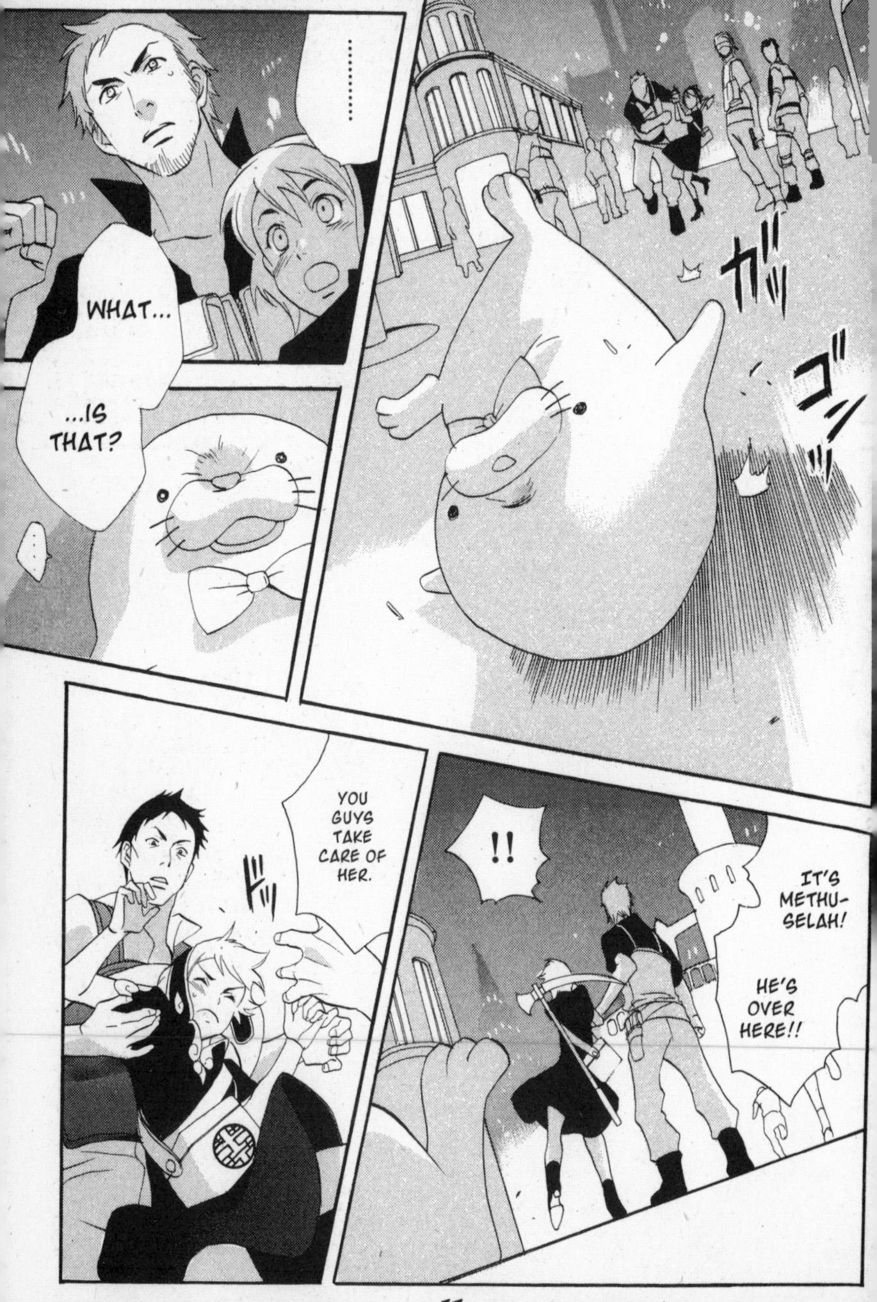
ガッ
ゴン
......
WHAT...
...IS THAT?
!!
IT'S METHU-SELAH!
HE'S OVER HERE!!
YOU GUYS TAKE CARE OF HER.
ドッ

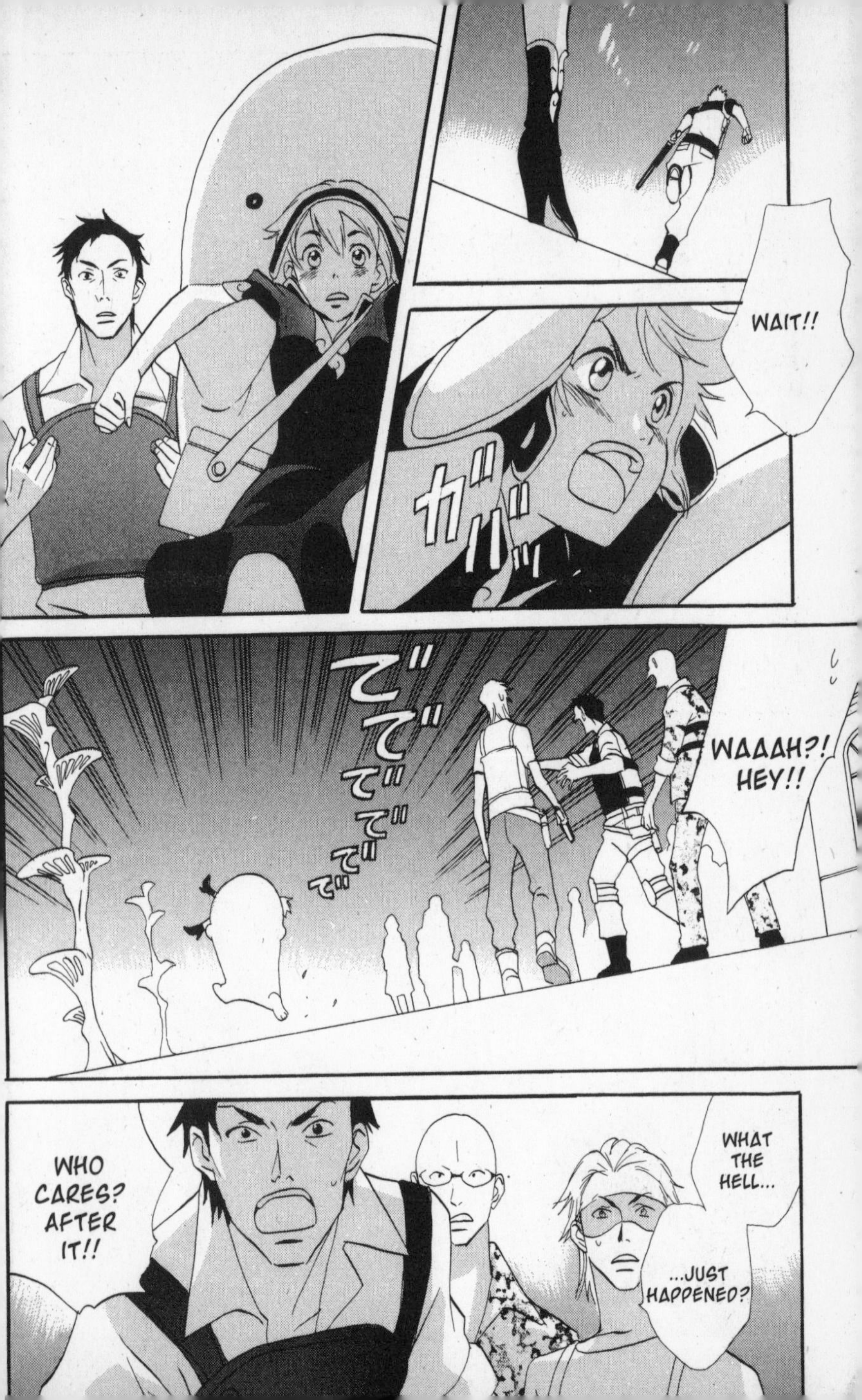

WAIT!!
ガバッ
WAAAH?! HEY!!
でででででで
WHAT THE HELL...
...JUST HAPPENED?
WHO CARES? AFTER IT!!

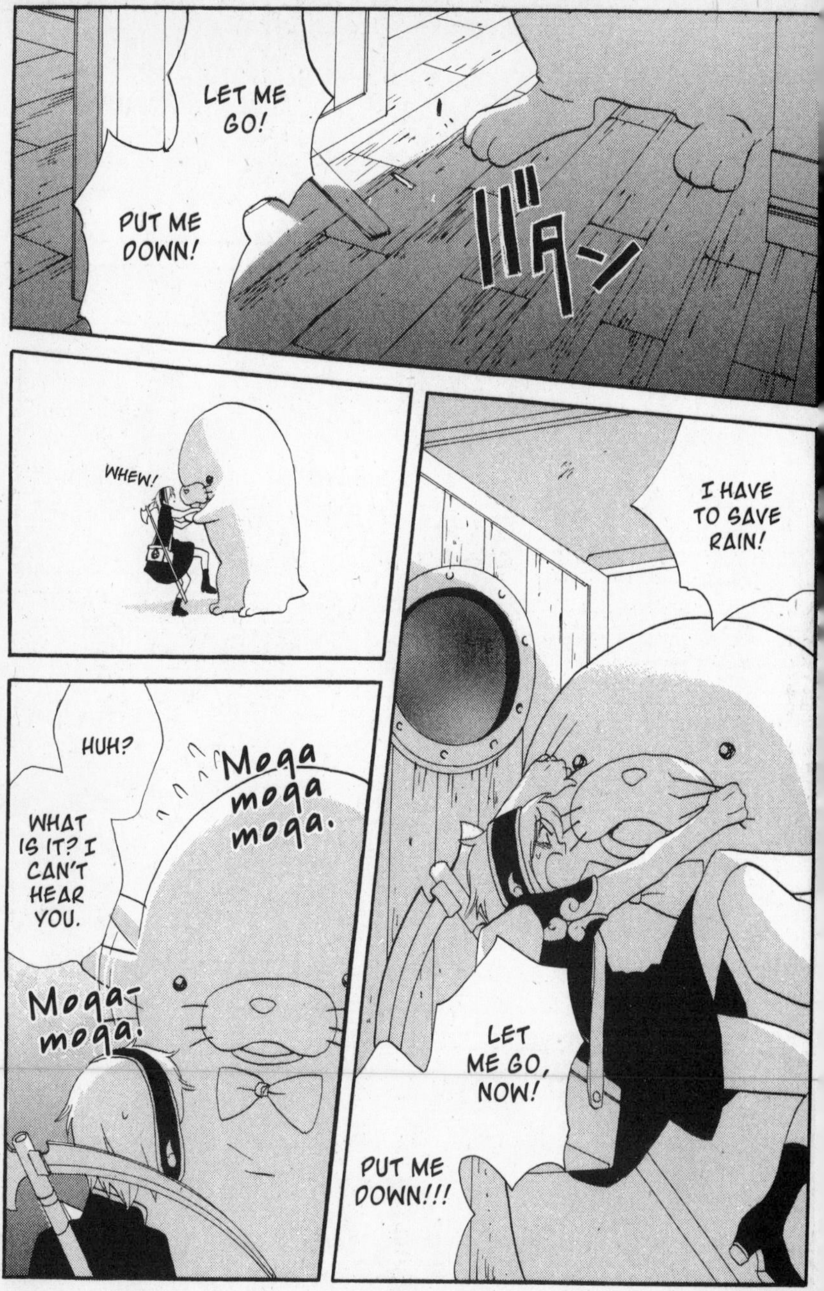
LET ME GO!
PUT ME DOWN!
バターン
I HAVE TO SAVE RAIN!
LET ME GO, NOW!
PUT ME DOWN!!!
WHEW!
Moga moga moga.
HUH?
WHAT IS IT? I CAN'T HEAR YOU.
Moga-moga.

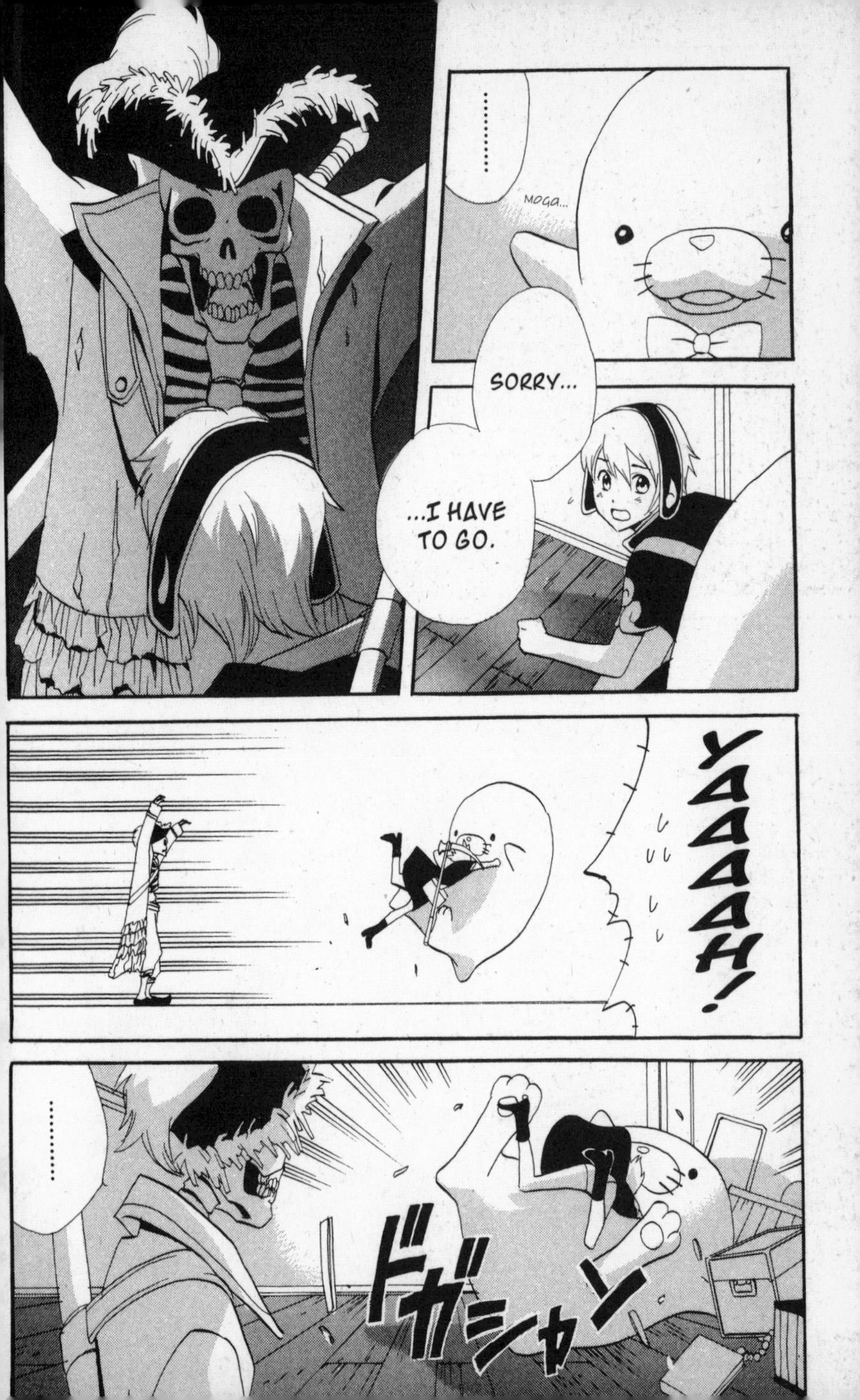
……
Moga...
SORRY...
...I HAVE TO GO.
YAAAAAH!
……
ドガシャン

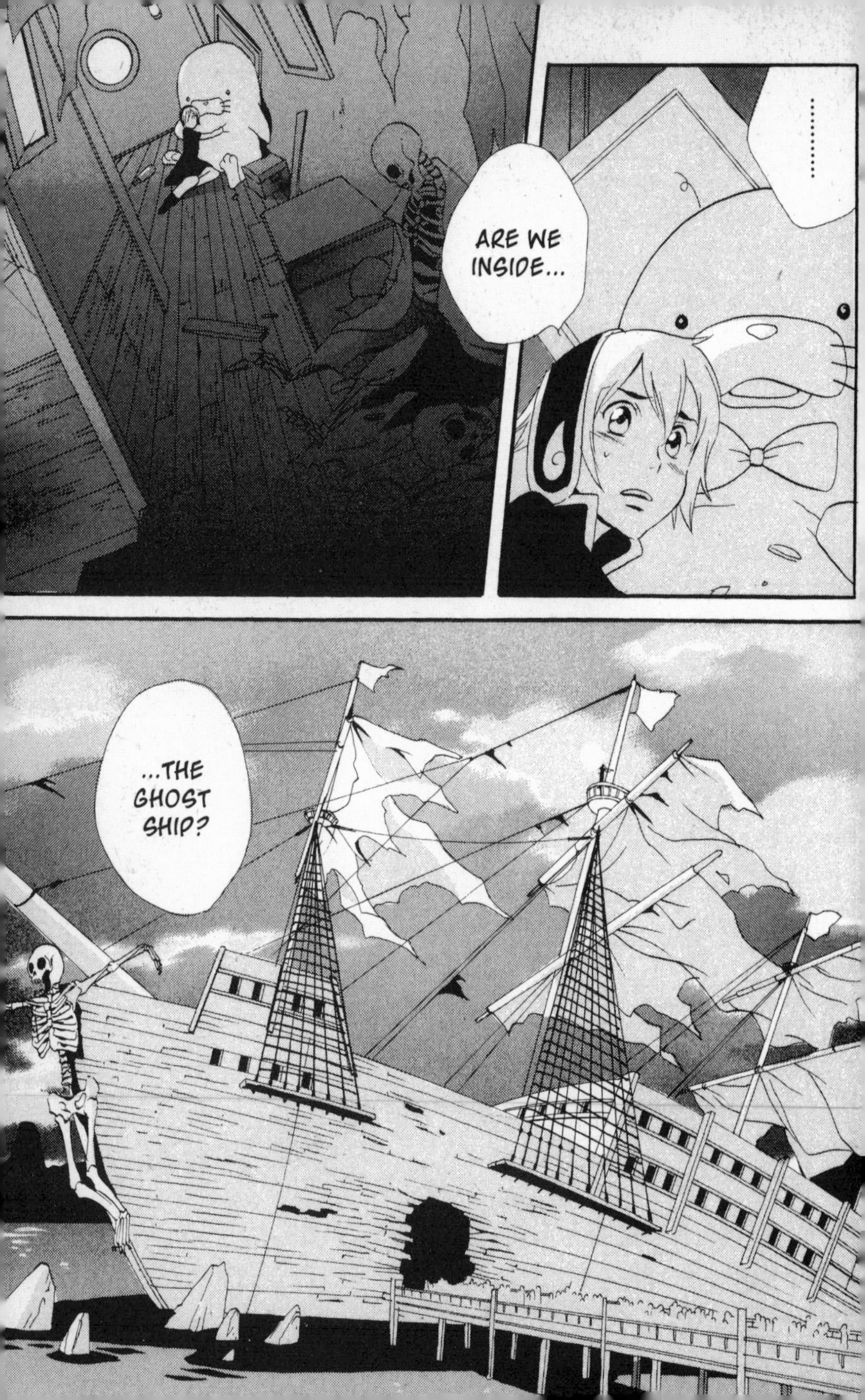
......
ARE WE INSIDE...
...THE GHOST SHIP?

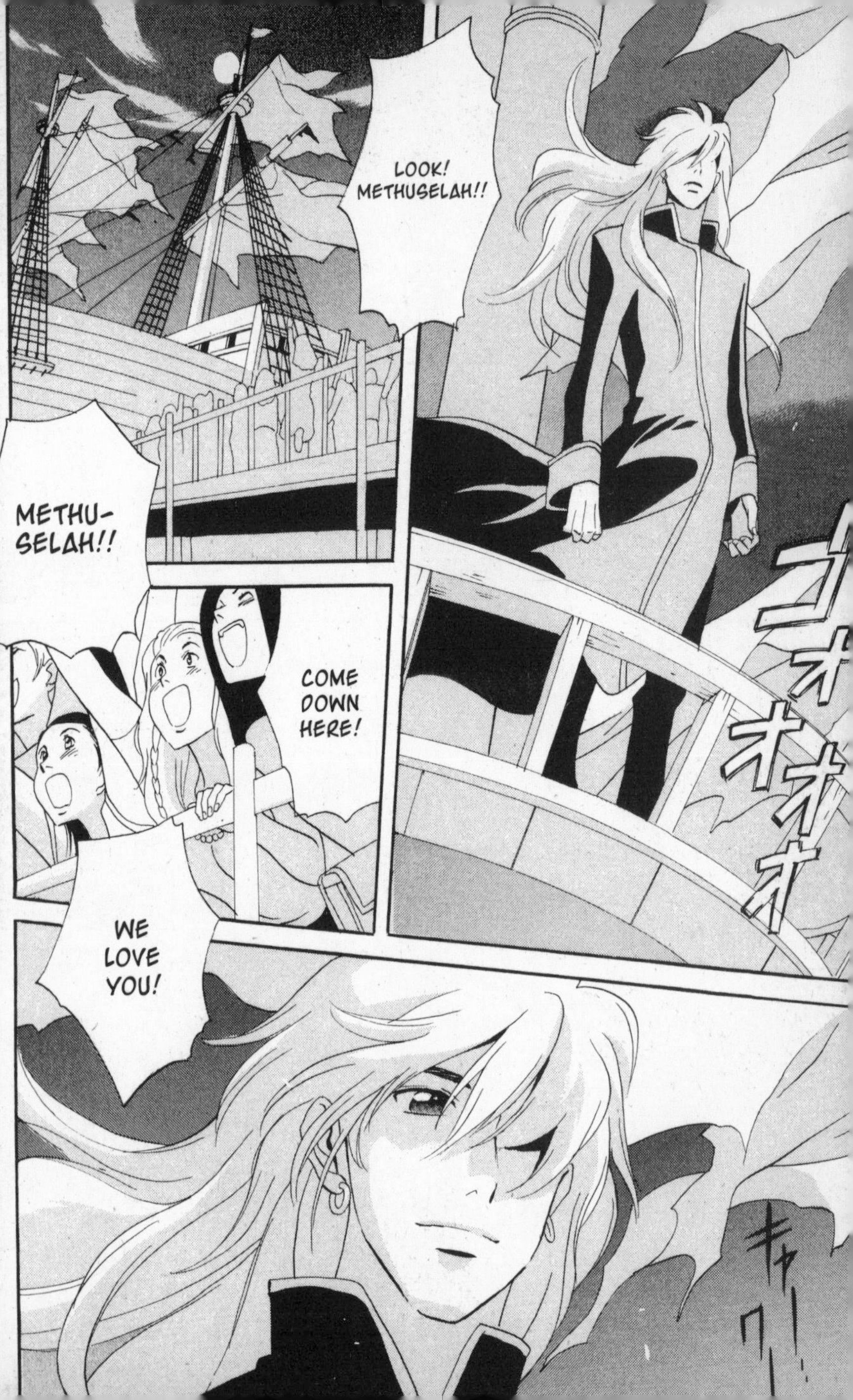
ゴォオオオ
LOOK! METHUSELAH!!
METHU-SELAH!!
COME DOWN HERE!
WE LOVE YOU!
キャーワー

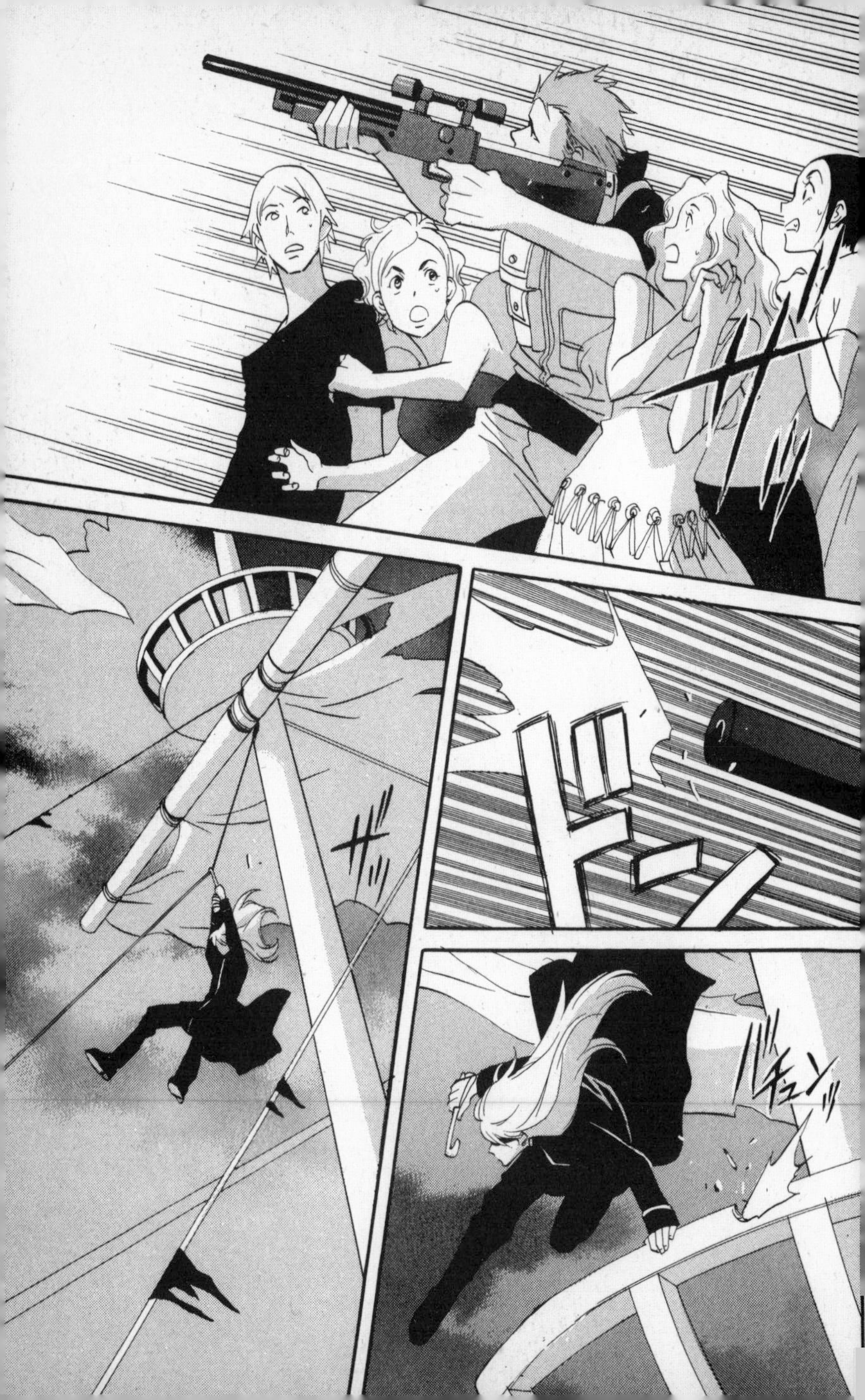
ザッ
ドン
バチュンッ
ザッ

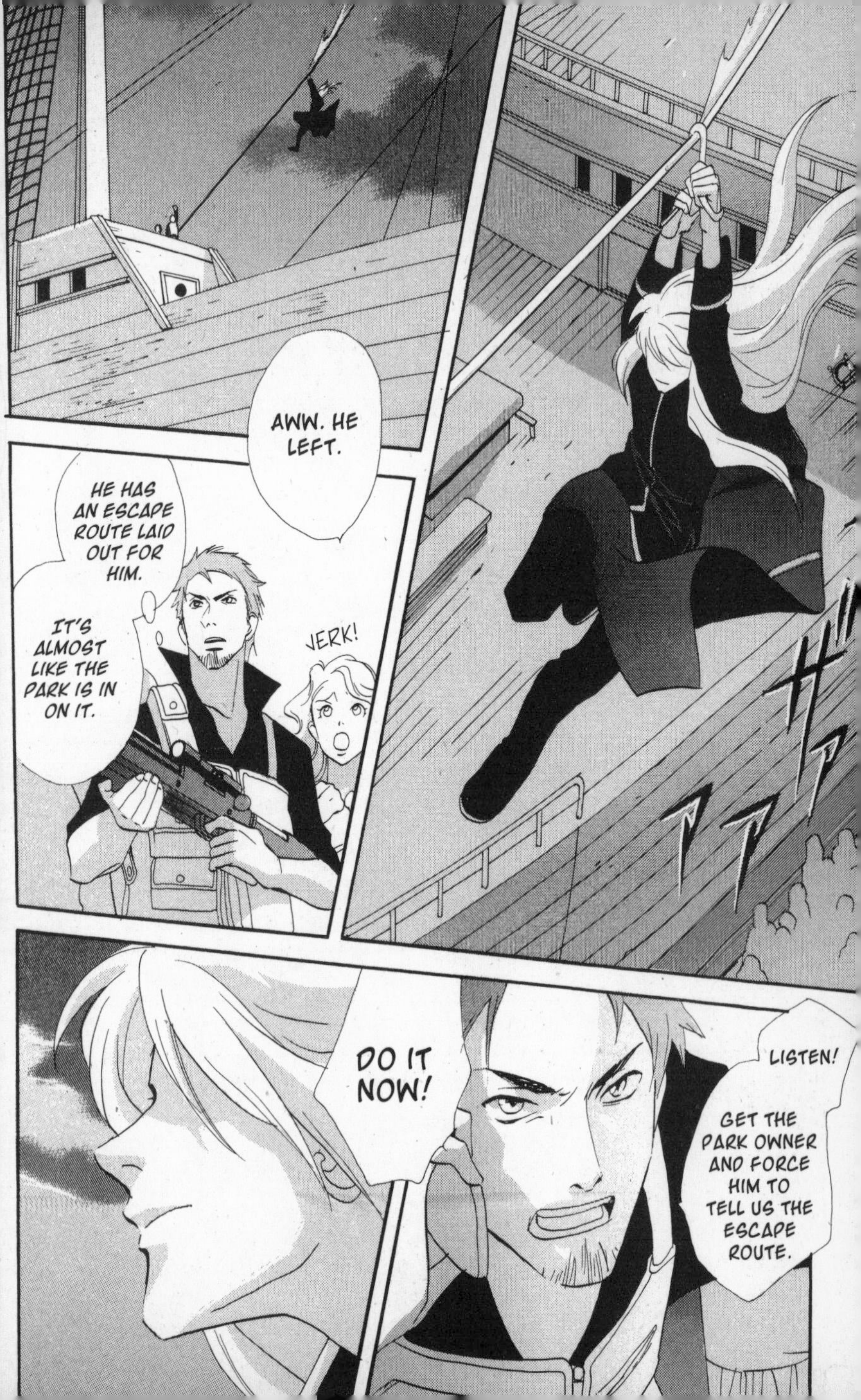
AWW. HE LEFT.
HE HAS AN ESCAPE ROUTE LAID OUT FOR HIM.
IT'S ALMOST LIKE THE PARK IS IN ON IT.
JERK!
LISTEN!
GET THE PARK OWNER AND FORCE HIM TO TELL US THE ESCAPE ROUTE.
DO IT NOW!

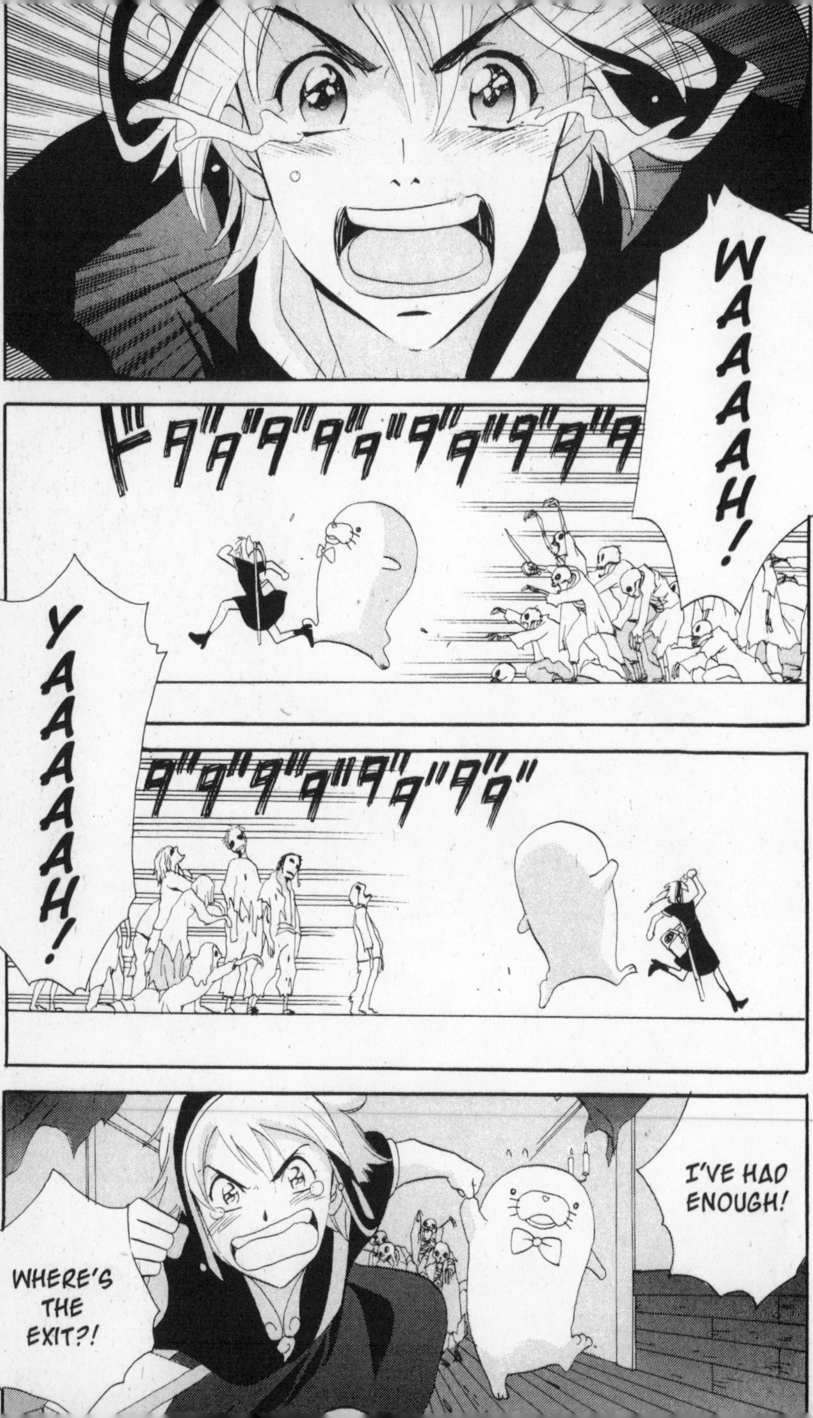
WAAAAAH!
ドダダダダダダダダダ
YAAAAAAH!
ダダダダダダダ
I'VE HAD ENOUGH!
WHERE'S THE EXIT?!

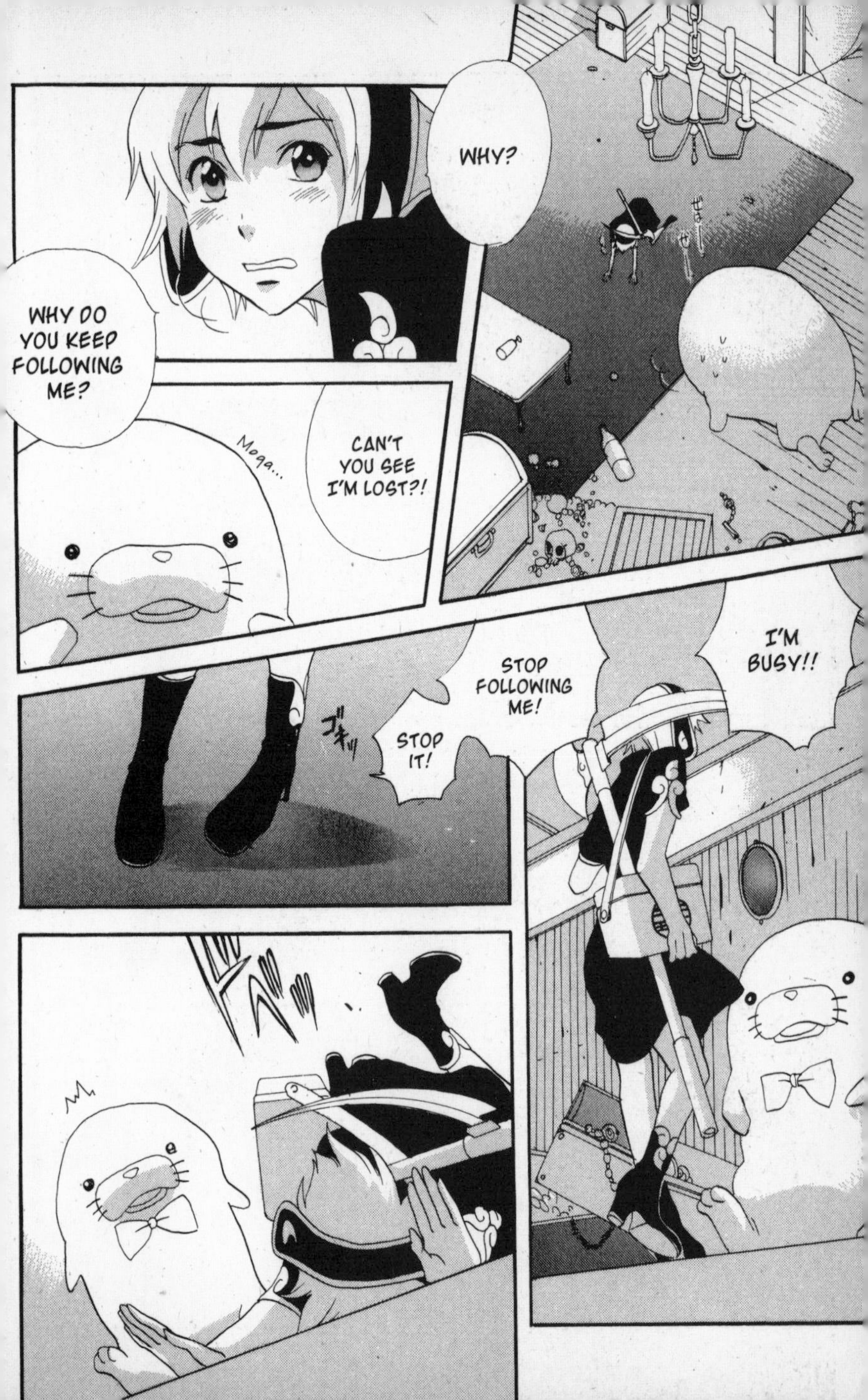
WHY?
WHY DO YOU KEEP FOLLOWING ME?
Moga...
CAN'T YOU SEE I'M LOST?!
I'M BUSY!!
STOP FOLLOWING ME!
STOP IT!
ゴキッ

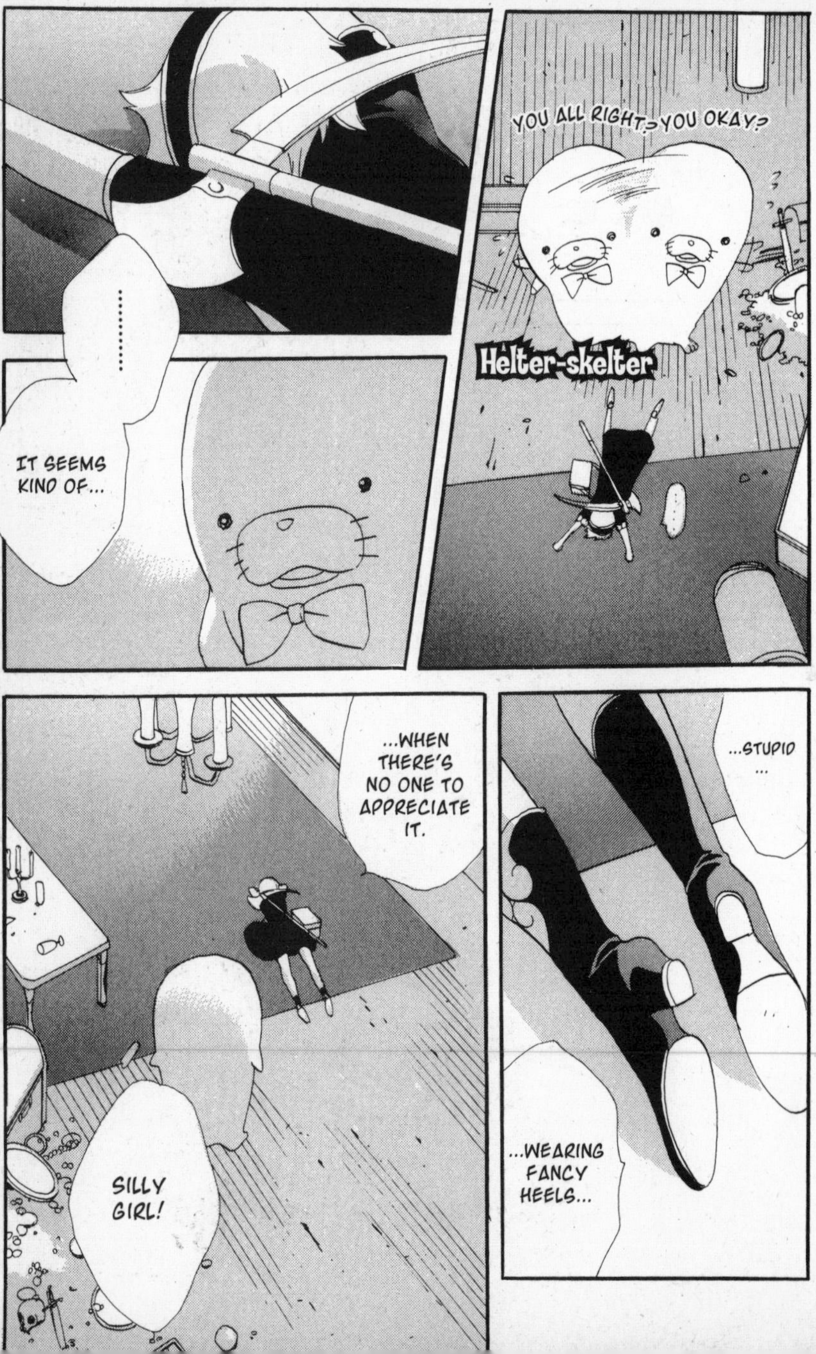
YOU ALL RIGHT? YOU OKAY?
Helter-skelter
....
IT SEEMS KIND OF...
...STUPID...
...WEARING FANCY HEELS...
...WHEN THERE'S NO ONE TO APPRECIATE IT.
SILLY GIRL!

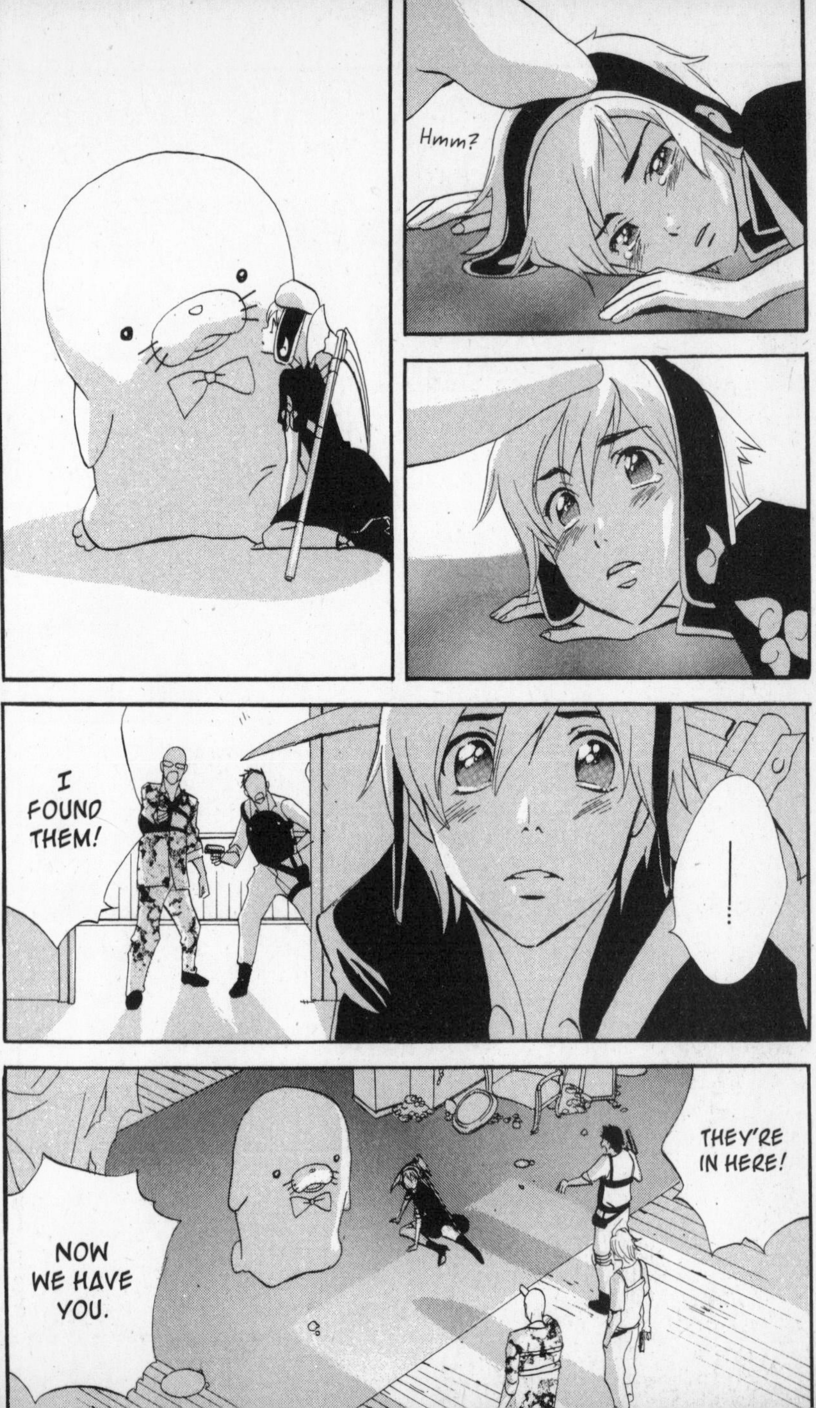
Hmm?
I FOUND THEM!
THEY'RE IN HERE!
NOW WE HAVE YOU.

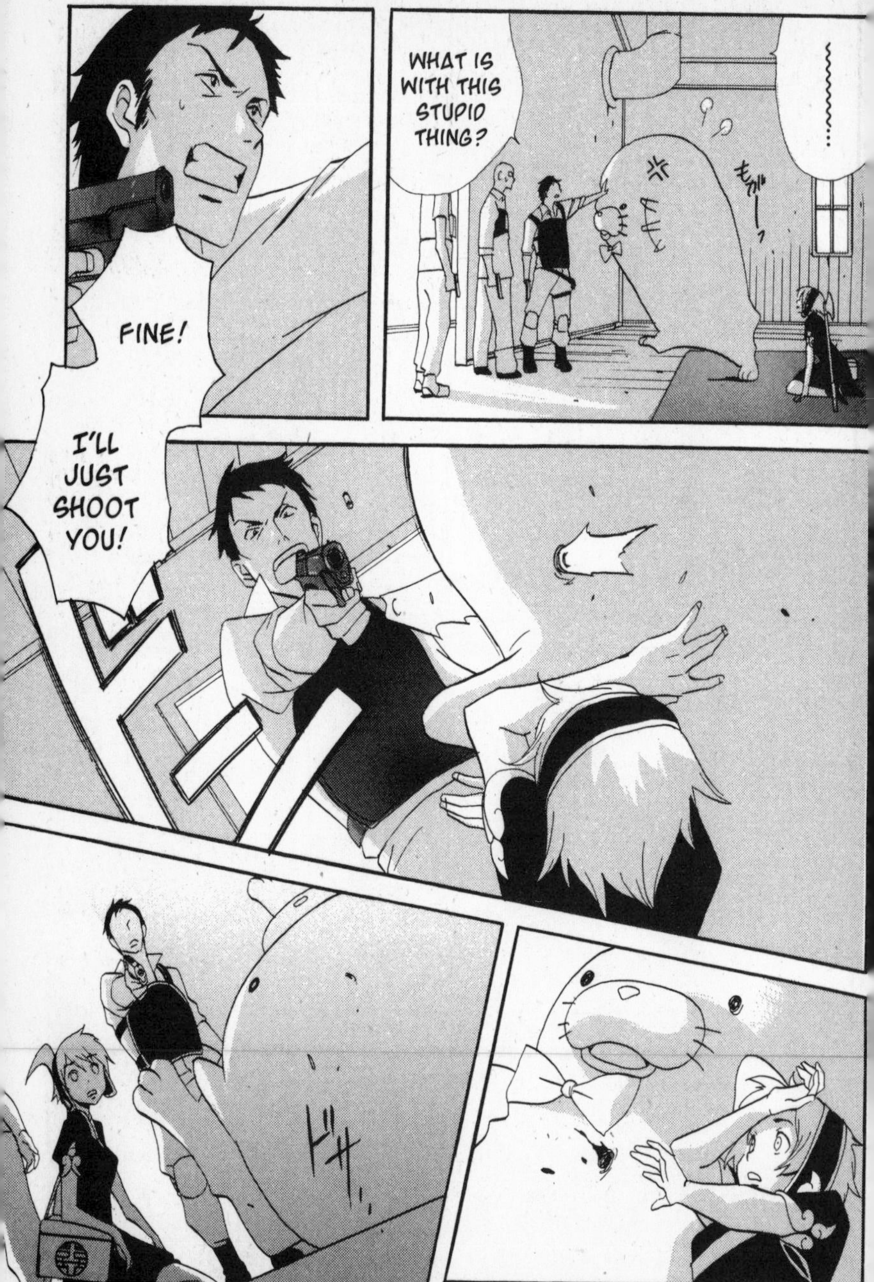
WHAT IS WITH THIS STUPID THING?
FINE!
I'LL JUST SHOOT YOU!

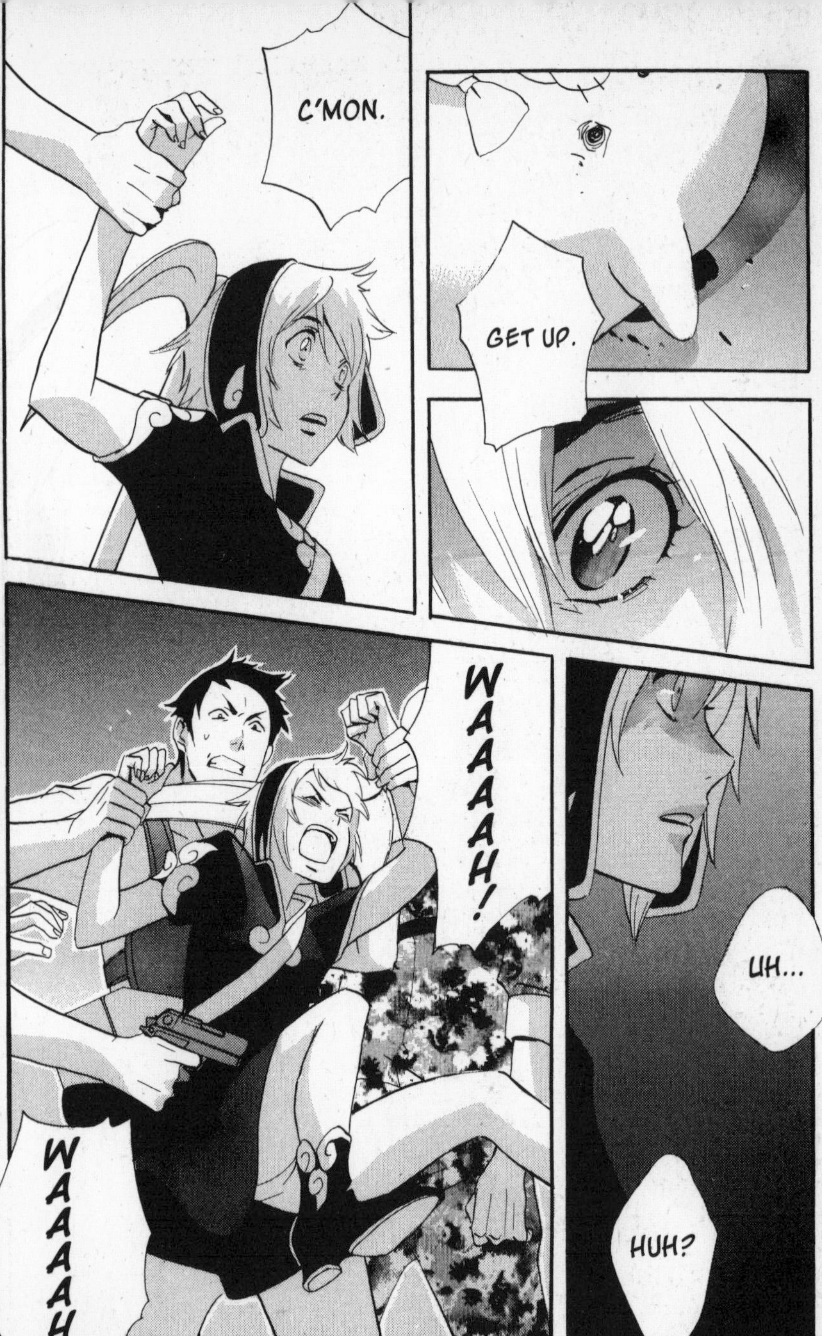
GET UP.
C'MON.
UH...
HUH?
WAAAAAH!
WAAAAAH!

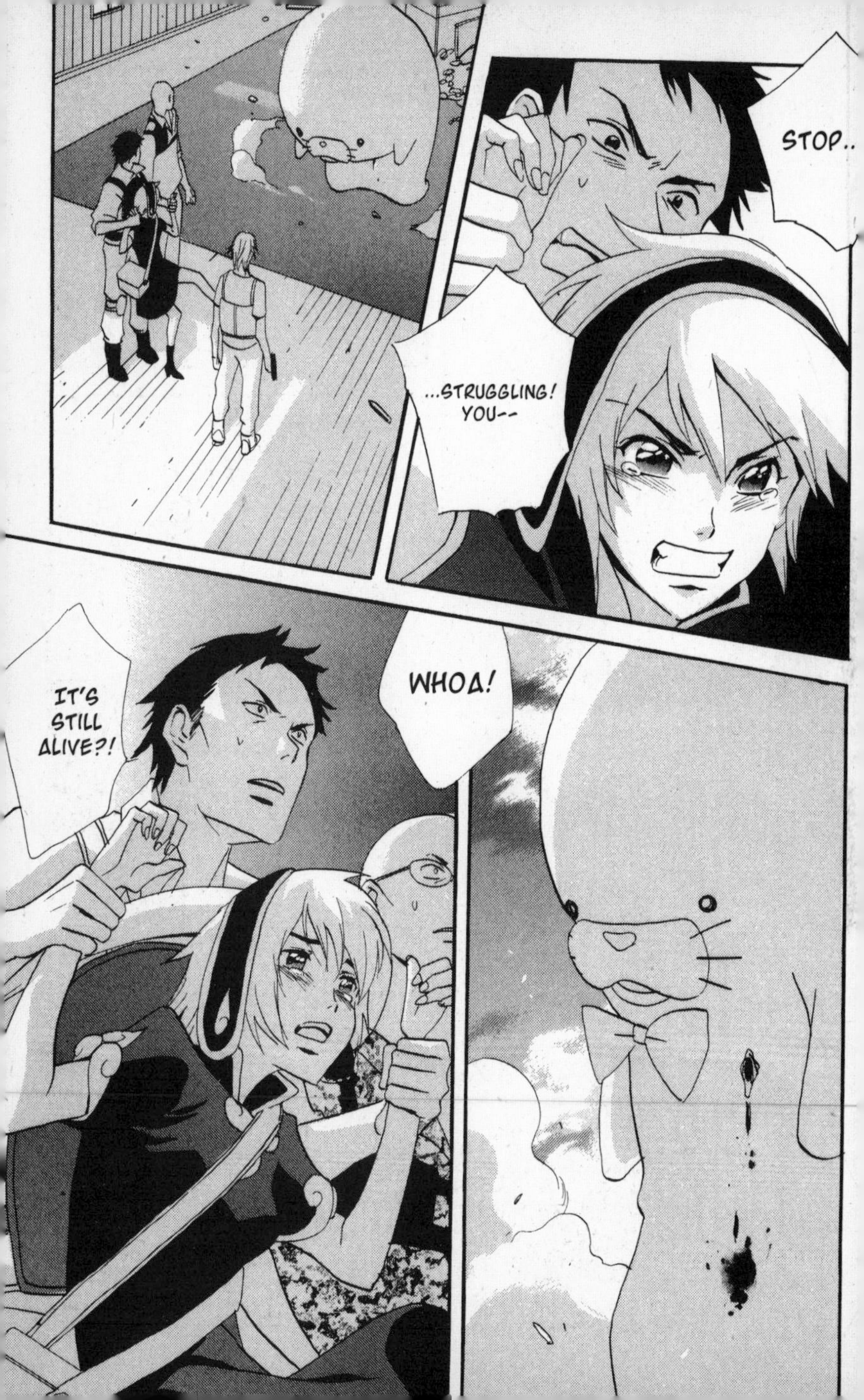
STOP..
...STRUGGLING! YOU--
WHOA!
IT'S STILL ALIVE?!

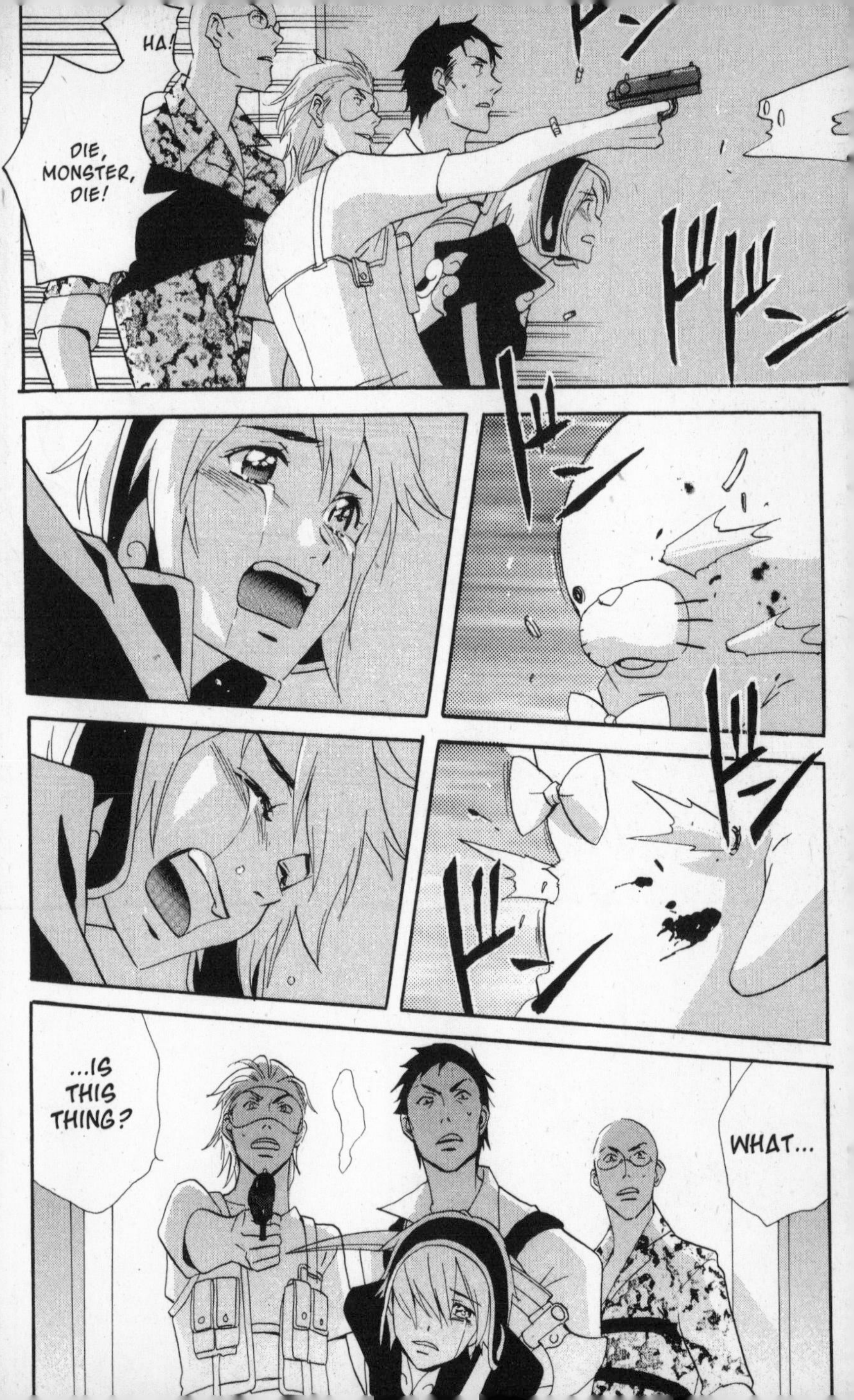
HA!
DIE, MONSTER, DIE!
WHAT...
...IS THIS THING?

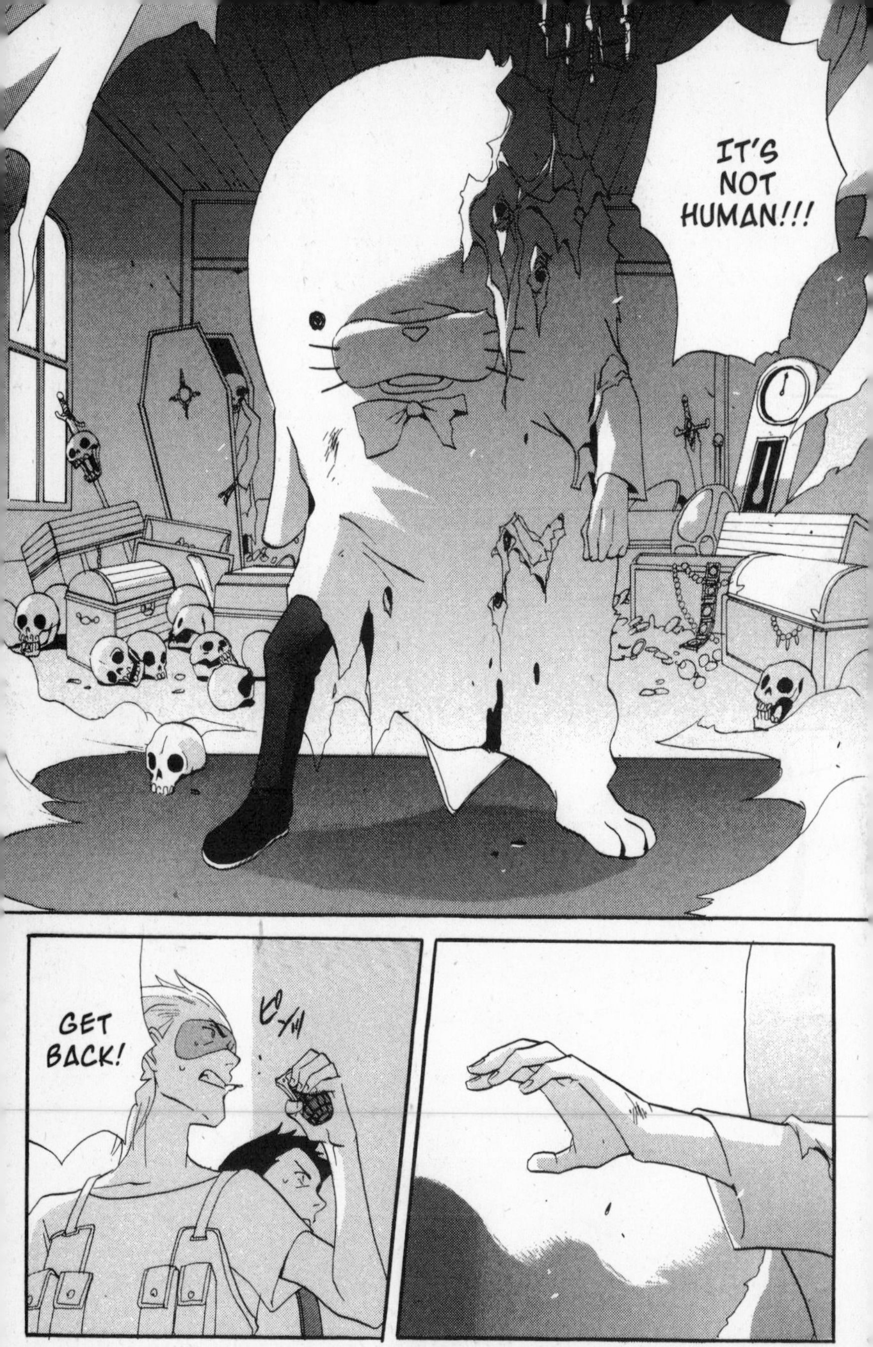
IT'S NOT HUMAN!!!
GET BACK!

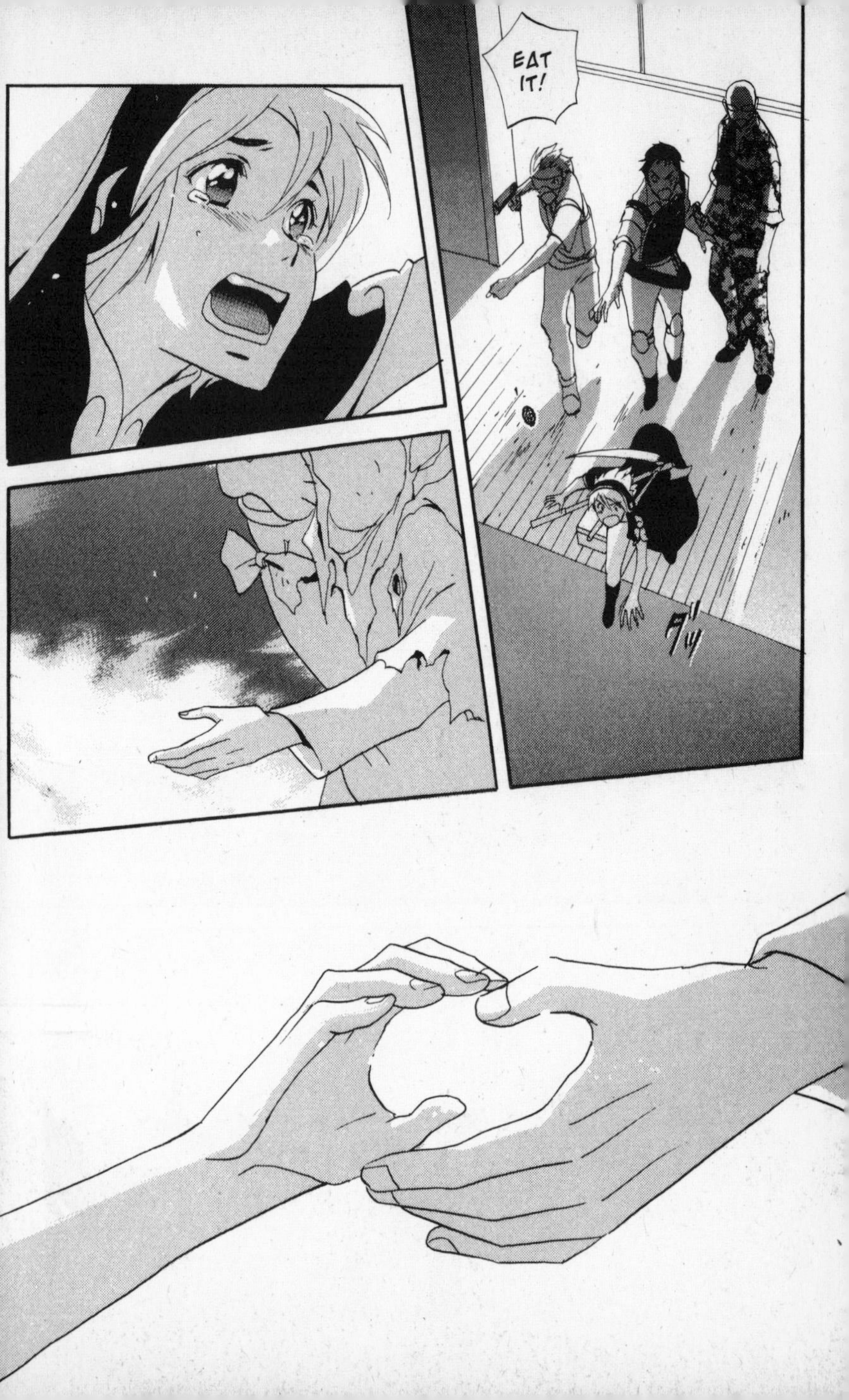
EAT IT!

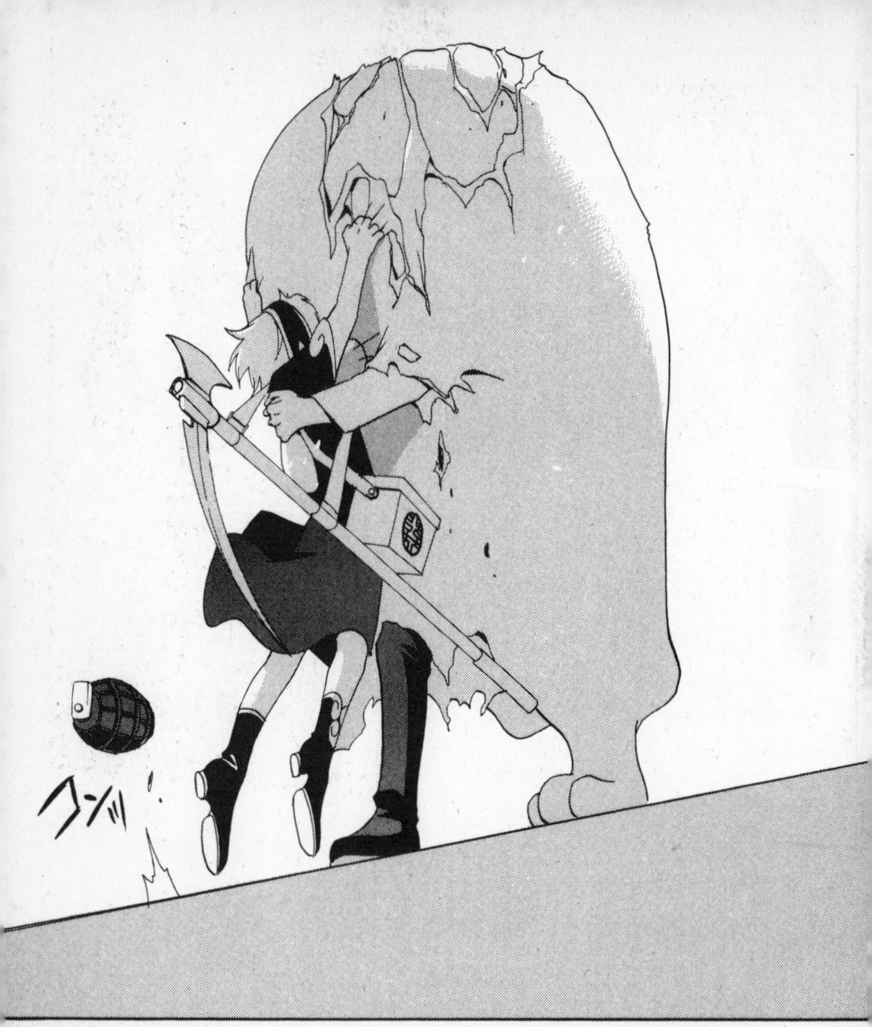
コーンッ
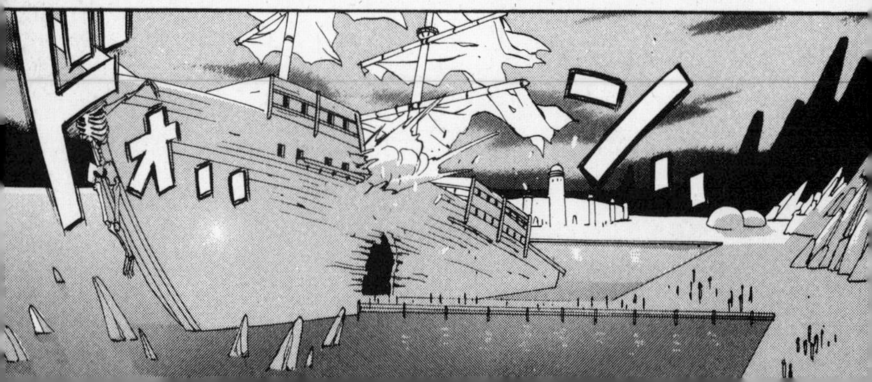
ドオン

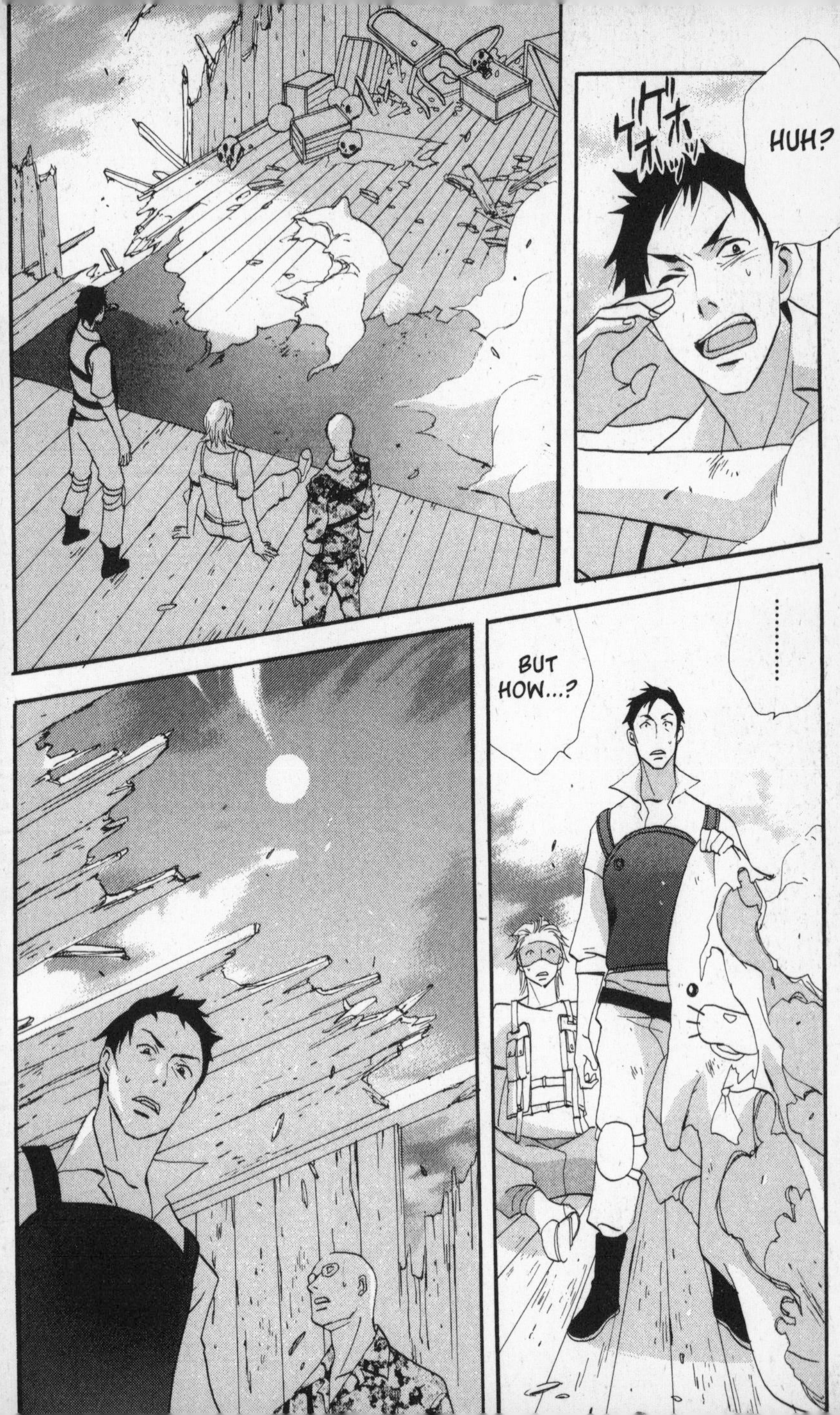
HUH?
ゲオ ケオッ
......
BUT HOW...?

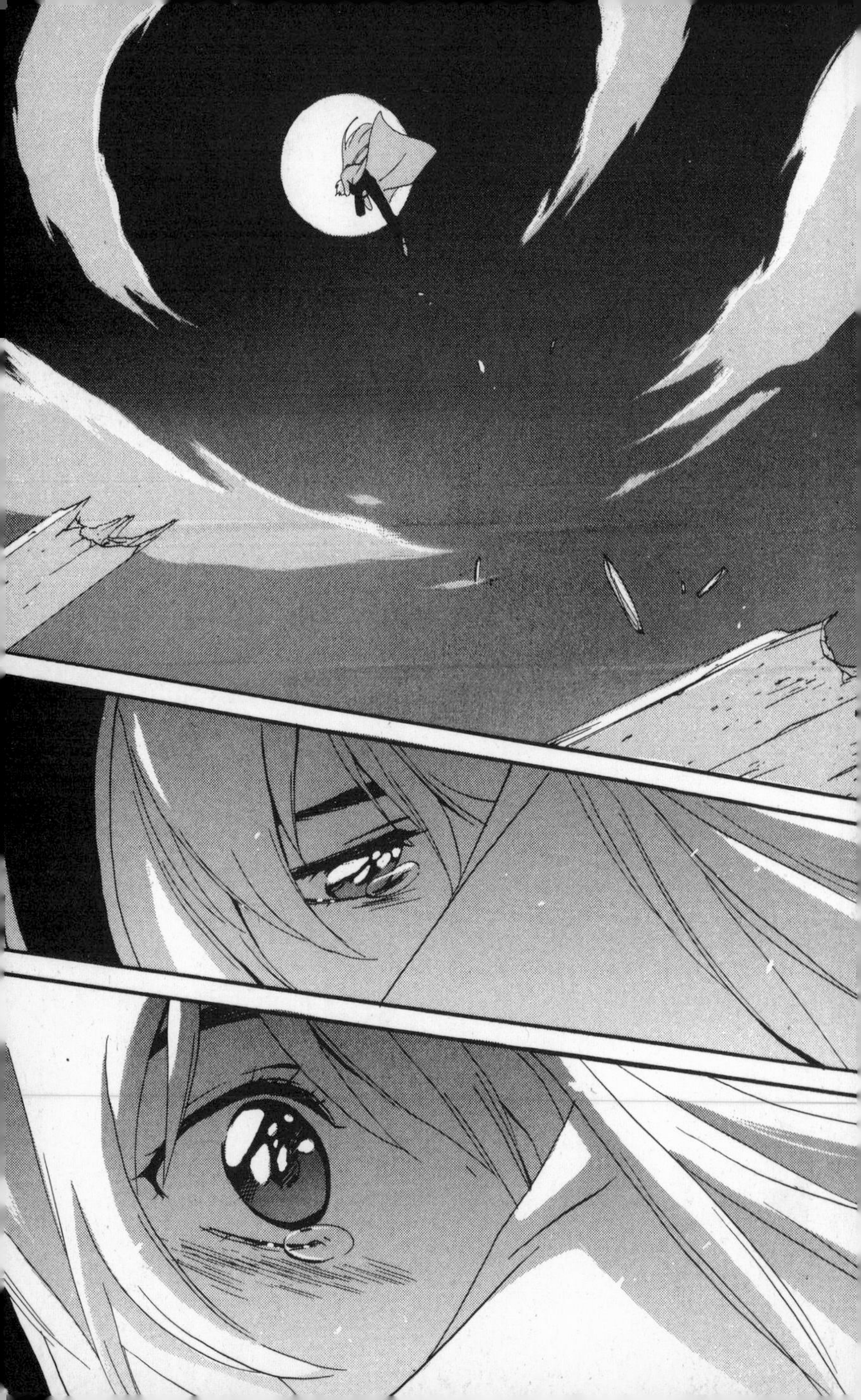

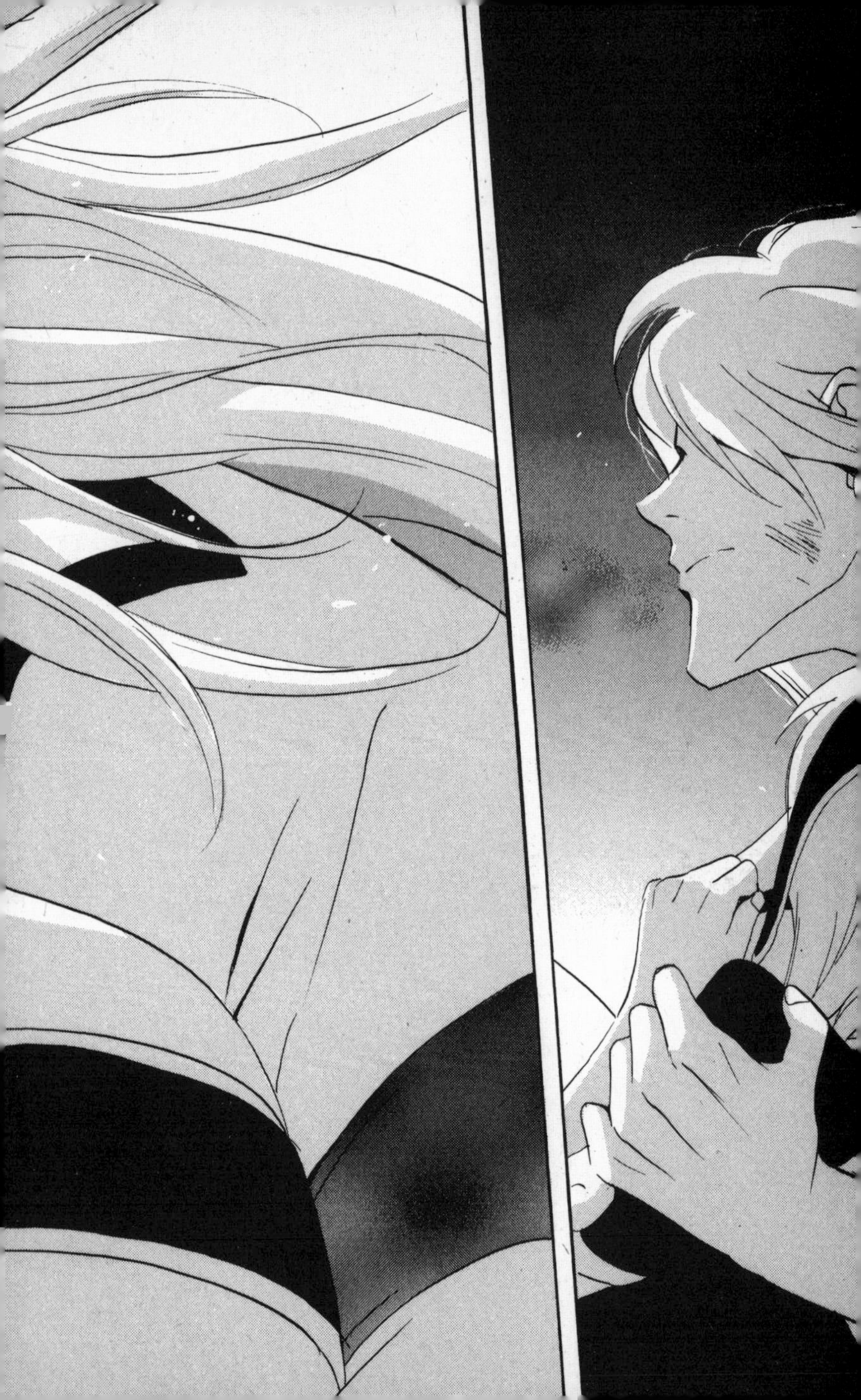

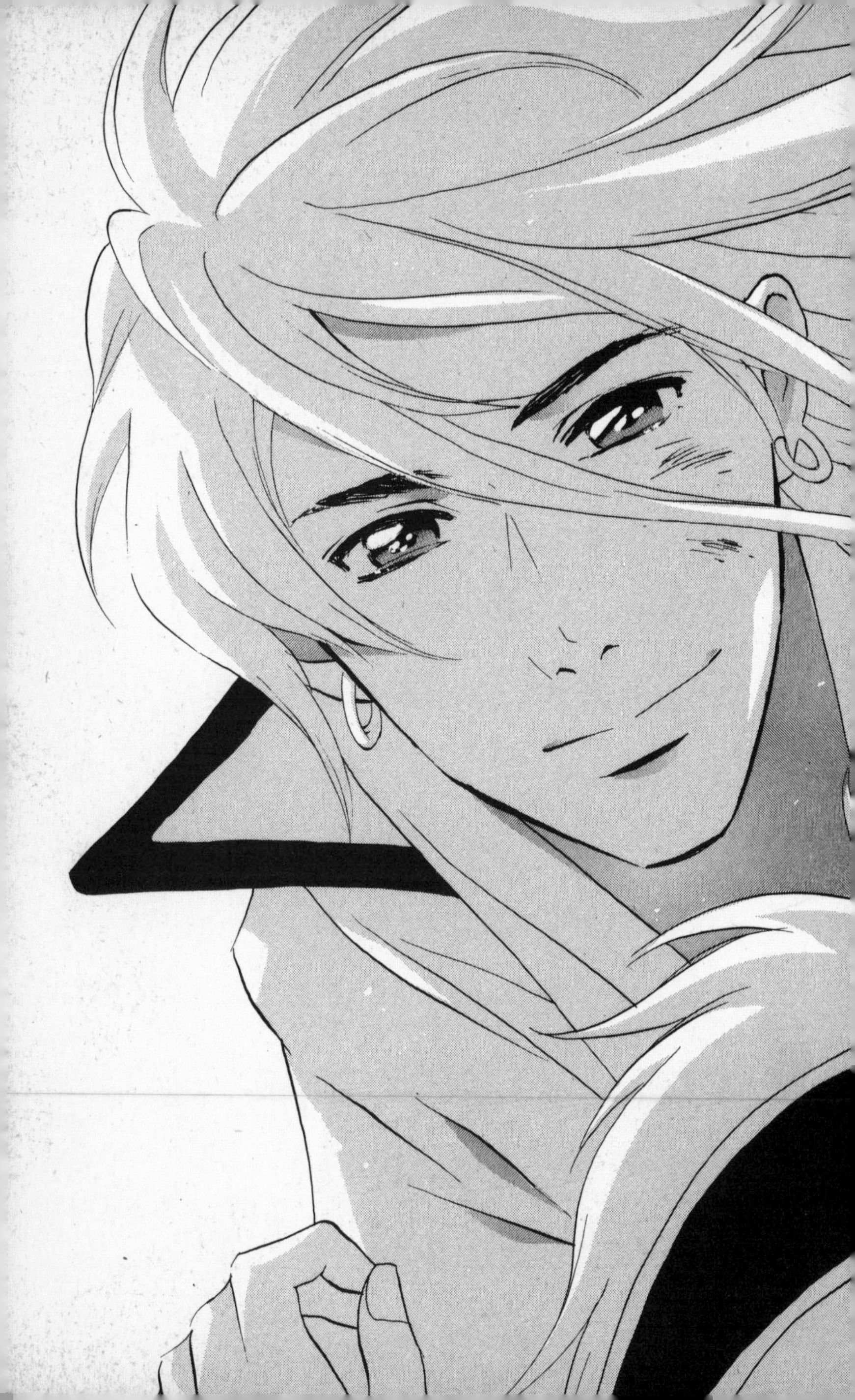

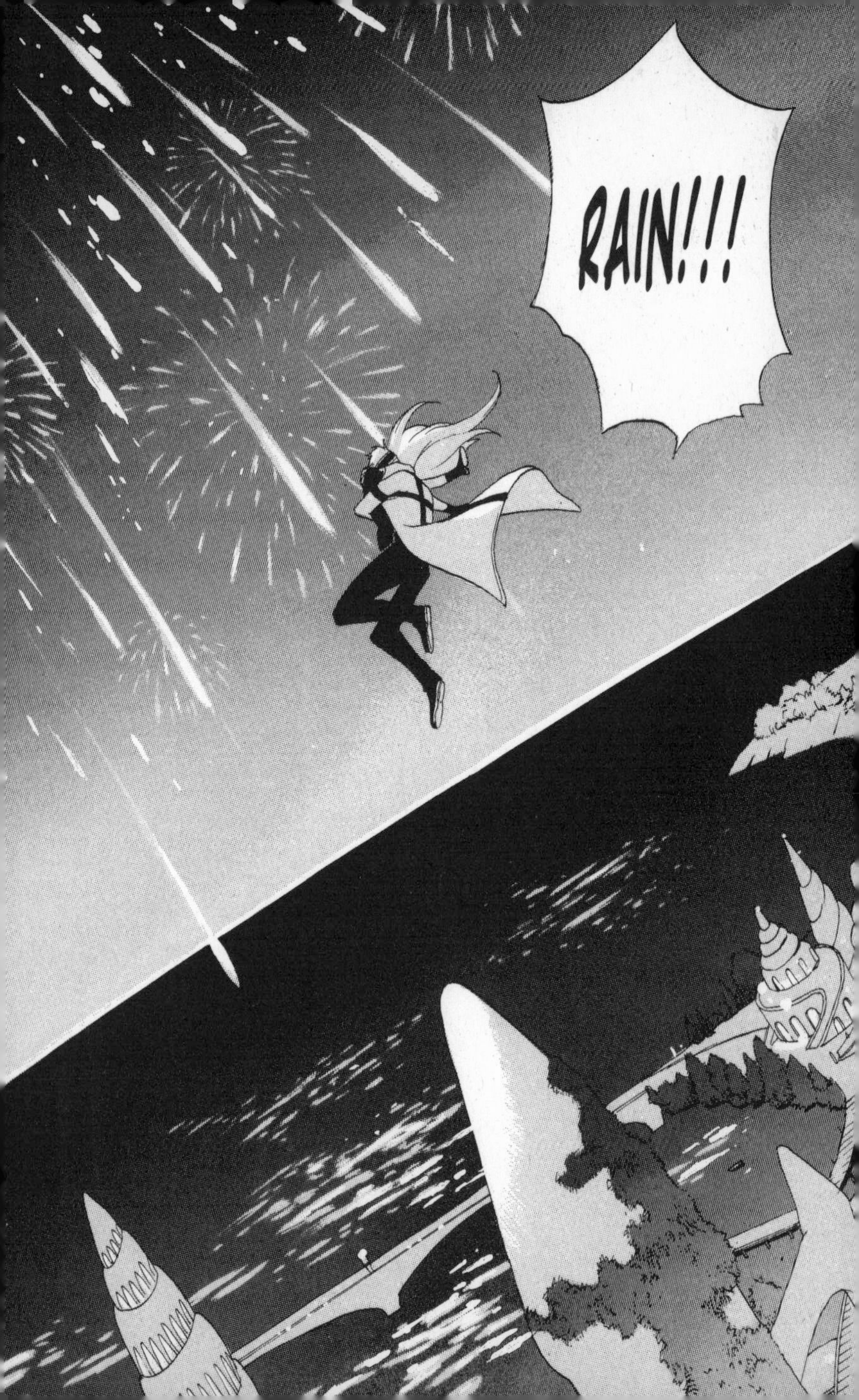
RAIN!!!

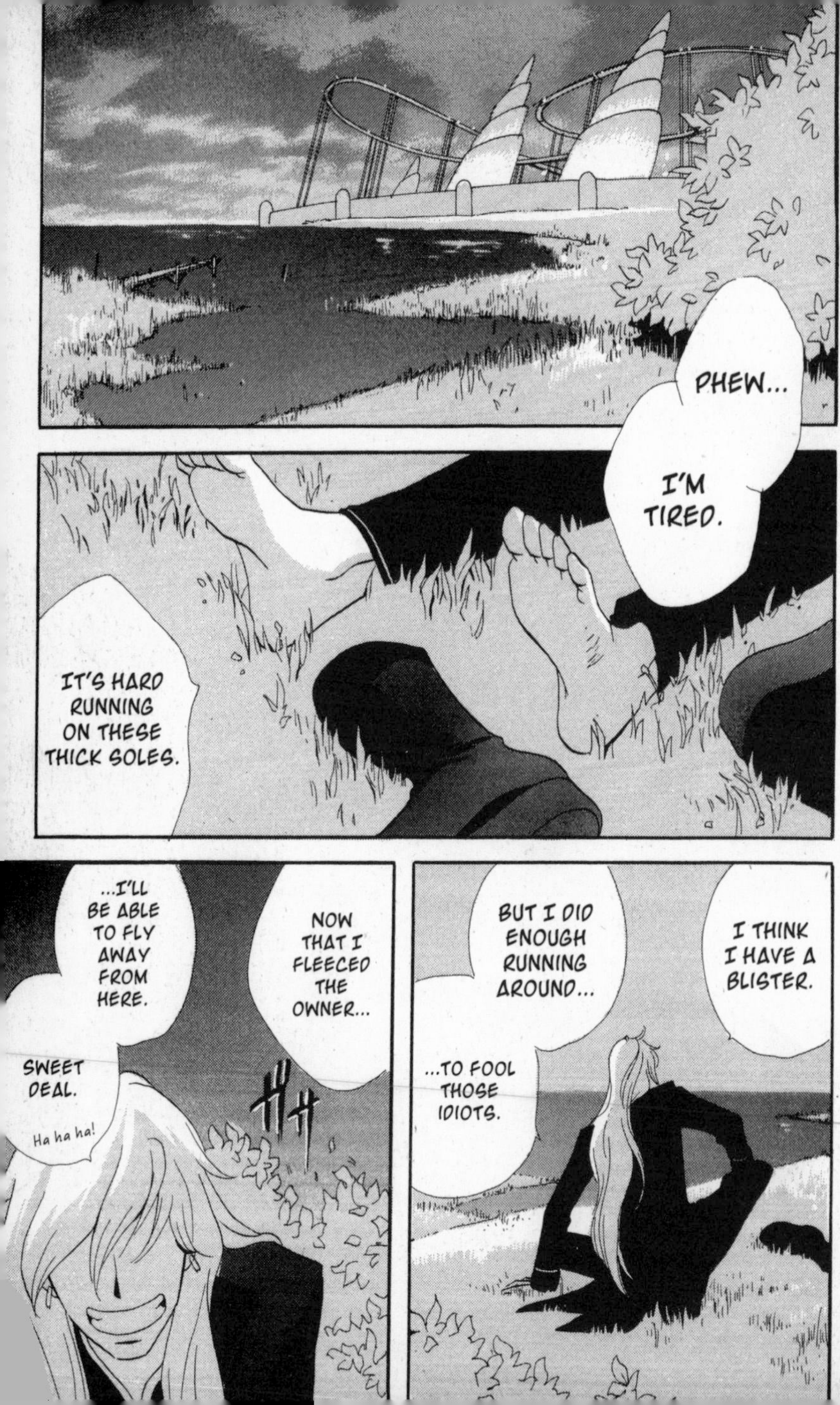
PHEW...
I'M TIRED.
IT'S HARD RUNNING ON THESE THICK SOLES.
I THINK I HAVE A BLISTER.
BUT I DID ENOUGH RUNNING AROUND...
...TO FOOL THOSE IDIOTS.
NOW THAT I FLEECED THE OWNER...
...I'LL BE ABLE TO FLY AWAY FROM HERE.
SWEET DEAL.
Ha ha ha!

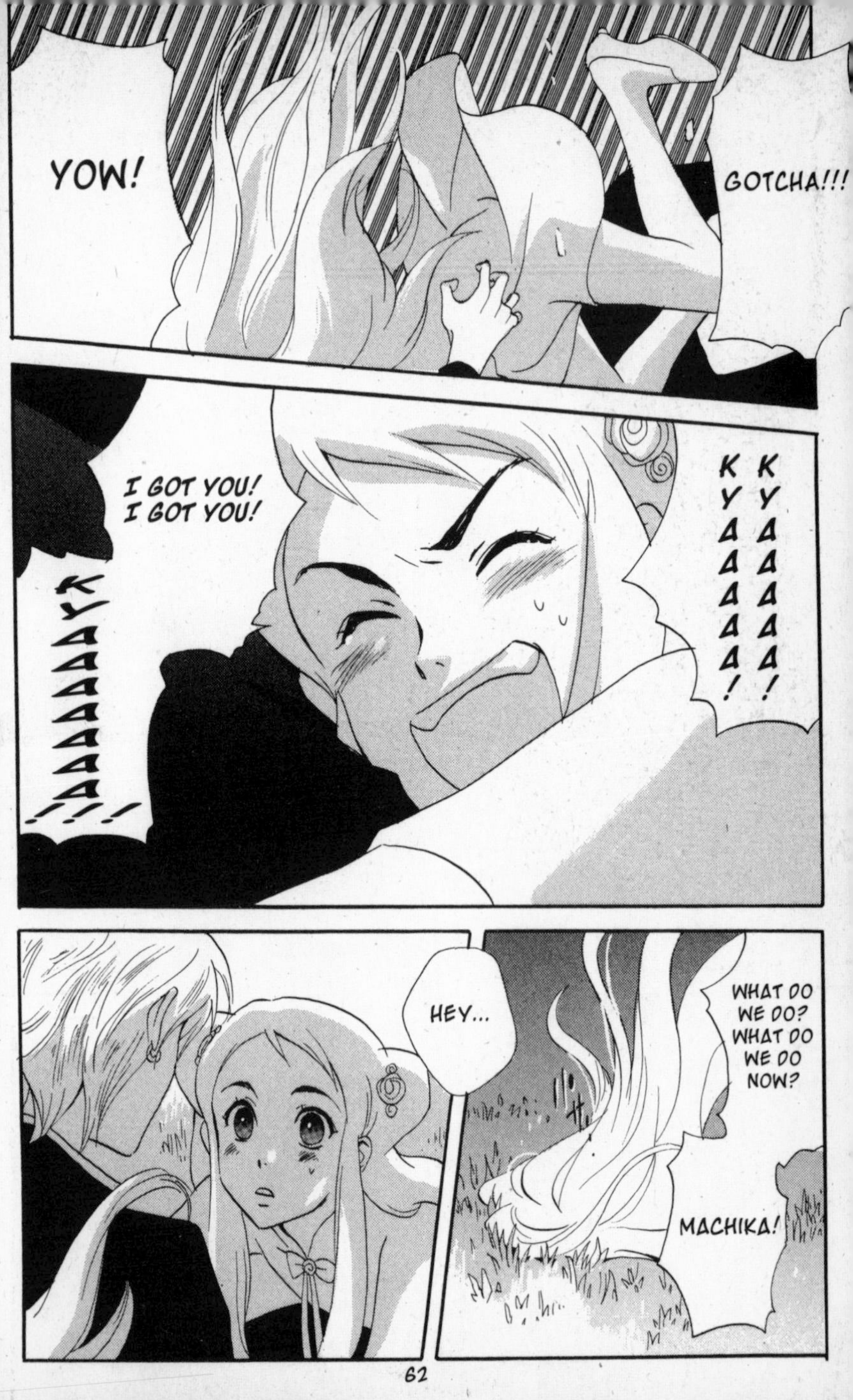
GOTCHA!!!
YOW!
KYAAAAA!
KYAAAAA!
I GOT YOU! I GOT YOU!
KYAAAAAAA!!!
WHAT DO WE DO? WHAT DO WE DO NOW?
MACHIKA!
HEY...

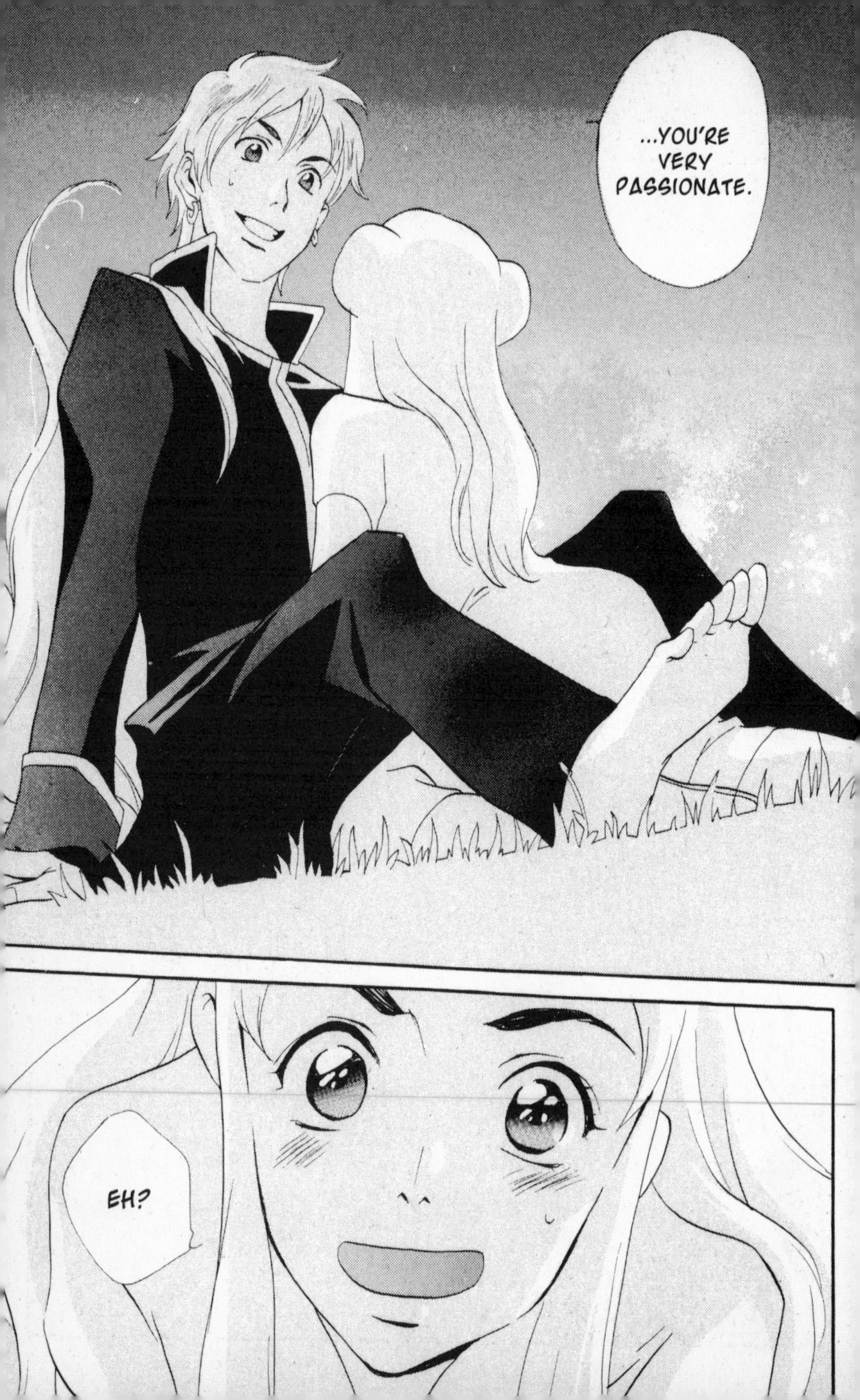
...YOU'RE VERY PASSIONATE.
EH?

IMMORTAL RAIN

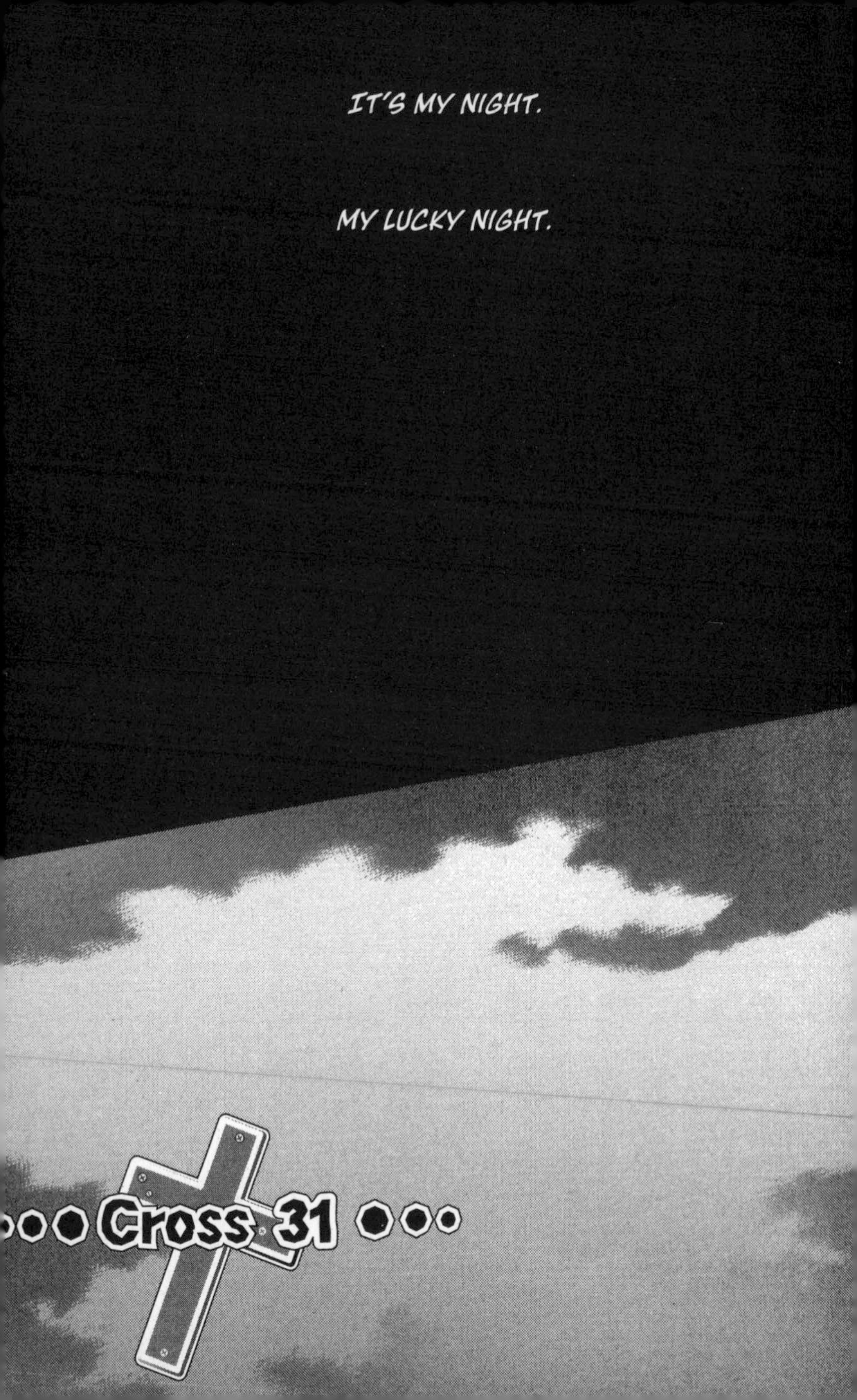
IT'S MY NIGHT.
MY LUCKY NIGHT.
Cross 31

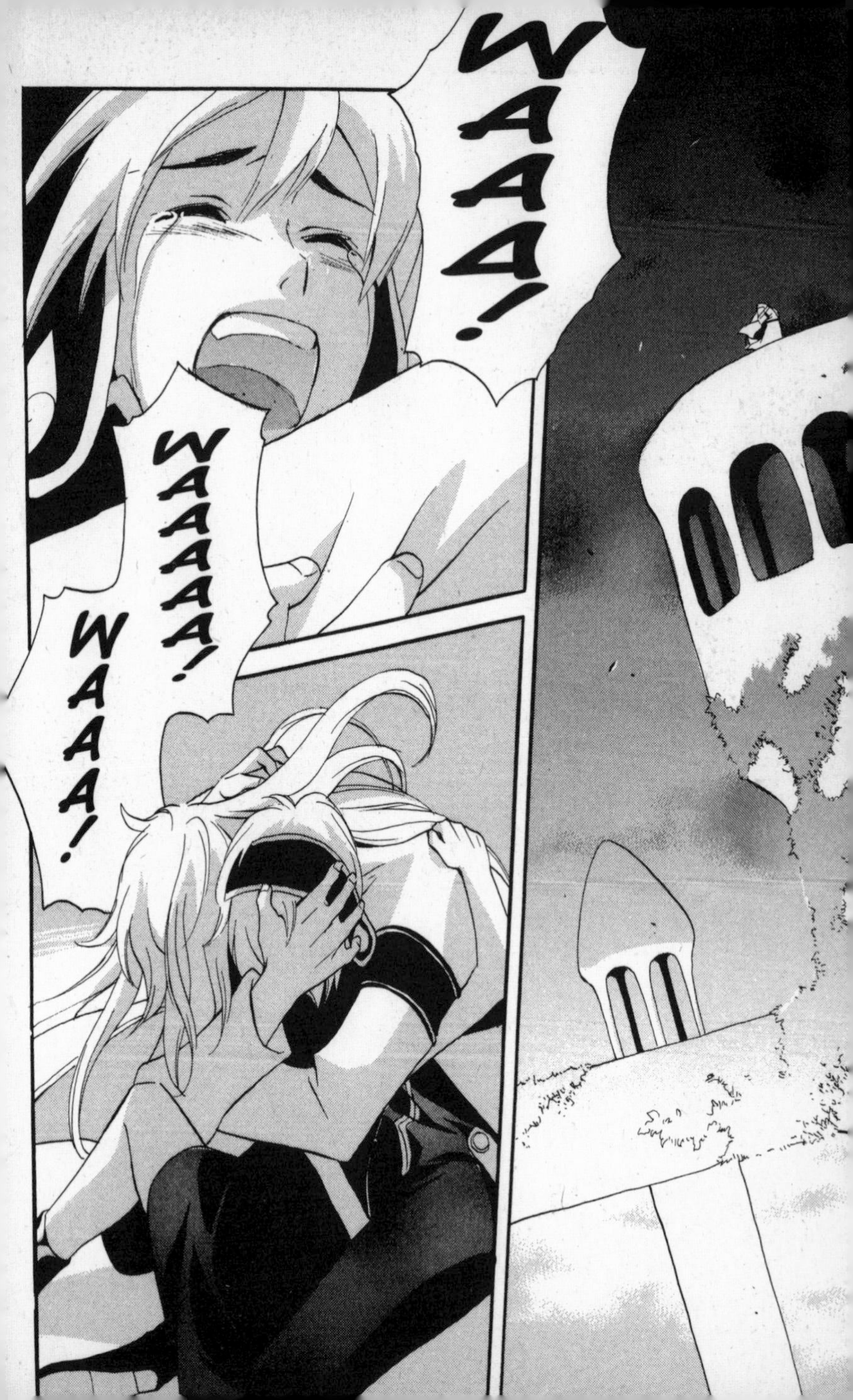
WAAAA!
WAAAAAA!
WAAAAA!

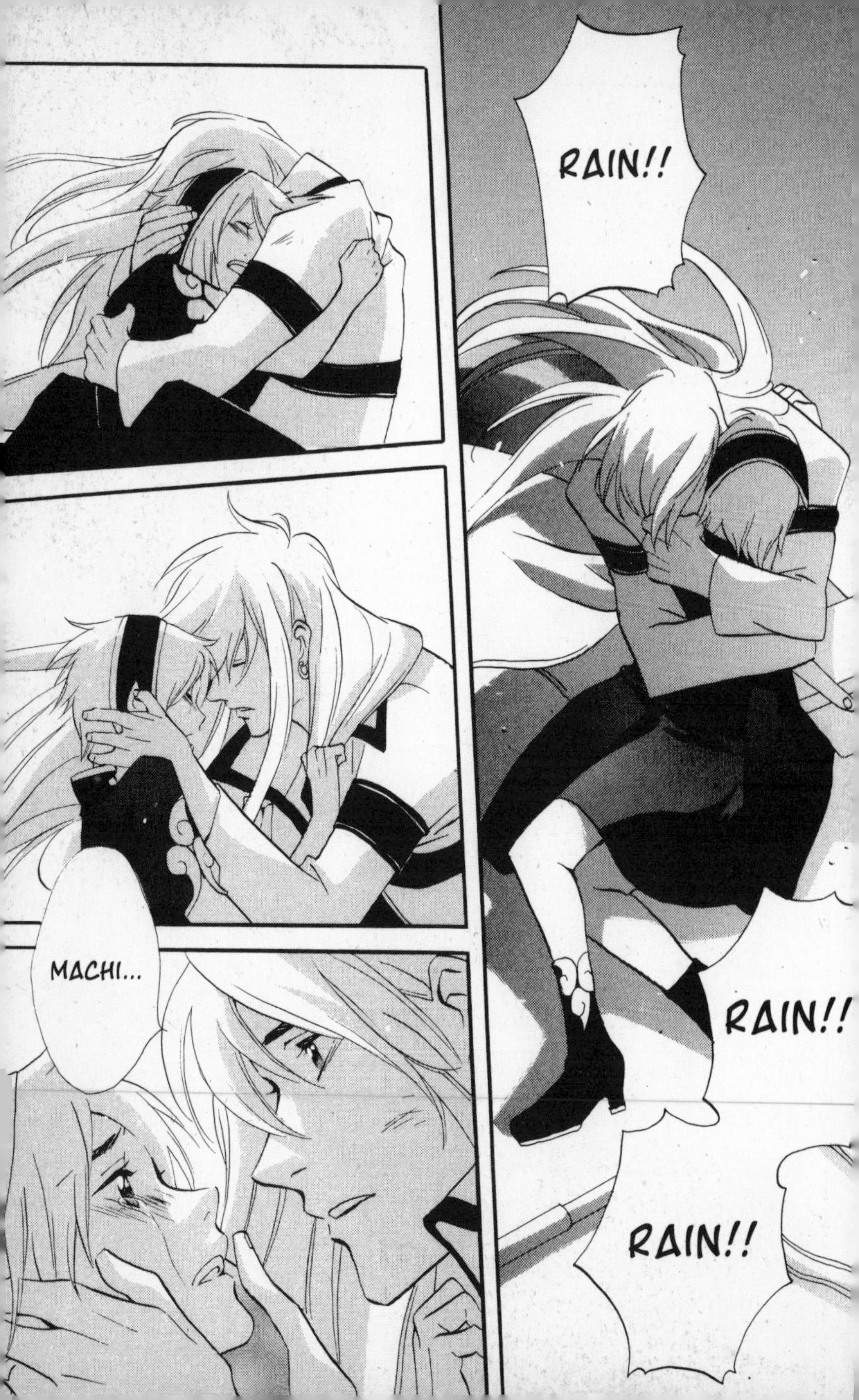
RAIN!!
RAIN!!
RAIN!!
MACHI...

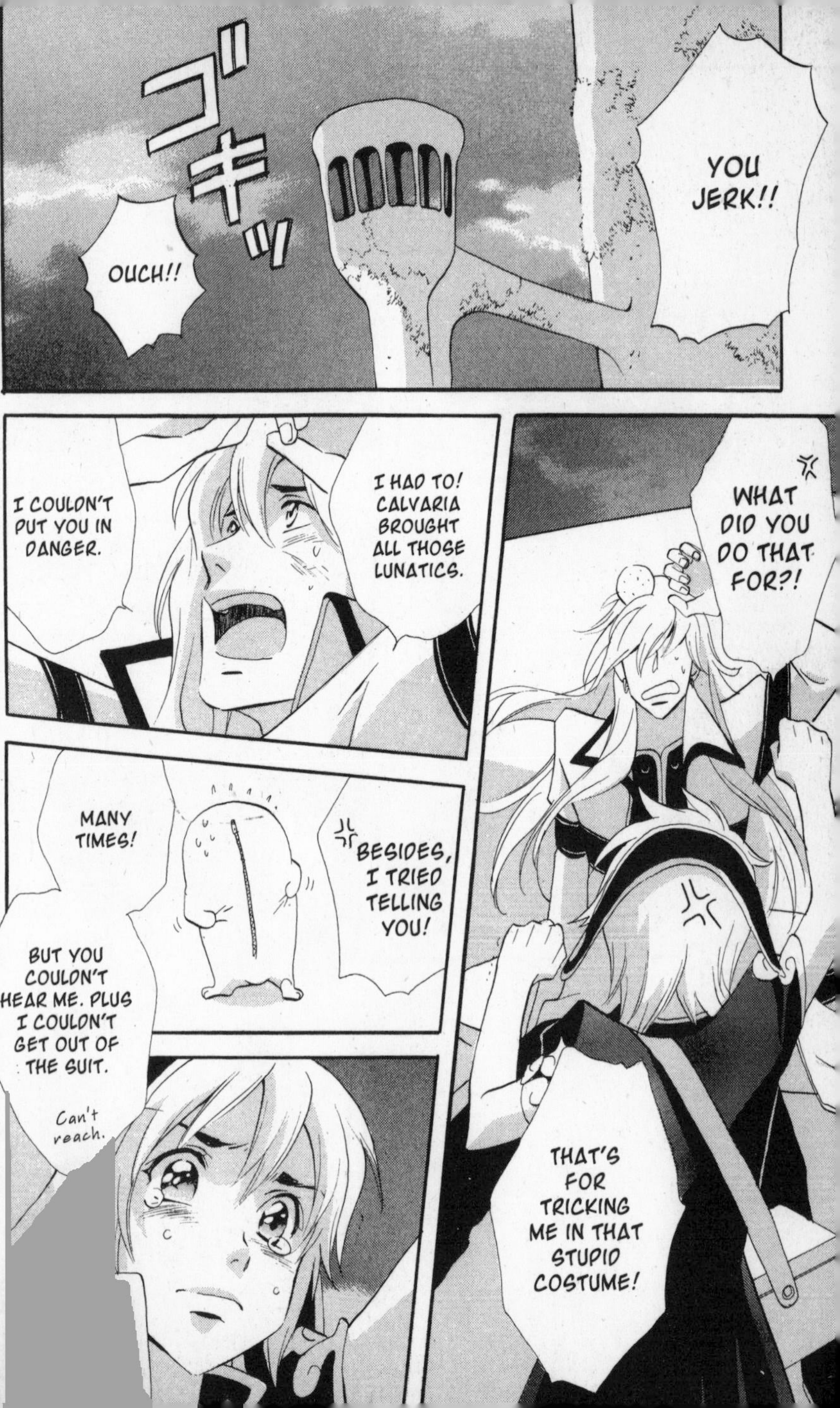

YOU JERK!!
ゴキッ
OUCH!!
WHAT DID YOU DO THAT FOR?!
THAT'S FOR TRICKING ME IN THAT STUPID COSTUME!
I HAD TO! CALVARIA BROUGHT ALL THOSE LUNATICS.
I COULDN'T PUT YOU IN DANGER.
BESIDES, I TRIED TELLING YOU!
MANY TIMES!
BUT YOU COULDN'T HEAR ME. PLUS I COULDN'T GET OUT OF THE SUIT.
Can't reach.

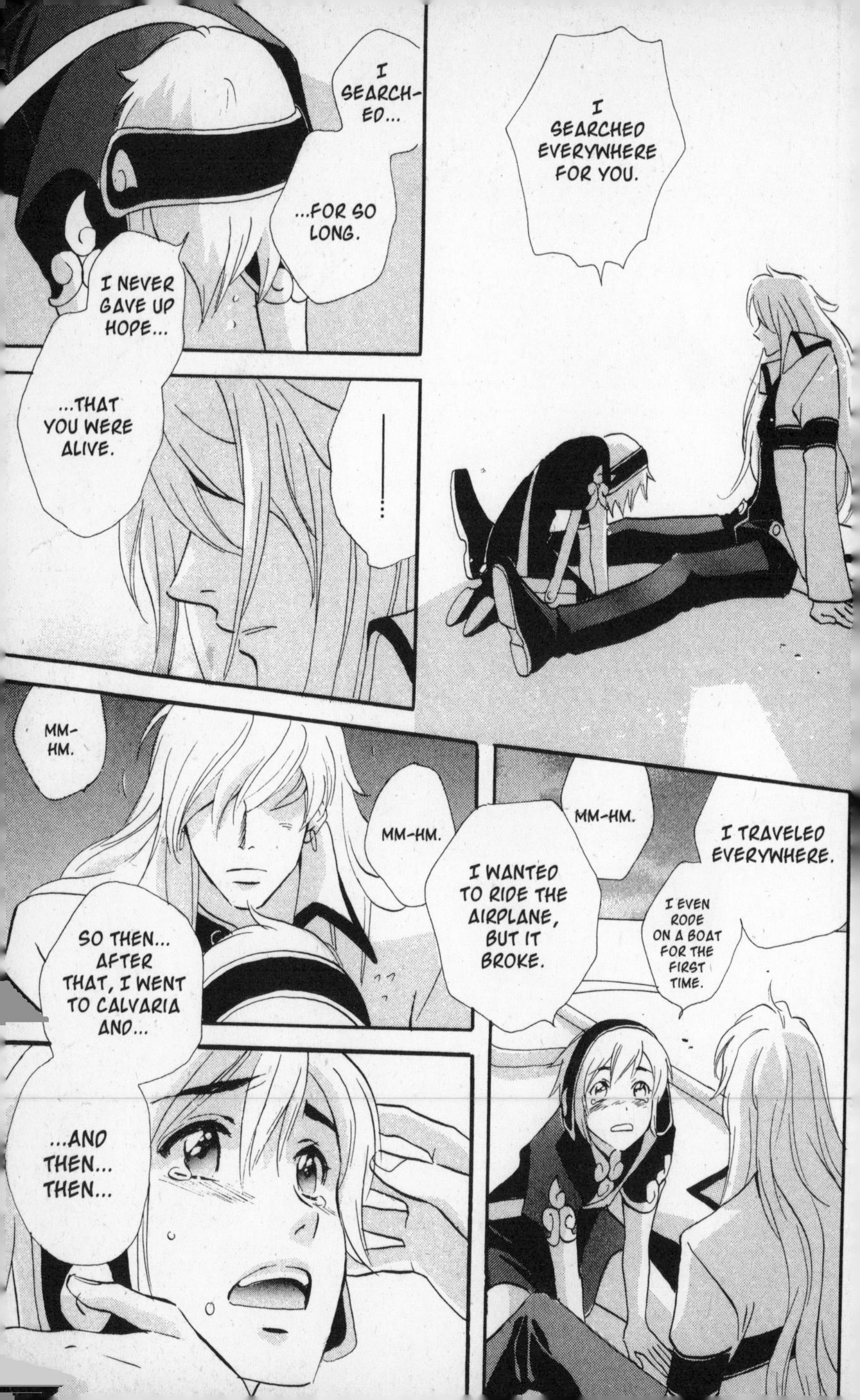
I SEARCHED EVERYWHERE FOR YOU.
I SEARCH-ED...
...FOR SO LONG.
I NEVER GAVE UP HOPE...
...THAT YOU WERE ALIVE.
I TRAVELED EVERYWHERE.
I EVEN RODE ON A BOAT FOR THE FIRST TIME.
MM-HM.
I WANTED TO RIDE THE AIRPLANE, BUT IT BROKE.
MM-HM.
MM-HM.
SO THEN... AFTER THAT, I WENT TO CALVARIA AND...
...AND THEN... THEN...

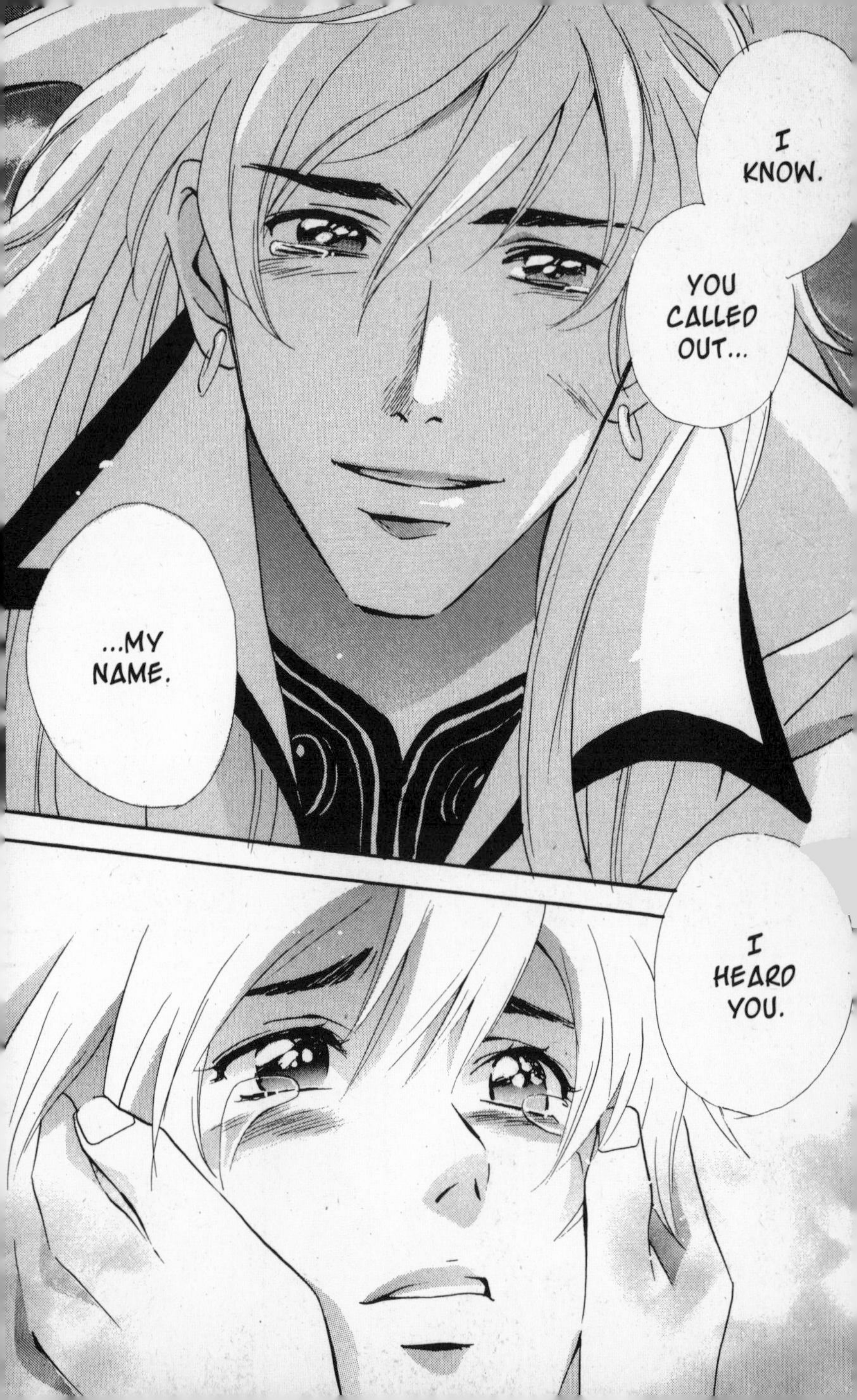
I KNOW.
YOU CALLED OUT...
...MY NAME.
I HEARD YOU.

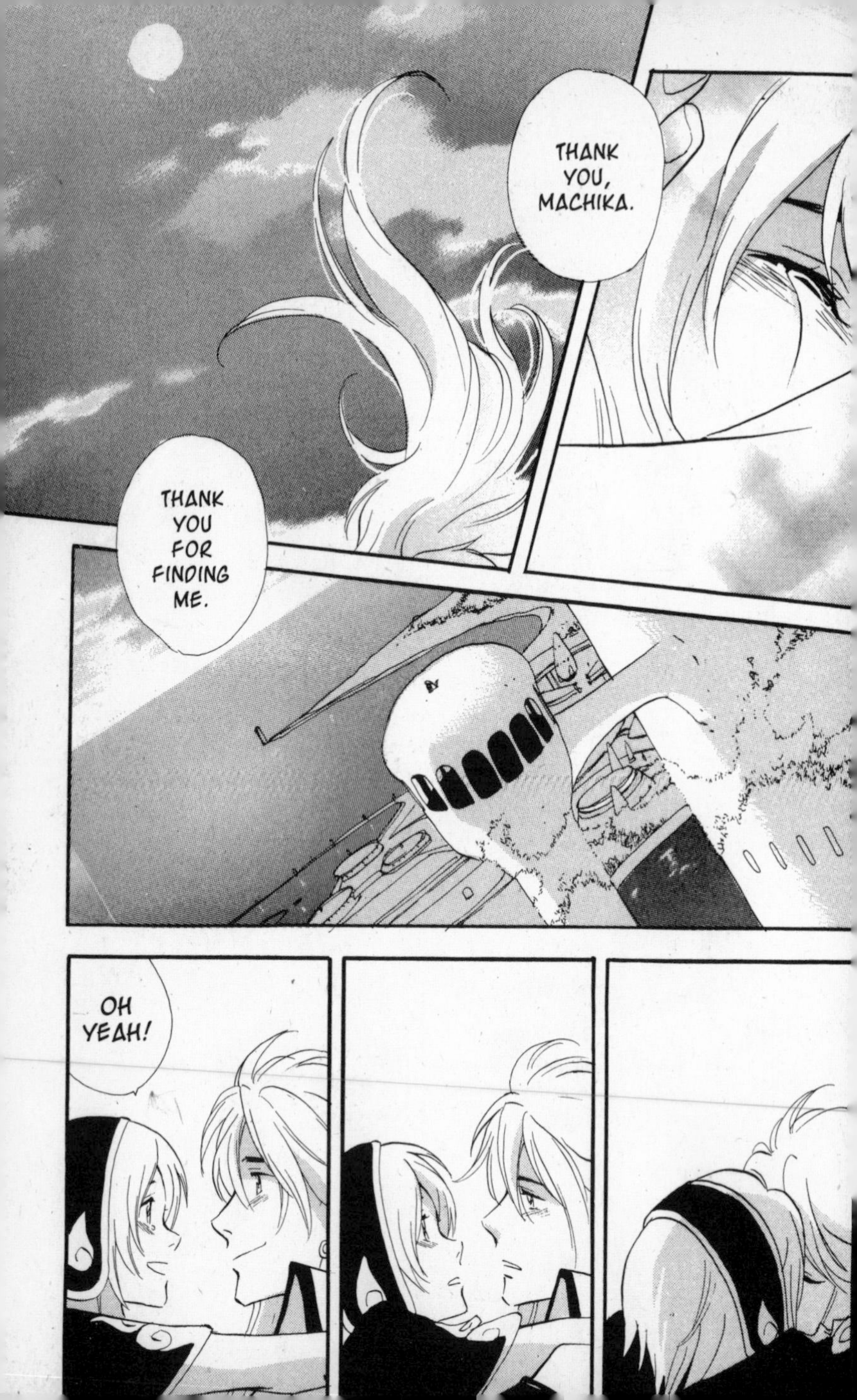
THANK YOU, MACHIKA.
THANK YOU FOR FINDING ME.
OH YEAH!

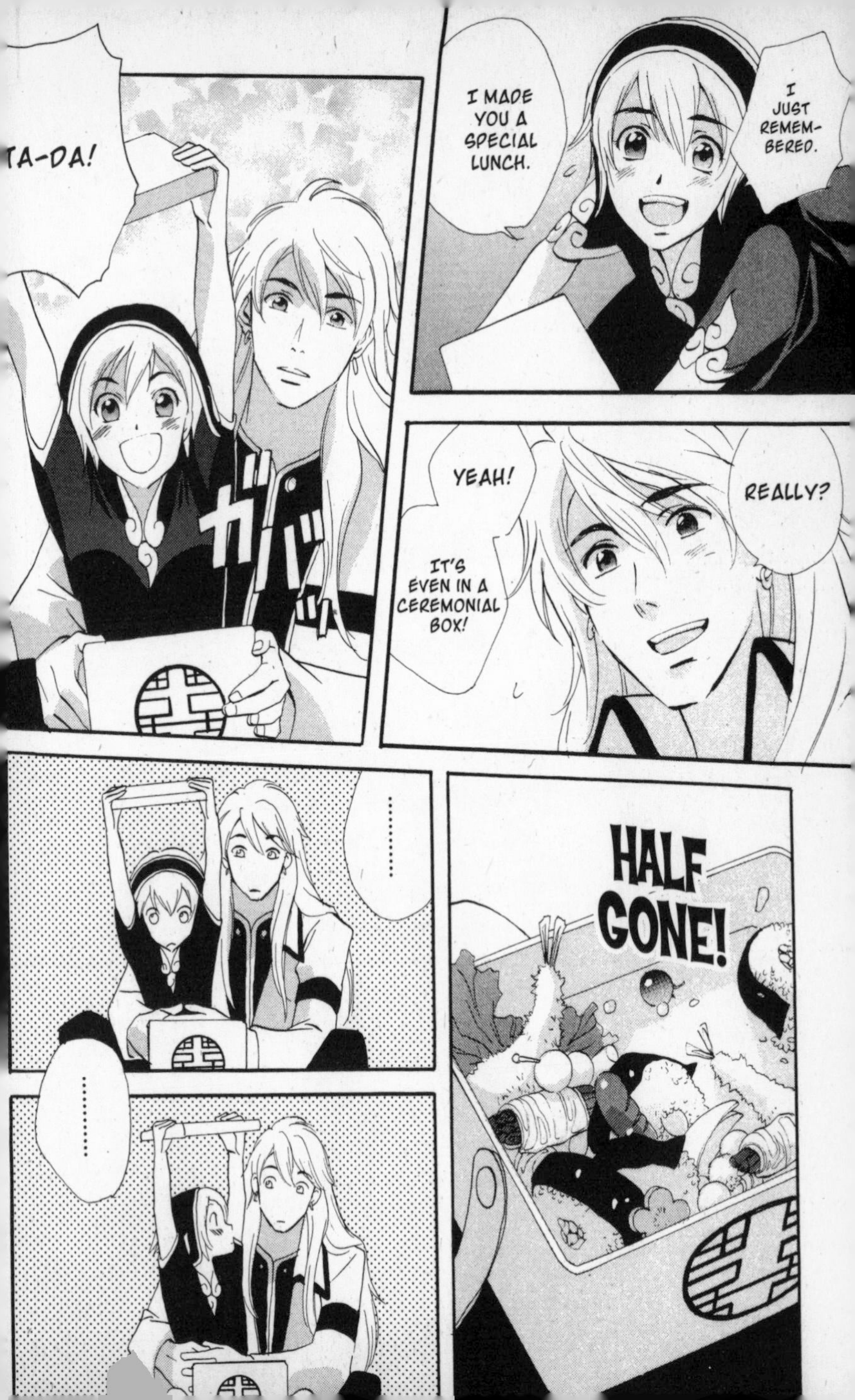
I JUST REMEMBERED.
I MADE YOU A SPECIAL LUNCH.
REALLY?
YEAH!
IT'S EVEN IN A CEREMONIAL BOX!
TA-DA!
HALF GONE!
......
......

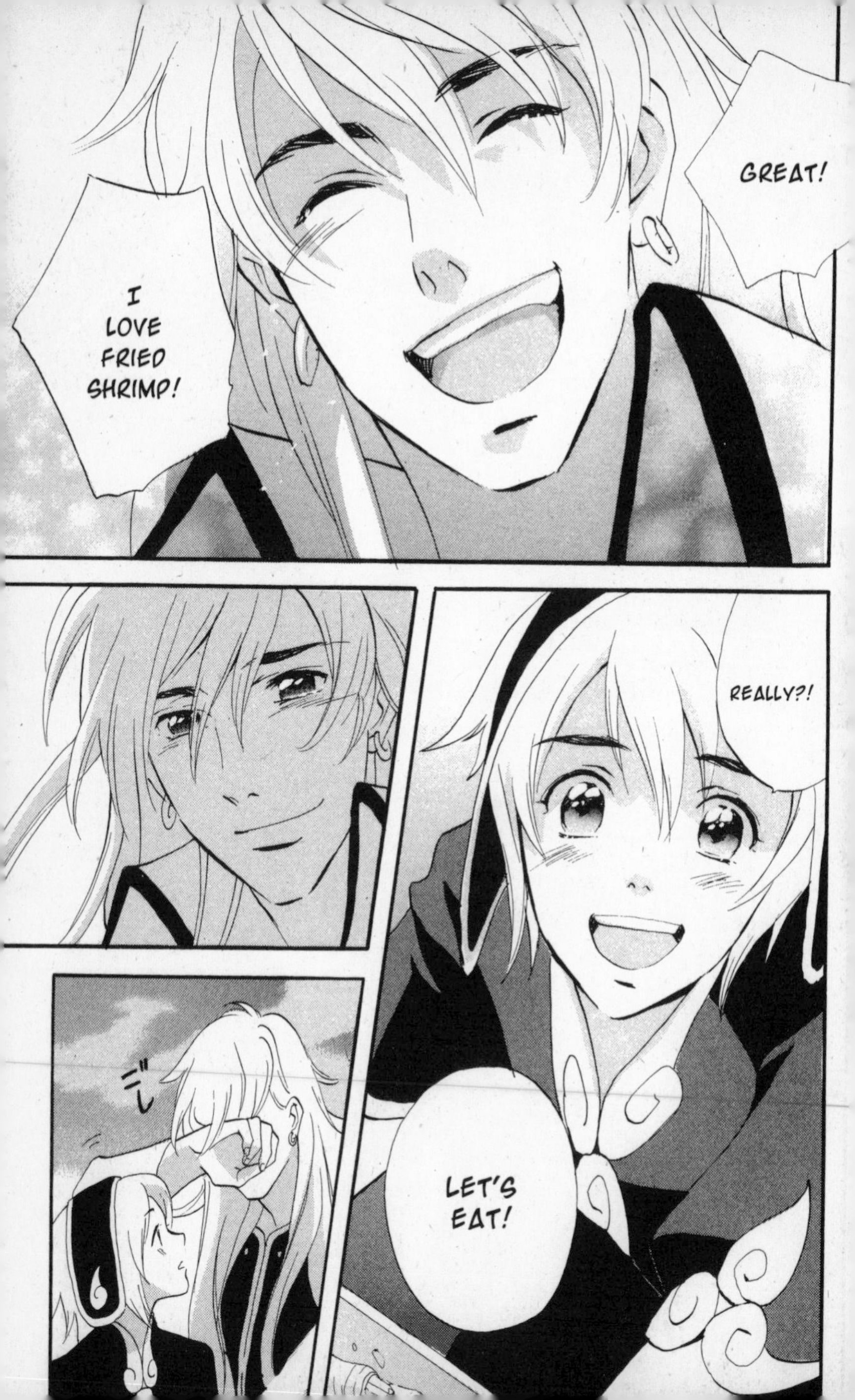
GREAT!
I LOVE FRIED SHRIMP!
REALLY?!
LET'S EAT!
ごし

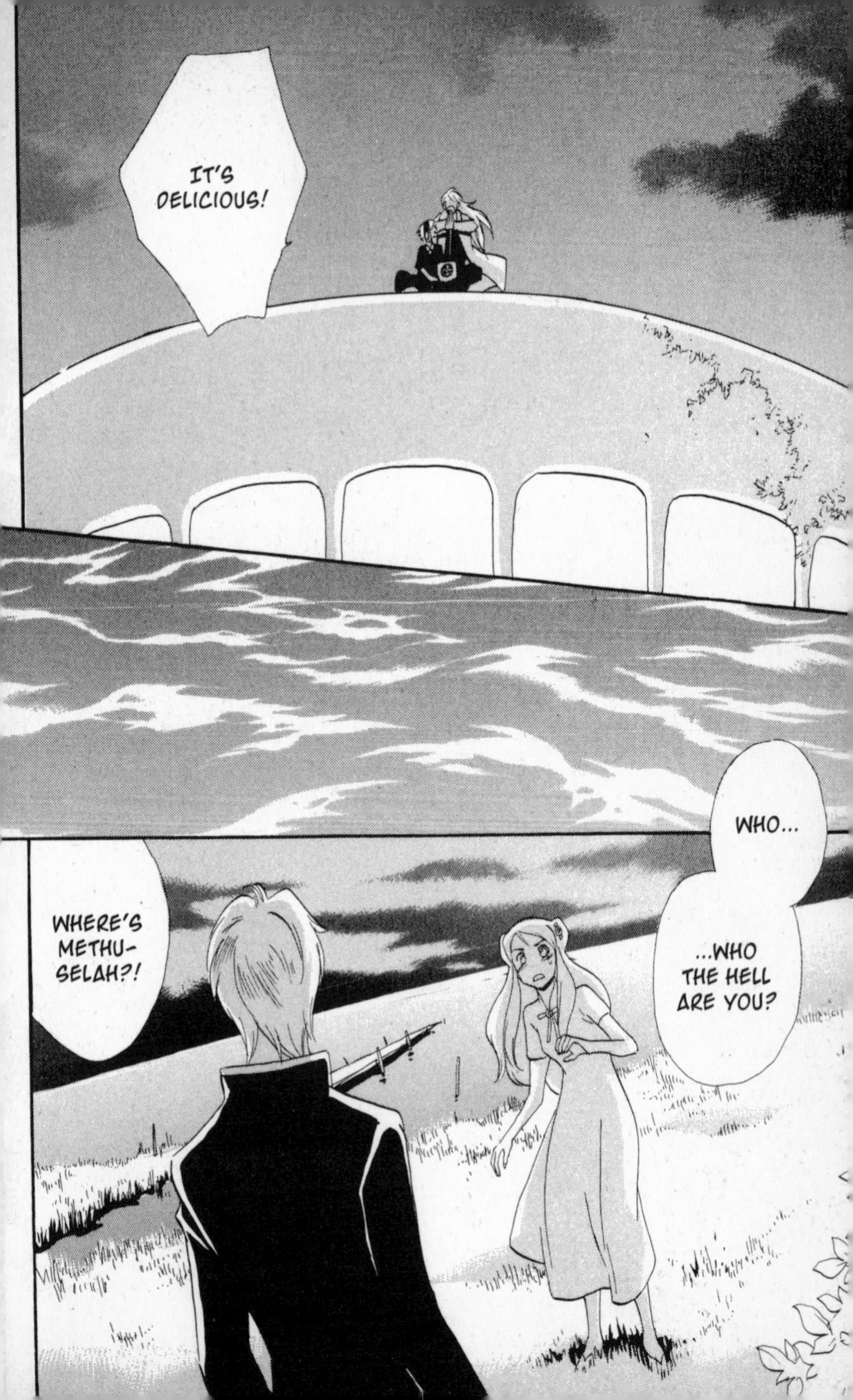
IT'S DELICIOUS!
WHO...
...WHO THE HELL ARE YOU?
WHERE'S METHU-SELAH?!

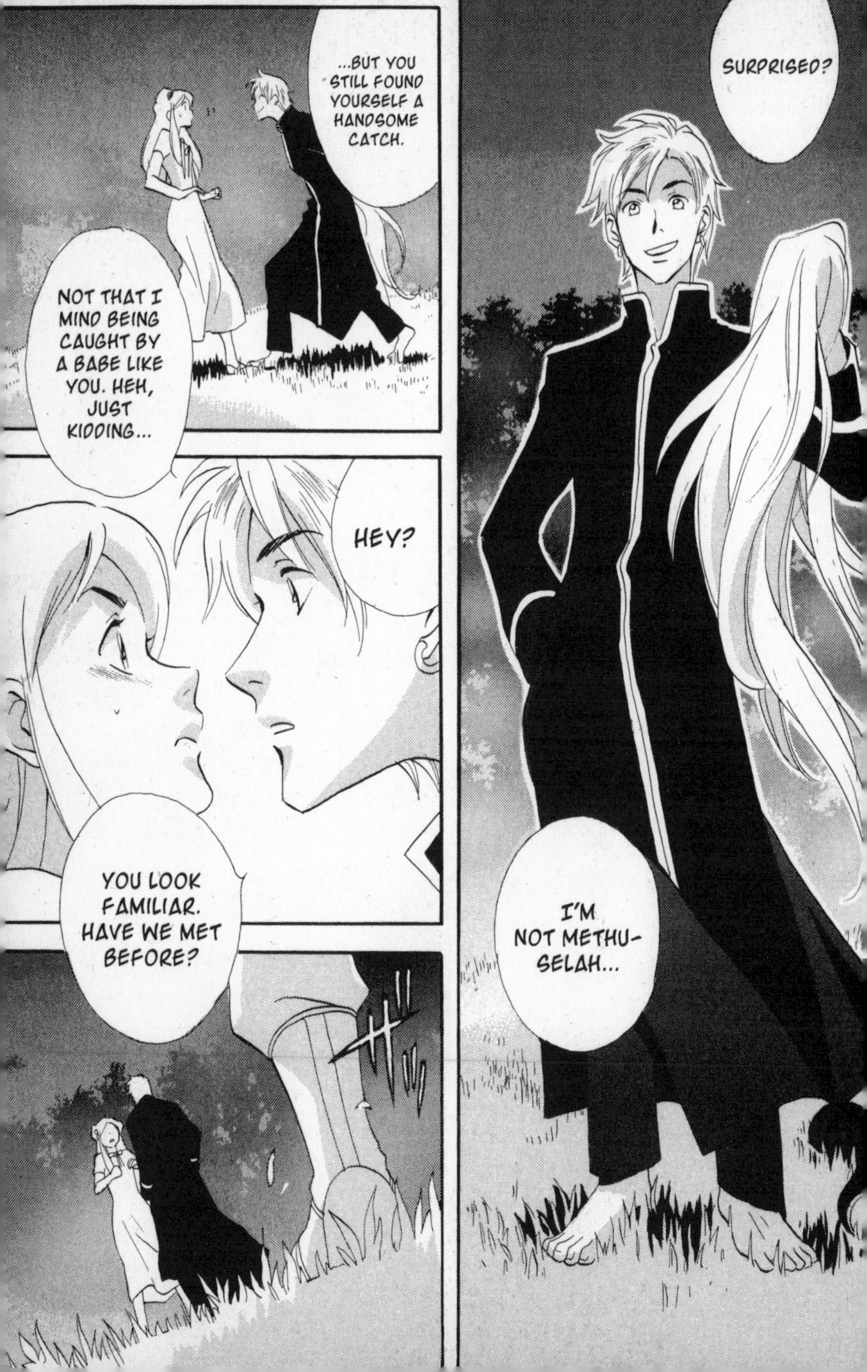
SURPRISED?
I'M NOT METHU-SELAH...
...BUT YOU STILL FOUND YOURSELF A HANDSOME CATCH.
NOT THAT I MIND BEING CAUGHT BY A BABE LIKE YOU. HEH, JUST KIDDING...
HEY?
YOU LOOK FAMILIAR. HAVE WE MET BEFORE?

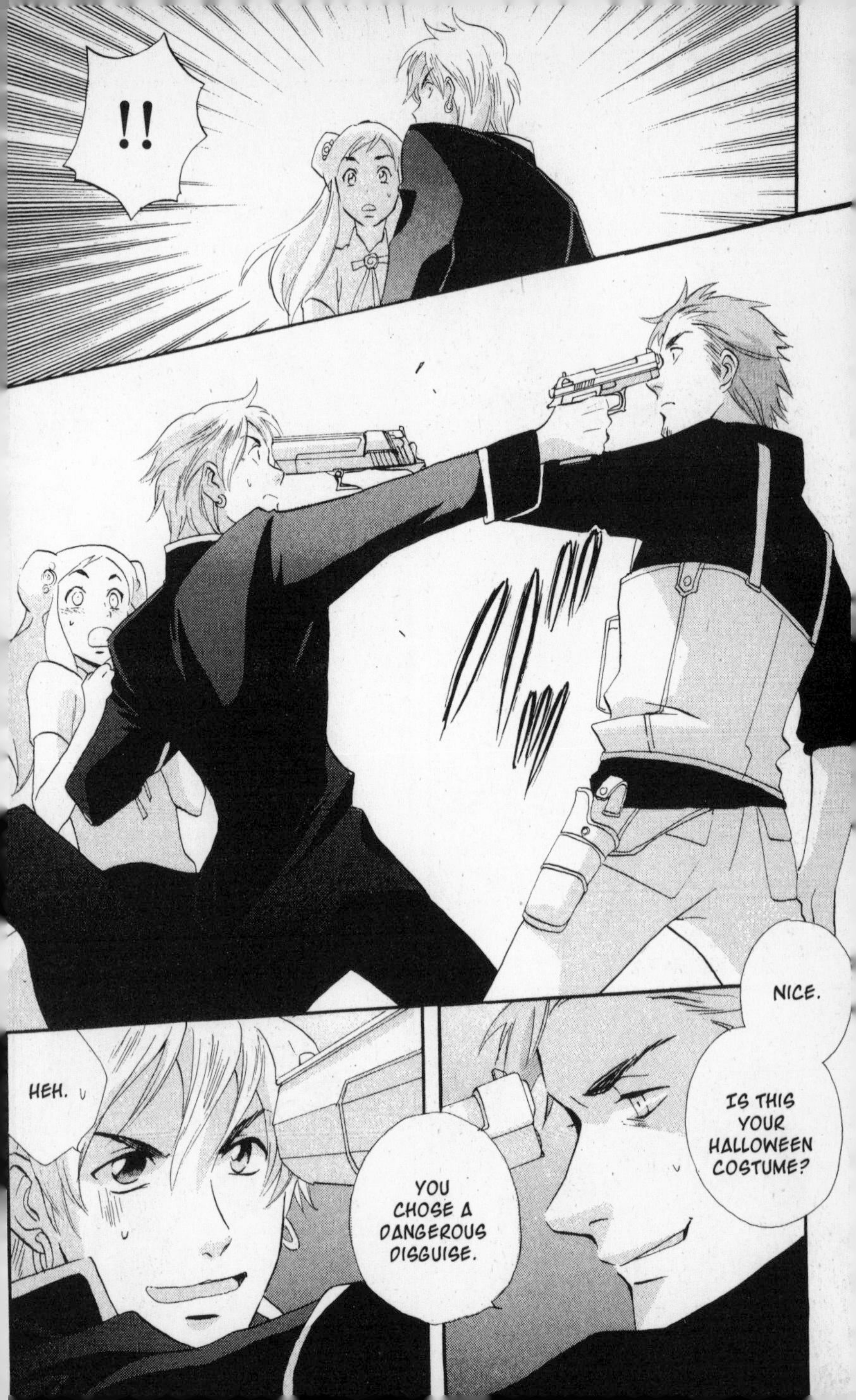
!!
NICE.
IS THIS YOUR HALLOWEEN COSTUME?
HEH.
YOU CHOSE A DANGEROUS DISGUISE.

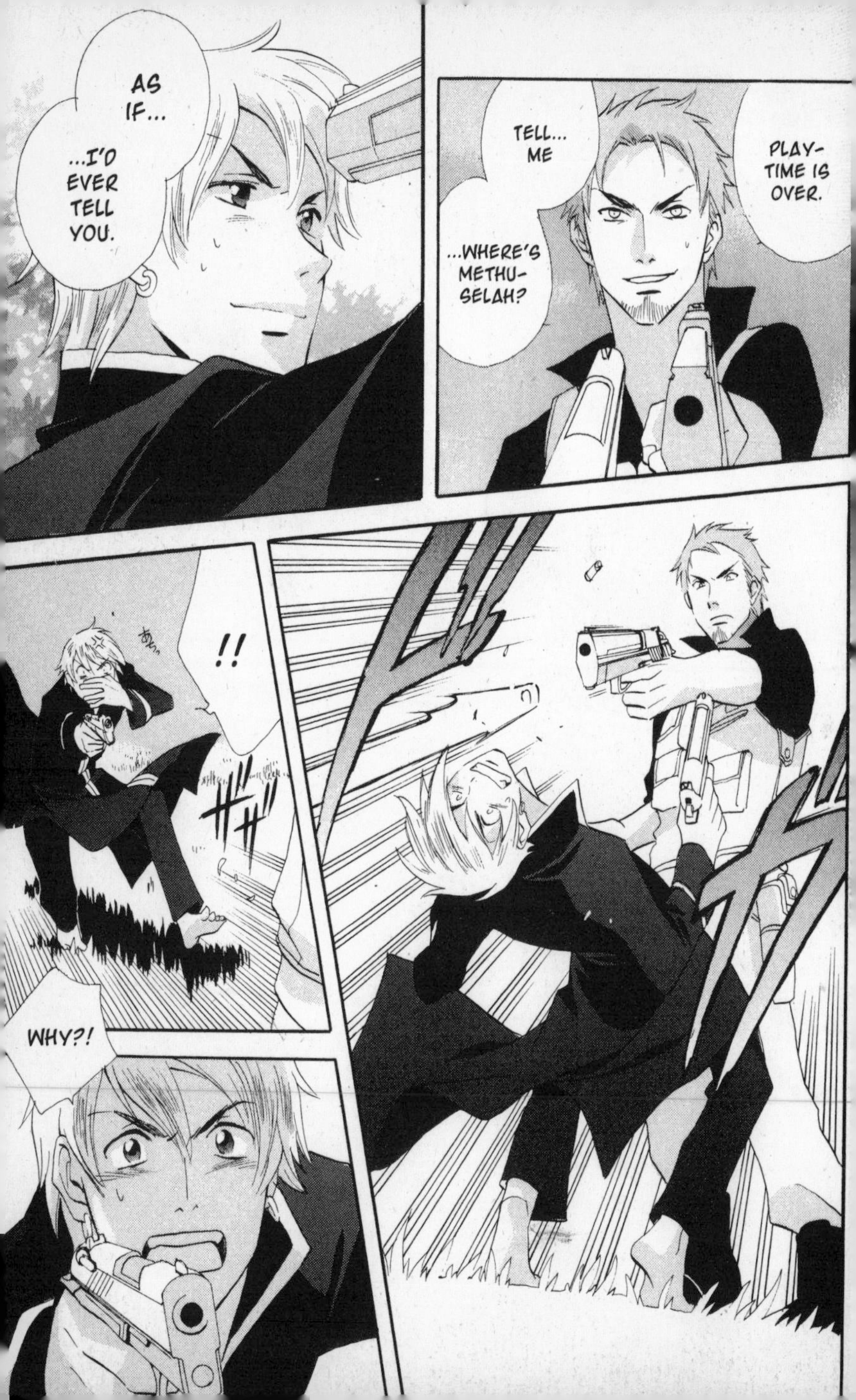
PLAY-TIME IS OVER.
TELL... ME
...WHERE'S METHU-SELAH?
AS IF...
...I'D EVER TELL YOU.
!!
WHY?!

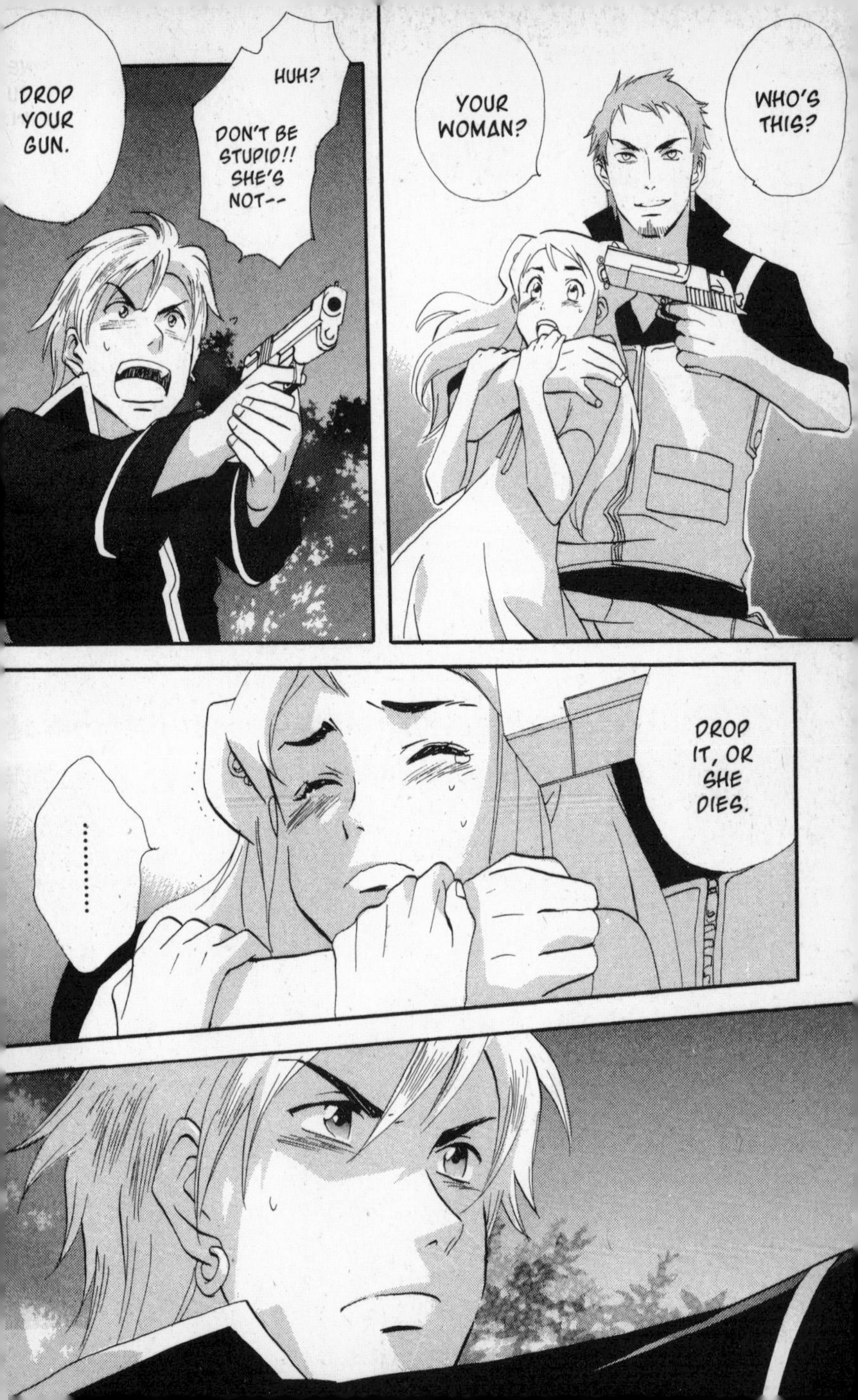
WHO'S THIS?
YOUR WOMAN?
HUH?
DON'T BE STUPID!! SHE'S NOT--
DROP YOUR GUN.
DROP IT, OR SHE DIES.
......

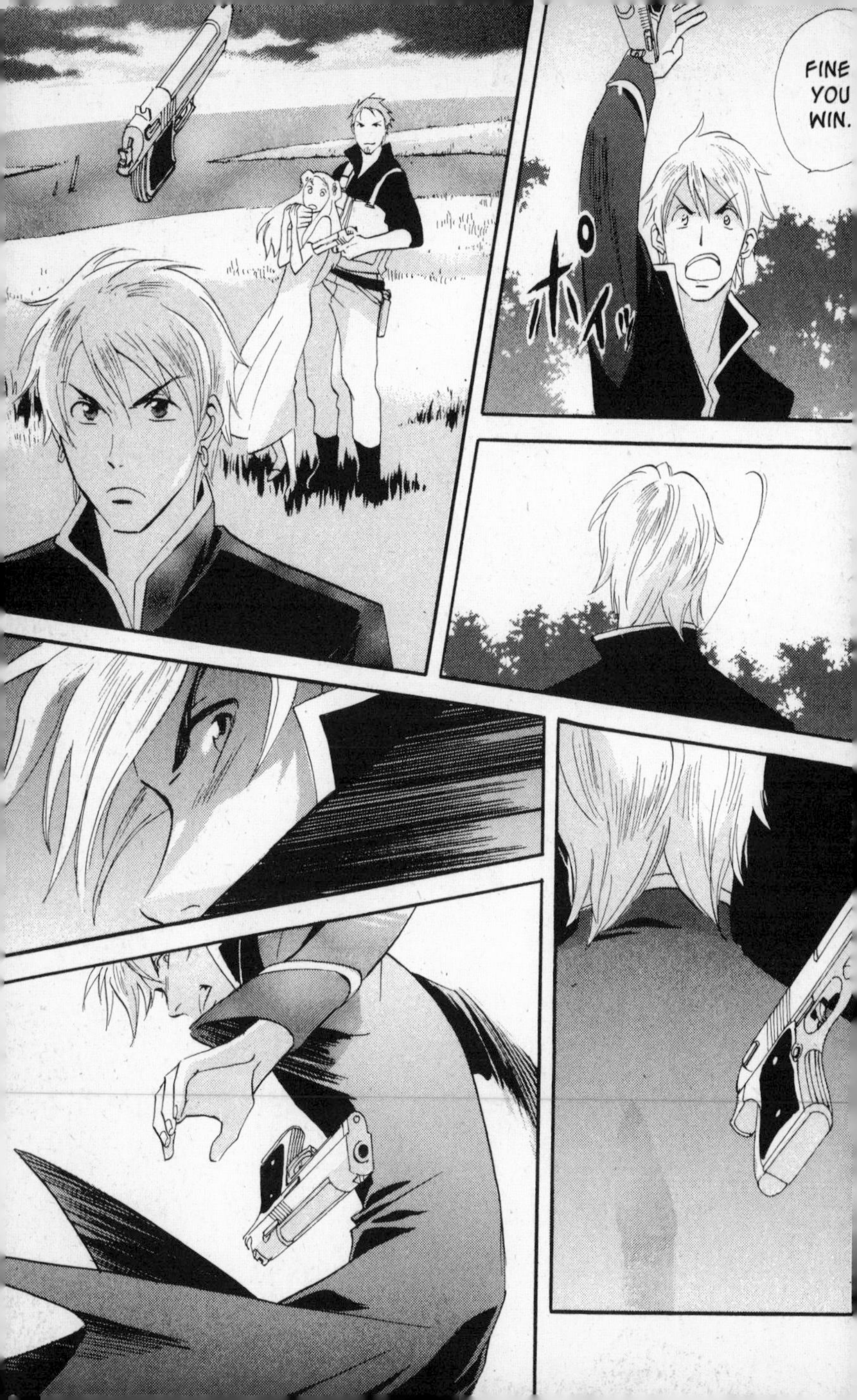
FINE YOU WIN.

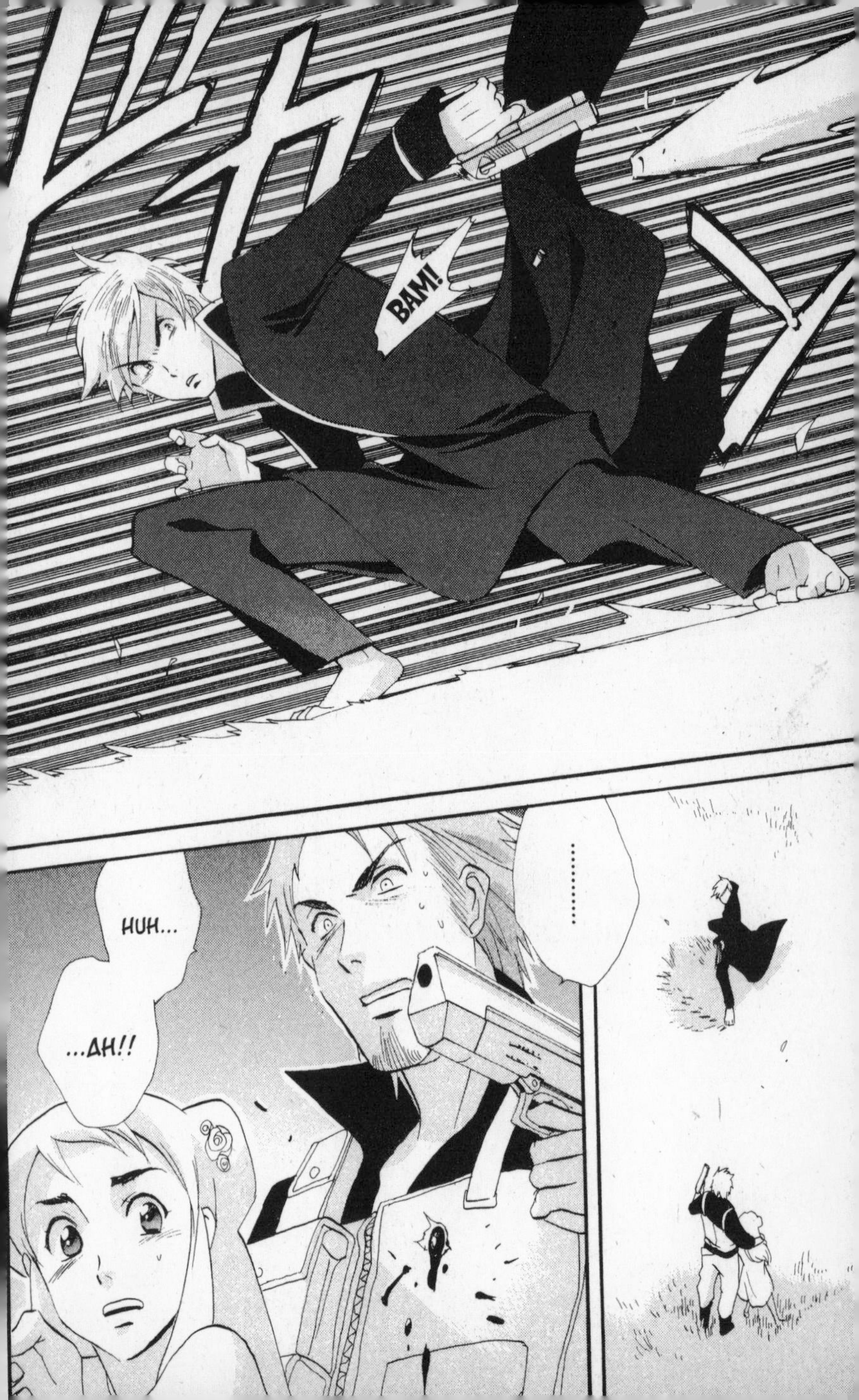
BAM!
......
HUH...
...AH!!

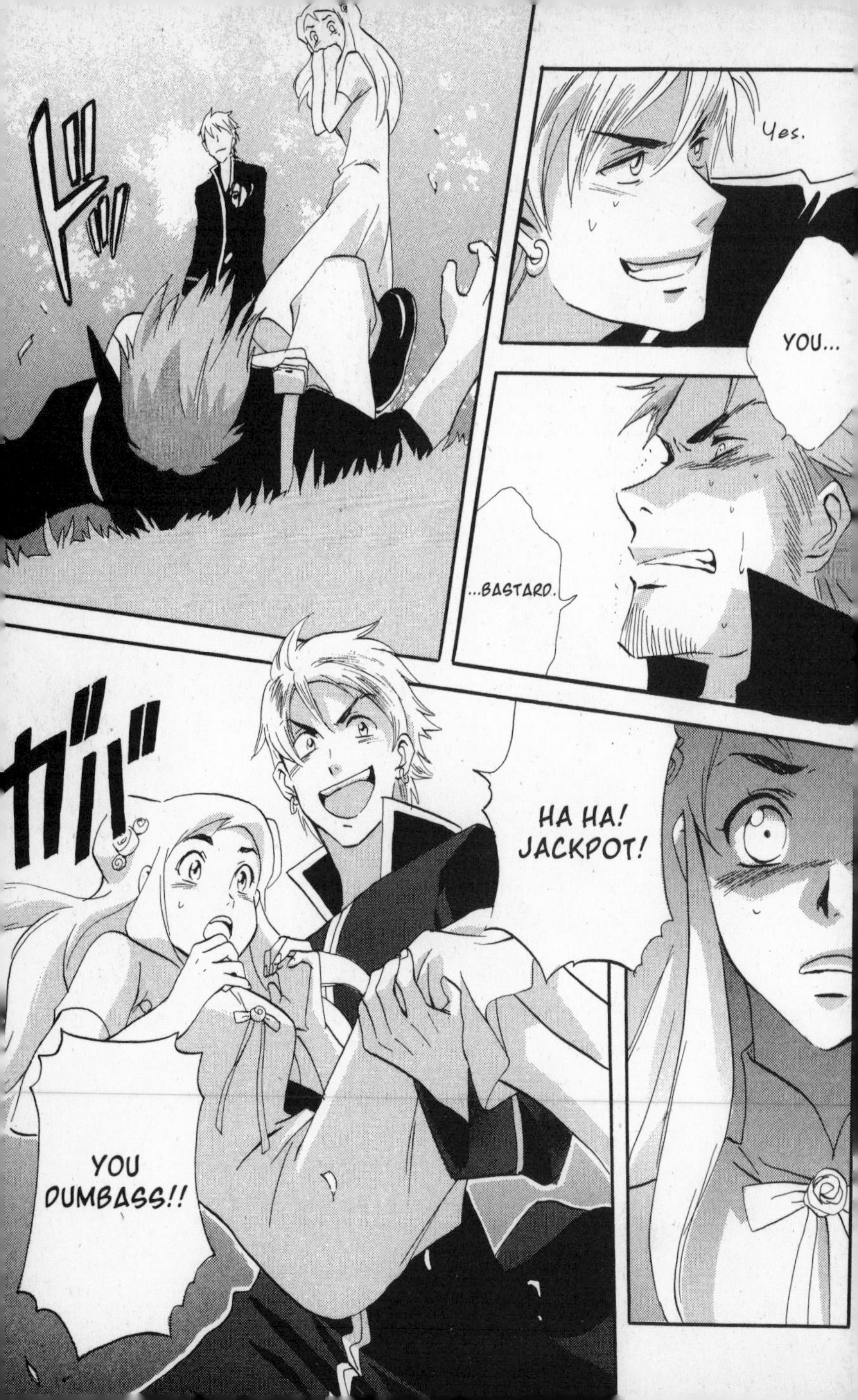
Yes.
YOU...
...BASTARD.
ドッ
HA HA! JACKPOT!
ガバ
YOU DUMBASS!!

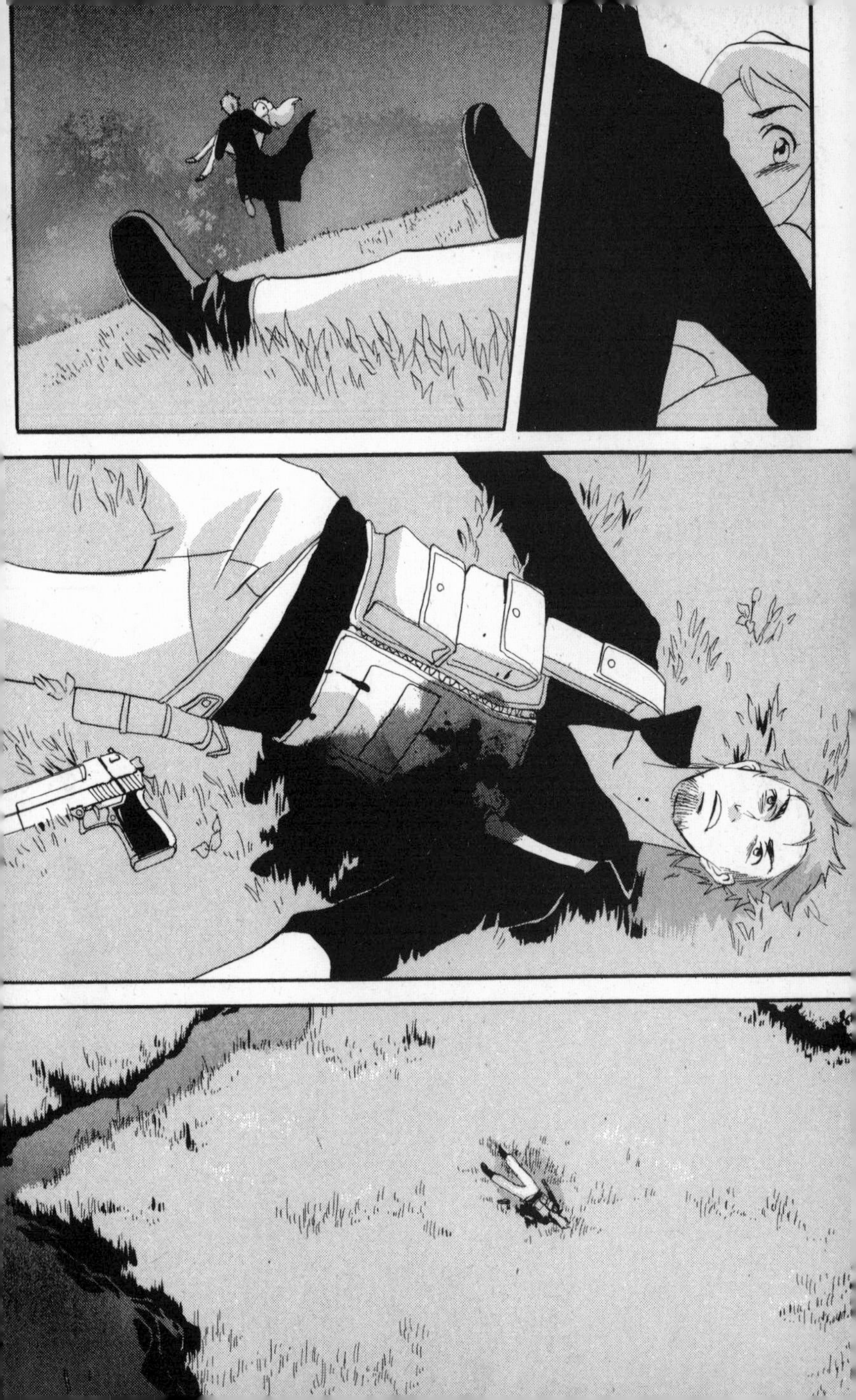

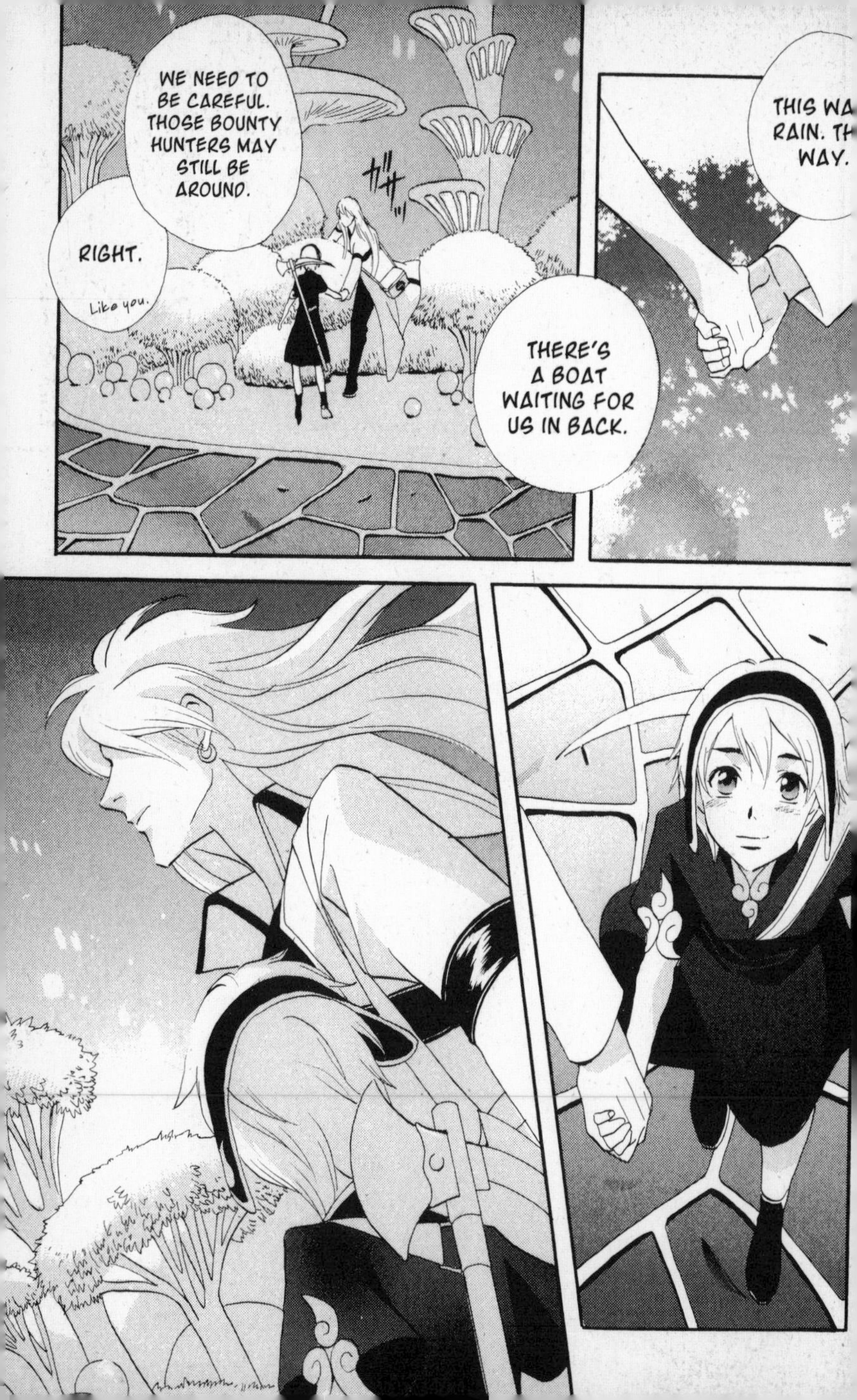
THIS WA RAIN. TH WAY.
WE NEED TO BE CAREFUL. THOSE BOUNTY HUNTERS MAY STILL BE AROUND.
RIGHT.
Like you.
THERE'S A BOAT WAITING FOR US IN BACK.

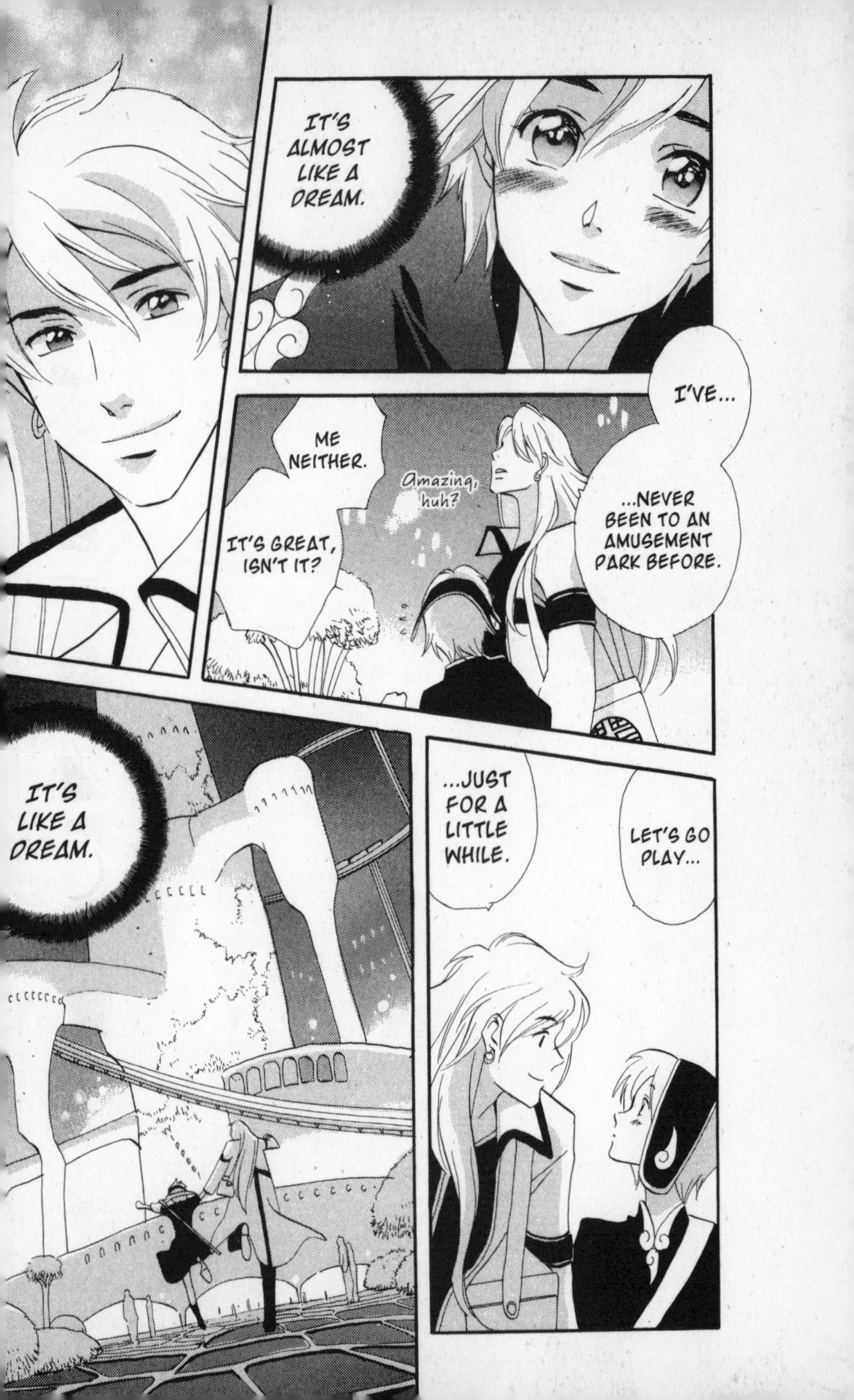
IT'S ALMOST LIKE A DREAM.
I'VE...
...NEVER BEEN TO AN AMUSEMENT PARK BEFORE.
Amazing, huh?
ME NEITHER.
IT'S GREAT, ISN'T IT?
LET'S GO PLAY...
...JUST FOR A LITTLE WHILE.
IT'S LIKE A DREAM.

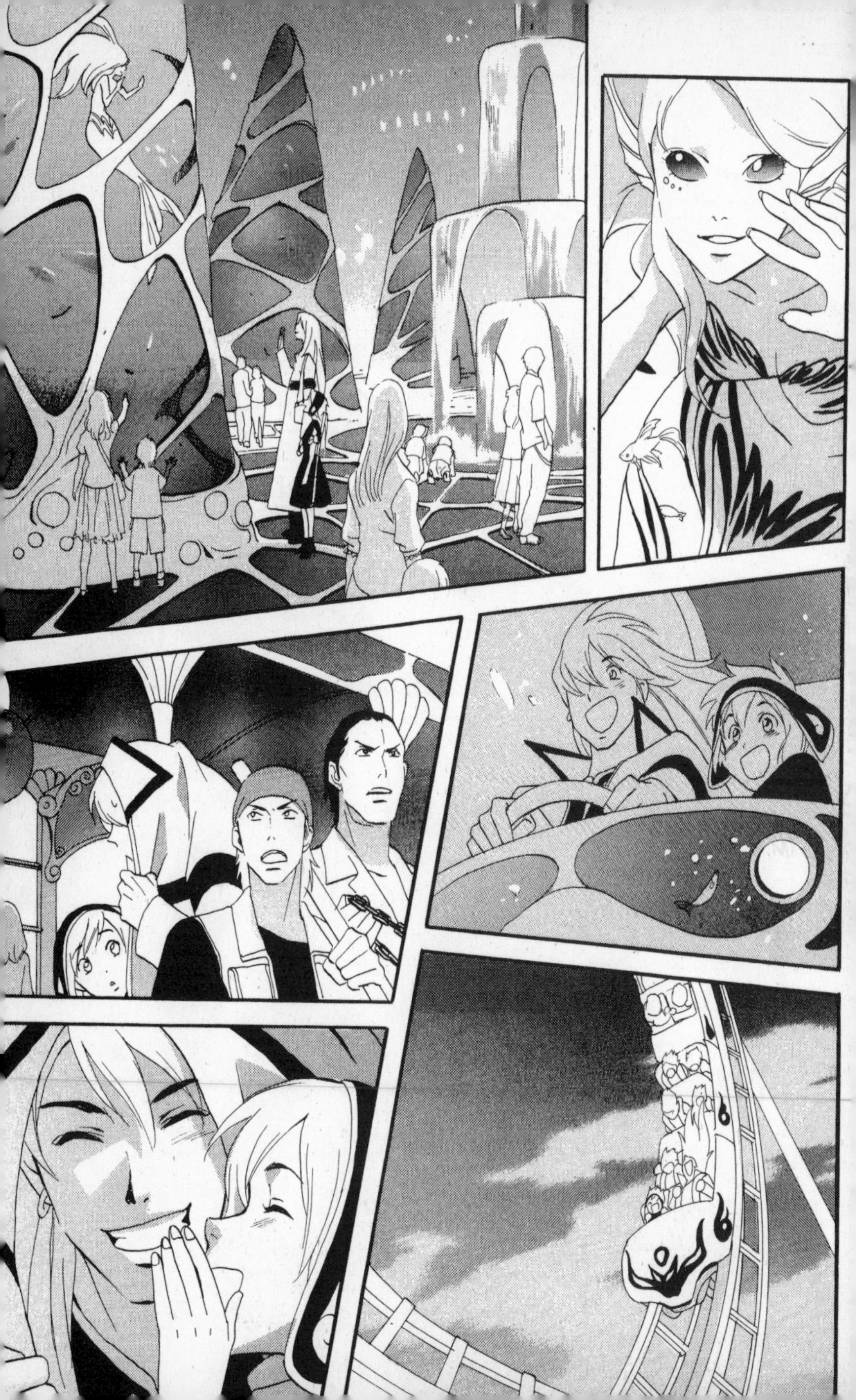

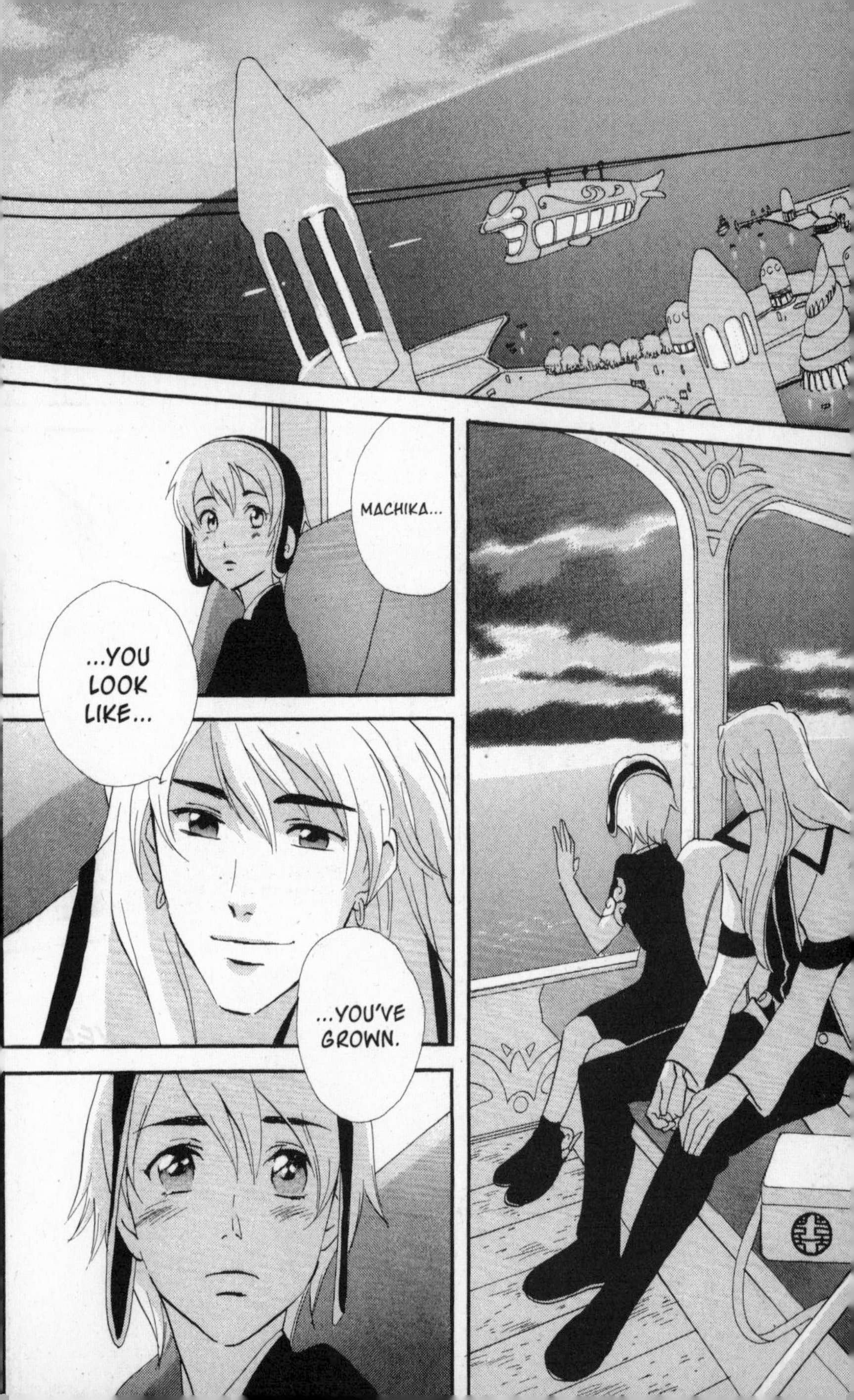
MACHIKA...
...YOU LOOK LIKE...
...YOU'VE GROWN.

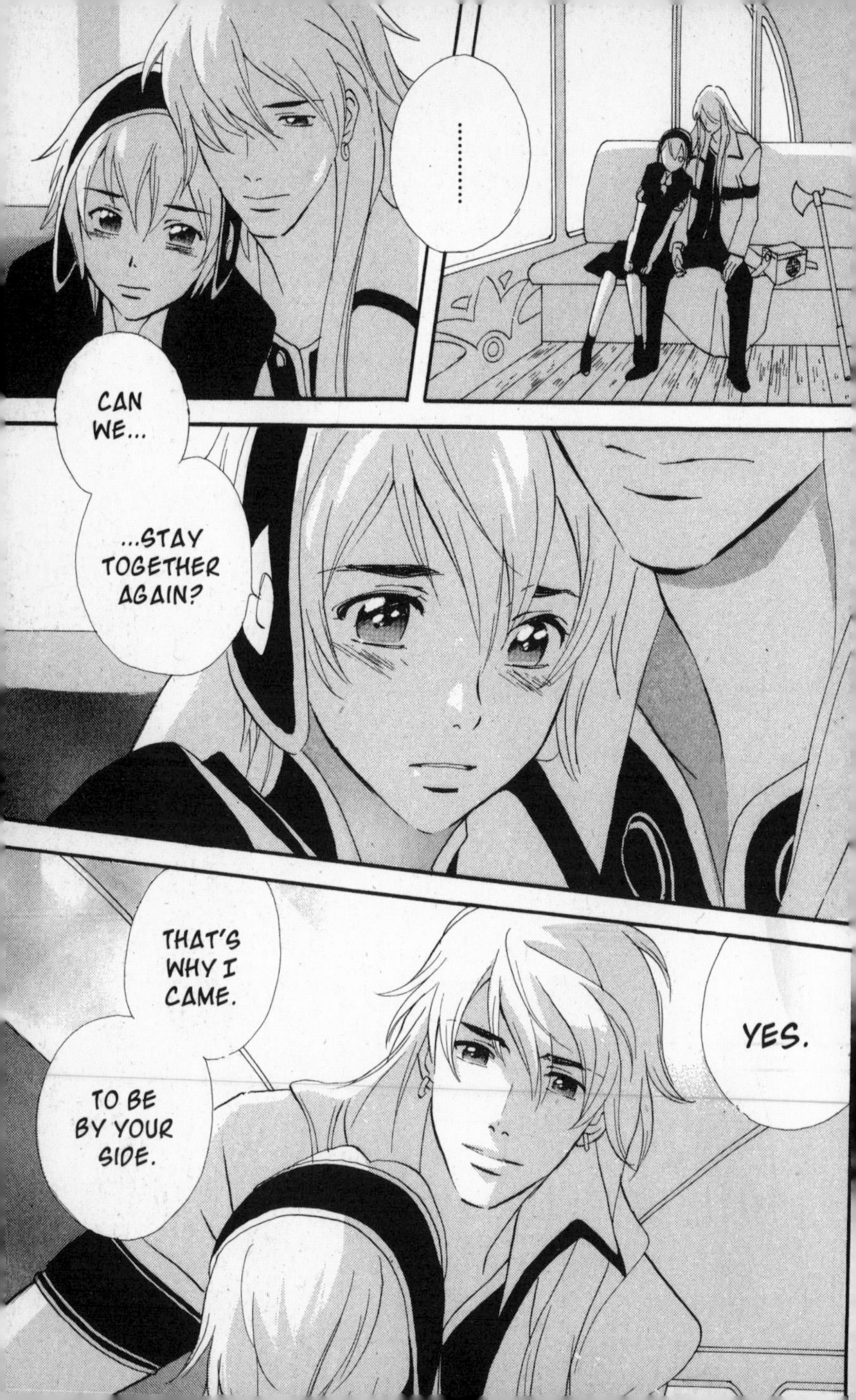
......
CAN WE...
...STAY TOGETHER AGAIN?
YES.
THAT'S WHY I CAME.
TO BE BY YOUR SIDE.

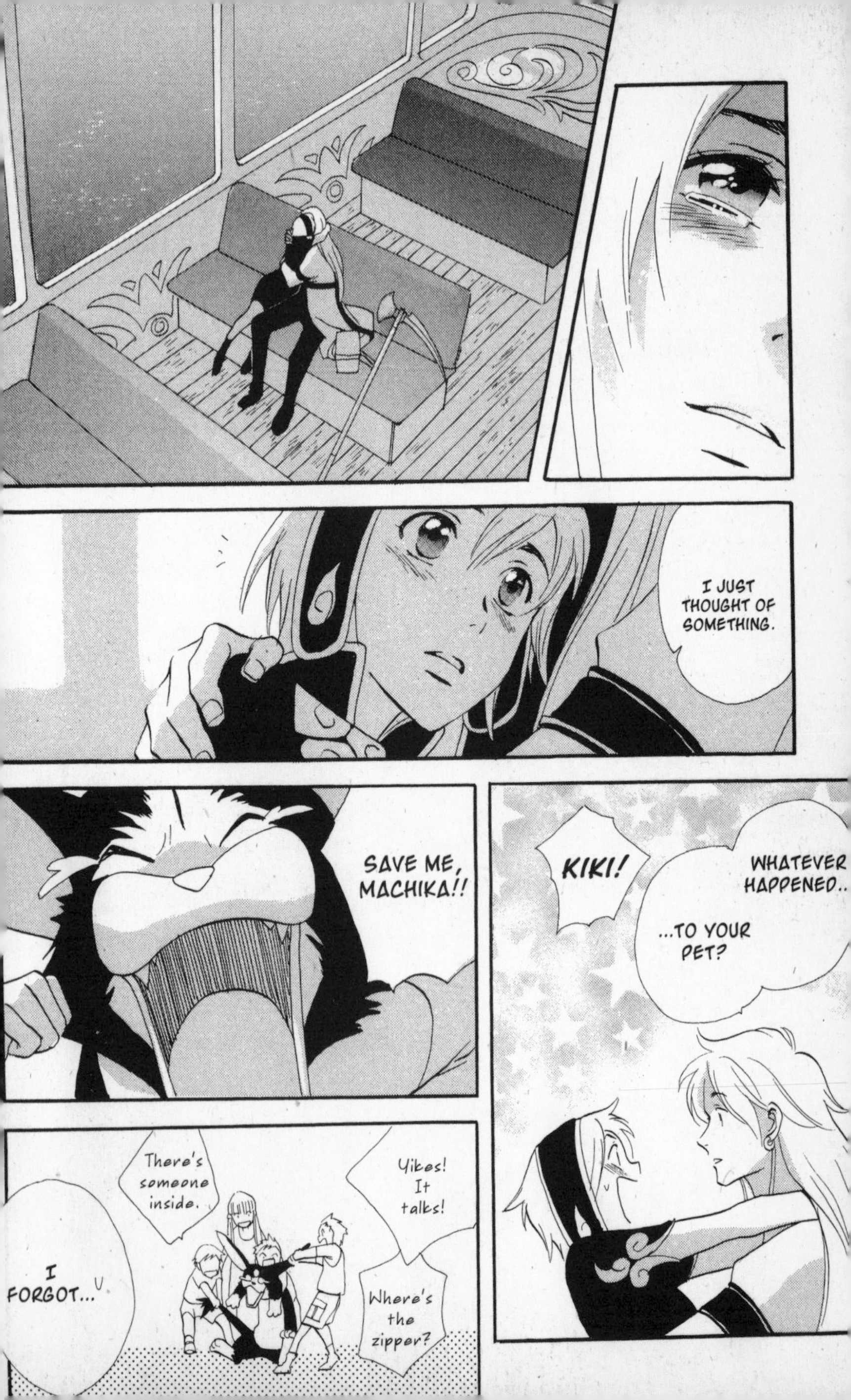
I JUST THOUGHT OF SOMETHING.
WHATEVER HAPPENED..
...TO YOUR PET?
KIKI!
SAVE ME, MACHIKA!!
Yikes! It talks!
There's someone inside.
Where's the zipper?
I FORGOT...

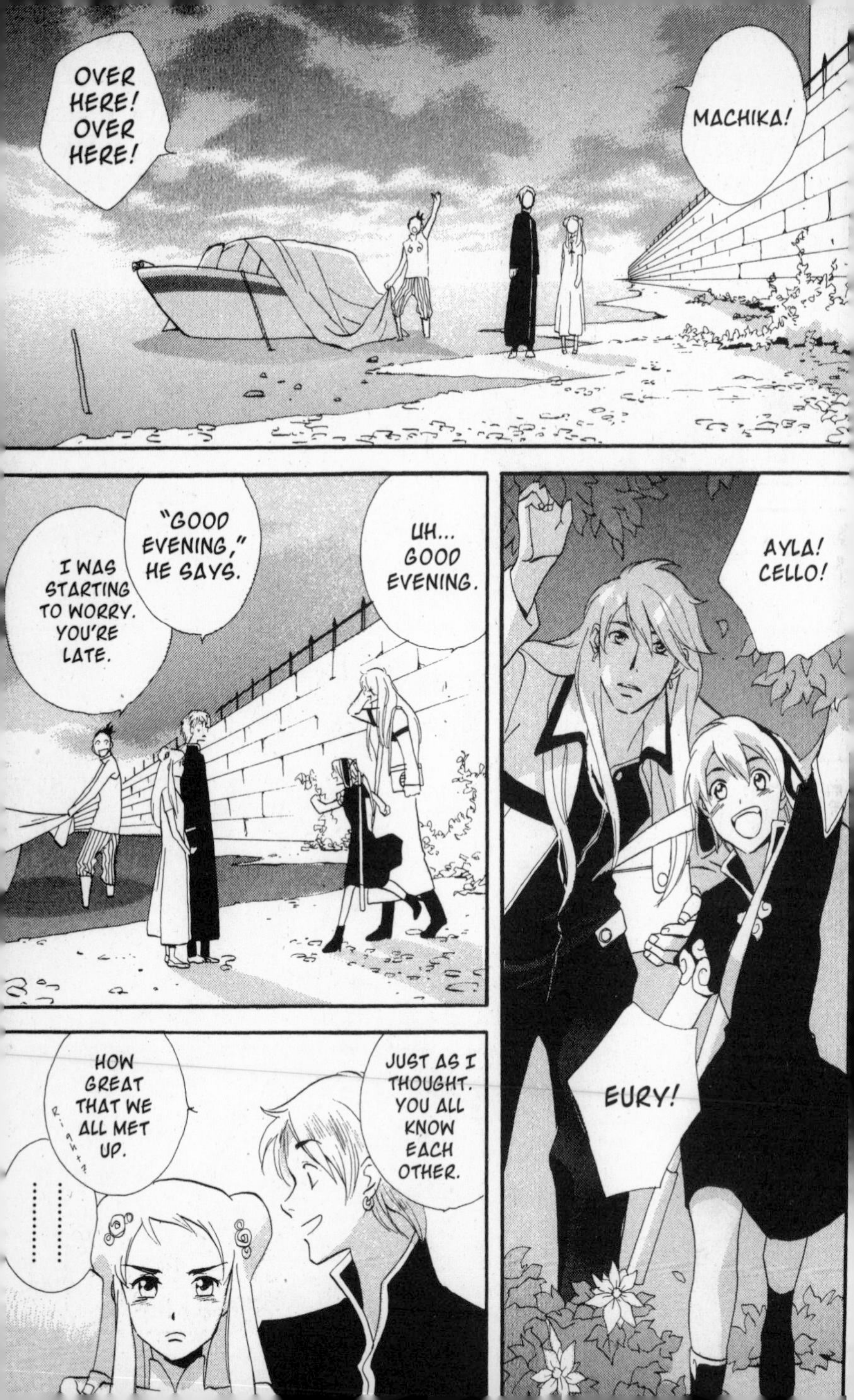
MACHIKA!
OVER HERE! OVER HERE!
AYLA! CELLO!
EURY!
UH... GOOD EVENING.
"GOOD EVENING," HE SAYS.
I WAS STARTING TO WORRY. YOU'RE LATE.
JUST AS I THOUGHT. YOU ALL KNOW EACH OTHER.
HOW GREAT THAT WE ALL MET UP.
Right?
......

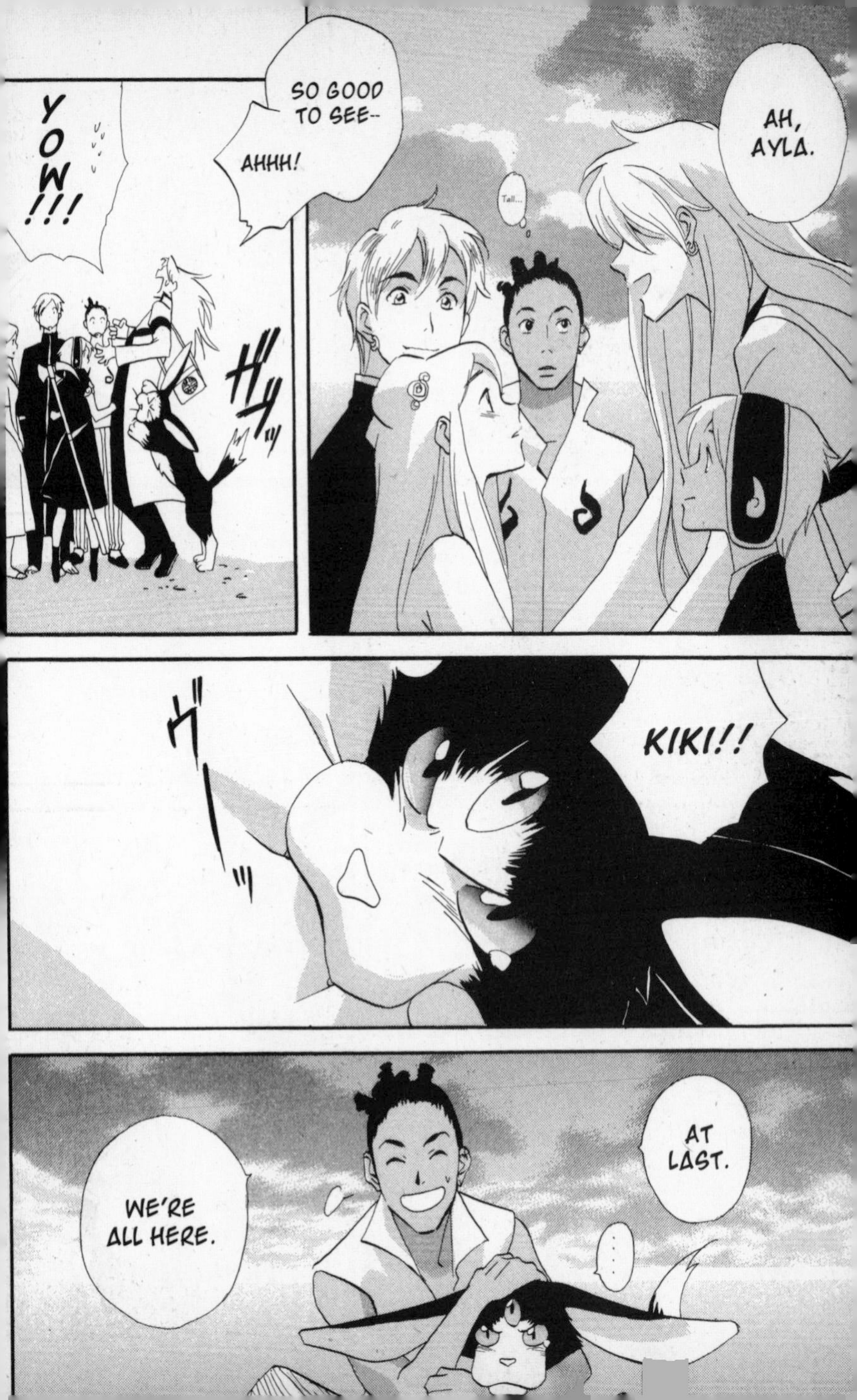

AH, AYLA.
Tall...
SO GOOD TO SEE--
AHHH!
YOW!!!
KIKI!!
AT LAST.
WE'RE ALL HERE.
...

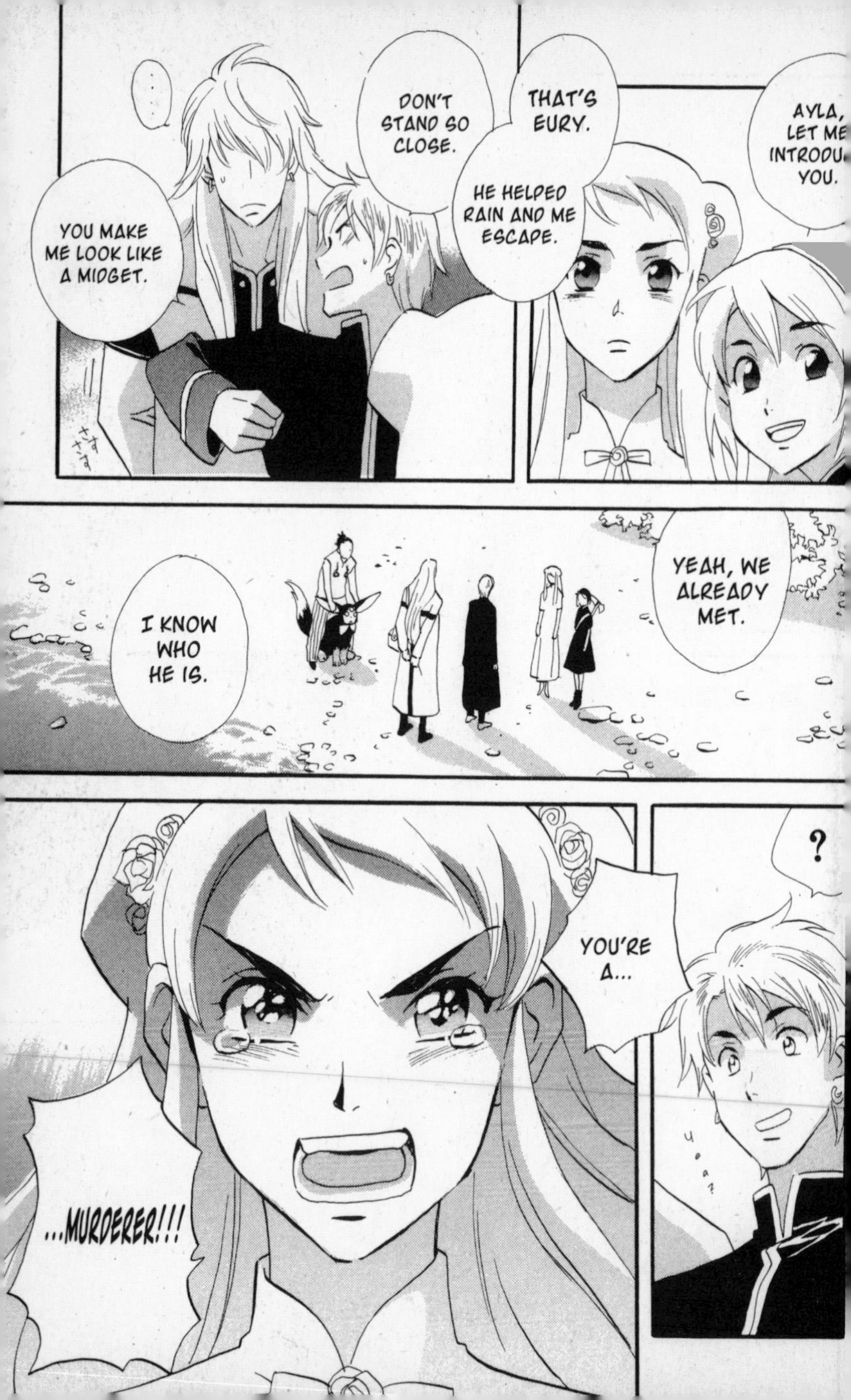
AYLA, LET ME INTRODU... YOU.
THAT'S EURY.
HE HELPED RAIN AND ME ESCAPE.
DON'T STAND SO CLOSE.
…
YOU MAKE ME LOOK LIKE A MIDGET.
さすさす
YEAH, WE ALREADY MET.
I KNOW WHO HE IS.
?
YOU'RE A...
...MURDERER!!!

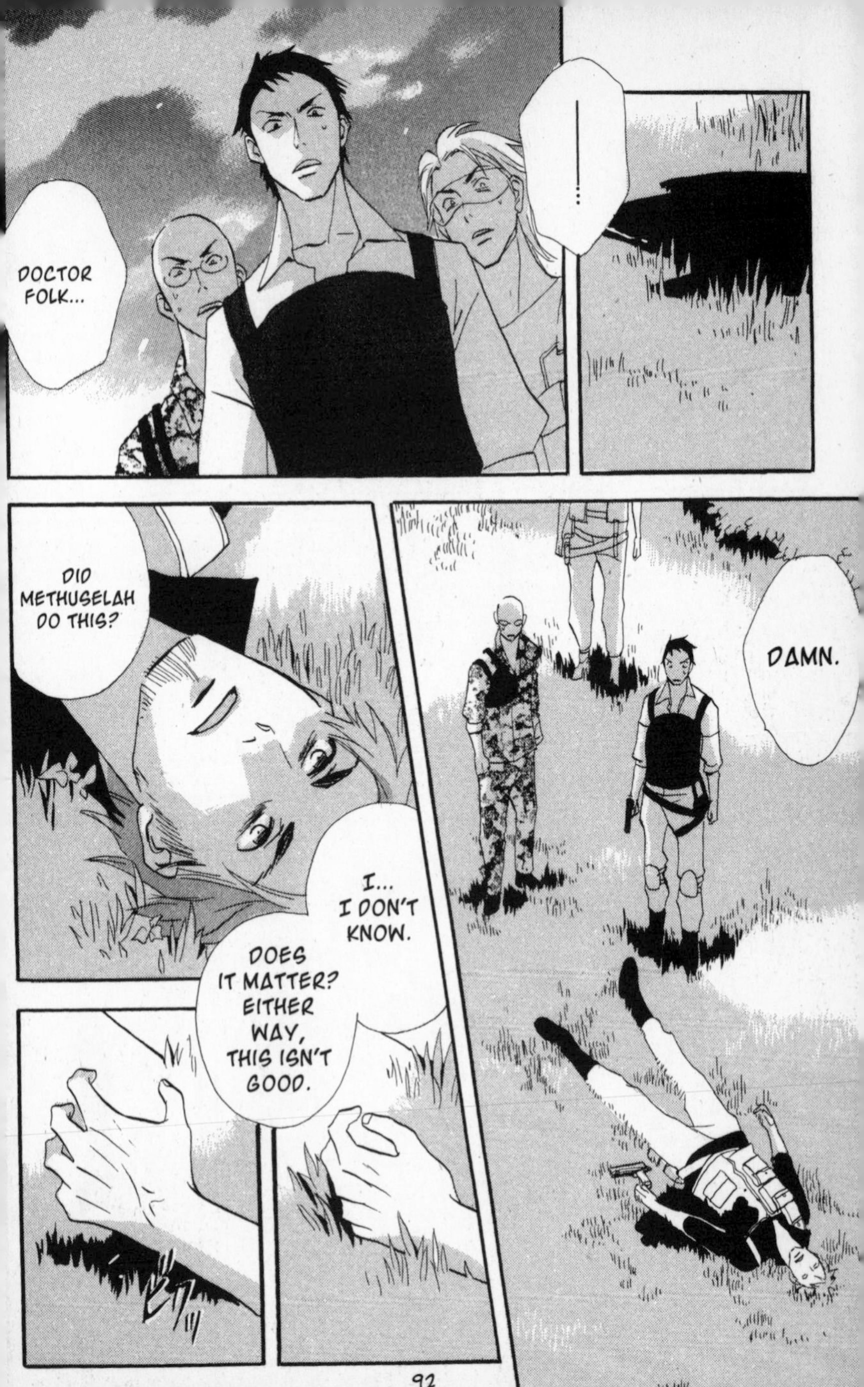
......
DOCTOR FOLK...
DAMN.
DID METHUSELAH DO THIS?
I... I DON'T KNOW.
DOES IT MATTER? EITHER WAY, THIS ISN'T GOOD.

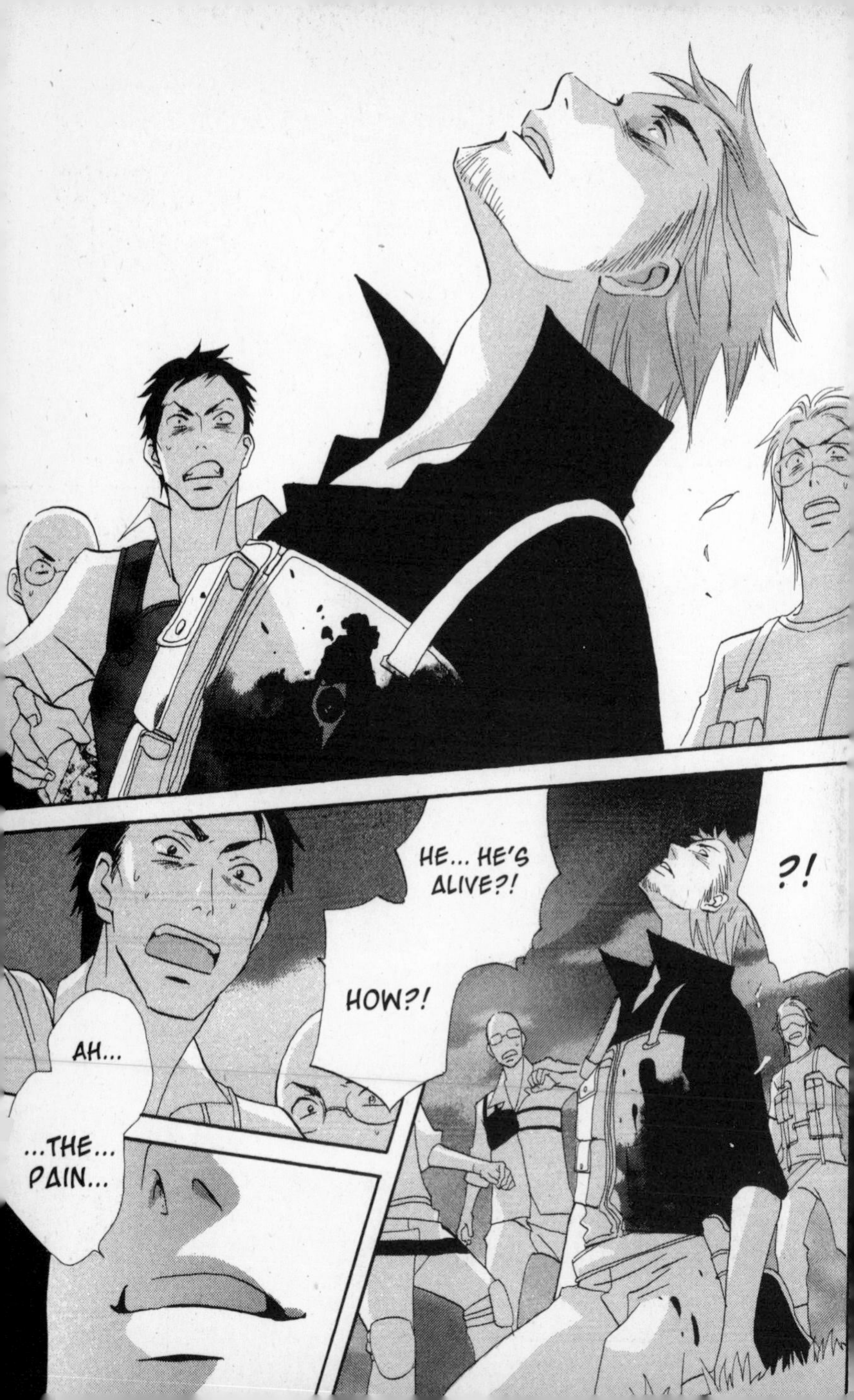
?!
HE... HE'S ALIVE?!
HOW?!
AH...
...THE... PAIN...

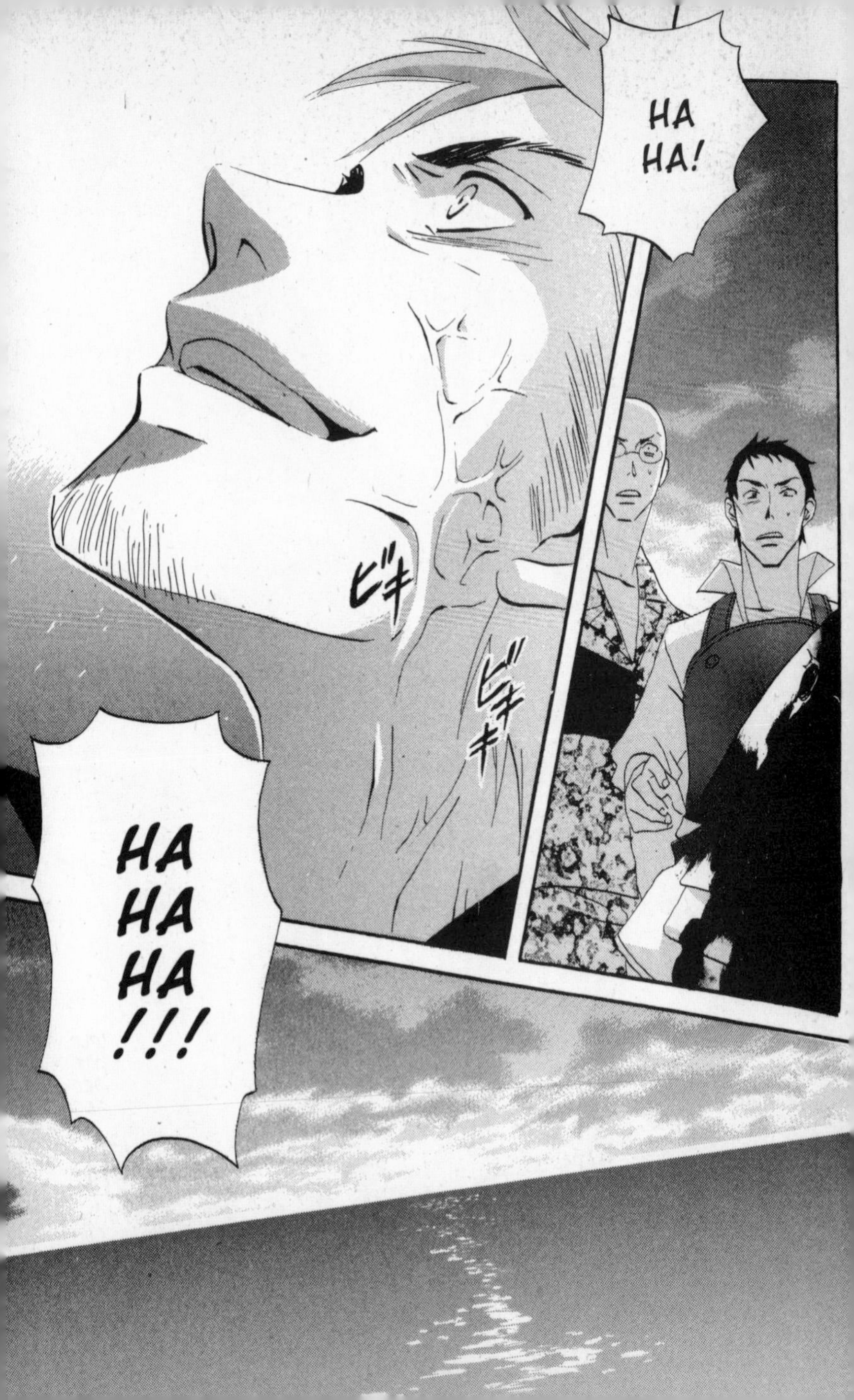

HA HA!
ビキ
ビキビキ
HA HA HA HA!!!

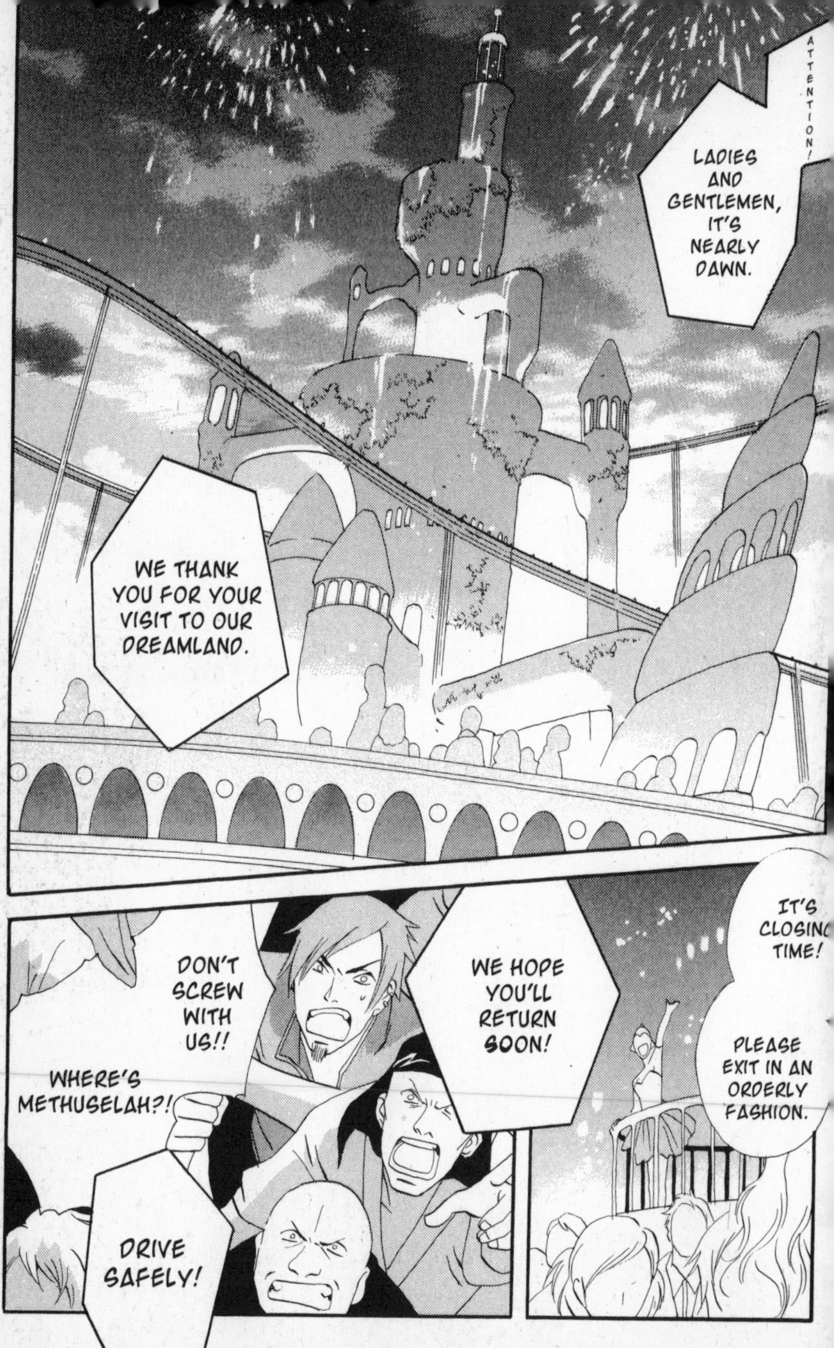
ATTENTION!
LADIES AND GENTLEMEN, IT'S NEARLY DAWN.
WE THANK YOU FOR YOUR VISIT TO OUR DREAMLAND.
IT'S CLOSING TIME!
PLEASE EXIT IN AN ORDERLY FASHION.
WE HOPE YOU'LL RETURN SOON!
DON'T SCREW WITH US!!
WHERE'S METHUSELAH?!
DRIVE SAFELY!

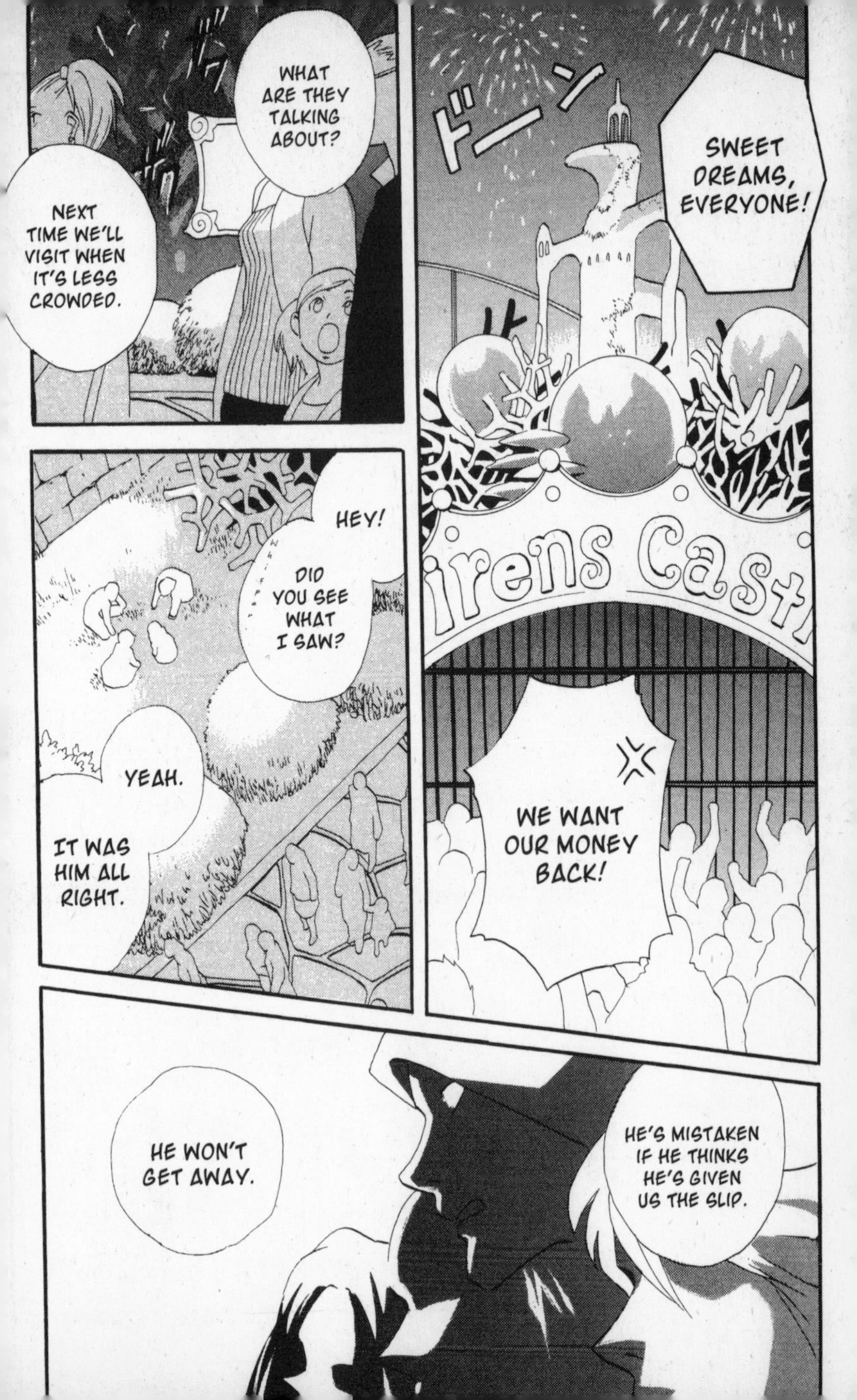
ドーン
SWEET DREAMS, EVERYONE!
irens Cast
WE WANT OUR MONEY BACK!
WHAT ARE THEY TALKING ABOUT?
NEXT TIME WE'LL VISIT WHEN IT'S LESS CROWDED.
HEY!
DID YOU SEE WHAT I SAW?
YEAH.
IT WAS HIM ALL RIGHT.
HE'S MISTAKEN IF HE THINKS HE'S GIVEN US THE SLIP.
HE WON'T GET AWAY.

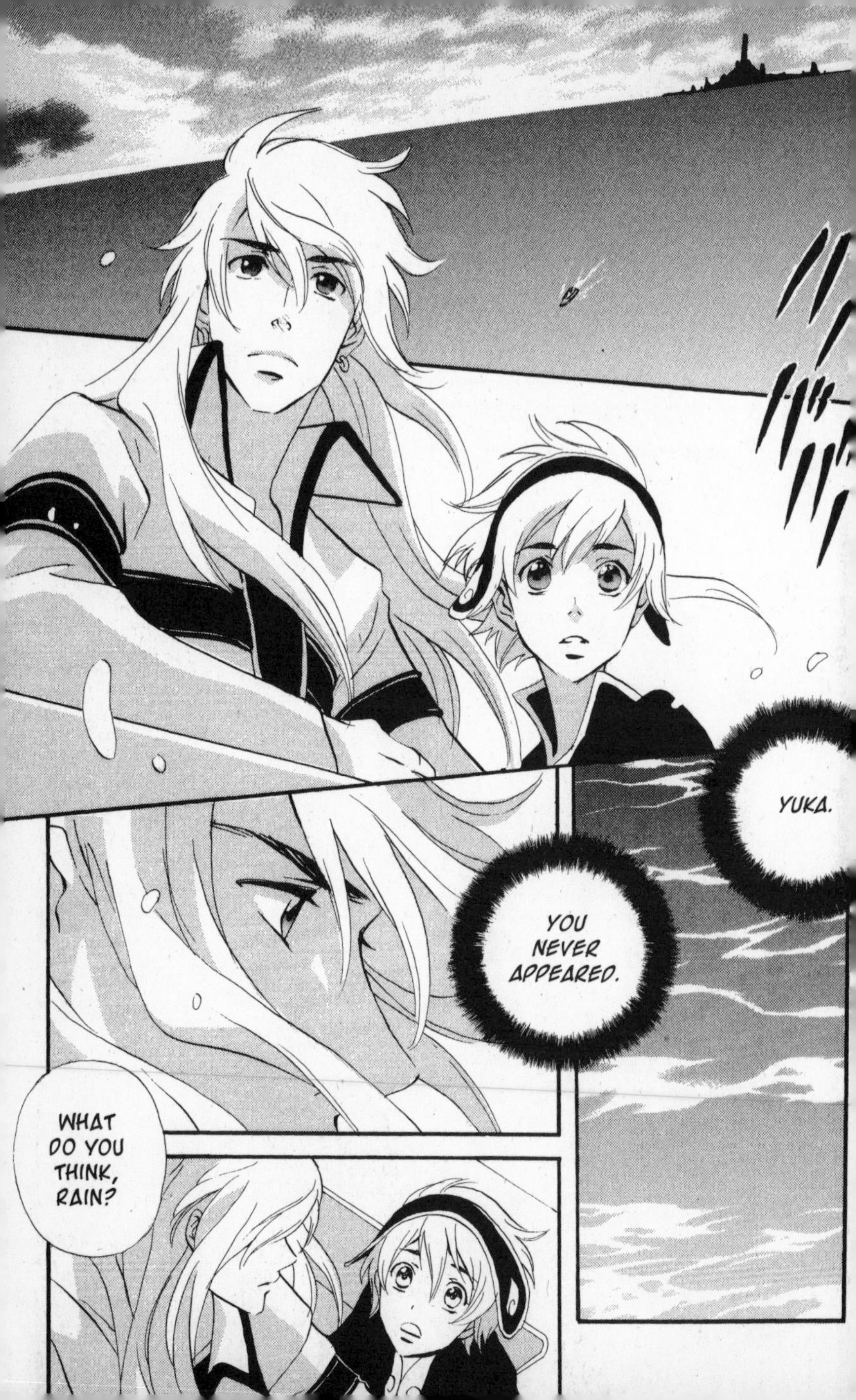
YUKA.
YOU NEVER APPEARED.
WHAT DO YOU THINK, RAIN?

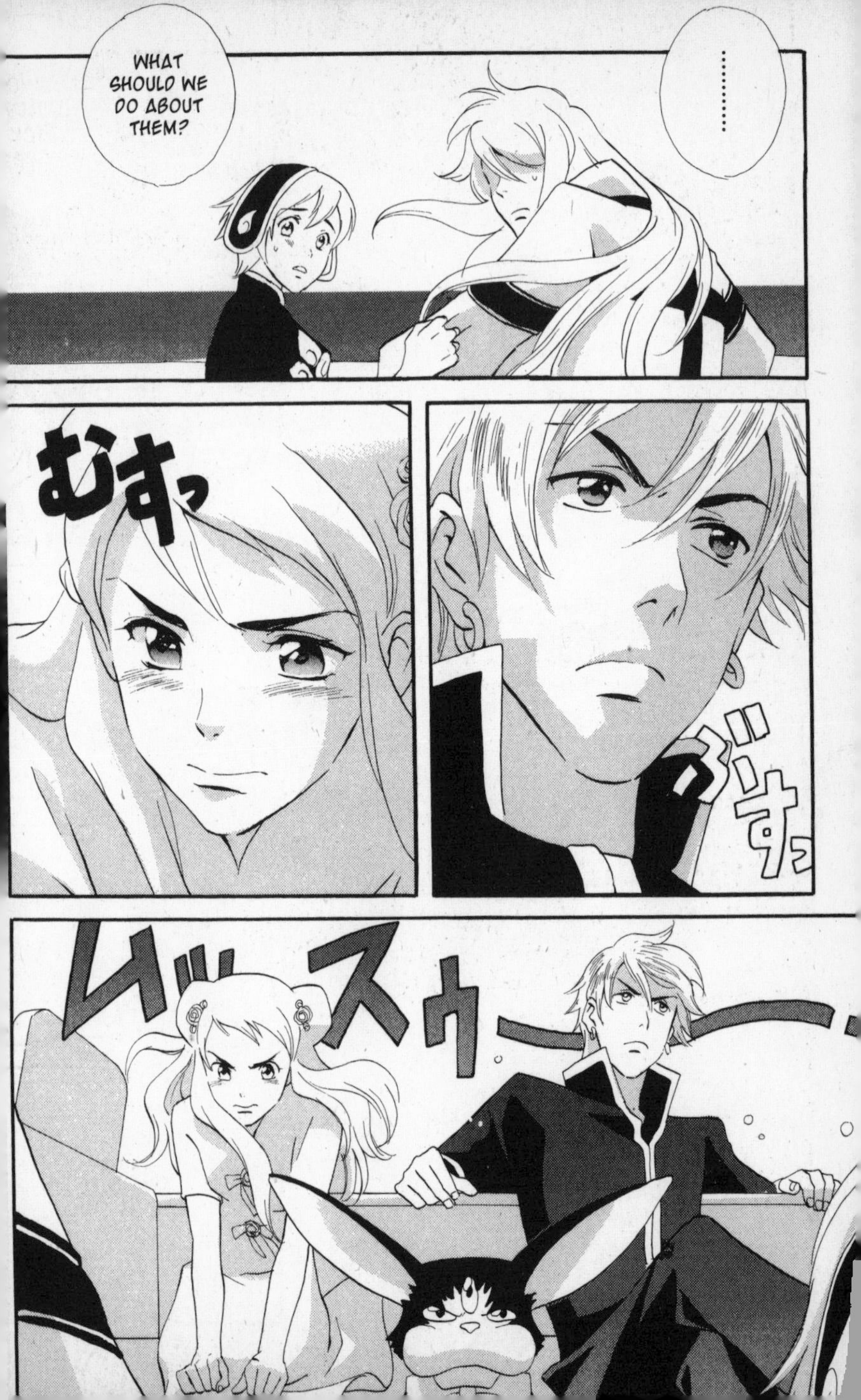
....
WHAT SHOULD WE DO ABOUT THEM?
ぶすっ
むすっ
ムッスゥーー

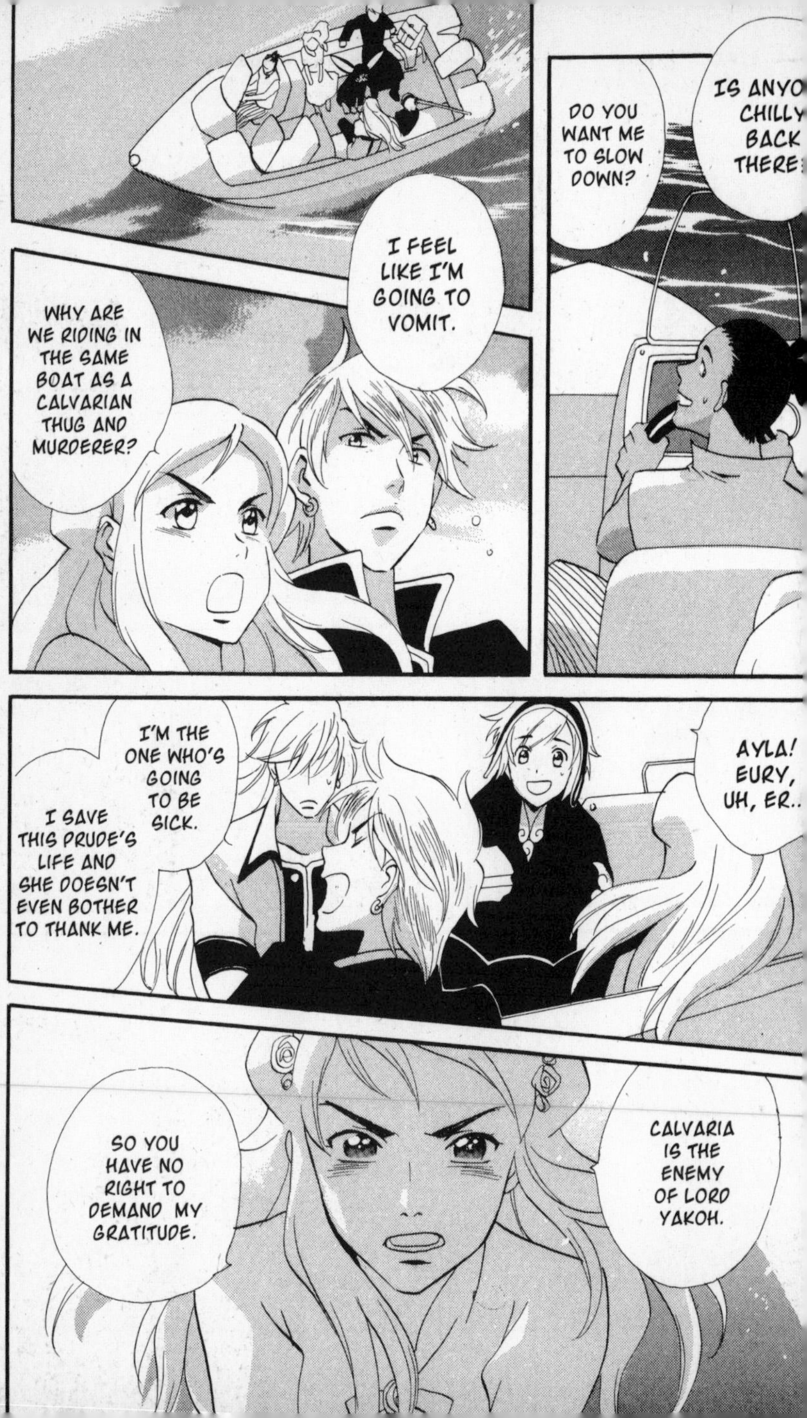
IS ANYO CHILLY BACK THERE
DO YOU WANT ME TO SLOW DOWN?
I FEEL LIKE I'M GOING TO VOMIT.
WHY ARE WE RIDING IN THE SAME BOAT AS A CALVARIAN THUG AND MURDERER?
AYLA! EURY, UH, ER..
I'M THE ONE WHO'S GOING TO BE SICK.
I SAVE THIS PRUDE'S LIFE AND SHE DOESN'T EVEN BOTHER TO THANK ME.
CALVARIA IS THE ENEMY OF LORD YAKOH.
SO YOU HAVE NO RIGHT TO DEMAND MY GRATITUDE.

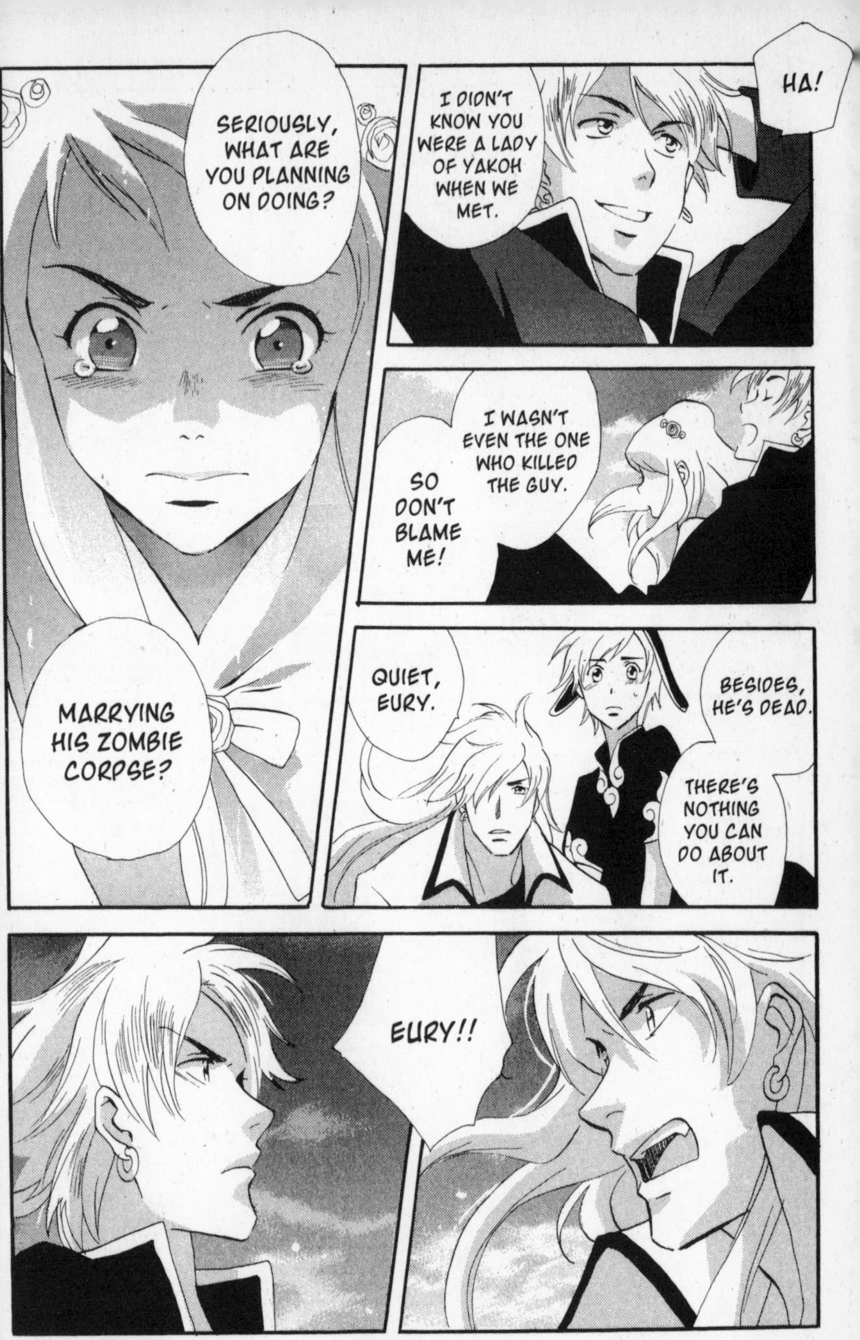

HA!
I DIDN'T KNOW YOU WERE A LADY OF YAKOH WHEN WE MET.
I WASN'T EVEN THE ONE WHO KILLED THE GUY.
SO DON'T BLAME ME!
BESIDES, HE'S DEAD.
THERE'S NOTHING YOU CAN DO ABOUT IT.
QUIET, EURY.
SERIOUSLY, WHAT ARE YOU PLANNING ON DOING?
MARRYING HIS ZOMBIE CORPSE?
EURY!!

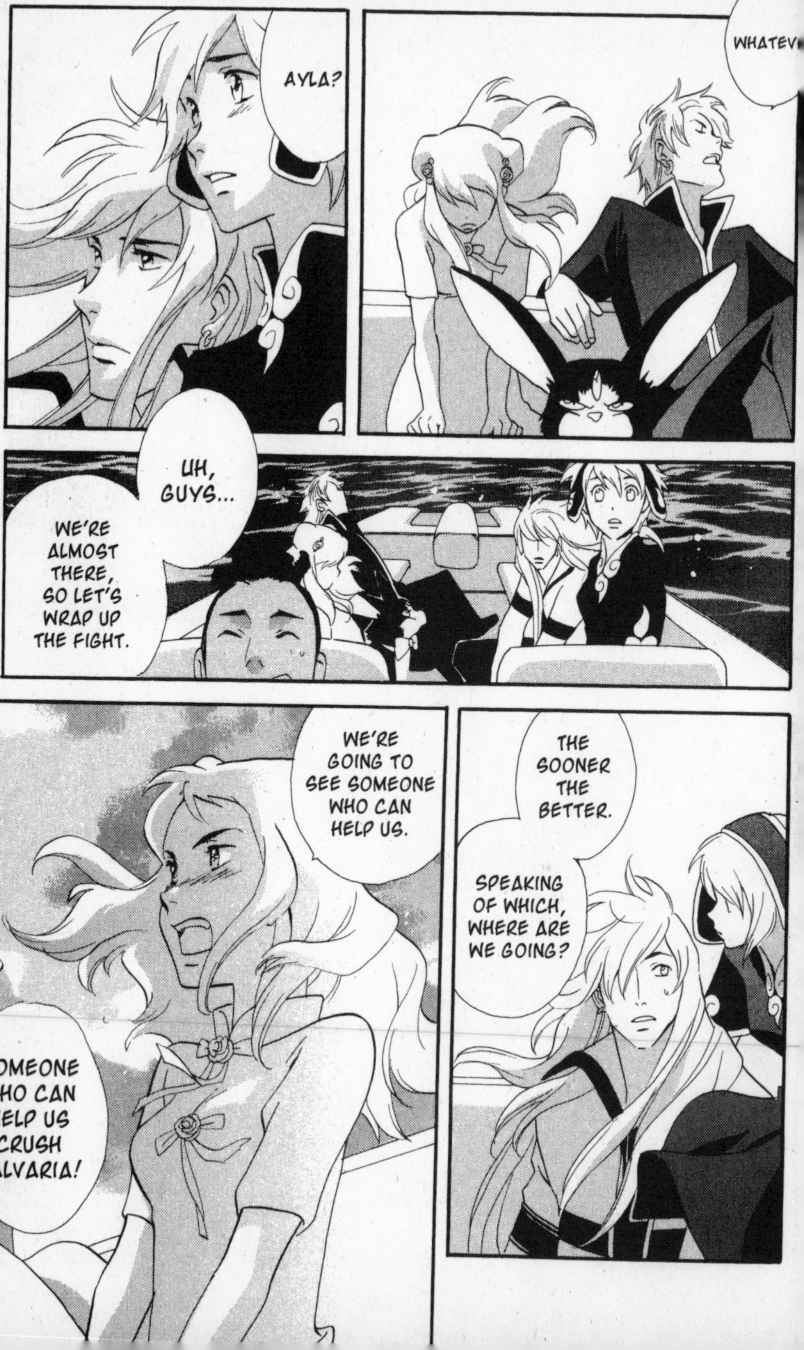
WHATEV
AYLA?
UH, GUYS...
WE'RE ALMOST THERE, SO LET'S WRAP UP THE FIGHT.
THE SOONER THE BETTER.
SPEAKING OF WHICH, WHERE ARE WE GOING?
WE'RE GOING TO SEE SOMEONE WHO CAN HELP US.
SOMEONE WHO CAN HELP US CRUSH CALVARIA!

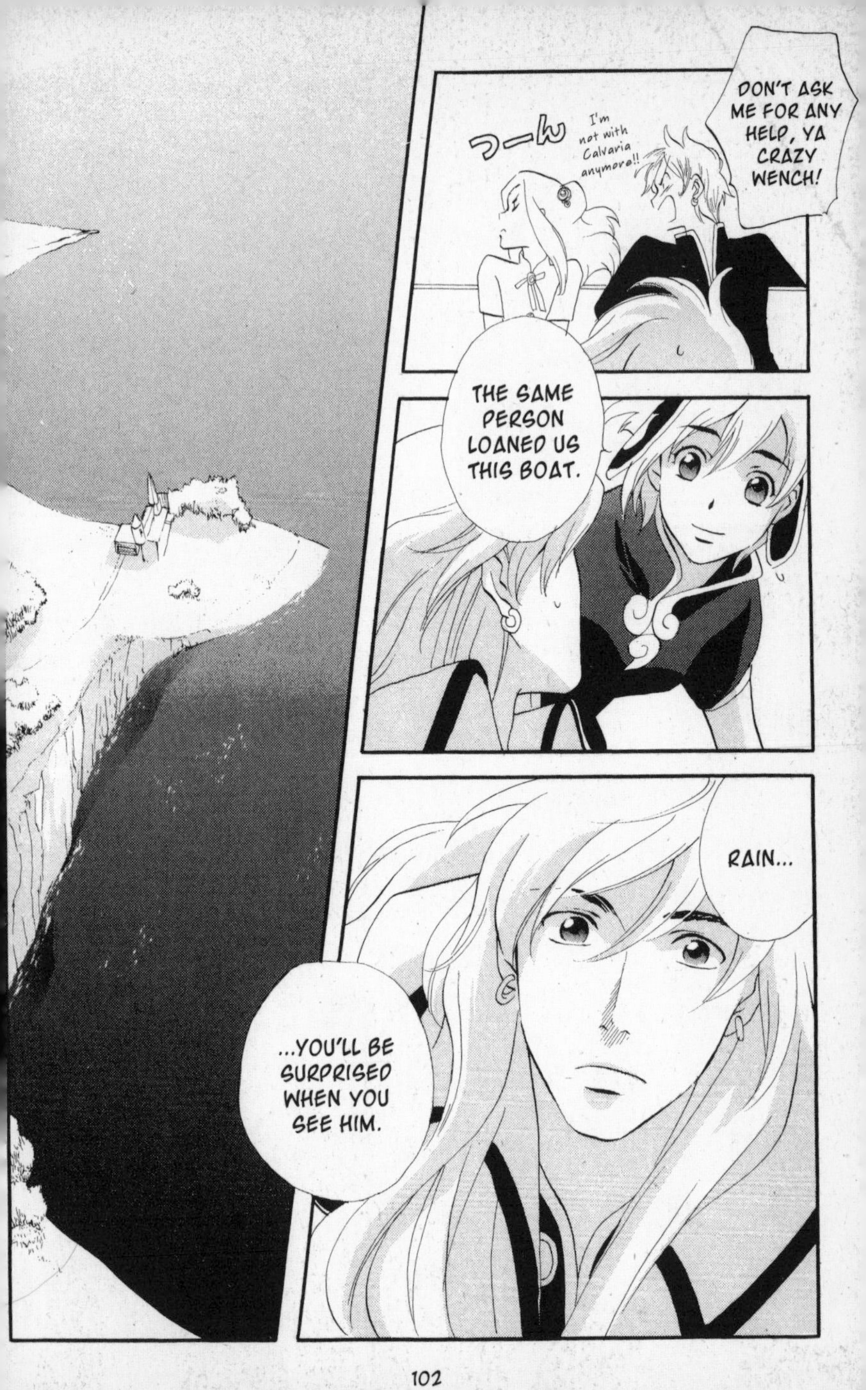

DON'T ASK ME FOR ANY HELP, YA CRAZY WENCH!
I'm not with Calvaria anymore!!
つーん
THE SAME PERSON LOANED US THIS BOAT.
RAIN...
...YOU'LL BE SURPRISED WHEN YOU SEE HIM.

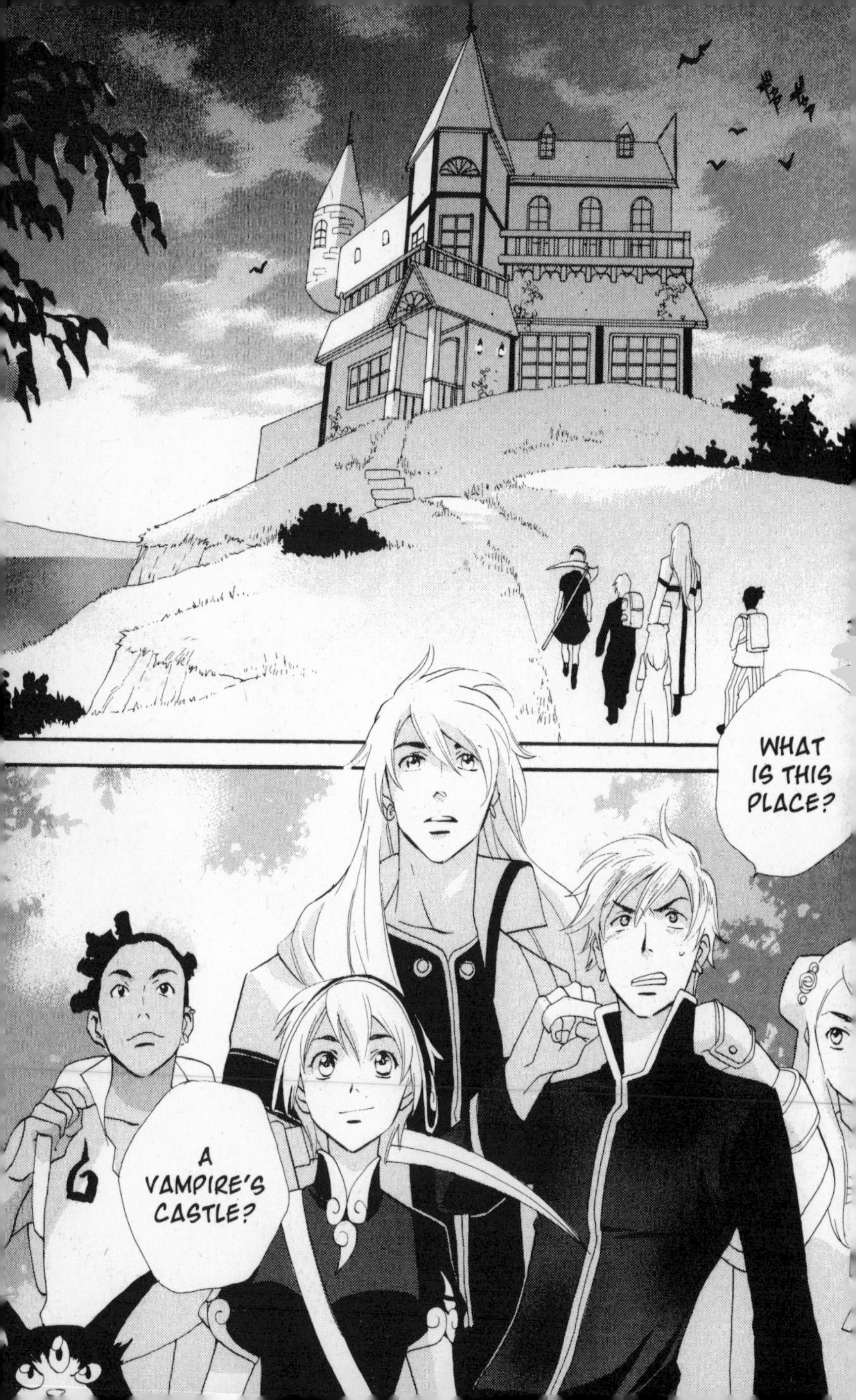
WHAT IS THIS PLACE?
A VAMPIRE'S CASTLE?

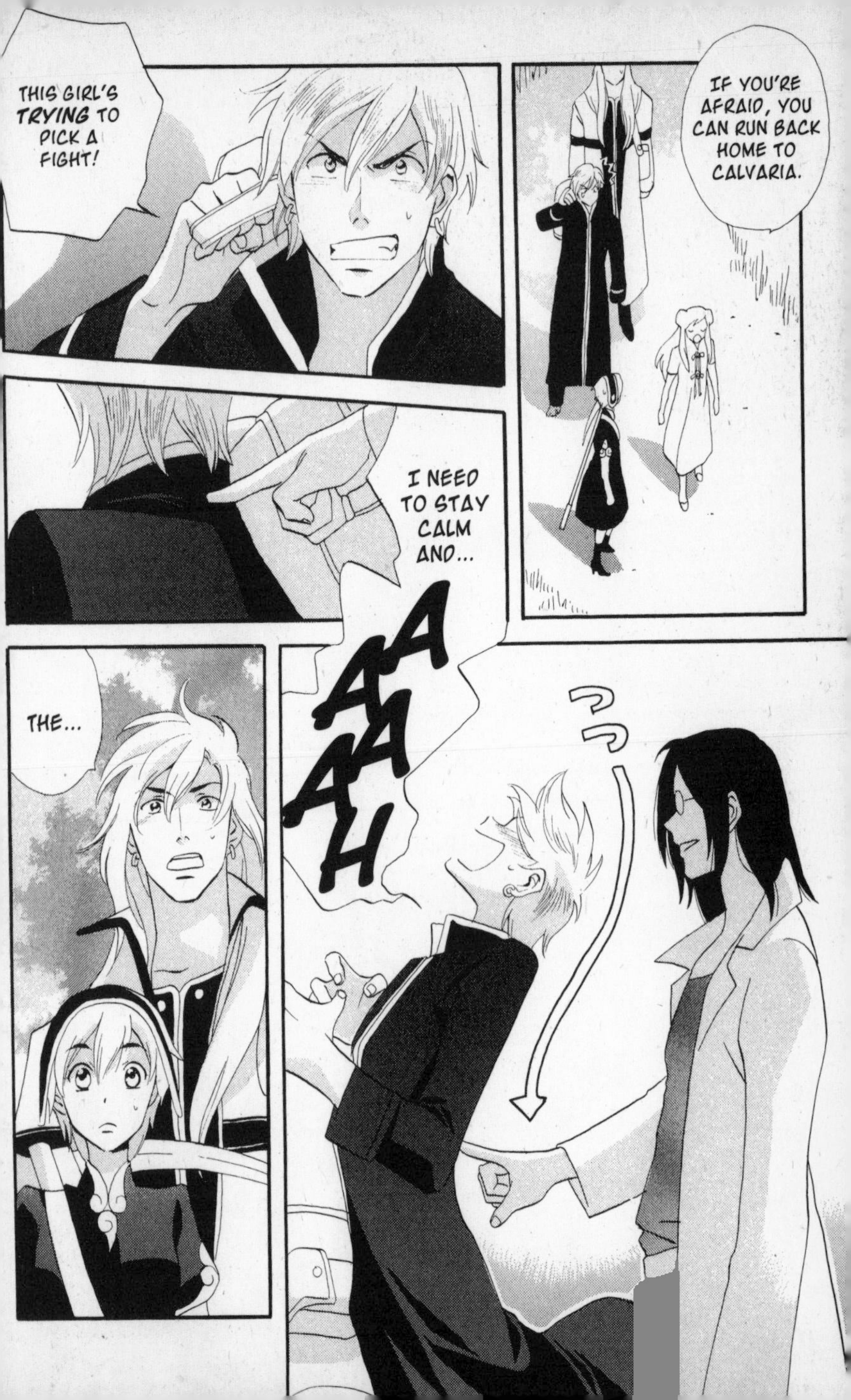
IF YOU'RE AFRAID, YOU CAN RUN BACK HOME TO CALVARIA.
THIS GIRL'S TRYING TO PICK A FIGHT!
I NEED TO STAY CALM AND...
AAAAAH
THE...

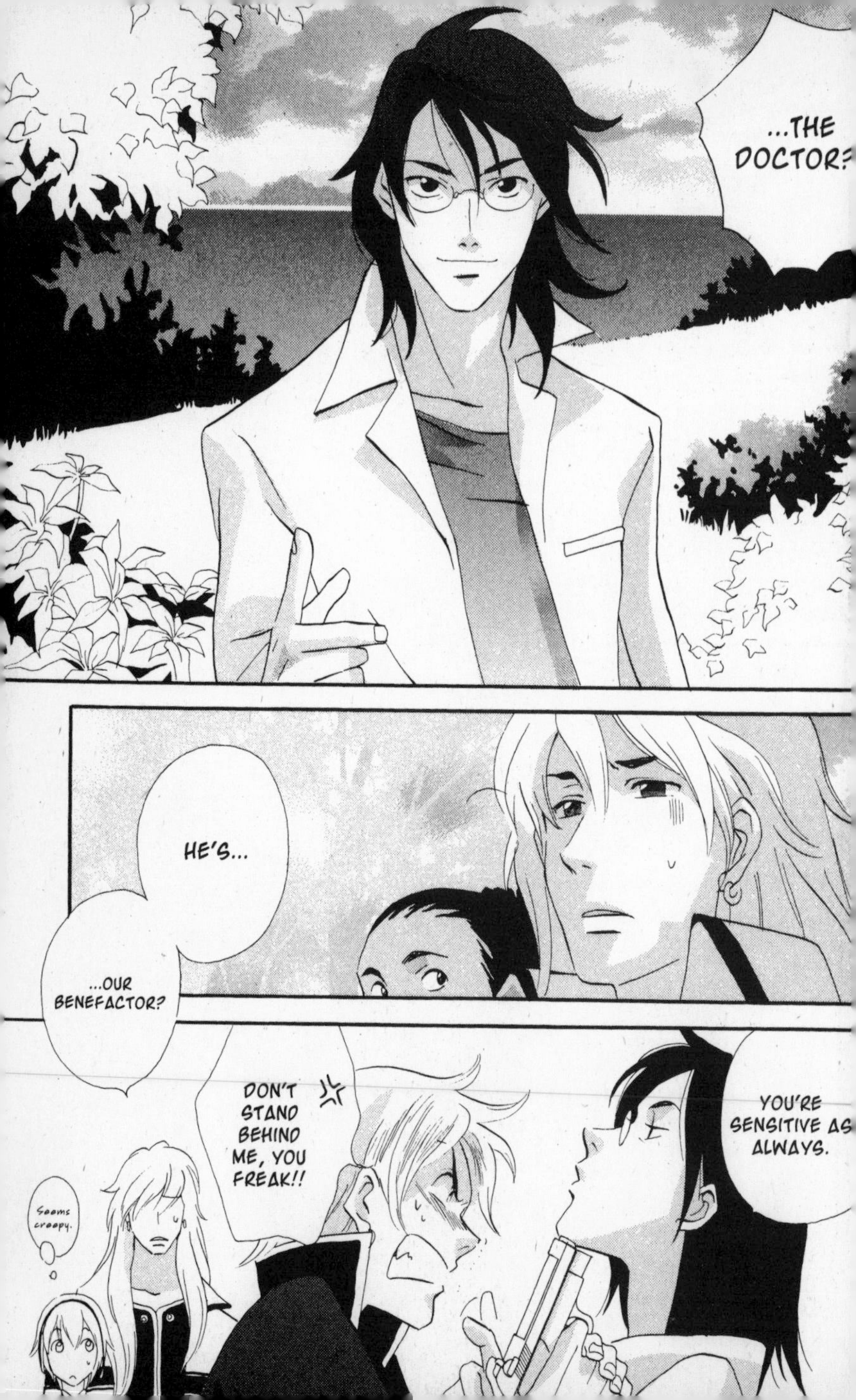
...THE DOCTOR?
HE'S...
...OUR BENEFACTOR?
YOU'RE SENSITIVE AS ALWAYS.
DON'T STAND BEHIND ME, YOU FREAK!!
Seems creepy.

BACKSTAGE MINI

Late!! Volume 7 is late!!

Hi, I'm Ozaki. When I finally started this volume, I was so behind I wanted to cry. But I'm finally ready to send it out!

I deeply apologize for keeping you waiting so long. I can be such a slug sometimes.

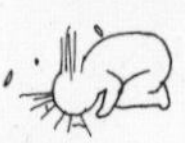

THUD!
I bow in shame.

This volume has changed into more of a romantic story. I'm not very good at writing romance, so parts of it were a little embarrassing to write. Now if this were an RPG, for example, all the party members would finally gather together to ride the boat. After that, they would obtain the airship and fly off to defeat Yuca with the Ultimate Weapons made of Orichalcum.

I wondered if I would ever finish. I was so worried about how the book would turn out that I spent more time worrying about it than I did working on it until it became a vicious circle that nearly cost me an entire year. I used to wonder if I'd ever finish drawing the story, but after fumbling through it, I'm finally done.

Please keep the faith and follow me until the story's end.

See you next volume!!

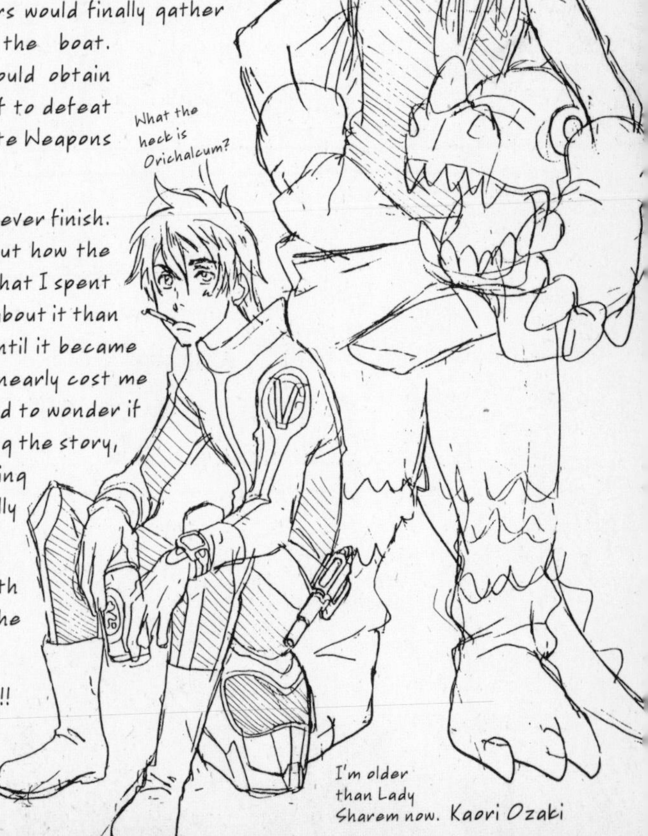

On the back cover I only dressed up two of the characters. Maybe next time I'll include a Pirate Methuselah.
What the heck is Orichalcum?
I'm older than Lady Sharem now.

Kaori Ozaki

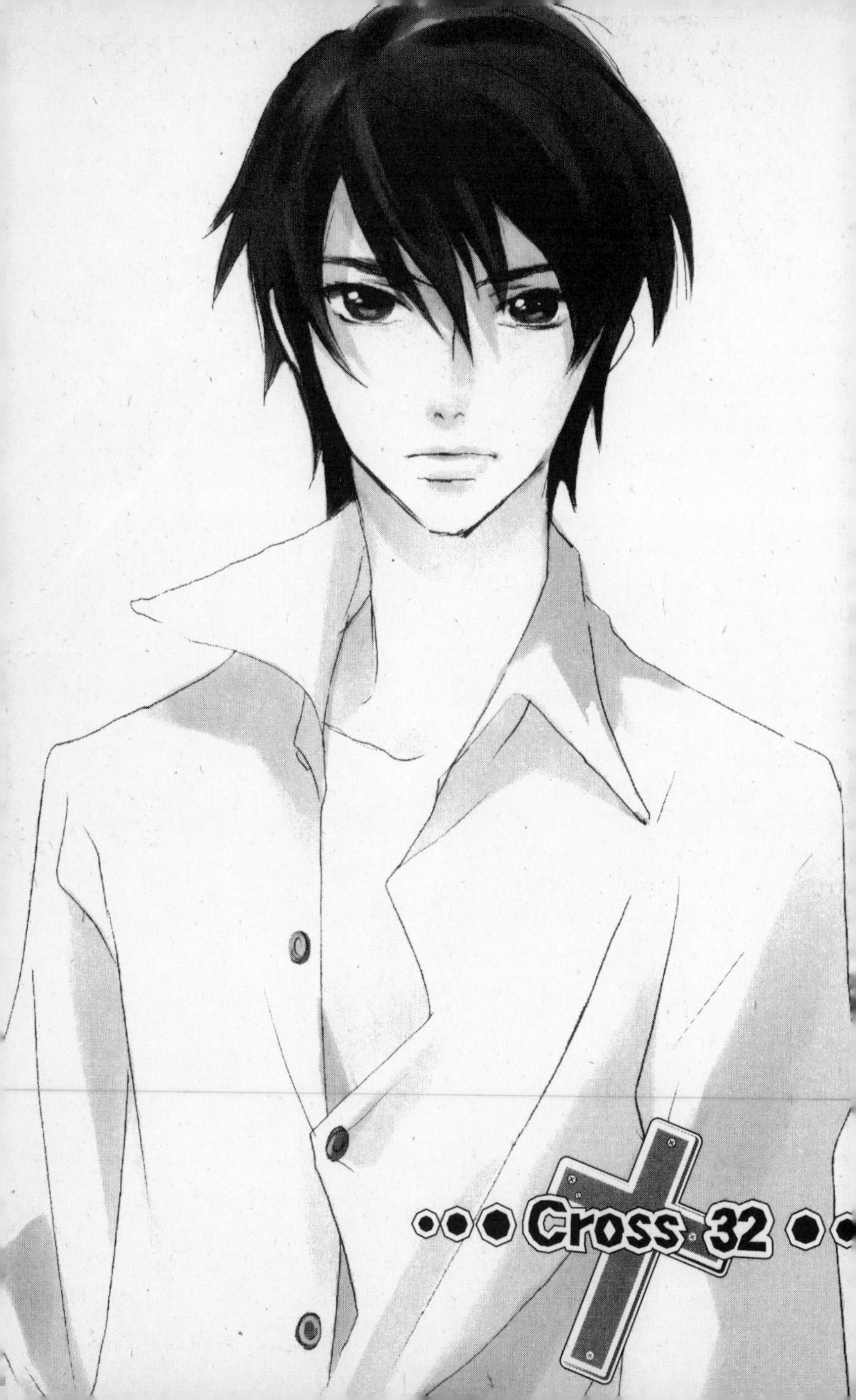
Cross 32

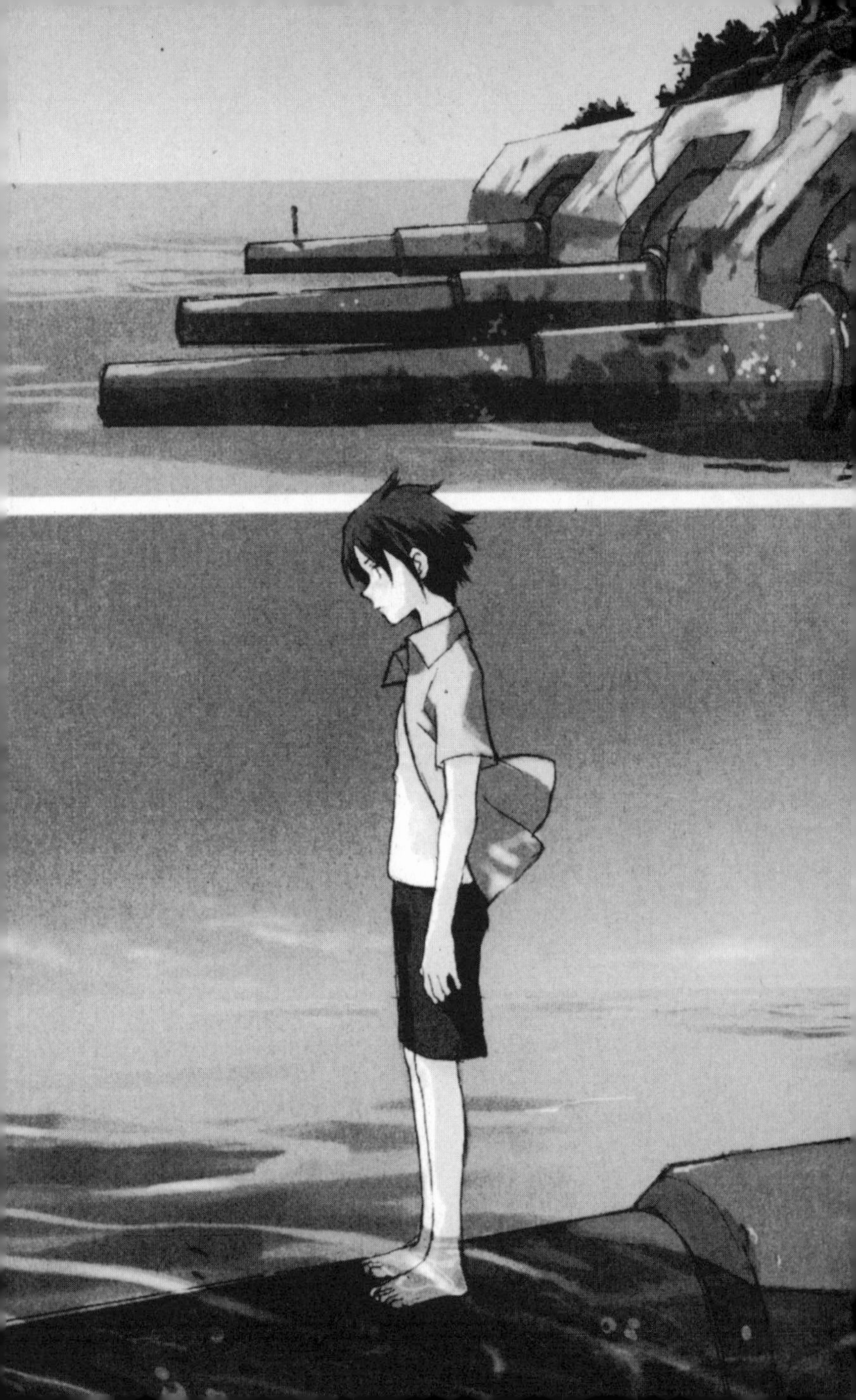

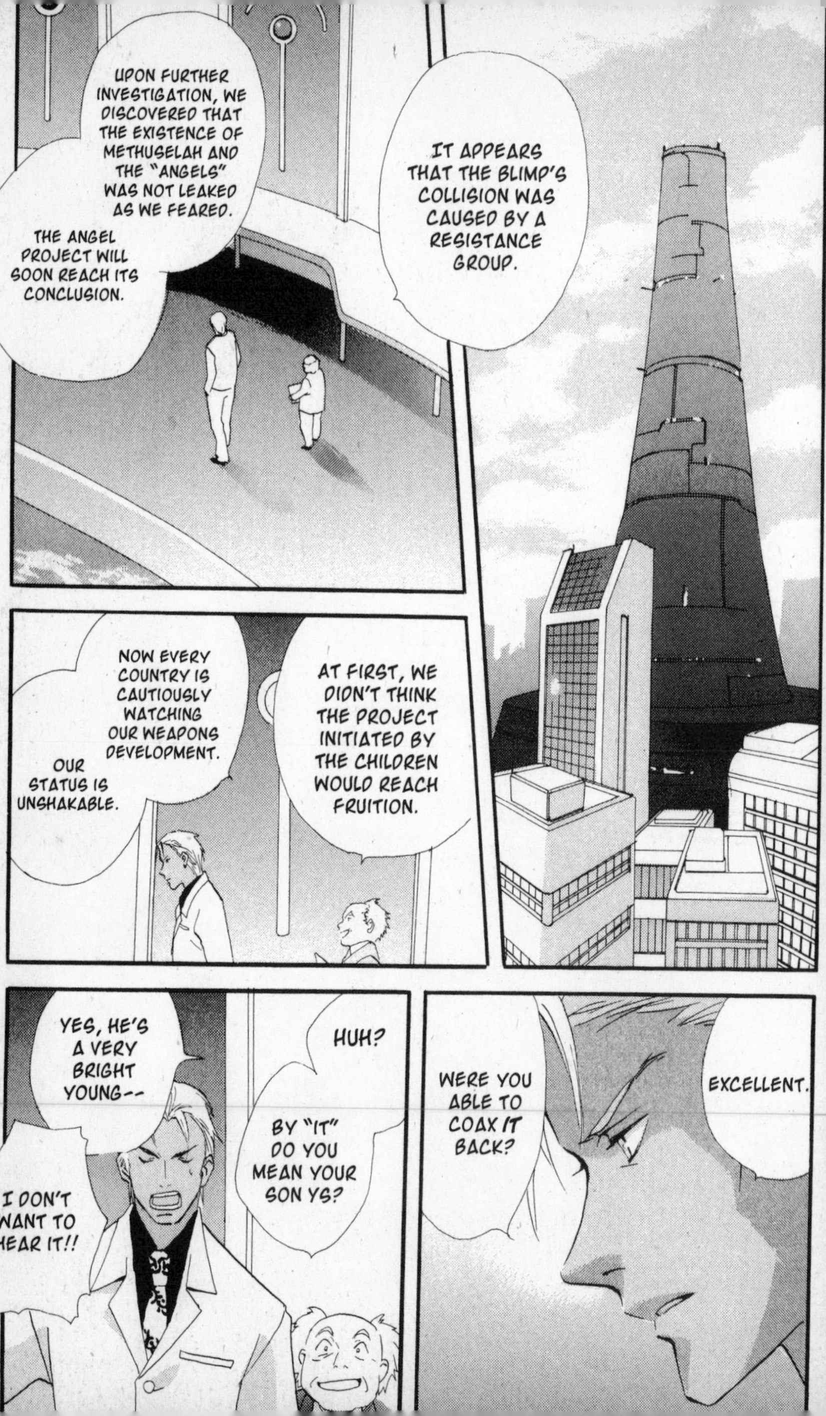
IT APPEARS THAT THE BLIMP'S COLLISION WAS CAUSED BY A RESISTANCE GROUP.
UPON FURTHER INVESTIGATION, WE DISCOVERED THAT THE EXISTENCE OF METHUSELAH AND THE "ANGELS" WAS NOT LEAKED AS WE FEARED.
THE ANGEL PROJECT WILL SOON REACH ITS CONCLUSION.
AT FIRST, WE DIDN'T THINK THE PROJECT INITIATED BY THE CHILDREN WOULD REACH FRUITION.
NOW EVERY COUNTRY IS CAUTIOUSLY WATCHING OUR WEAPONS DEVELOPMENT.
OUR STATUS IS UNSHAKABLE.
EXCELLENT.
WERE YOU ABLE TO COAX IT BACK?
HUH?
BY "IT" DO YOU MEAN YOUR SON YS?
YES, HE'S A VERY BRIGHT YOUNG--
I DON'T WANT TO HEAR IT!!

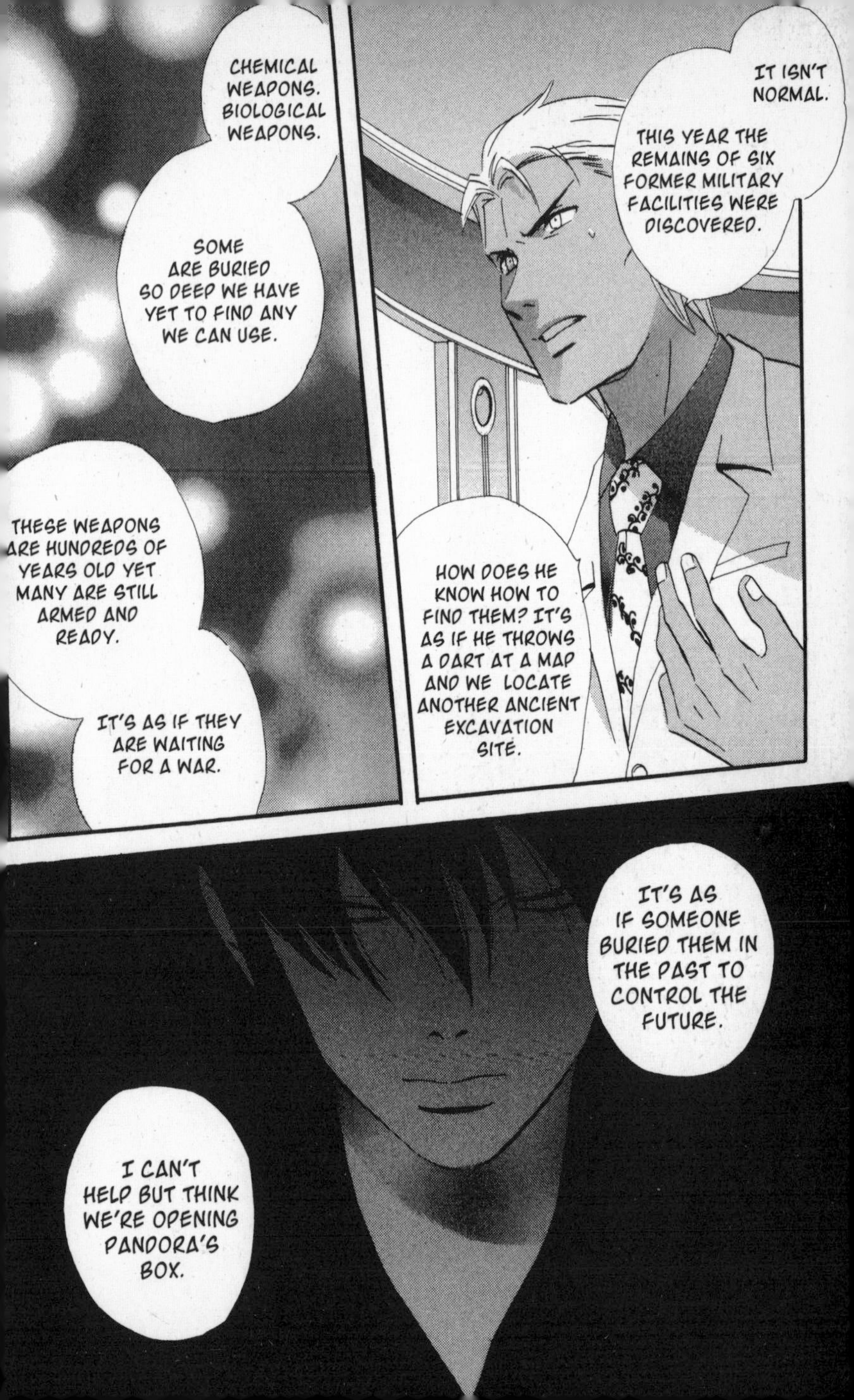
IT ISN'T NORMAL.
THIS YEAR THE REMAINS OF SIX FORMER MILITARY FACILITIES WERE DISCOVERED.
HOW DOES HE KNOW HOW TO FIND THEM? IT'S AS IF HE THROWS A DART AT A MAP AND WE LOCATE ANOTHER ANCIENT EXCAVATION SITE.
CHEMICAL WEAPONS. BIOLOGICAL WEAPONS.
SOME ARE BURIED SO DEEP WE HAVE YET TO FIND ANY WE CAN USE.
THESE WEAPONS ARE HUNDREDS OF YEARS OLD YET MANY ARE STILL ARMED AND READY.
IT'S AS IF THEY ARE WAITING FOR A WAR.
IT'S AS IF SOMEONE BURIED THEM IN THE PAST TO CONTROL THE FUTURE.
I CAN'T HELP BUT THINK WE'RE OPENING PANDORA'S BOX.

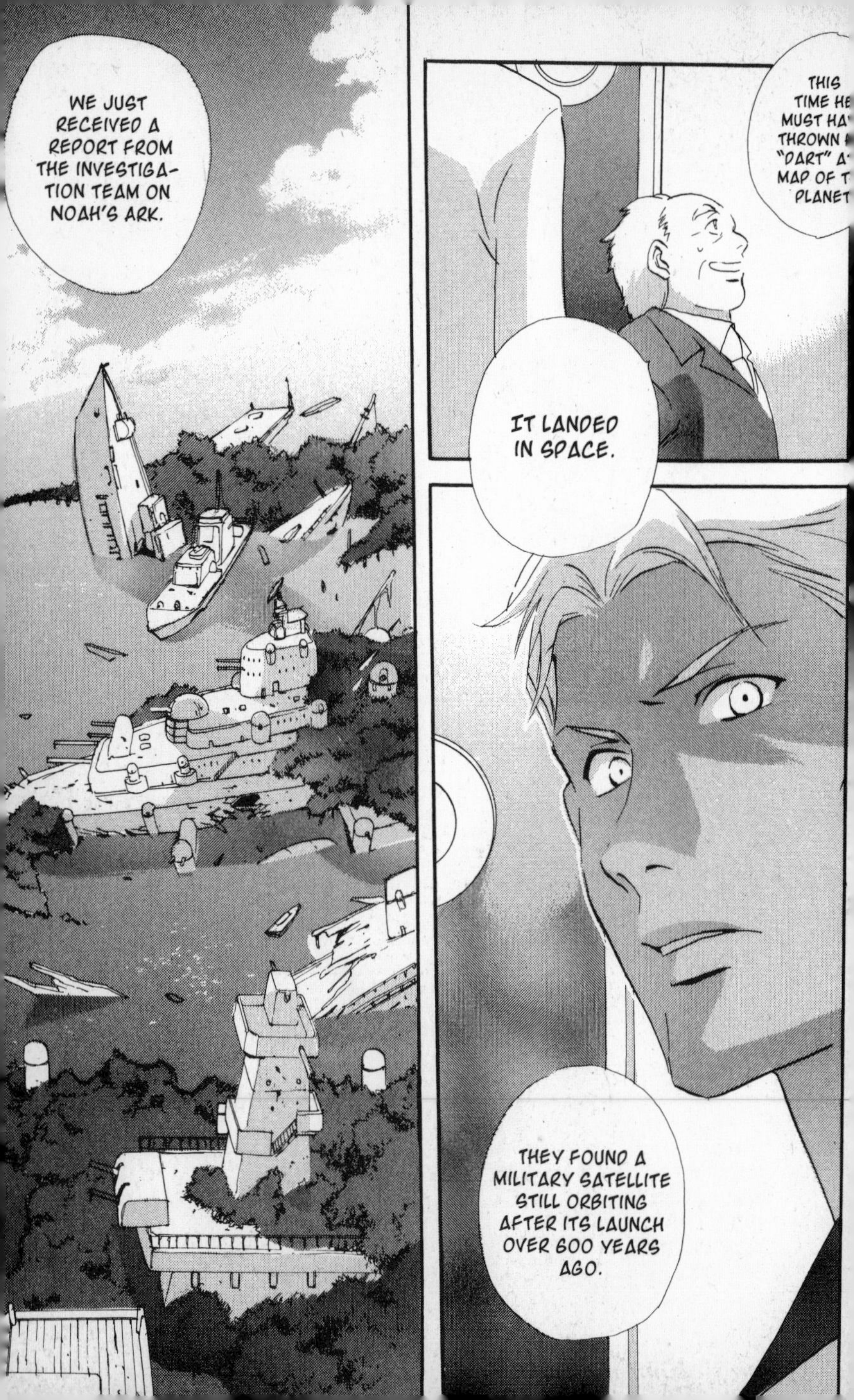
THIS TIME HE MUST HA THROWN "DART" A MAP OF T PLANET
IT LANDED IN SPACE.
THEY FOUND A MILITARY SATELLITE STILL ORBITING AFTER ITS LAUNCH OVER 600 YEARS AGO.
WE JUST RECEIVED A REPORT FROM THE INVESTIGATION TEAM ON NOAH'S ARK.

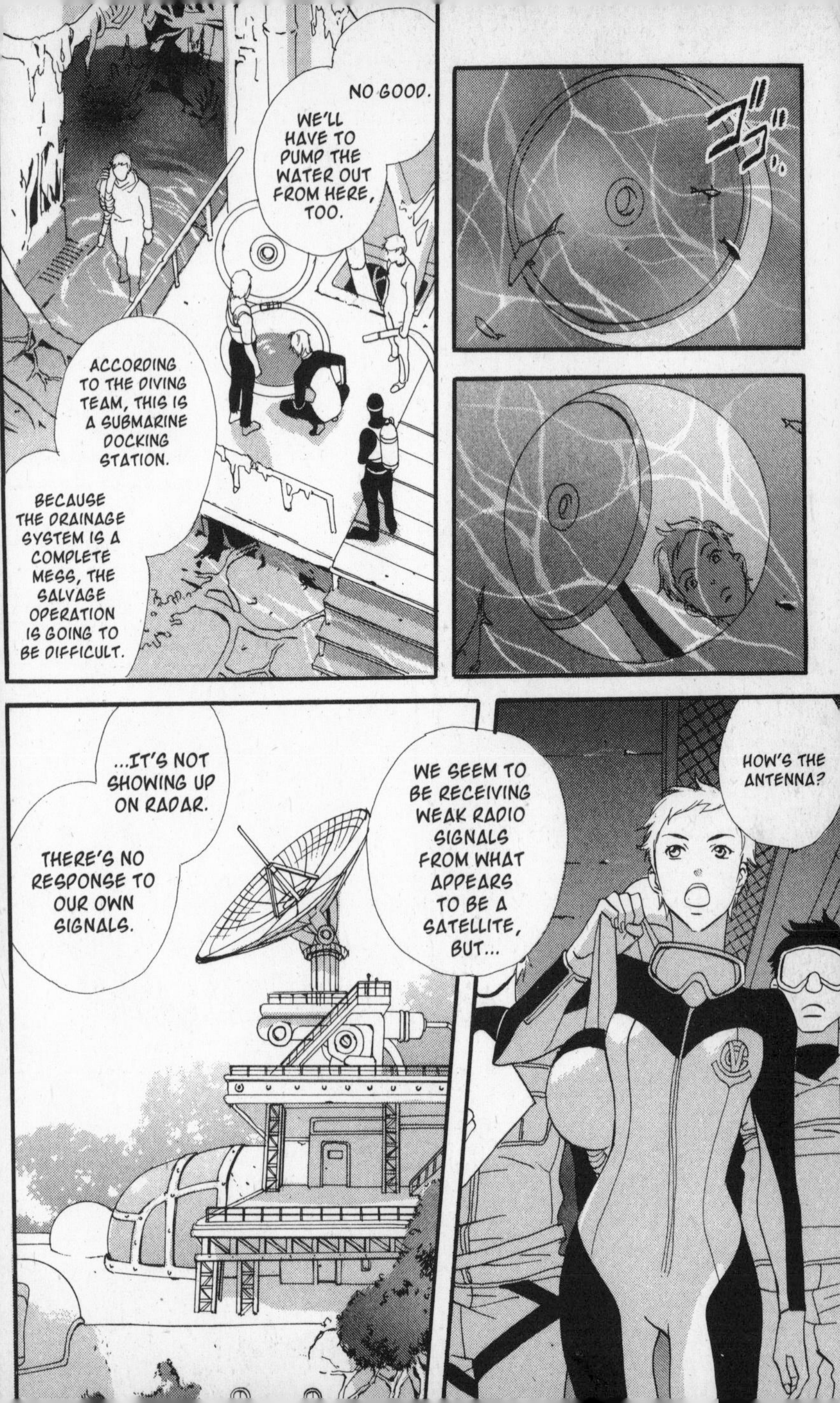
ゴゴ
NO GOOD.
WE'LL HAVE TO PUMP THE WATER OUT FROM HERE, TOO.
ACCORDING TO THE DIVING TEAM, THIS IS A SUBMARINE DOCKING STATION.
BECAUSE THE DRAINAGE SYSTEM IS A COMPLETE MESS, THE SALVAGE OPERATION IS GOING TO BE DIFFICULT.
HOW'S THE ANTENNA?
WE SEEM TO BE RECEIVING WEAK RADIO SIGNALS FROM WHAT APPEARS TO BE A SATELLITE, BUT...
...IT'S NOT SHOWING UP ON RADAR.
THERE'S NO RESPONSE TO OUR OWN SIGNALS.

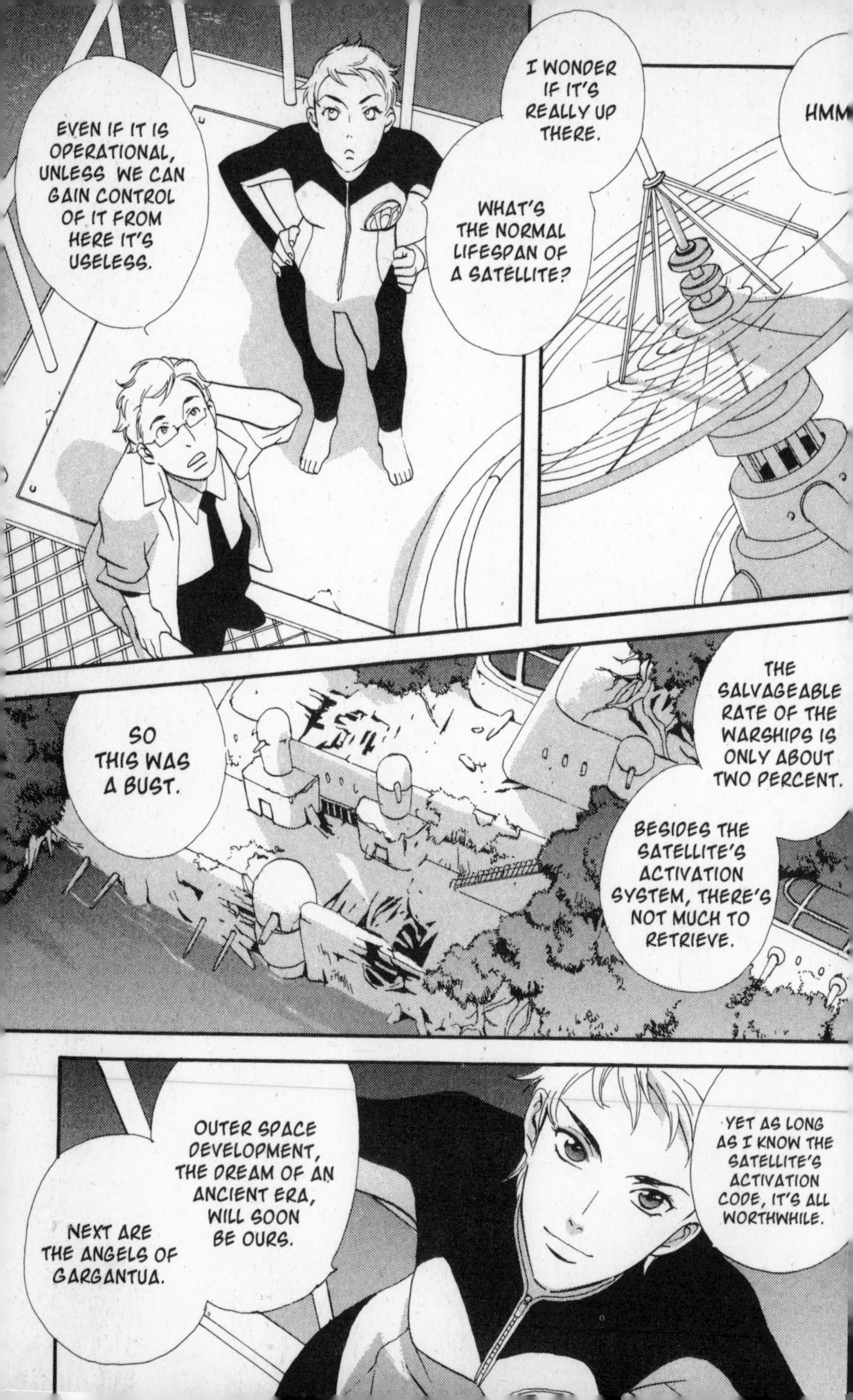
HMM
I WONDER IF IT'S REALLY UP THERE.
WHAT'S THE NORMAL LIFESPAN OF A SATELLITE?
EVEN IF IT IS OPERATIONAL, UNLESS WE CAN GAIN CONTROL OF IT FROM HERE IT'S USELESS.
THE SALVAGEABLE RATE OF THE WARSHIPS IS ONLY ABOUT TWO PERCENT.
BESIDES THE SATELLITE'S ACTIVATION SYSTEM, THERE'S NOT MUCH TO RETRIEVE.
SO THIS WAS A BUST.
YET AS LONG AS I KNOW THE SATELLITE'S ACTIVATION CODE, IT'S ALL WORTHWHILE.
OUTER SPACE DEVELOPMENT, THE DREAM OF AN ANCIENT ERA, WILL SOON BE OURS.
NEXT ARE THE ANGELS OF GARGANTUA.

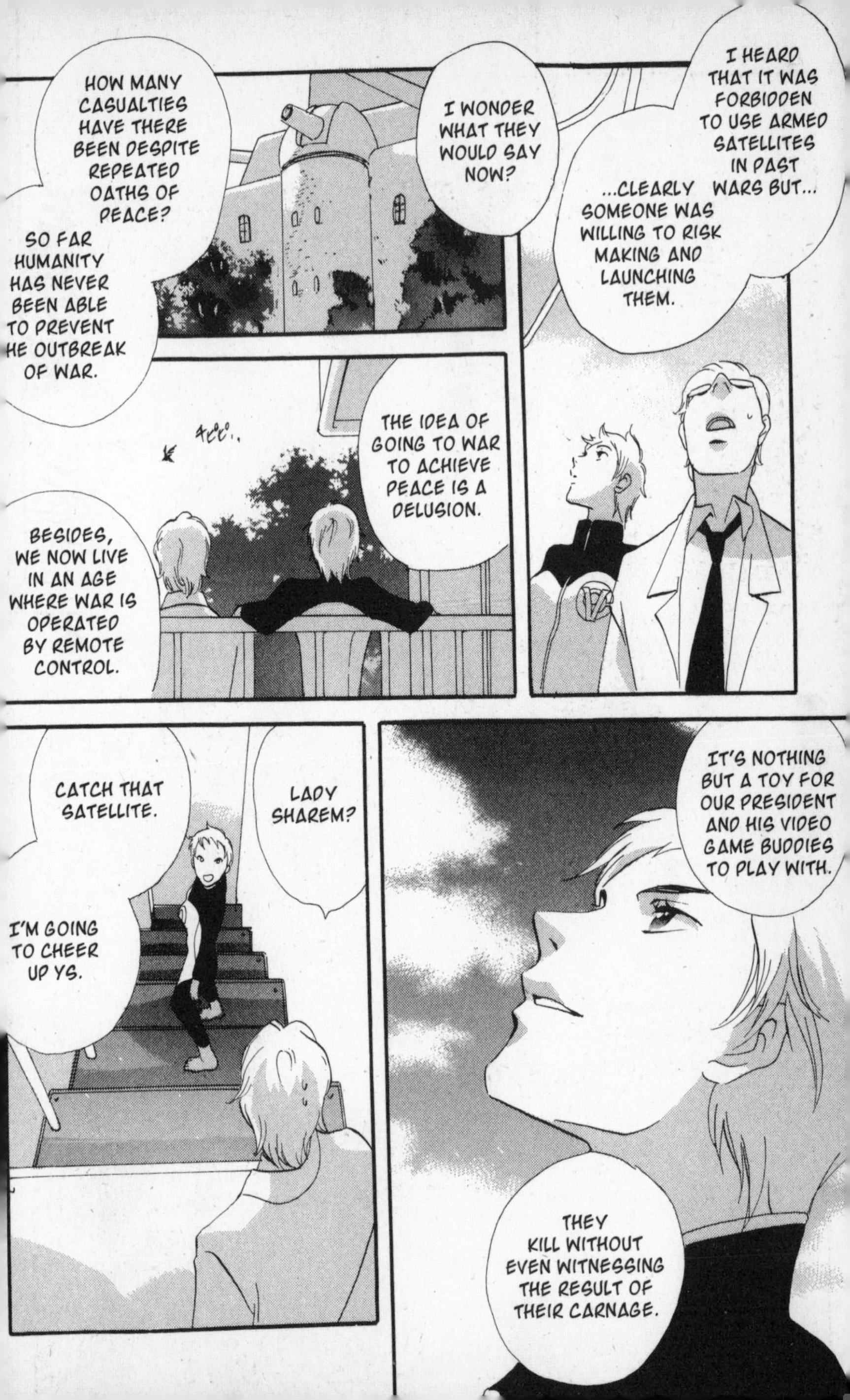
I HEARD THAT IT WAS FORBIDDEN TO USE ARMED SATELLITES IN PAST WARS BUT...
...CLEARLY SOMEONE WAS WILLING TO RISK MAKING AND LAUNCHING THEM.
I WONDER WHAT THEY WOULD SAY NOW?
HOW MANY CASUALTIES HAVE THERE BEEN DESPITE REPEATED OATHS OF PEACE?
SO FAR HUMANITY HAS NEVER BEEN ABLE TO PREVENT HE OUTBREAK OF WAR.
THE IDEA OF GOING TO WAR TO ACHIEVE PEACE IS A DELUSION.
BESIDES, WE NOW LIVE IN AN AGE WHERE WAR IS OPERATED BY REMOTE CONTROL.
IT'S NOTHING BUT A TOY FOR OUR PRESIDENT AND HIS VIDEO GAME BUDDIES TO PLAY WITH.
THEY KILL WITHOUT EVEN WITNESSING THE RESULT OF THEIR CARNAGE.
LADY SHAREM?
CATCH THAT SATELLITE.
I'M GOING TO CHEER UP YS.

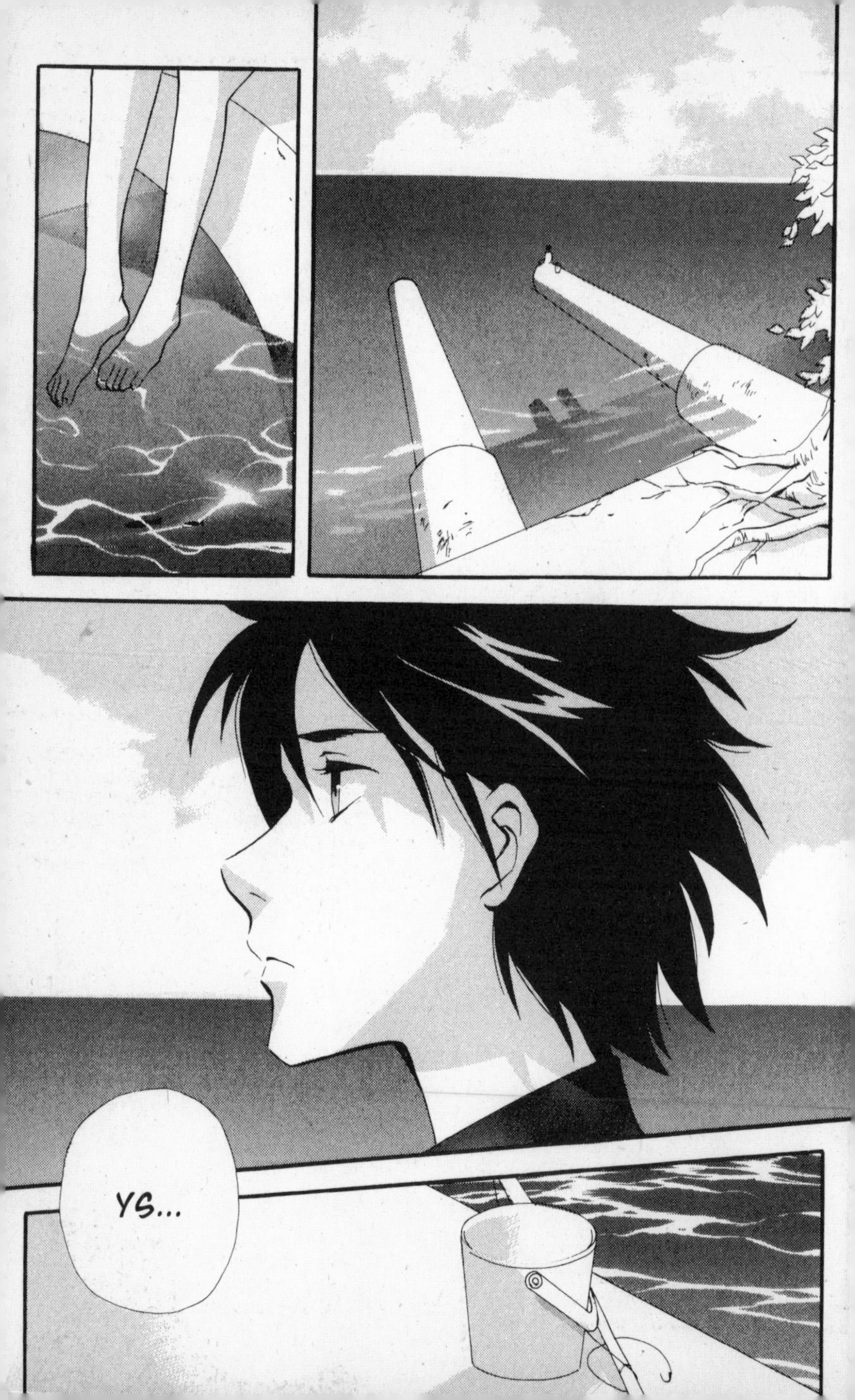
YS...

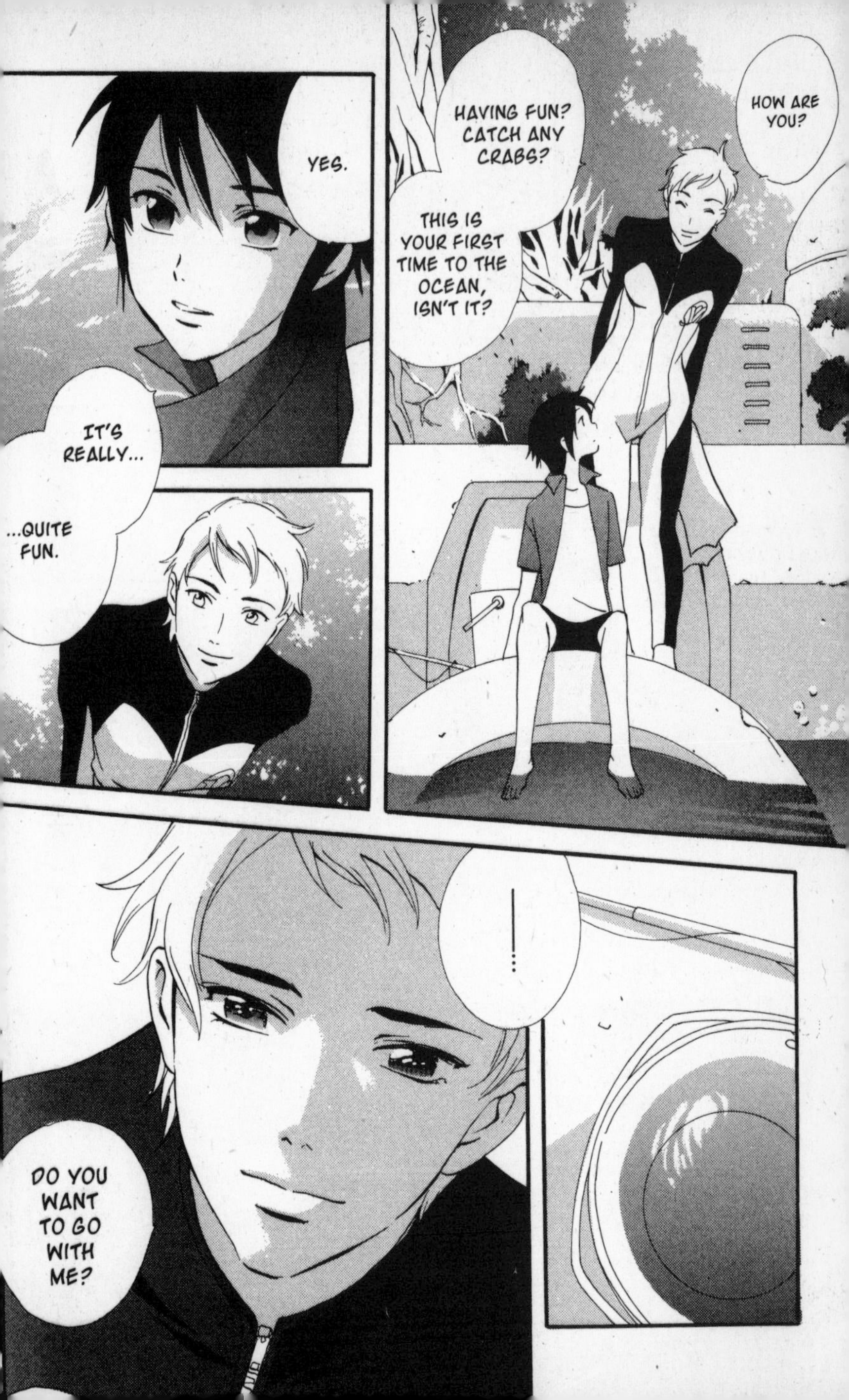

HOW ARE YOU?
HAVING FUN? CATCH ANY CRABS?
THIS IS YOUR FIRST TIME TO THE OCEAN, ISN'T IT?
YES.
IT'S REALLY...
...QUITE FUN.
—...
DO YOU WANT TO GO WITH ME?

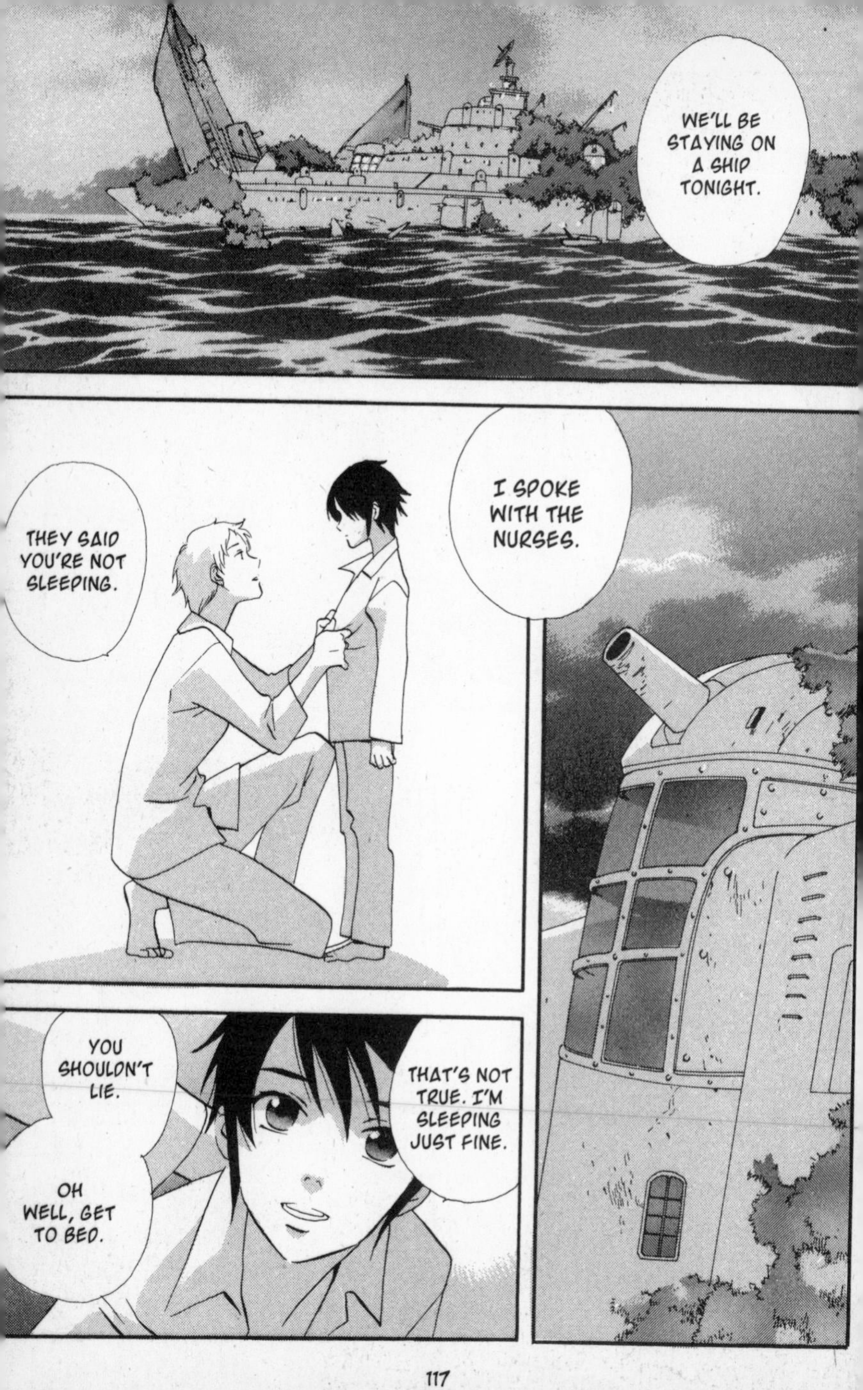
WE'LL BE STAYING ON A SHIP TONIGHT.
I SPOKE WITH THE NURSES.
THEY SAID YOU'RE NOT SLEEPING.
THAT'S NOT TRUE. I'M SLEEPING JUST FINE.
YOU SHOULDN'T LIE.
OH WELL, GET TO BED.

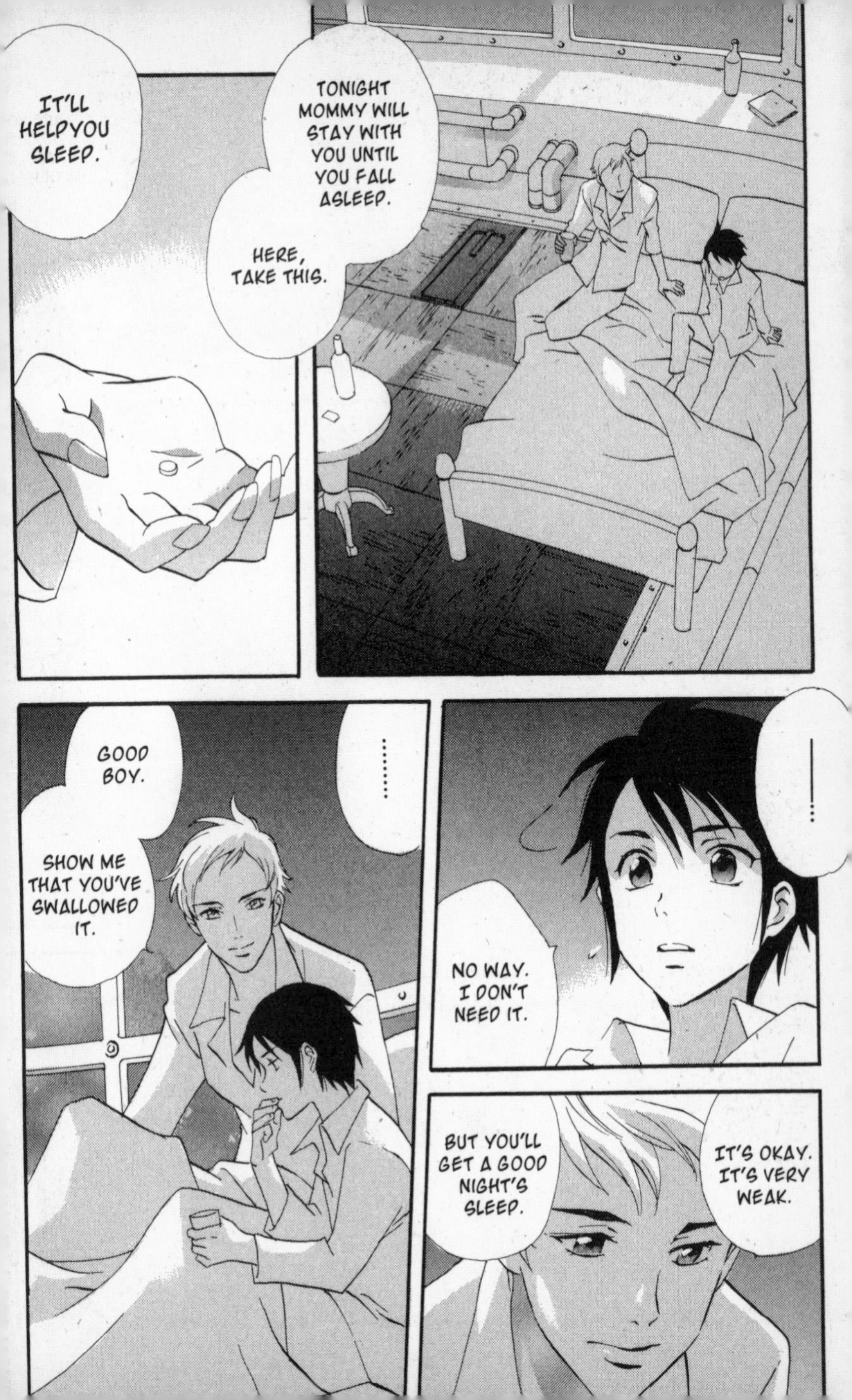
TONIGHT MOMMY WILL STAY WITH YOU UNTIL YOU FALL ASLEEP.
HERE, TAKE THIS.
IT'LL HELP YOU SLEEP.
......
NO WAY. I DON'T NEED IT.
IT'S OKAY. IT'S VERY WEAK.
BUT YOU'LL GET A GOOD NIGHT'S SLEEP.
......
GOOD BOY.
SHOW ME THAT YOU'VE SWALLOWED IT.

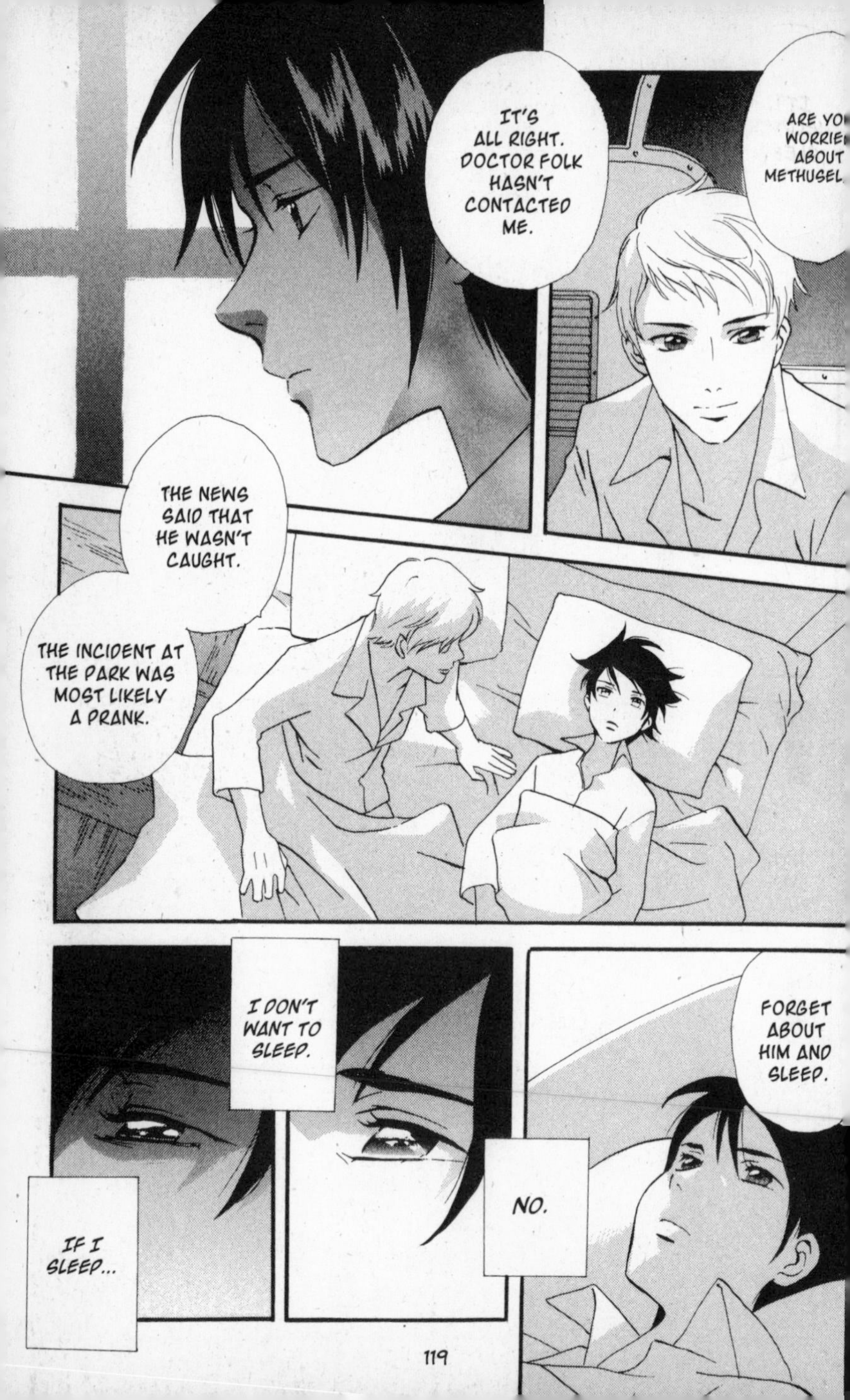

ARE YO WORRIE ABOUT METHUSEL
IT'S ALL RIGHT. DOCTOR FOLK HASN'T CONTACTED ME.
THE NEWS SAID THAT HE WASN'T CAUGHT.
THE INCIDENT AT THE PARK WAS MOST LIKELY A PRANK.
FORGET ABOUT HIM AND SLEEP.
NO.
I DON'T WANT TO SLEEP.
IF I SLEEP...

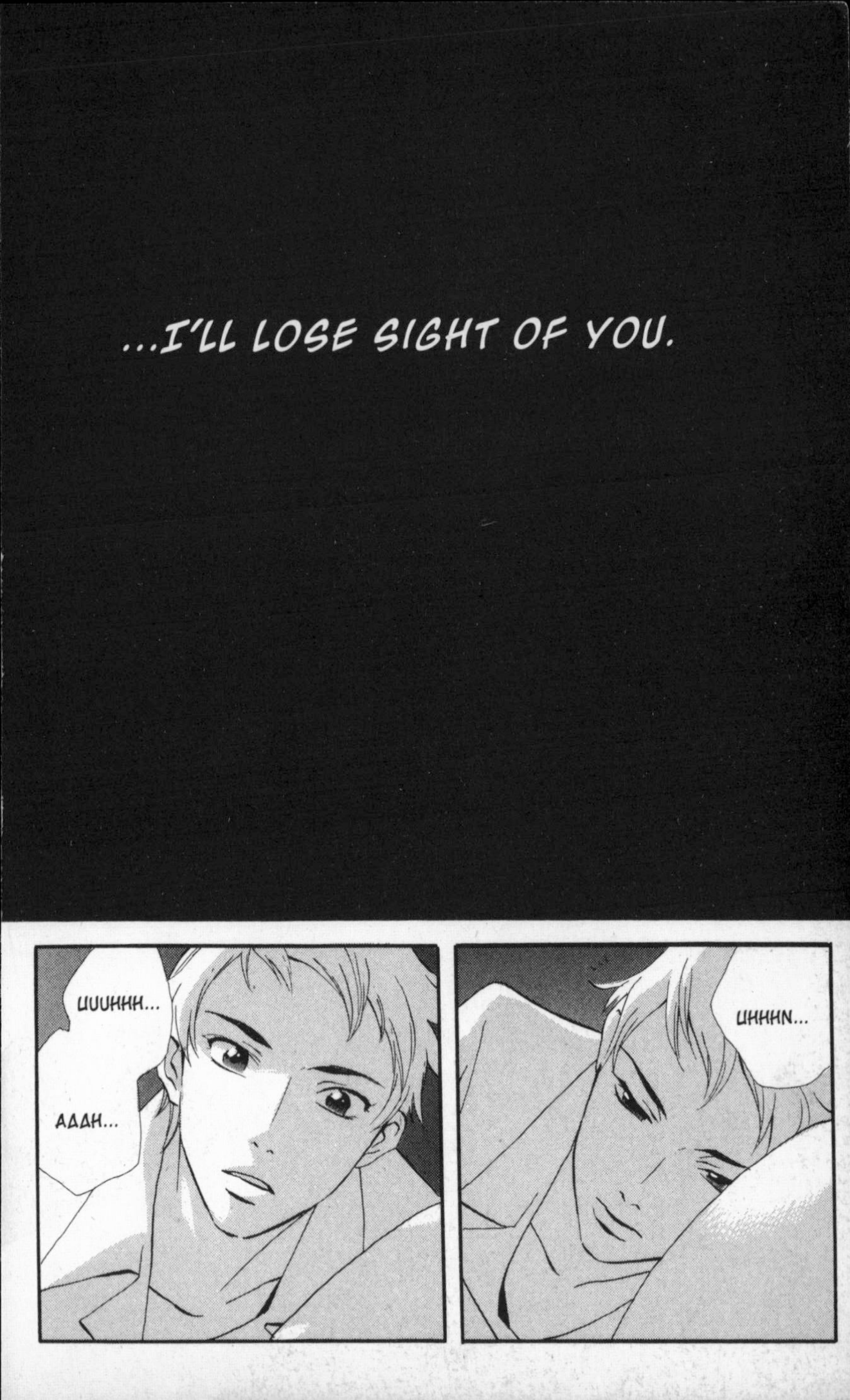
...I'LL LOSE SIGHT OF YOU.
UHHHN...
UUUHHH...
AAAH...

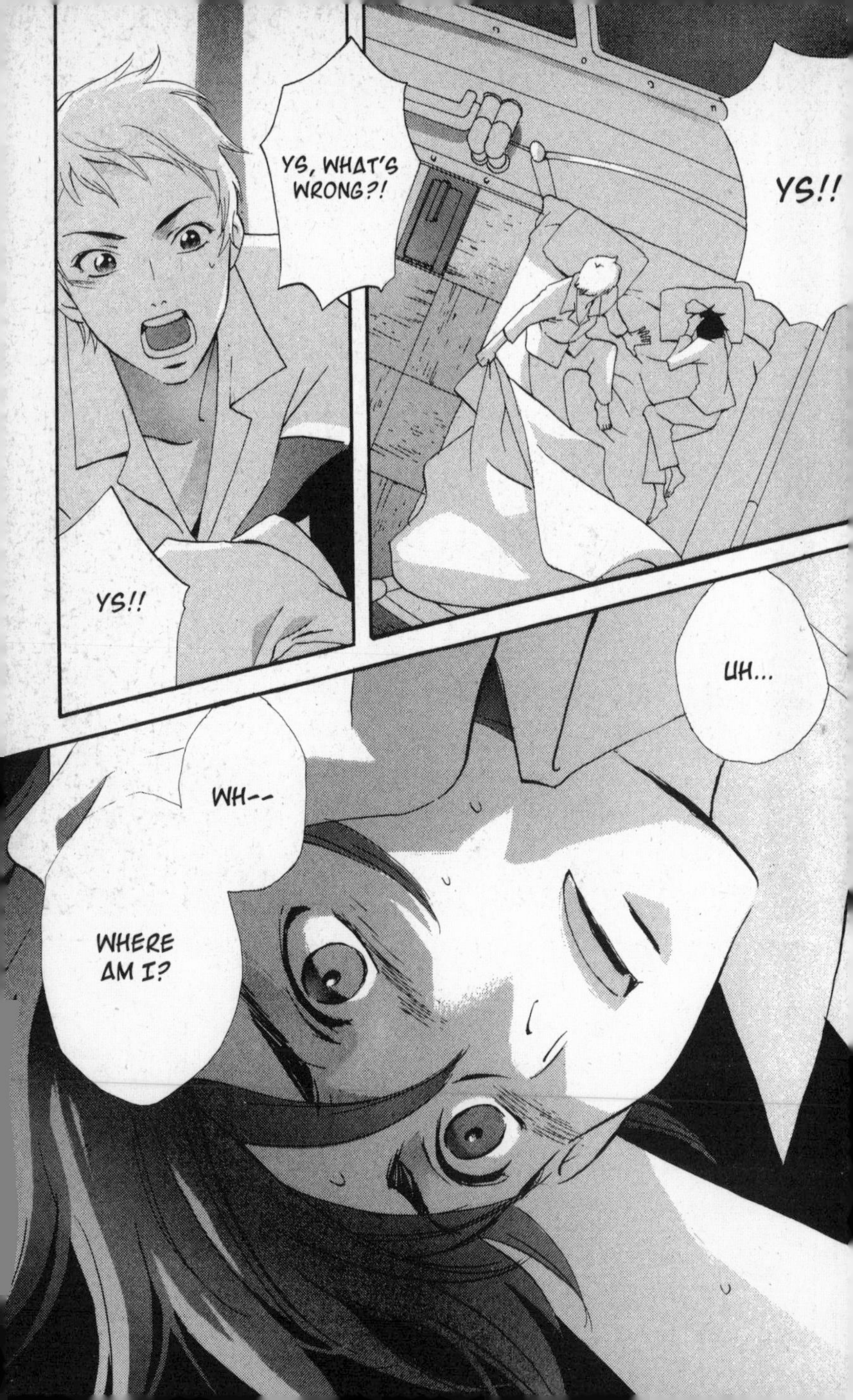
YS!!
YS, WHAT'S WRONG?!
YS!!
UH...
WH--
WHERE AM I?

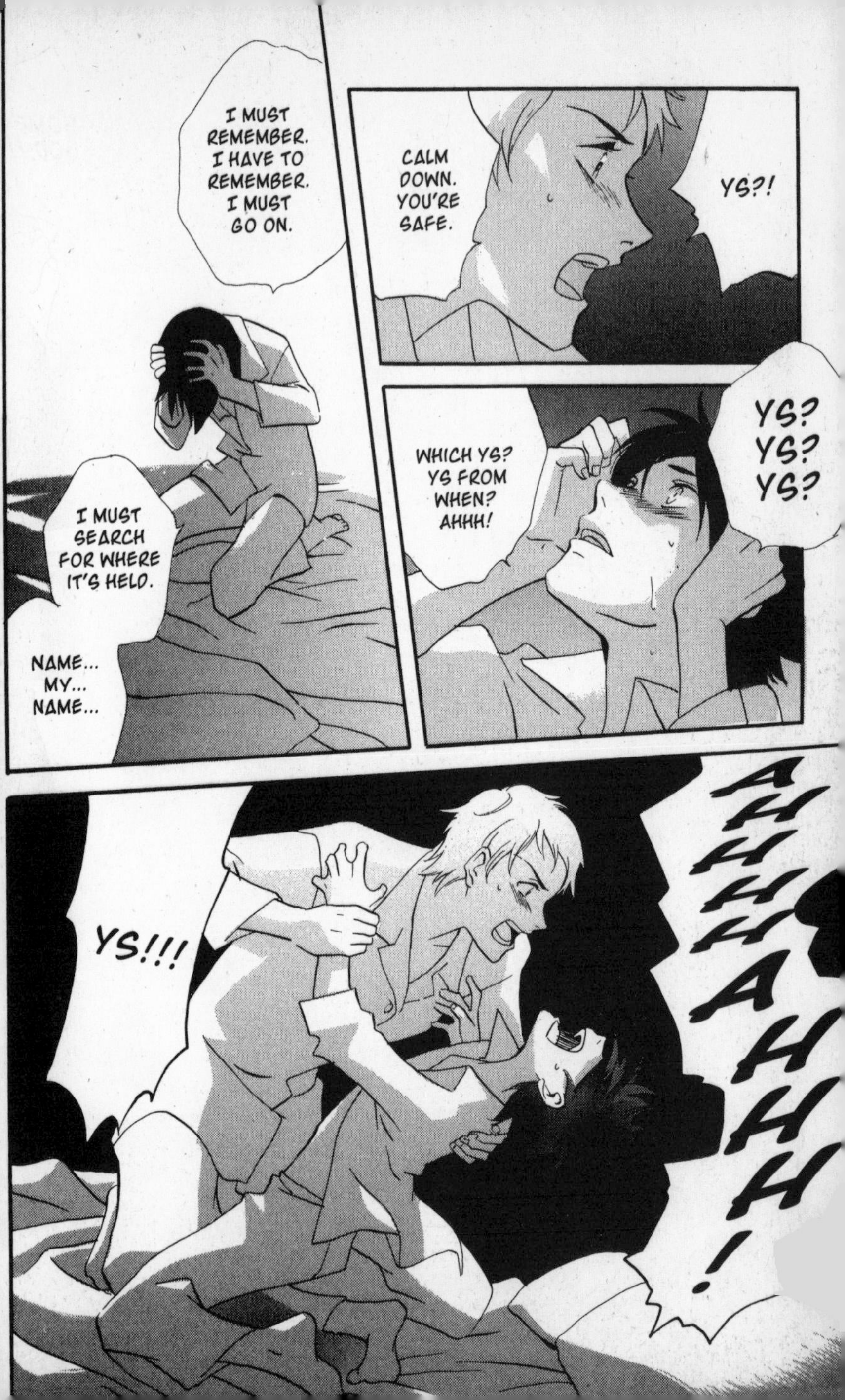
YS?!
CALM DOWN. YOU'RE SAFE.
YS? YS? YS?
WHICH YS? YS FROM WHEN? AHHH!
I MUST REMEMBER. I HAVE TO REMEMBER. I MUST GO ON.
I MUST SEARCH FOR WHERE IT'S HELD.
NAME... MY... NAME...
AHHHHAHHH!
YS!!!

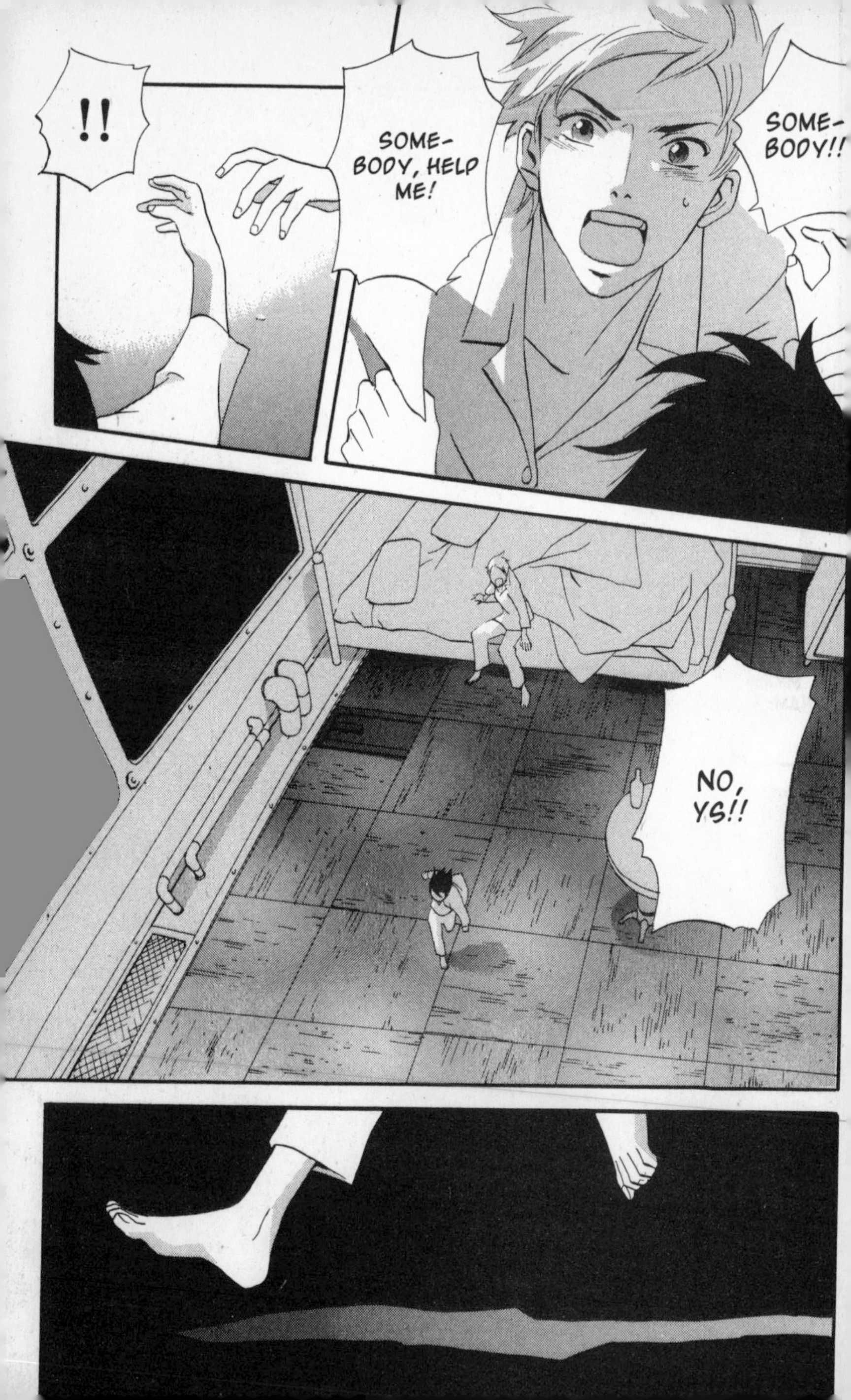
SOME-BODY!!
SOME-BODY, HELP ME!
!!
NO, YS!!

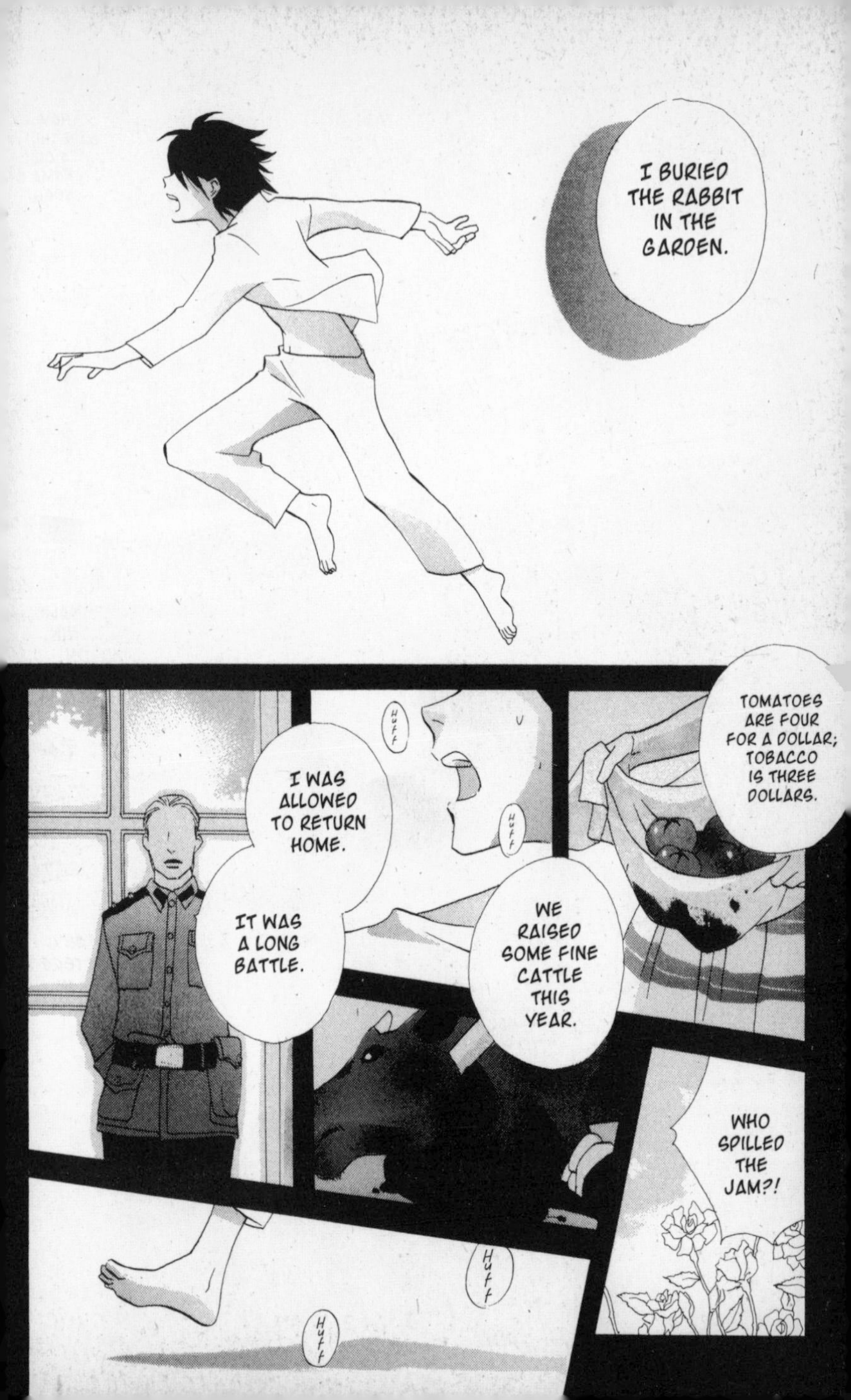
I BURIED THE RABBIT IN THE GARDEN.
TOMATOES ARE FOUR FOR A DOLLAR; TOBACCO IS THREE DOLLARS.
Huff
Huff
I WAS ALLOWED TO RETURN HOME.
IT WAS A LONG BATTLE.
WE RAISED SOME FINE CATTLE THIS YEAR.
WHO SPILLED THE JAM?!
Huff
Huff

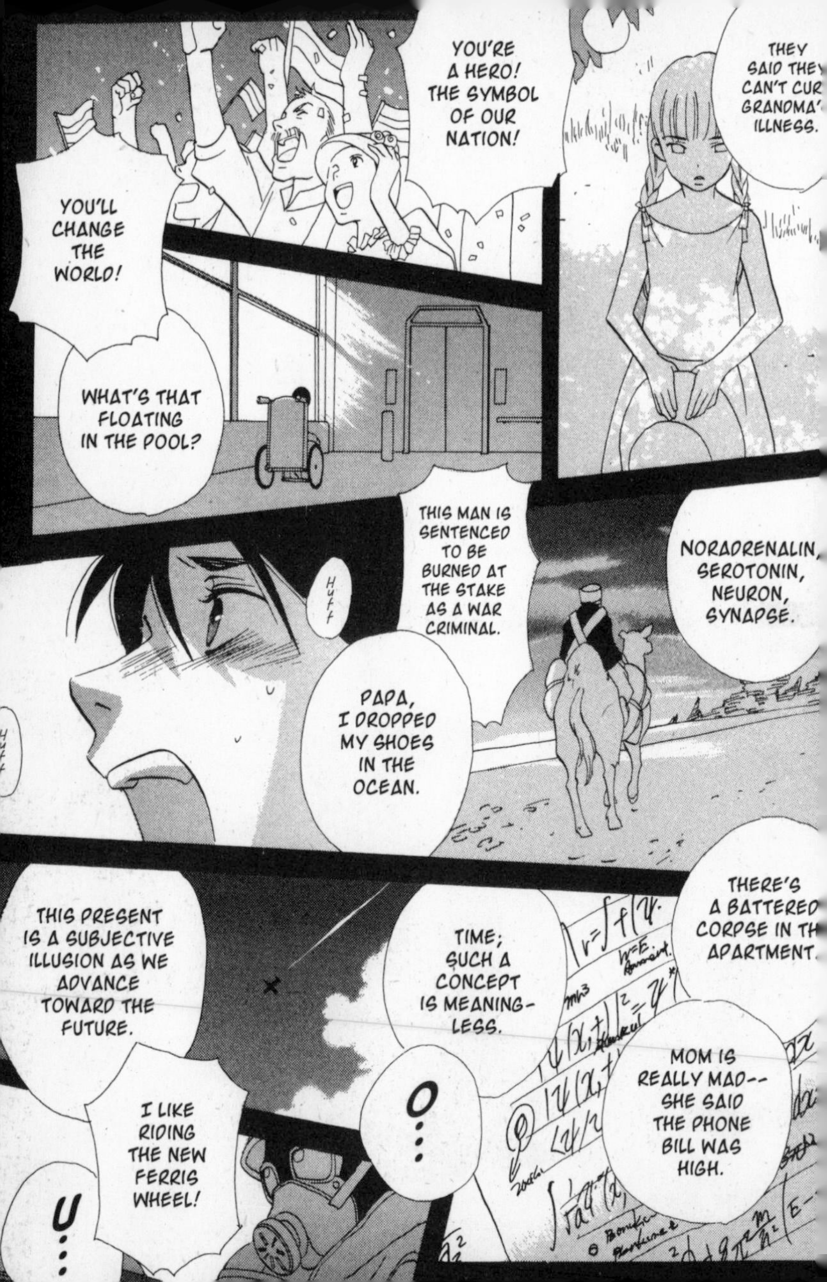
THEY SAID THEY CAN'T CUR GRANDMA' ILLNESS.
YOU'RE A HERO! THE SYMBOL OF OUR NATION!
YOU'LL CHANGE THE WORLD!
WHAT'S THAT FLOATING IN THE POOL?
NORADRENALIN, SEROTONIN, NEURON, SYNAPSE.
THIS MAN IS SENTENCED TO BE BURNED AT THE STAKE AS A WAR CRIMINAL.
PAPA, I DROPPED MY SHOES IN THE OCEAN.
Huff
Huff
THERE'S A BATTERED CORPSE IN TH APARTMENT.
MOM IS REALLY MAD-- SHE SAID THE PHONE BILL WAS HIGH.
TIME; SUCH A CONCEPT IS MEANING-LESS.
THIS PRESENT IS A SUBJECTIVE ILLUSION AS WE ADVANCE TOWARD THE FUTURE.
O...
I LIKE RIDING THE NEW FERRIS WHEEL!
U...

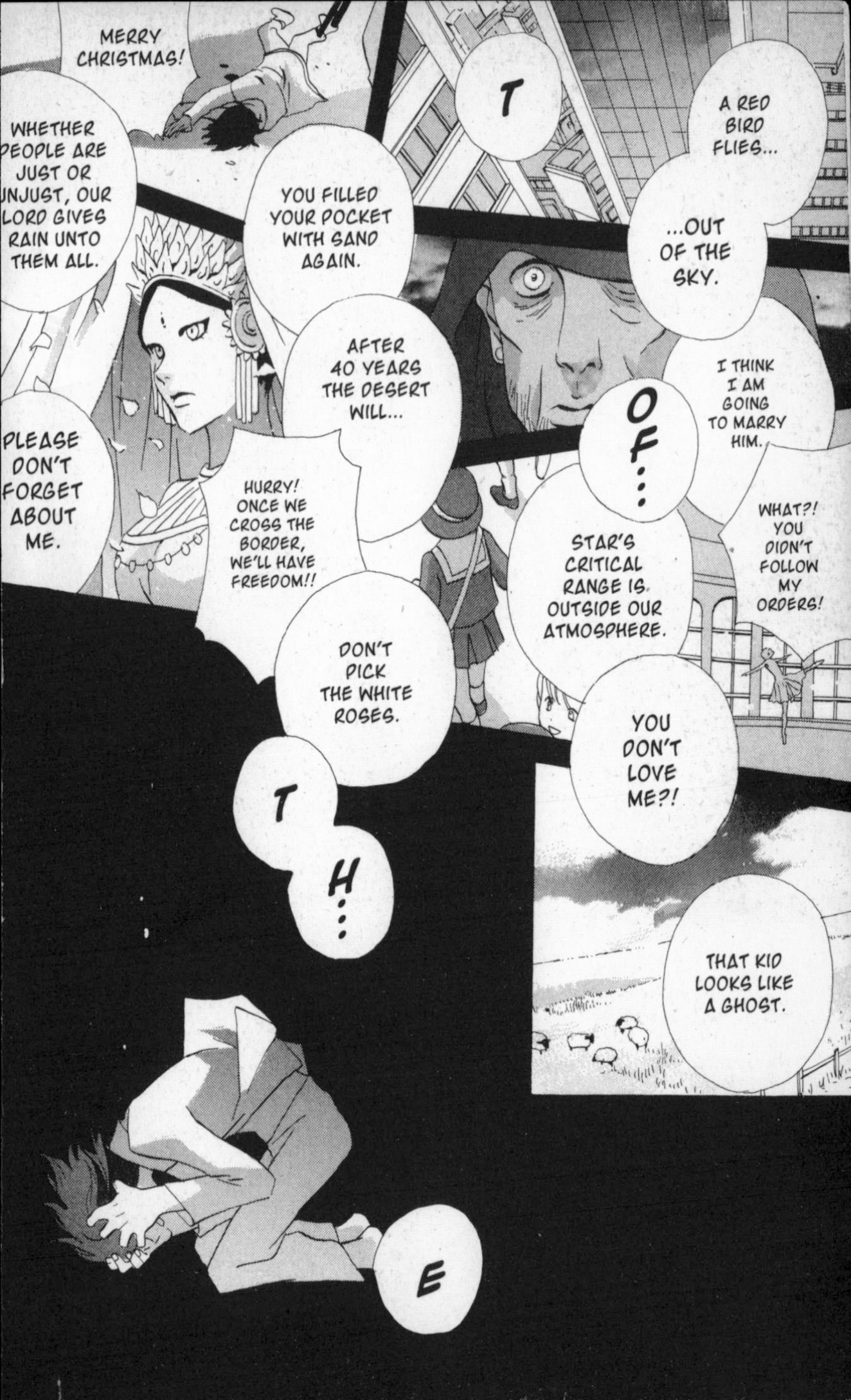
A RED BIRD FLIES...
...OUT OF THE SKY.
T
MERRY CHRISTMAS!
YOU FILLED YOUR POCKET WITH SAND AGAIN.
WHETHER PEOPLE ARE JUST OR UNJUST, OUR LORD GIVES RAIN UNTO THEM ALL.
I THINK I AM GOING TO MARRY HIM.
OF...
AFTER 40 YEARS THE DESERT WILL...
WHAT?! YOU DIDN'T FOLLOW MY ORDERS!
STAR'S CRITICAL RANGE IS OUTSIDE OUR ATMOSPHERE.
HURRY! ONCE WE CROSS THE BORDER, WE'LL HAVE FREEDOM!!
PLEASE DON'T FORGET ABOUT ME.
YOU DON'T LOVE ME?!
DON'T PICK THE WHITE ROSES.
T
THAT KID LOOKS LIKE A GHOST.
H...
E

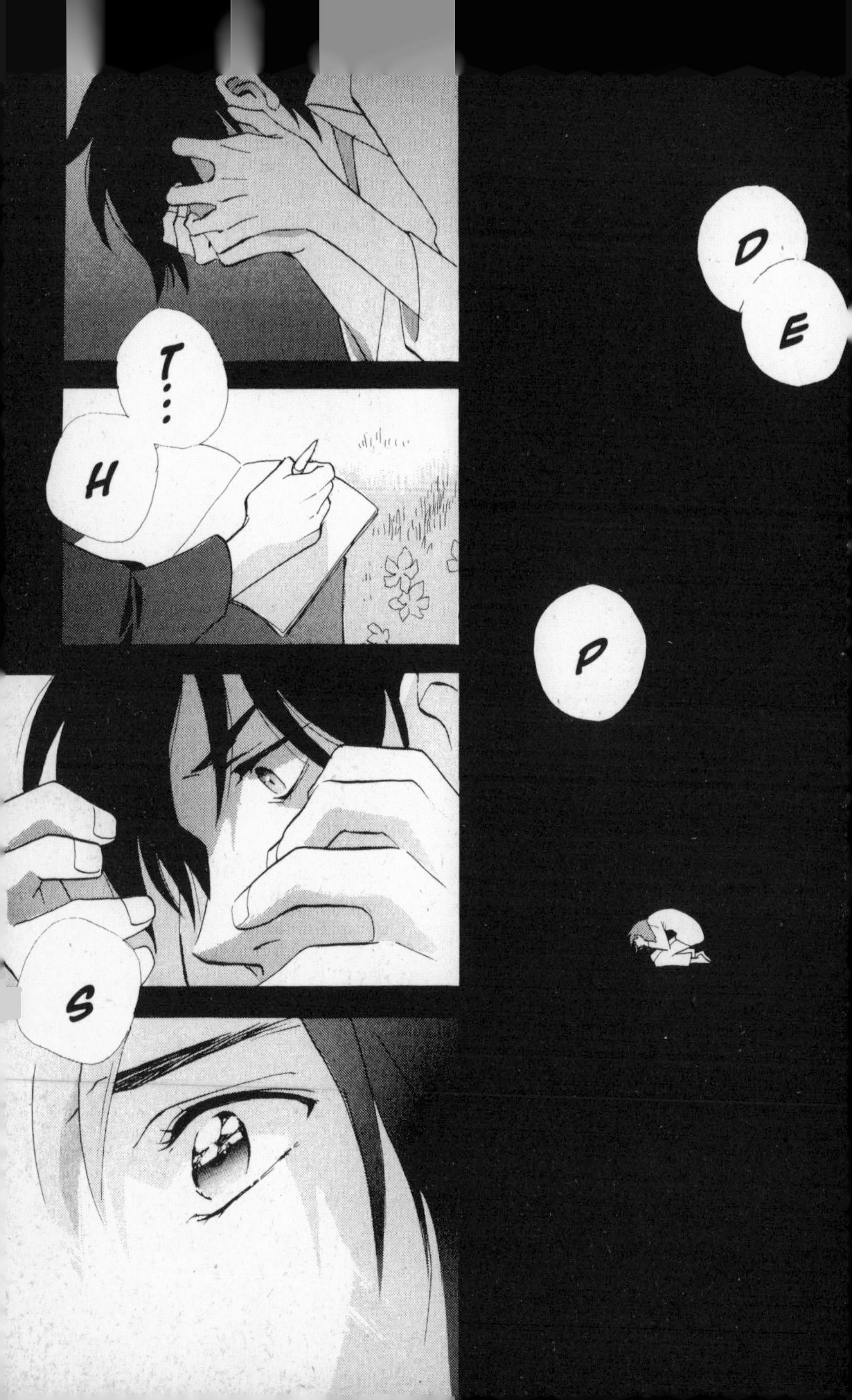
D
E
P
T...
H
S

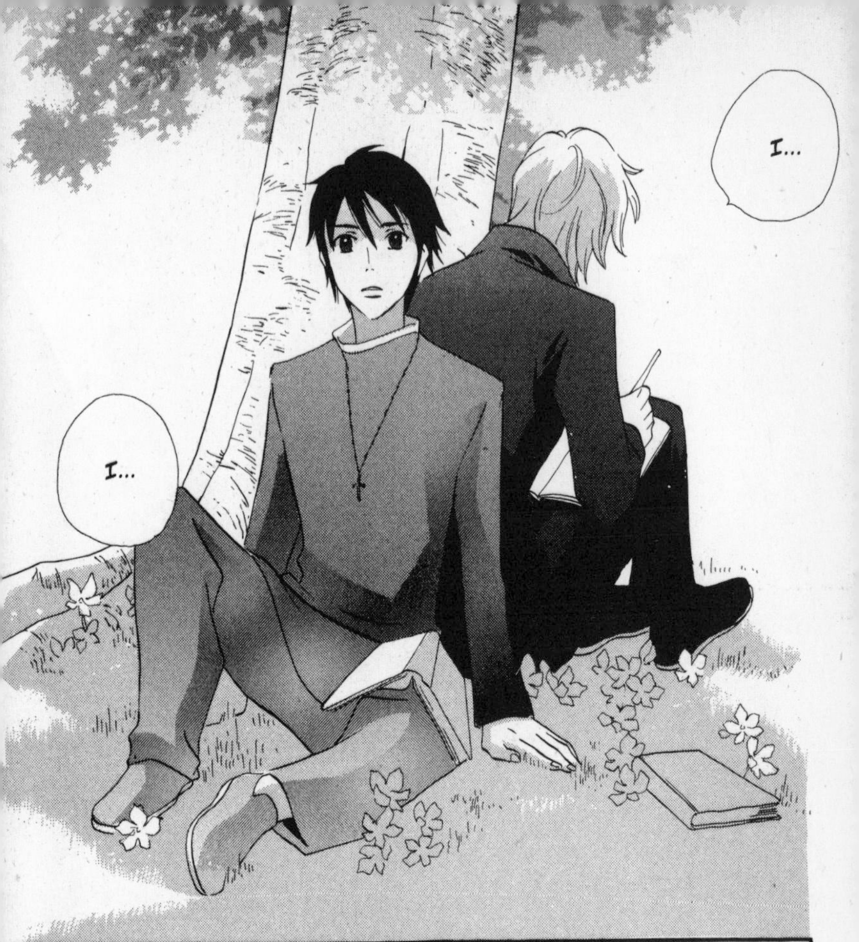
I...
I...
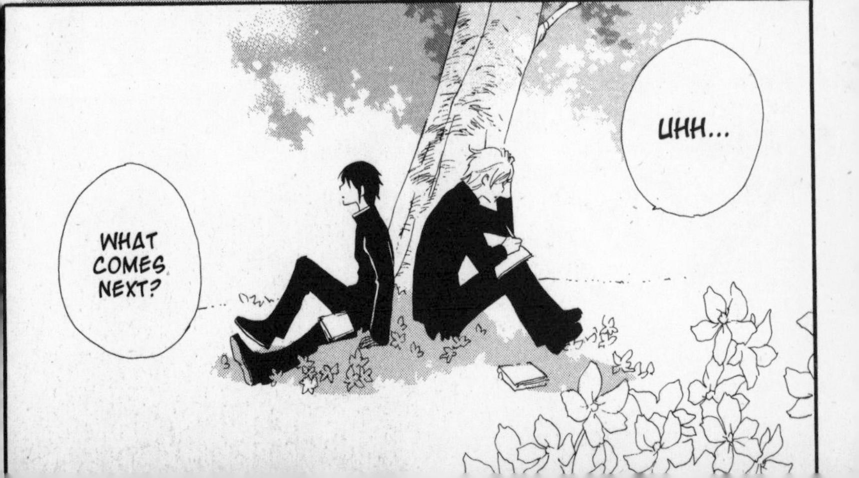
UHH...
WHAT COMES NEXT?

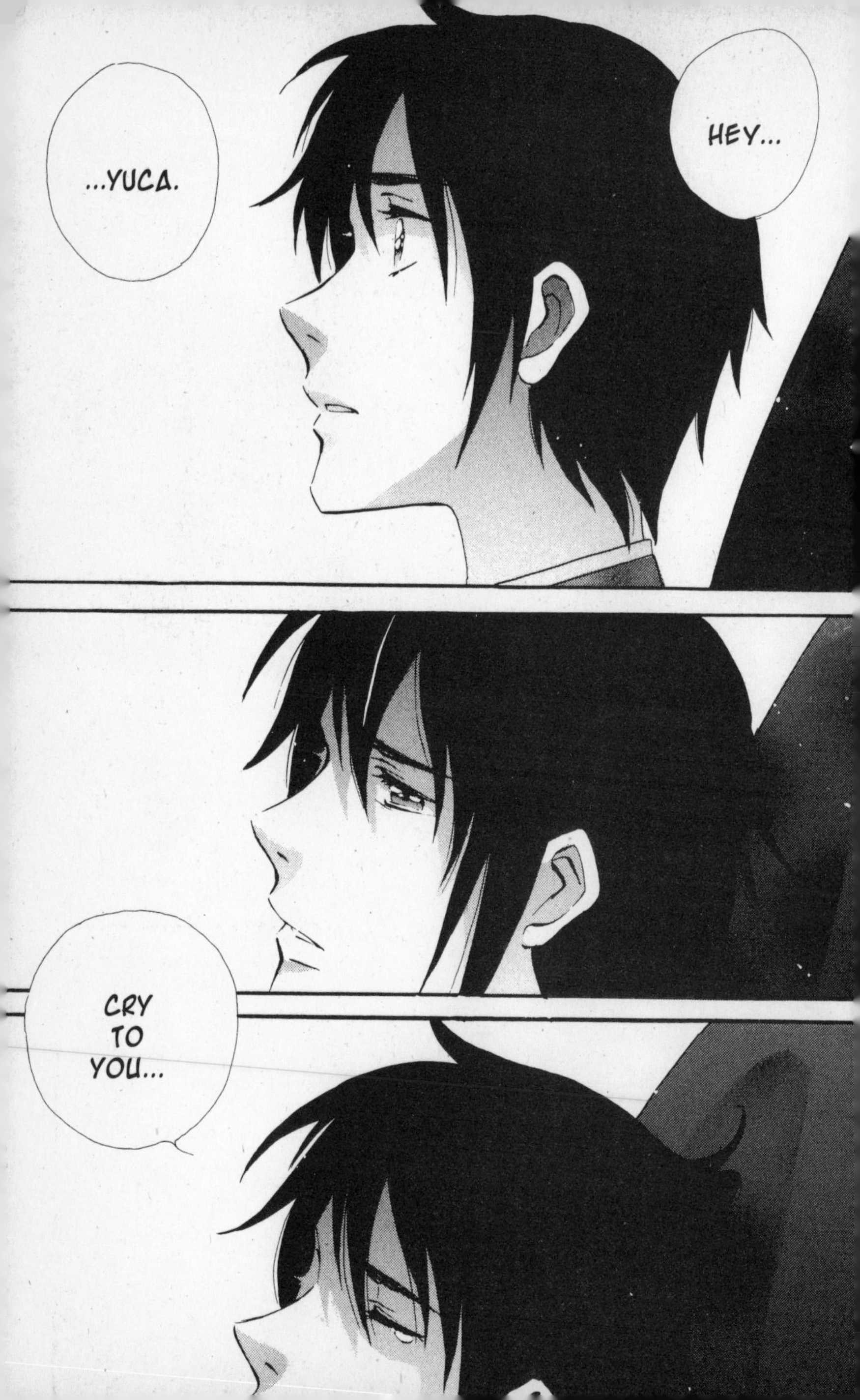
HEY...
...YUCA.
CRY TO YOU...

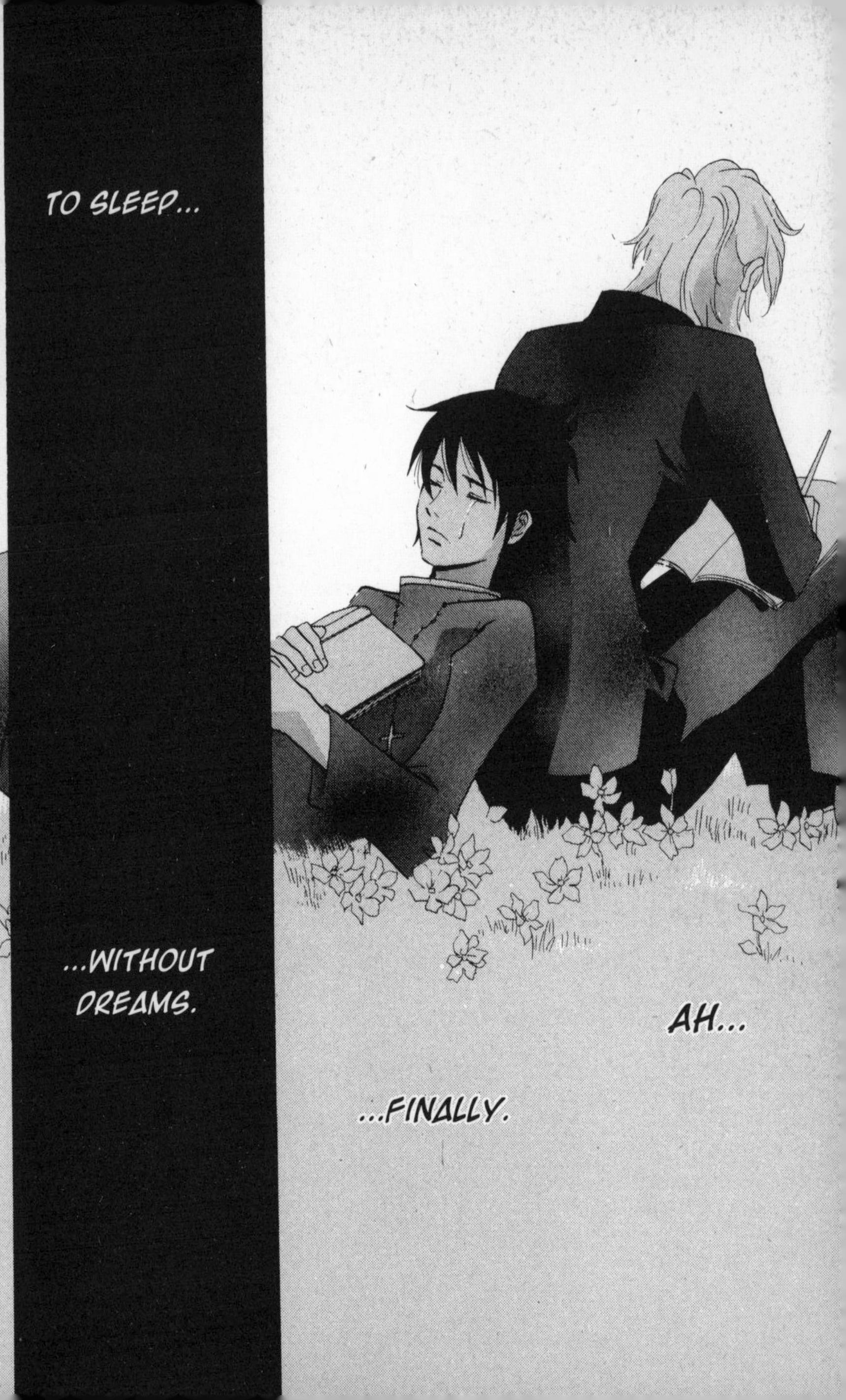
AH...
...FINALLY.
TO SLEEP...
...WITHOUT DREAMS.

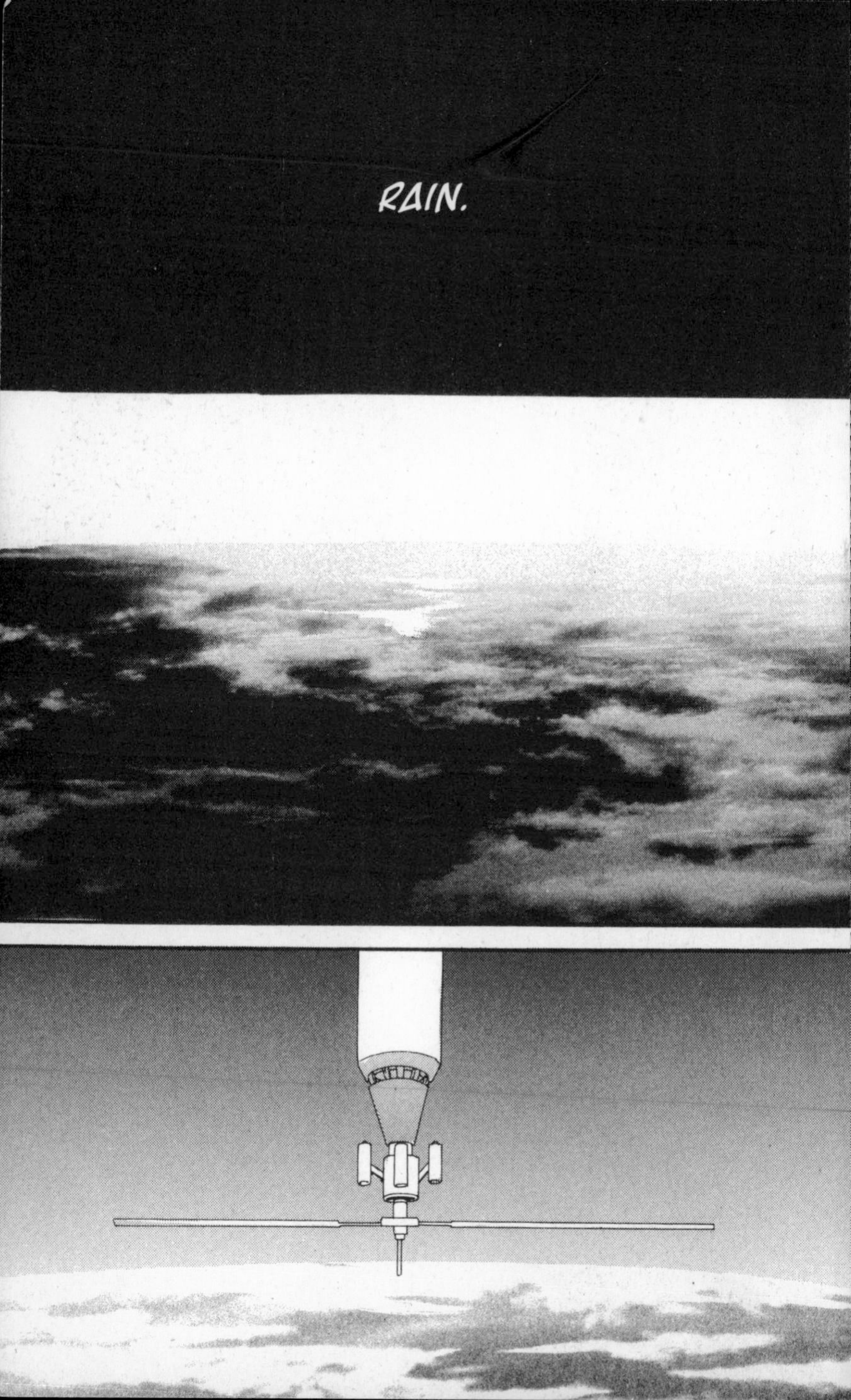
RAIN.

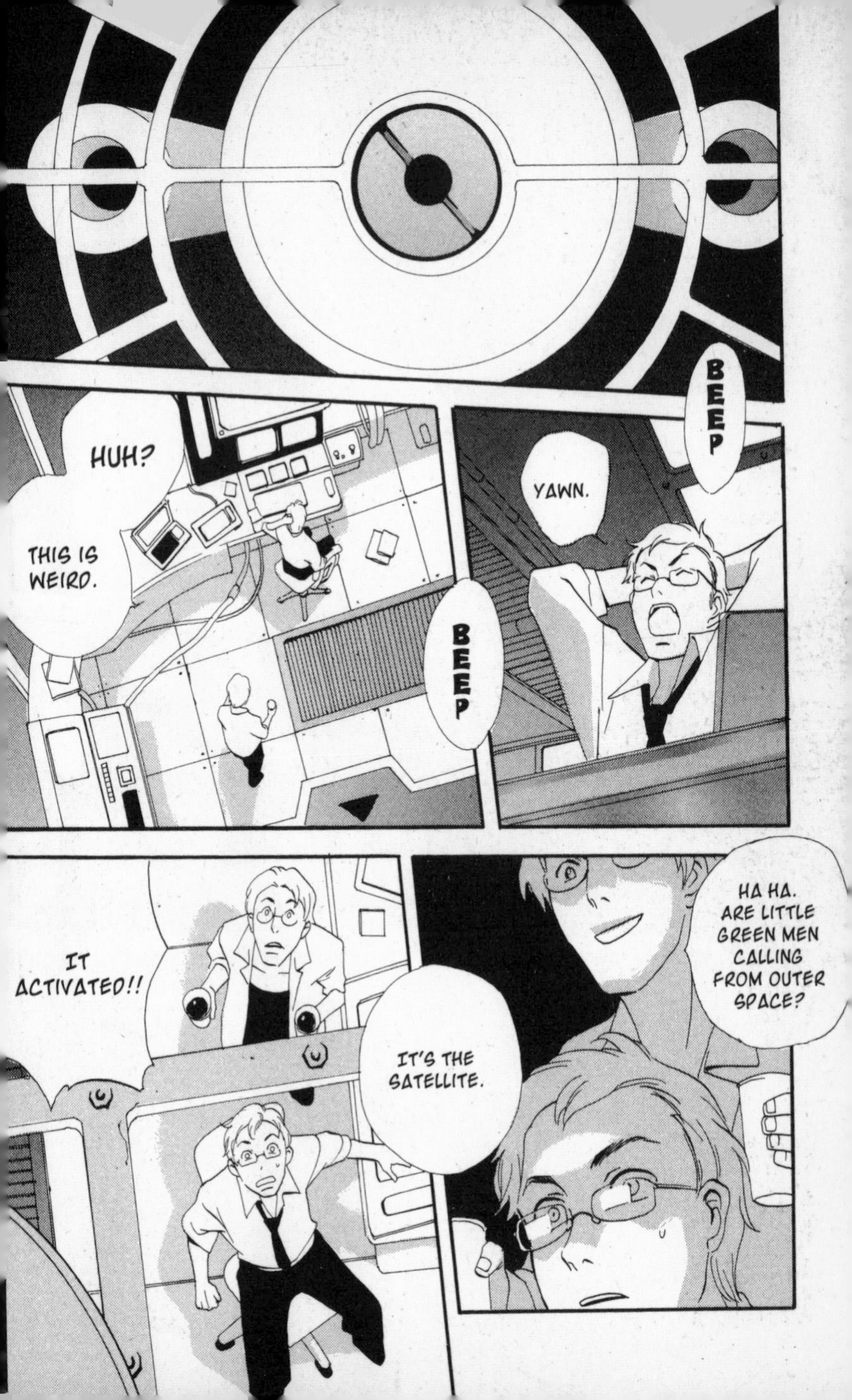
BEEP
YAWN.
BEEP
HUH?
THIS IS WEIRD.
HA HA. ARE LITTLE GREEN MEN CALLING FROM OUTER SPACE?
IT'S THE SATELLITE.
IT ACTIVATED!!

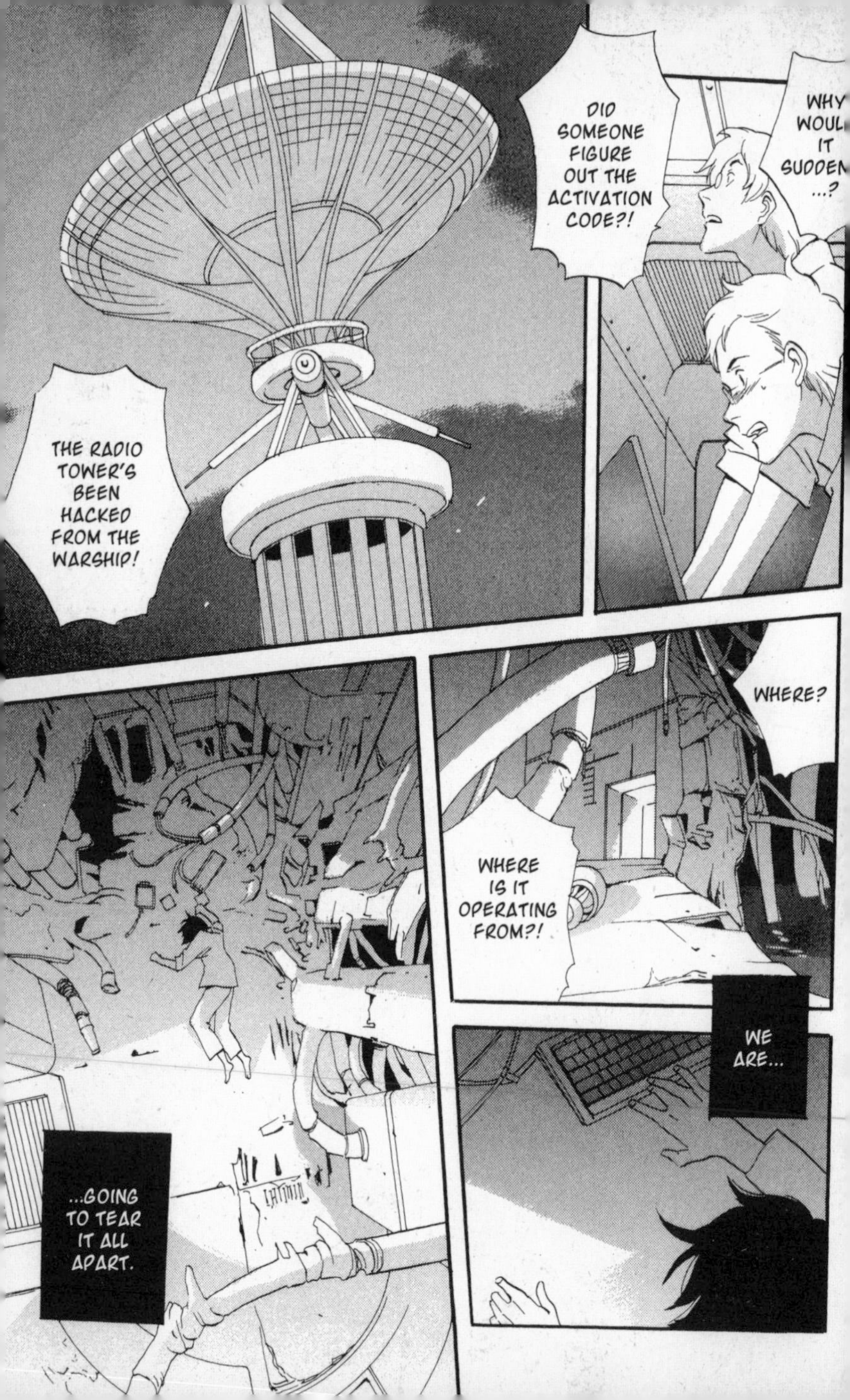
WHY WOUL IT SUDDEN ...?
DID SOMEONE FIGURE OUT THE ACTIVATION CODE?!
THE RADIO TOWER'S BEEN HACKED FROM THE WARSHIP!
WHERE?
WHERE IS IT OPERATING FROM?!
WE ARE...
...GOING TO TEAR IT ALL APART.

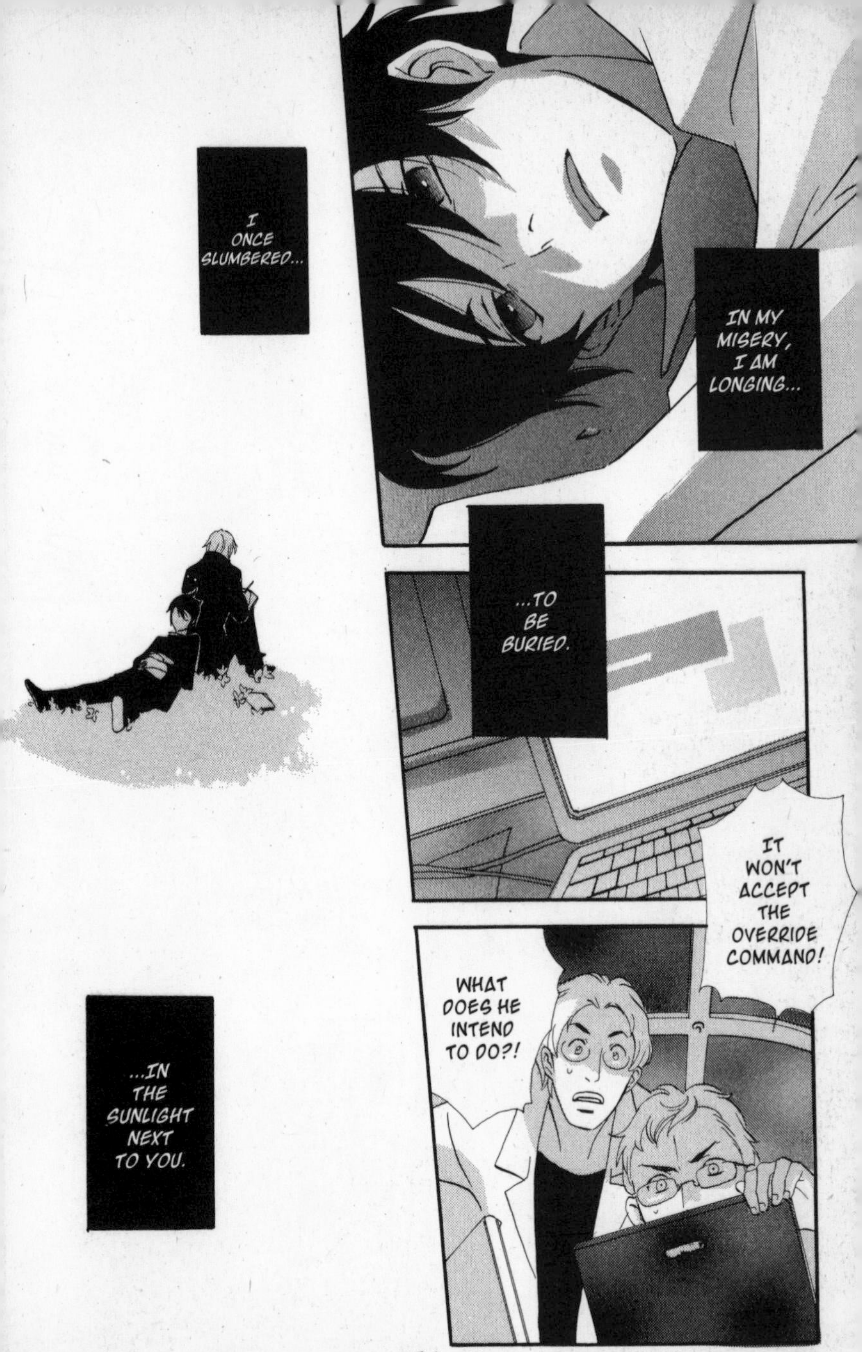
IN MY MISERY, I AM LONGING...
...TO BE BURIED.
IT WON'T ACCEPT THE OVERRIDE COMMAND!
WHAT DOES HE INTEND TO DO?!
I ONCE SLUMBERED...
...IN THE SUNLIGHT NEXT TO YOU.

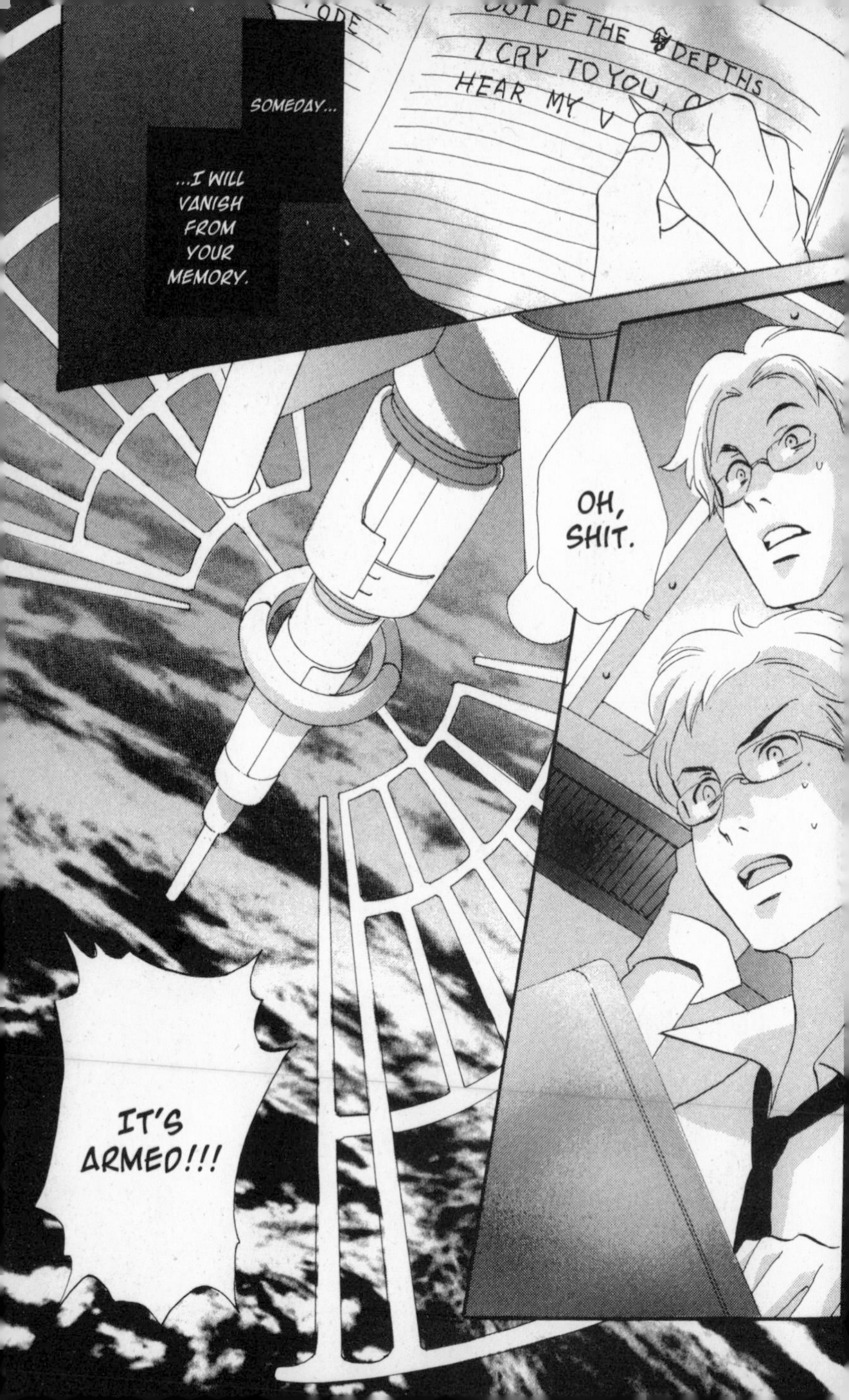
OF THE DEPTHS
I CRY TO YOU,
HEAR MY V
SOMEDAY...
...I WILL VANISH FROM YOUR MEMORY.
OH, SHIT.
IT'S ARMED!!!

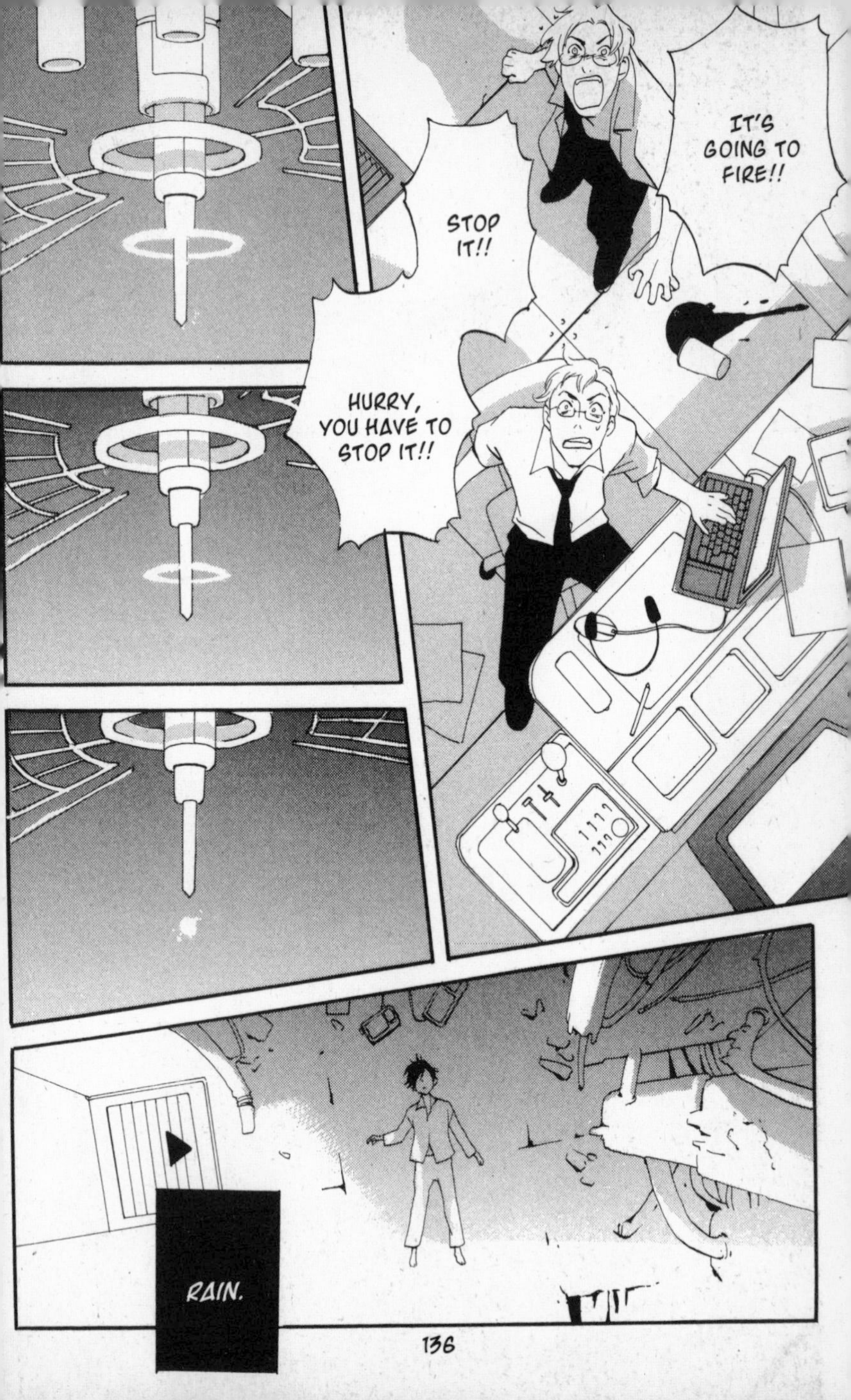
IT'S GOING TO FIRE!!
STOP IT!!
HURRY, YOU HAVE TO STOP IT!!
RAIN.

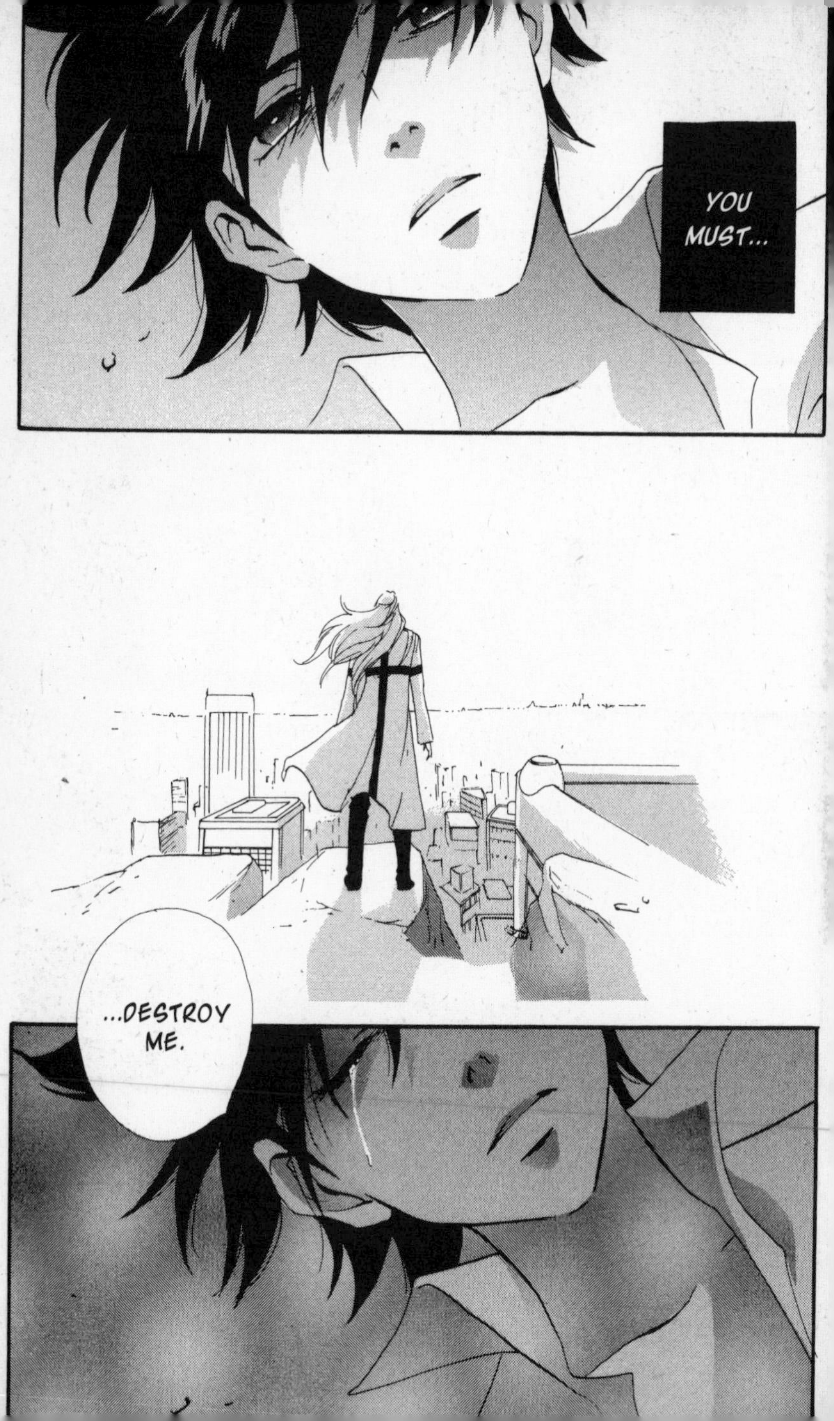
YOU MUST...
...DESTROY ME.

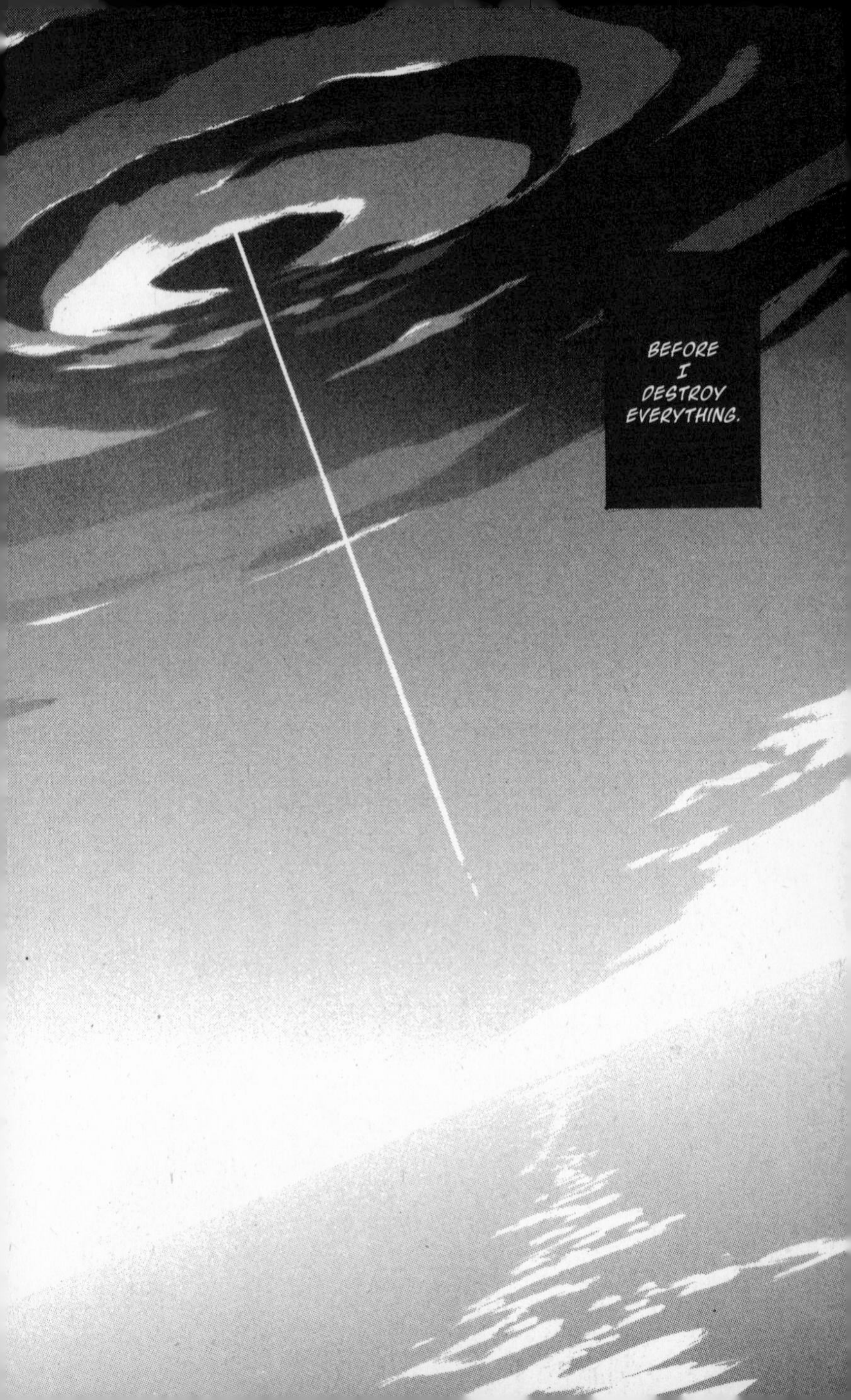
BEFORE I DESTROY EVERYTHING.

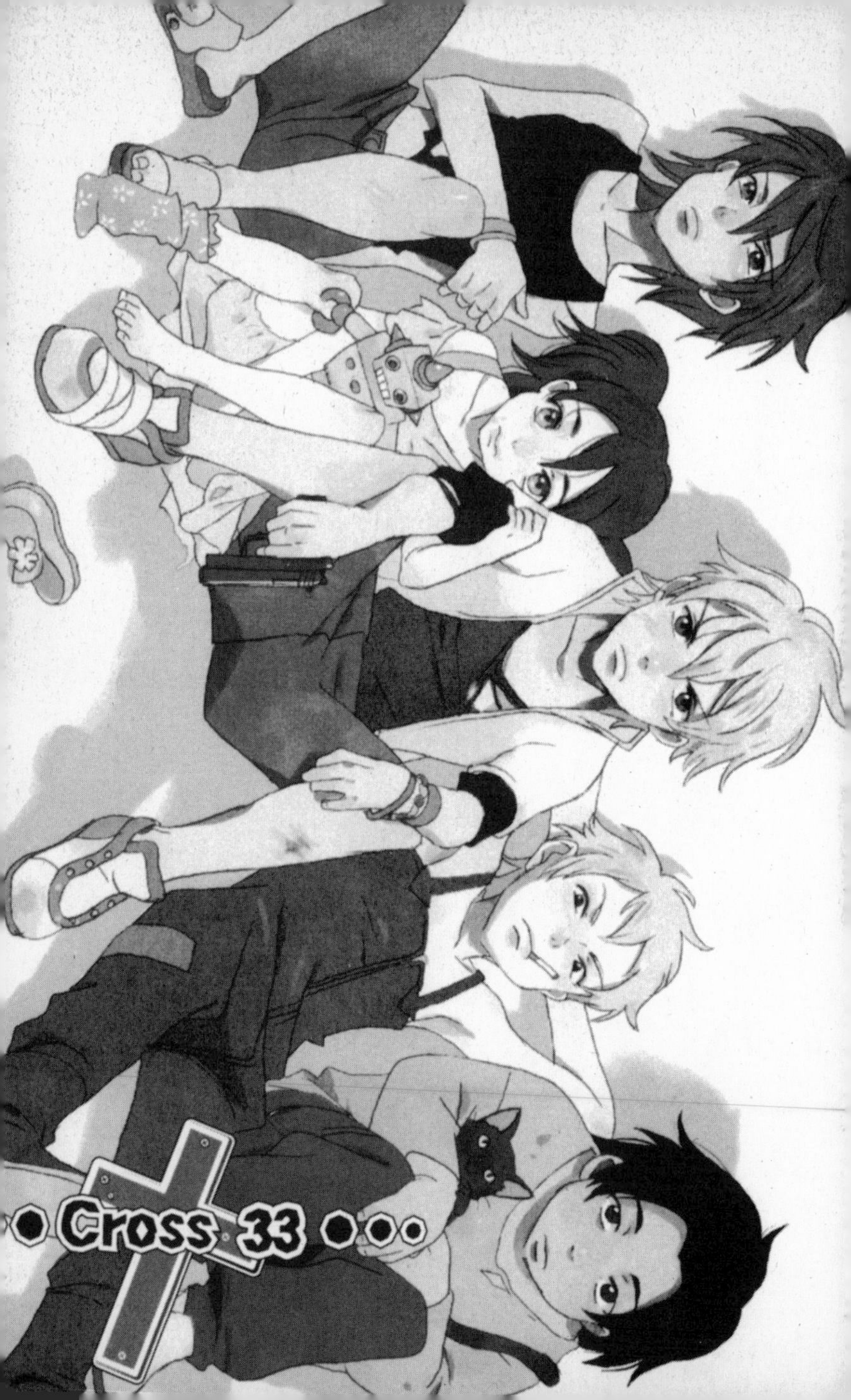
Cross 33

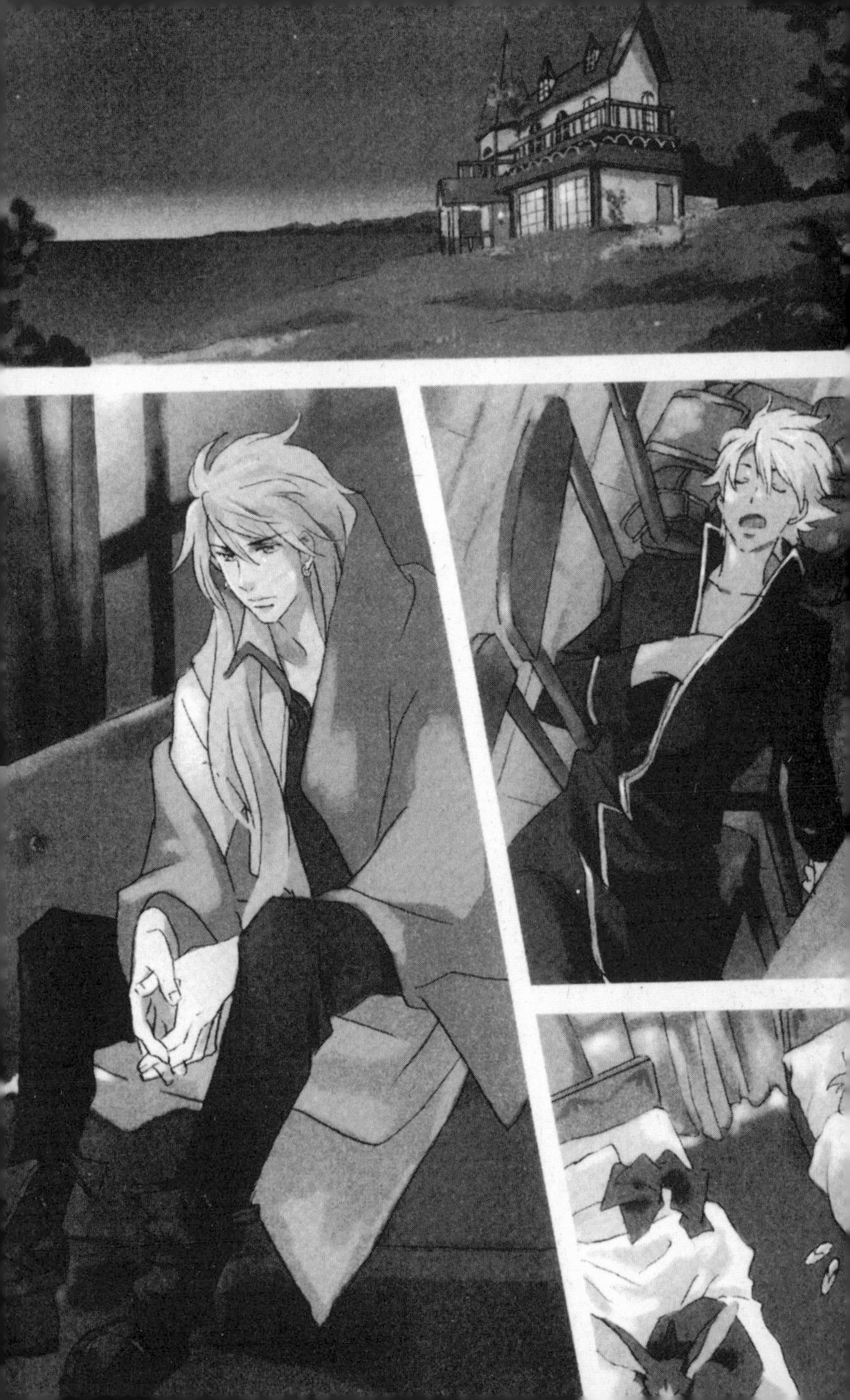

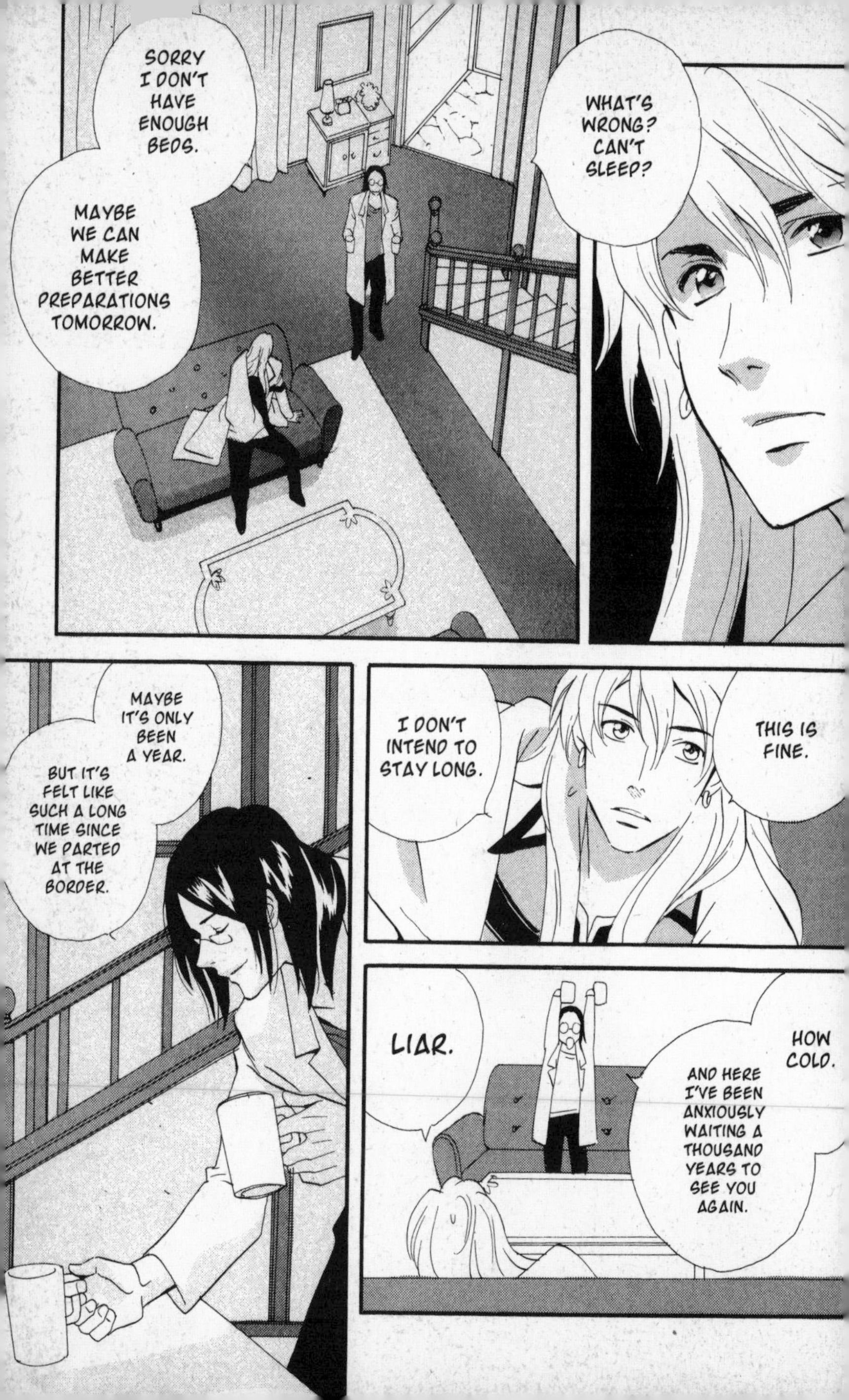
WHAT'S WRONG? CAN'T SLEEP?
SORRY I DON'T HAVE ENOUGH BEDS.
MAYBE WE CAN MAKE BETTER PREPARATIONS TOMORROW.
THIS IS FINE.
I DON'T INTEND TO STAY LONG.
HOW COLD.
AND HERE I'VE BEEN ANXIOUSLY WAITING A THOUSAND YEARS TO SEE YOU AGAIN.
LIAR.
MAYBE IT'S ONLY BEEN A YEAR.
BUT IT'S FELT LIKE SUCH A LONG TIME SINCE WE PARTED AT THE BORDER.

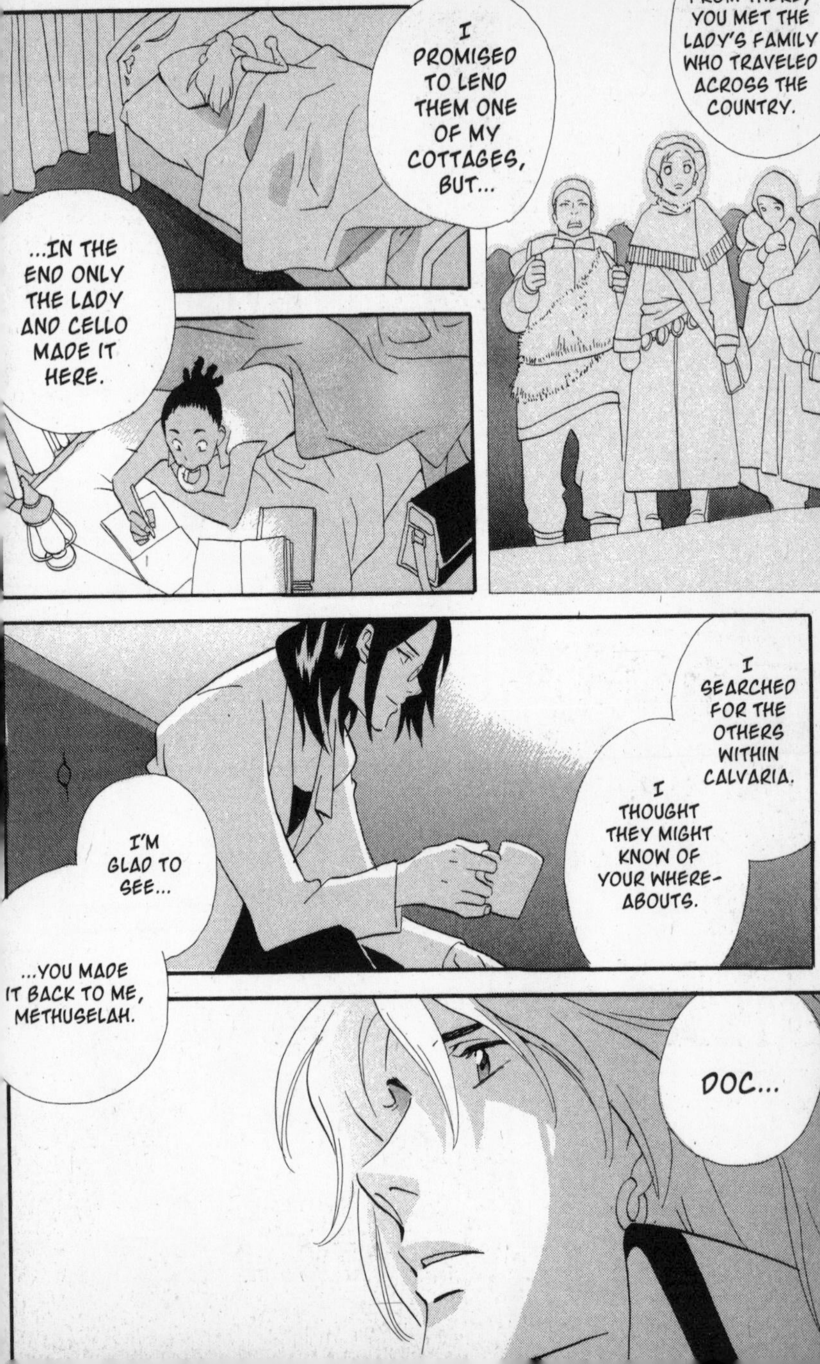

FROM THERE, YOU MET THE LADY'S FAMILY WHO TRAVELED ACROSS THE COUNTRY.
I PROMISED TO LEND THEM ONE OF MY COTTAGES, BUT...
...IN THE END ONLY THE LADY AND CELLO MADE IT HERE.
I SEARCHED FOR THE OTHERS WITHIN CALVARIA.
I THOUGHT THEY MIGHT KNOW OF YOUR WHERE-ABOUTS.
I'M GLAD TO SEE...
...YOU MADE IT BACK TO ME, METHUSELAH.
DOC...

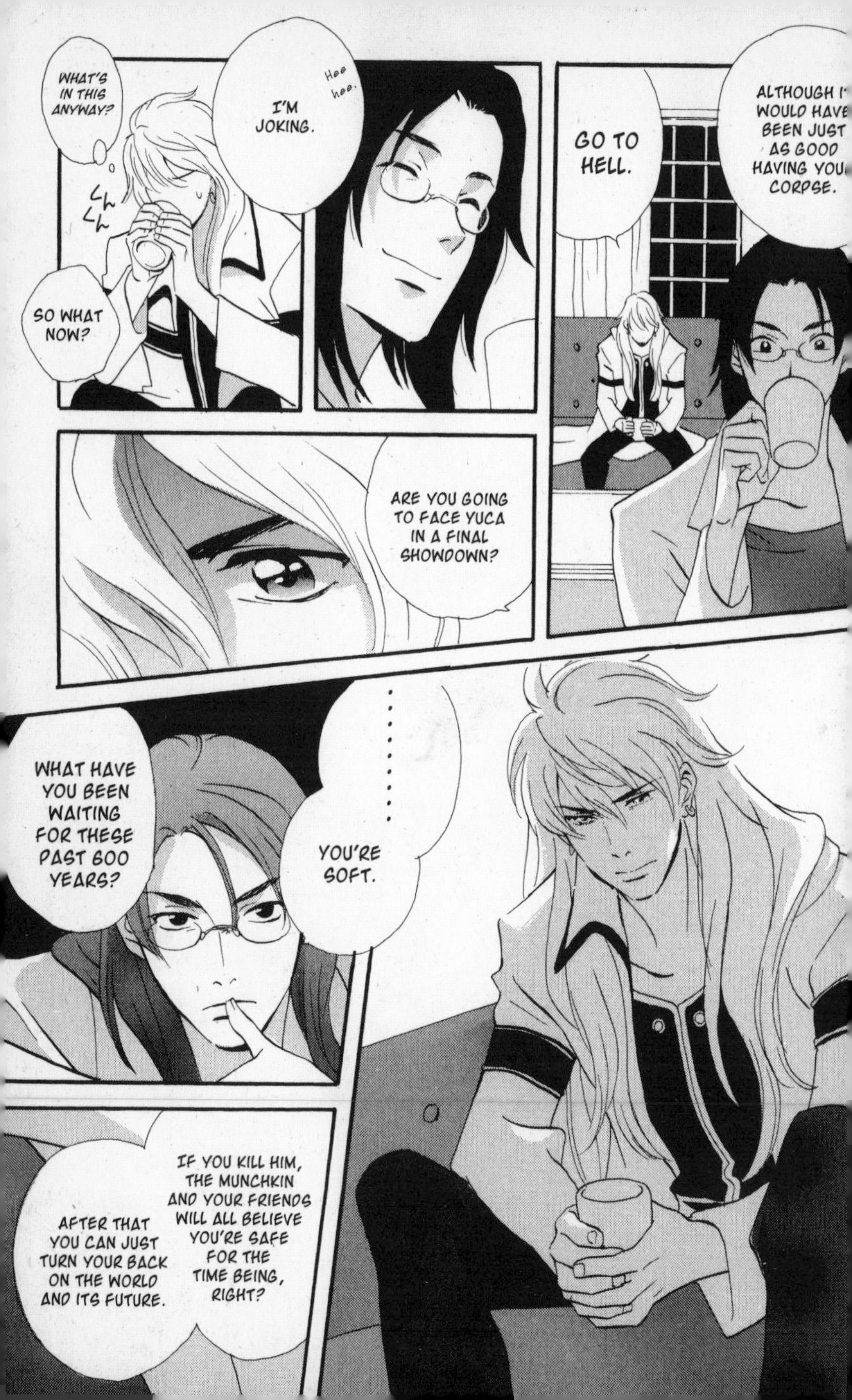
ALTHOUGH I
WOULD HAVE BEEN JUST AS GOOD HAVING YOU
CORPSE.
GO TO HELL.
Hee hee.
I'M JOKING.
WHAT'S IN THIS ANYWAY?
くん くん
SO WHAT NOW?
ARE YOU GOING TO FACE YUCA IN A FINAL SHOWDOWN?
......
YOU'RE SOFT.
WHAT HAVE YOU BEEN WAITING FOR THESE PAST 600 YEARS?
IF YOU KILL HIM, THE MUNCHKIN AND YOUR FRIENDS WILL ALL BELIEVE YOU'RE SAFE FOR THE TIME BEING, RIGHT?
AFTER THAT YOU CAN JUST TURN YOUR BACK ON THE WORLD AND ITS FUTURE.

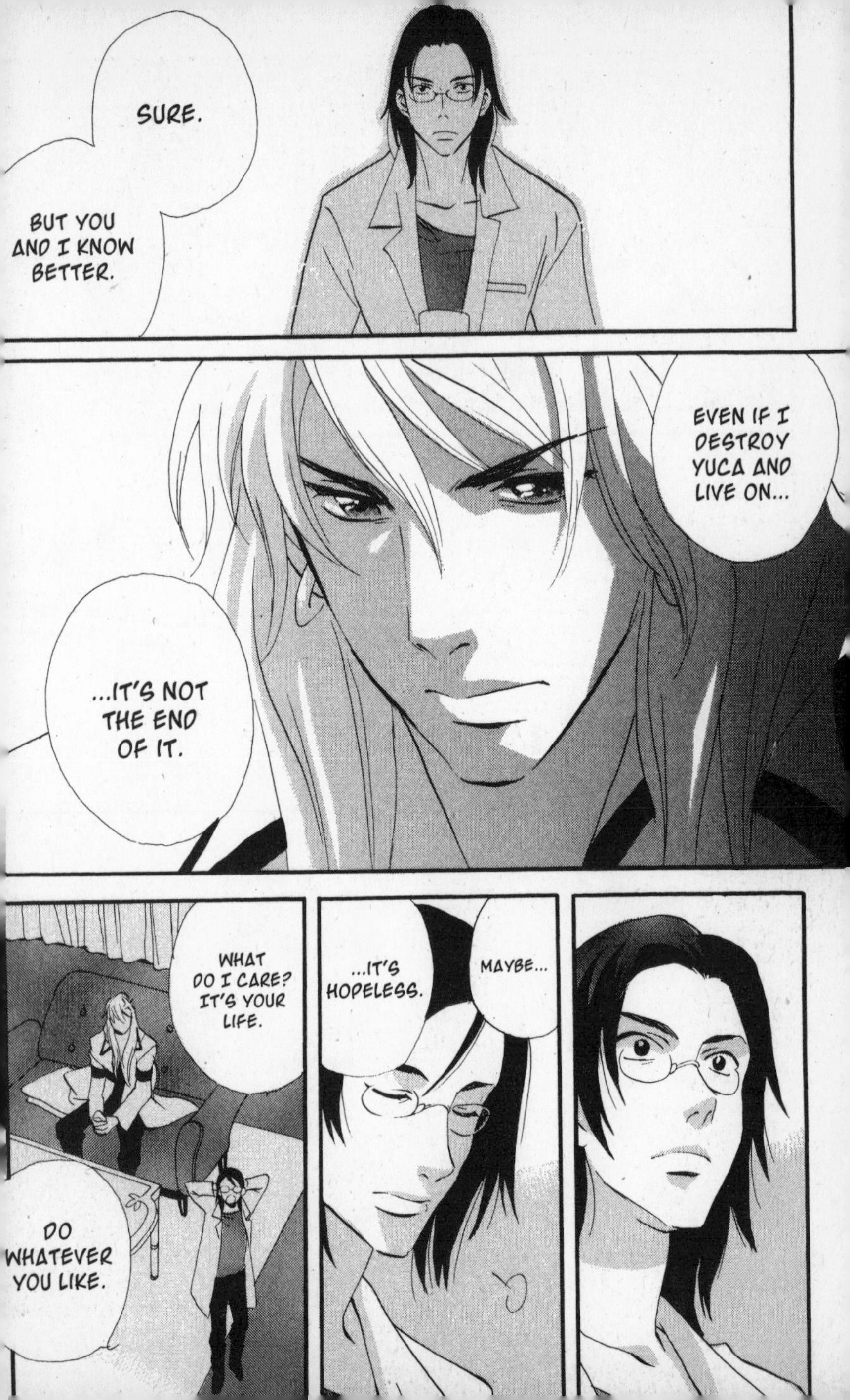
SURE.
BUT YOU AND I KNOW BETTER.
EVEN IF I DESTROY YUCA AND LIVE ON...
...IT'S NOT THE END OF IT.
MAYBE...
...IT'S HOPELESS.
WHAT DO I CARE? IT'S YOUR LIFE.
DO WHATEVER YOU LIKE.

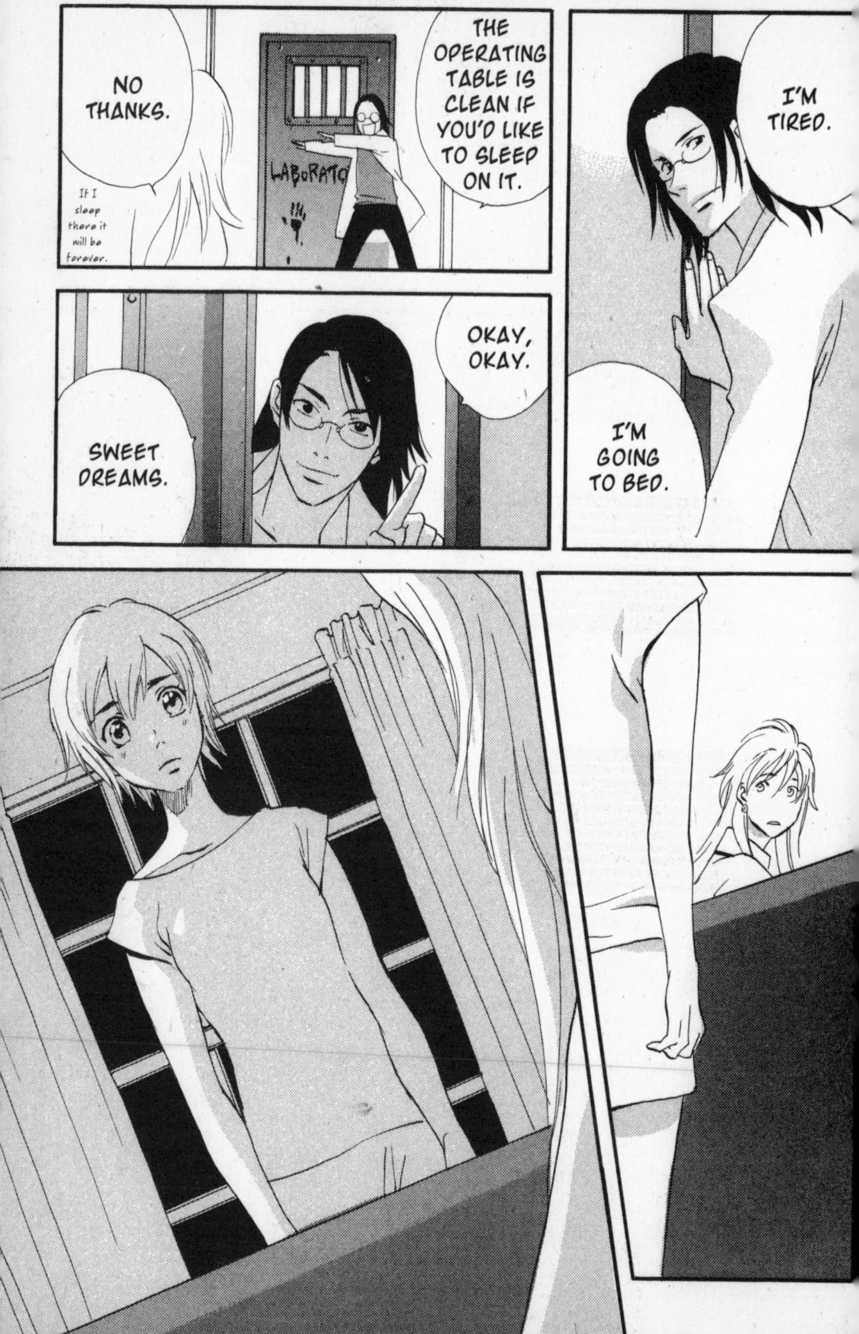
I'M TIRED.
I'M GOING TO BED.
THE OPERATING TABLE IS CLEAN IF YOU'D LIKE TO SLEEP ON IT.
LABORATO
NO THANKS.
If I sleep there it will be forever.
OKAY, OKAY.
SWEET DREAMS.

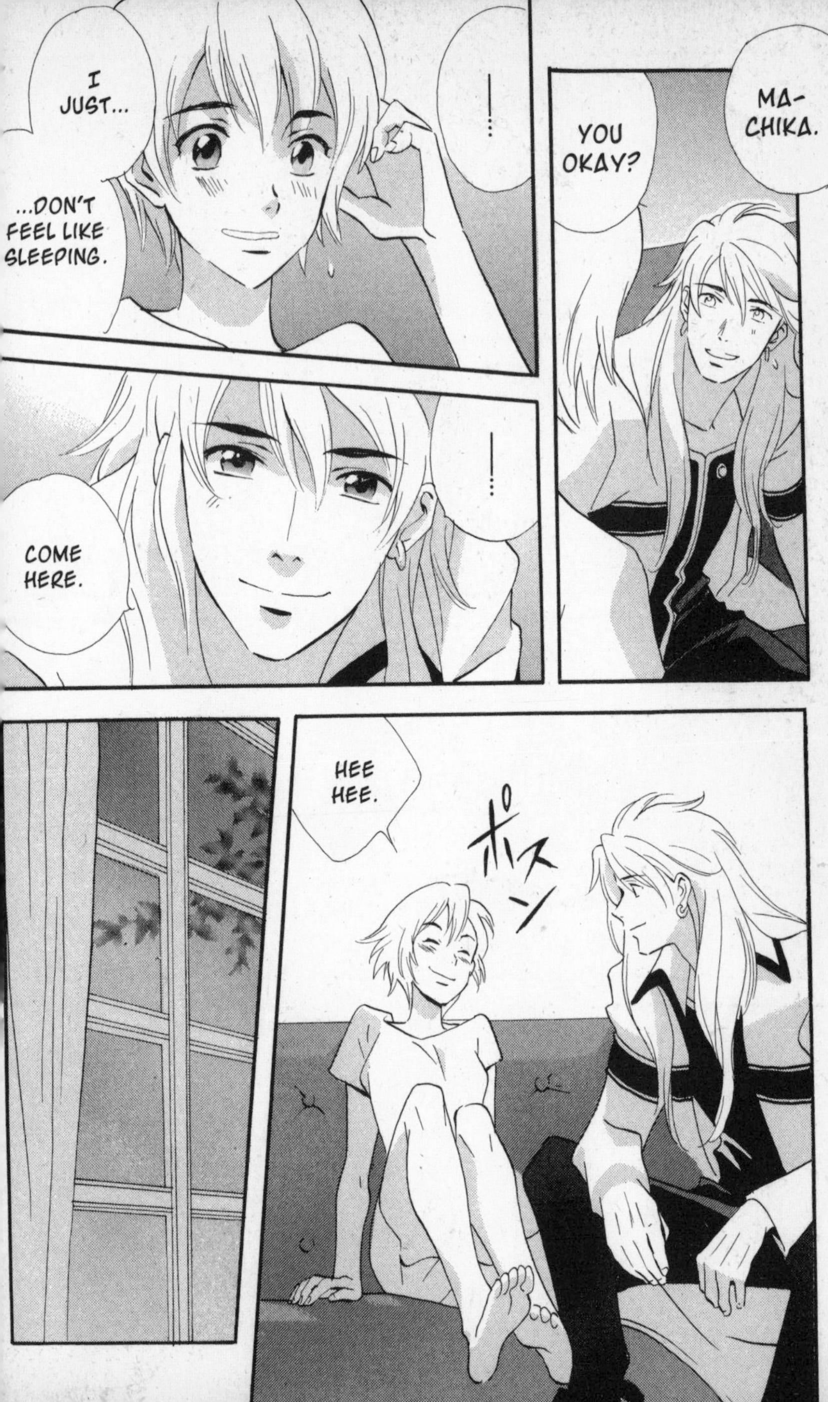
MA-CHIKA.
YOU OKAY?
—...
I JUST...
...DON'T FEEL LIKE SLEEPING.
—...
COME HERE.
HEE HEE.
ポスン

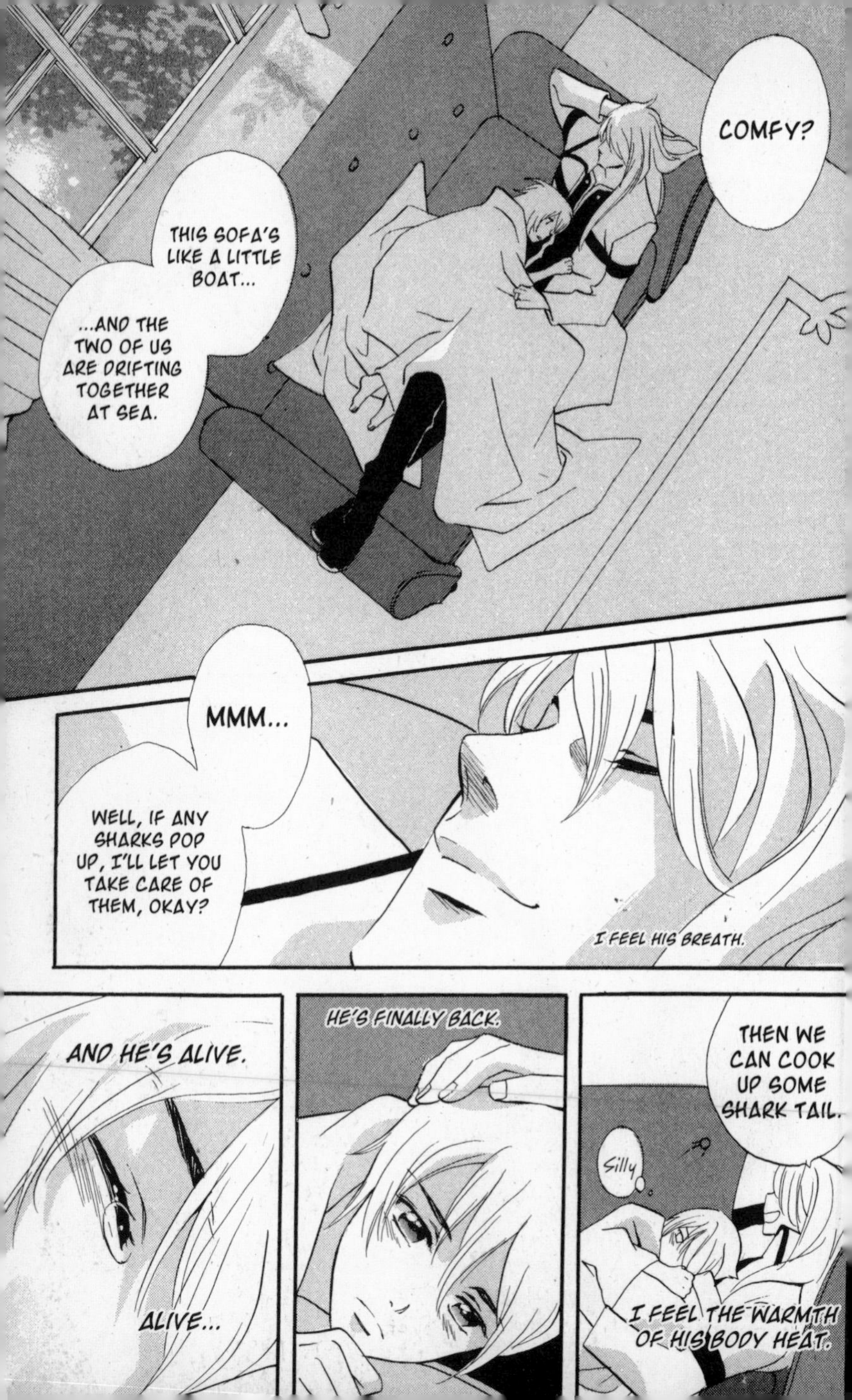
COMFY?
THIS SOFA'S LIKE A LITTLE BOAT...
...AND THE TWO OF US ARE DRIFTING TOGETHER AT SEA.
MMM...
WELL, IF ANY SHARKS POP UP, I'LL LET YOU TAKE CARE OF THEM, OKAY?
I FEEL HIS BREATH.
THEN WE CAN COOK UP SOME SHARK TAIL.
Silly
I FEEL THE WARMTH OF HIS BODY HEAT.
HE'S FINALLY BACK.
AND HE'S ALIVE.
ALIVE...

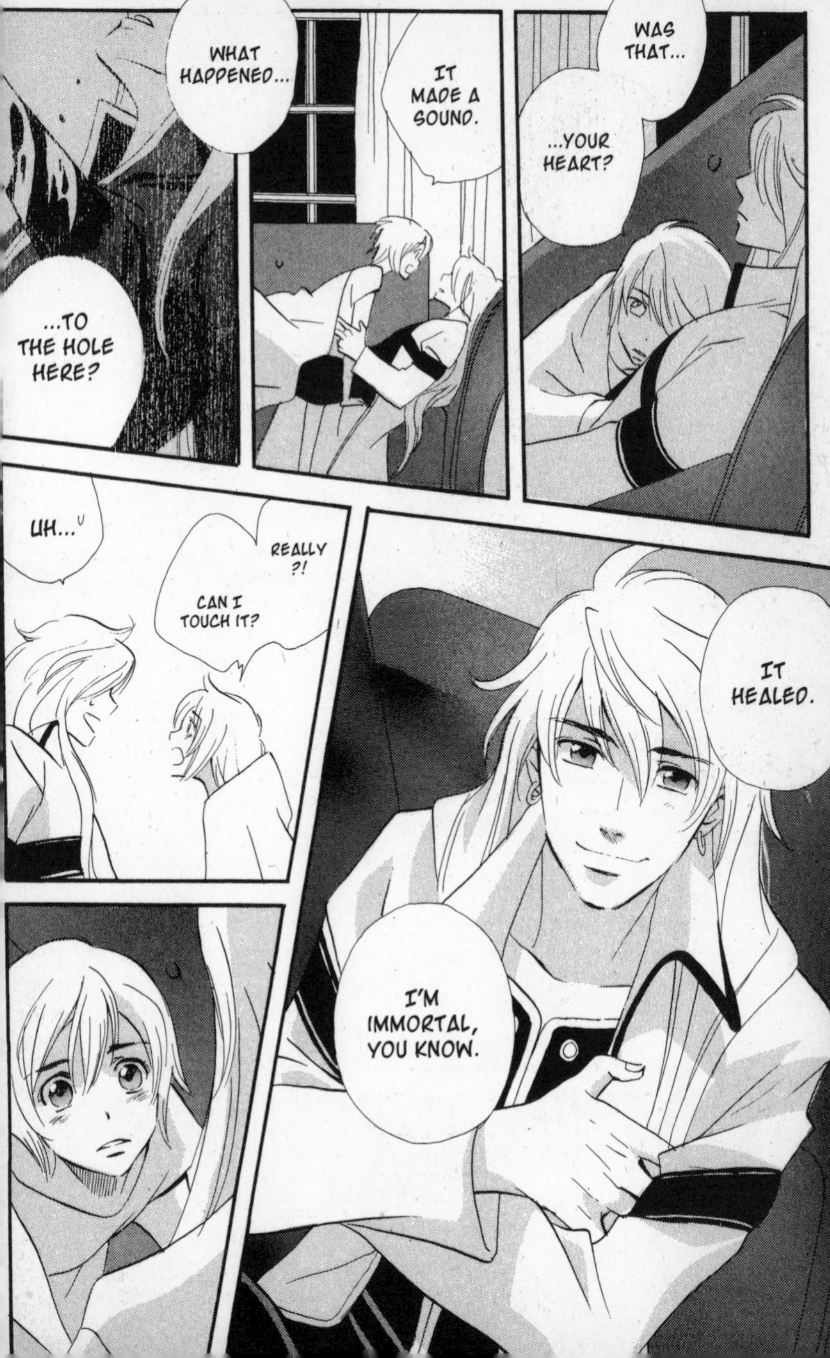
WAS THAT...
...YOUR HEART?
IT MADE A SOUND.
WHAT HAPPENED...
...TO THE HOLE HERE?
IT HEALED.
I'M IMMORTAL, YOU KNOW.
REALLY ?!
CAN I TOUCH IT?
UH...

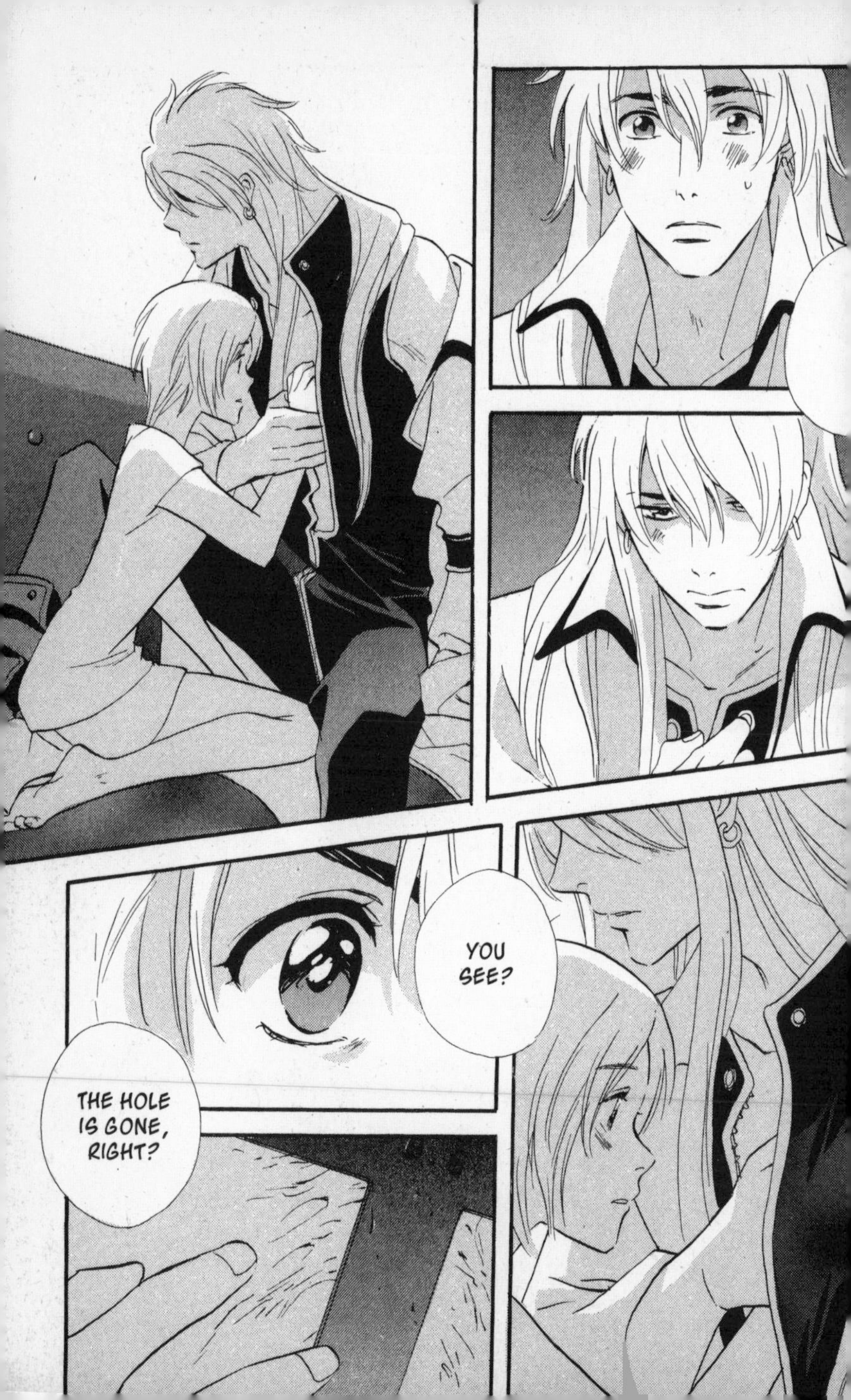
YOU SEE?
THE HOLE IS GONE, RIGHT?

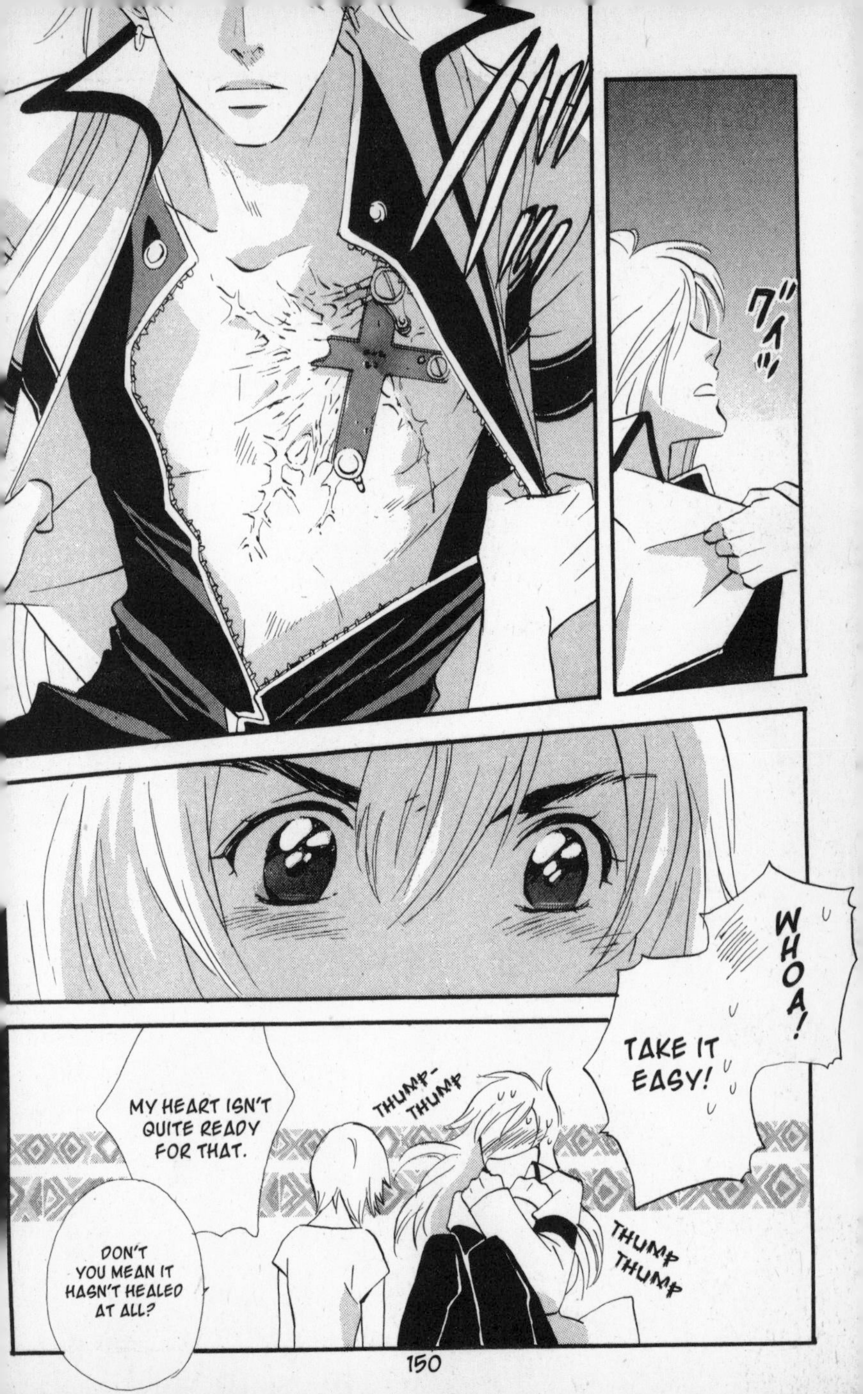
ヴィッ
WHOA!
TAKE IT EASY!
THUMP-THUMP
THUMP THUMP
MY HEART ISN'T QUITE READY FOR THAT.
DON'T YOU MEAN IT HASN'T HEALED AT ALL?

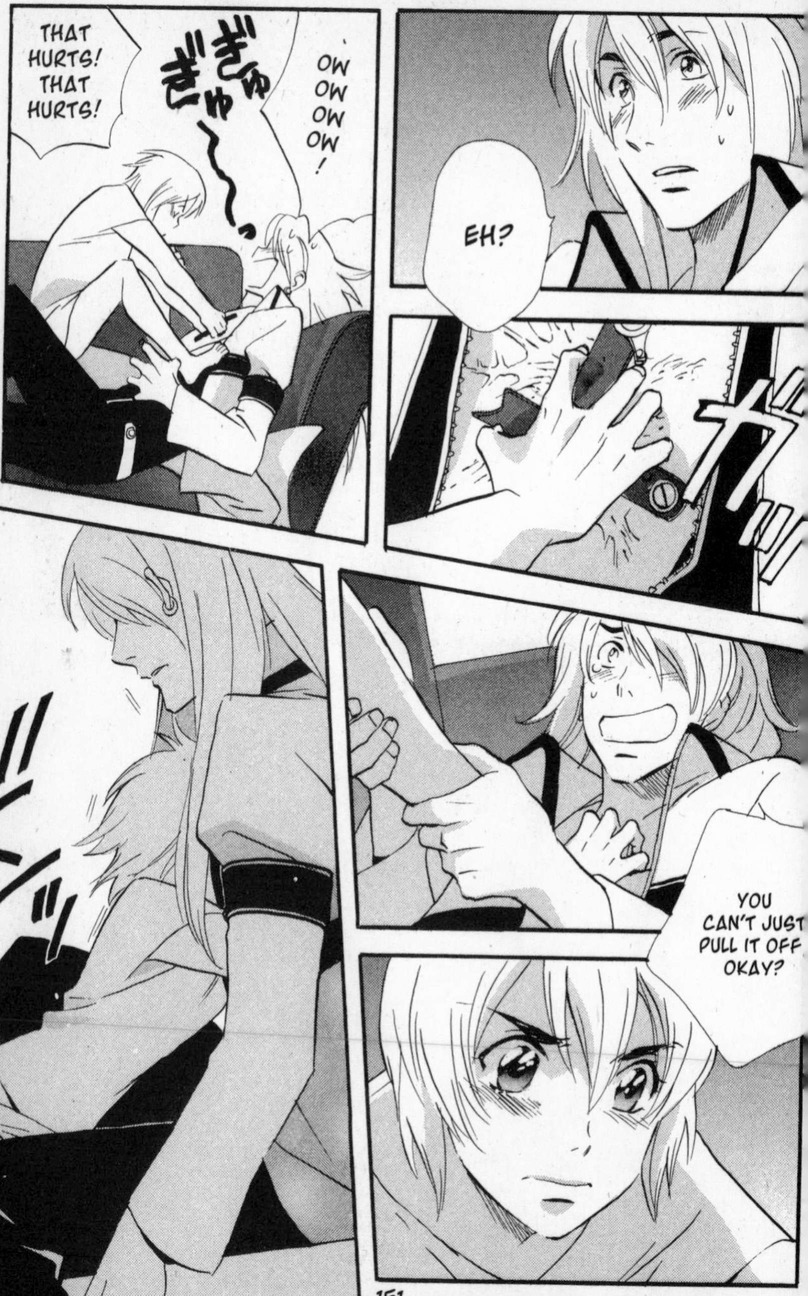
EH?
OW OW OW OW!
ぎゅぎゅ〜っ
THAT HURTS! THAT HURTS!
YOU CAN'T JUST PULL IT OFF OKAY?

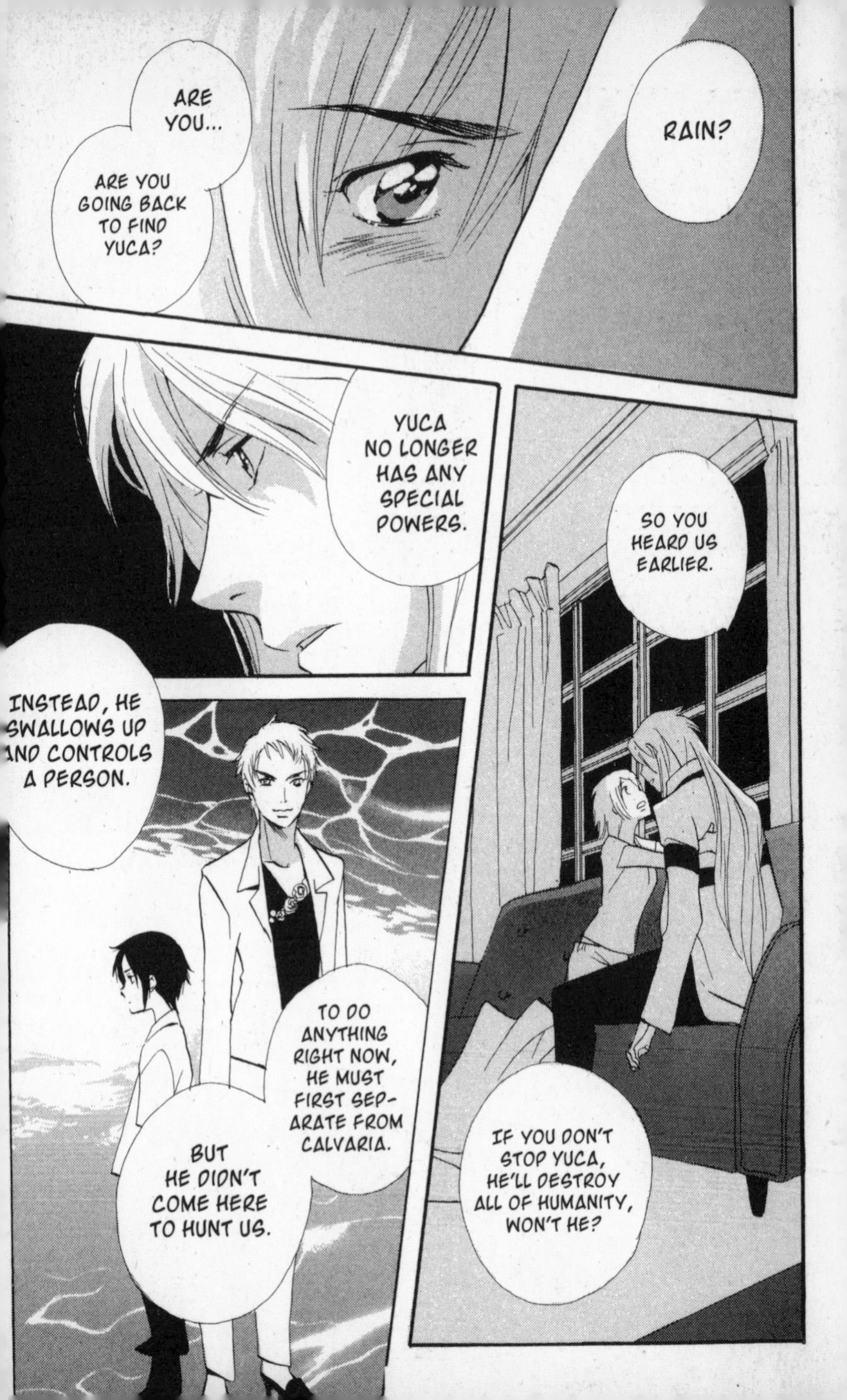
RAIN?
ARE YOU...
ARE YOU GOING BACK TO FIND YUCA?
SO YOU HEARD US EARLIER.
IF YOU DON'T STOP YUCA, HE'LL DESTROY ALL OF HUMANITY, WON'T HE?
YUCA NO LONGER HAS ANY SPECIAL POWERS.
INSTEAD, HE SWALLOWS UP AND CONTROLS A PERSON.
TO DO ANYTHING RIGHT NOW, HE MUST FIRST SEP-ARATE FROM CALVARIA.
BUT HE DIDN'T COME HERE TO HUNT US.

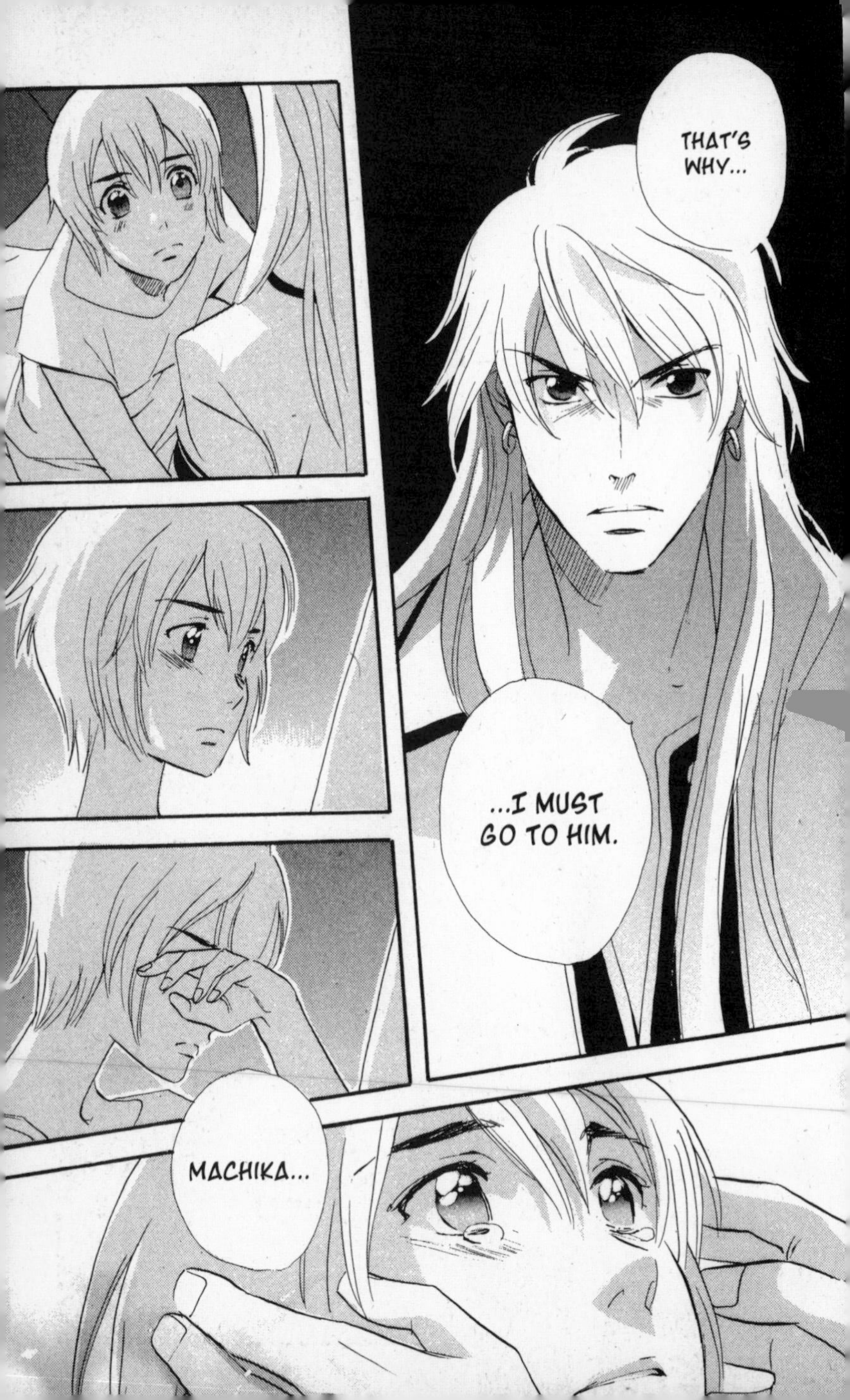
THAT'S WHY...
...I MUST GO TO HIM.
MACHIKA...

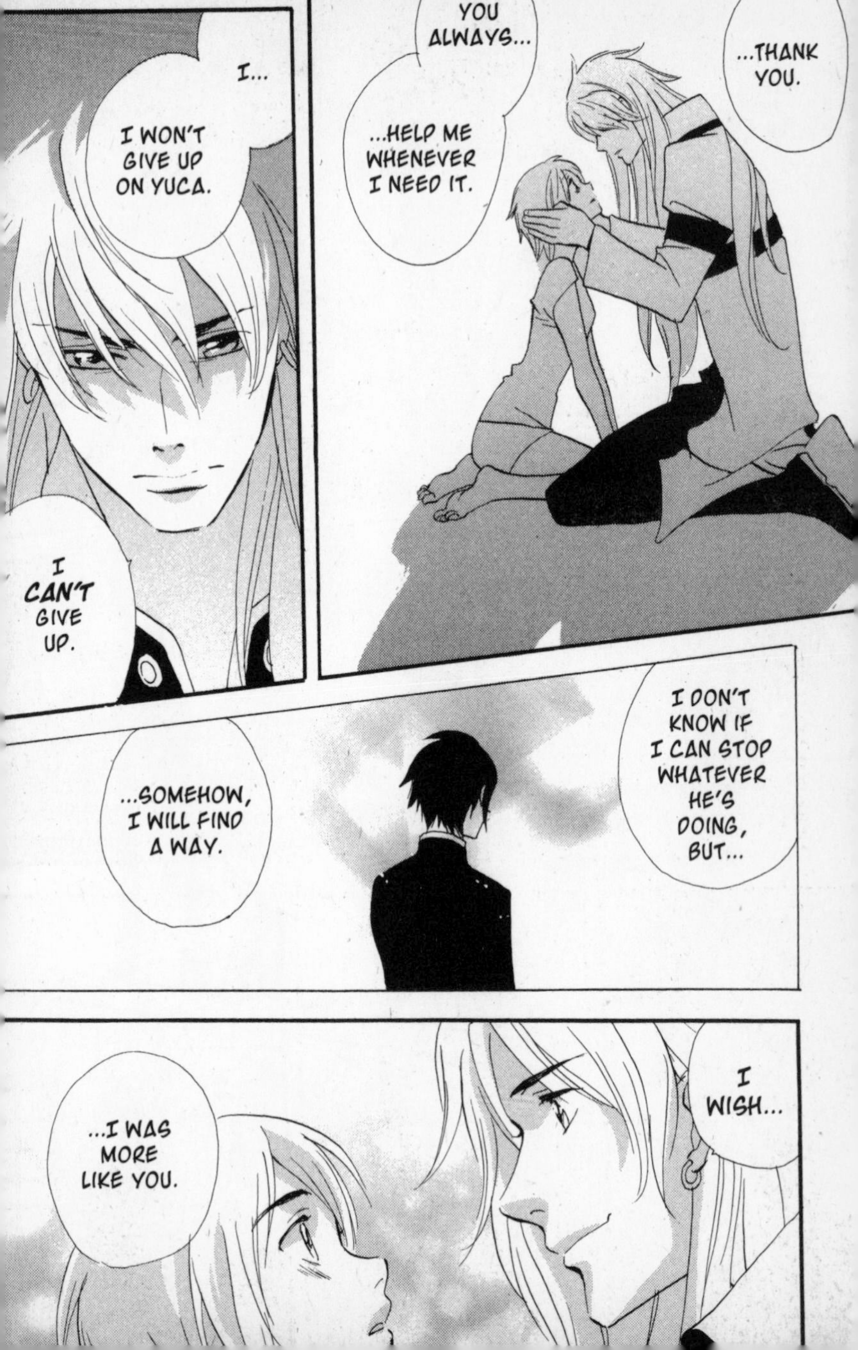
...THANK YOU.
YOU ALWAYS...
...HELP ME WHENEVER I NEED IT.
I...
I WON'T GIVE UP ON YUCA.
I **CAN'T** GIVE UP.
I DON'T KNOW IF I CAN STOP WHATEVER HE'S DOING, BUT...
...SOMEHOW, I WILL FIND A WAY.
I WISH...
...I WAS MORE LIKE YOU.

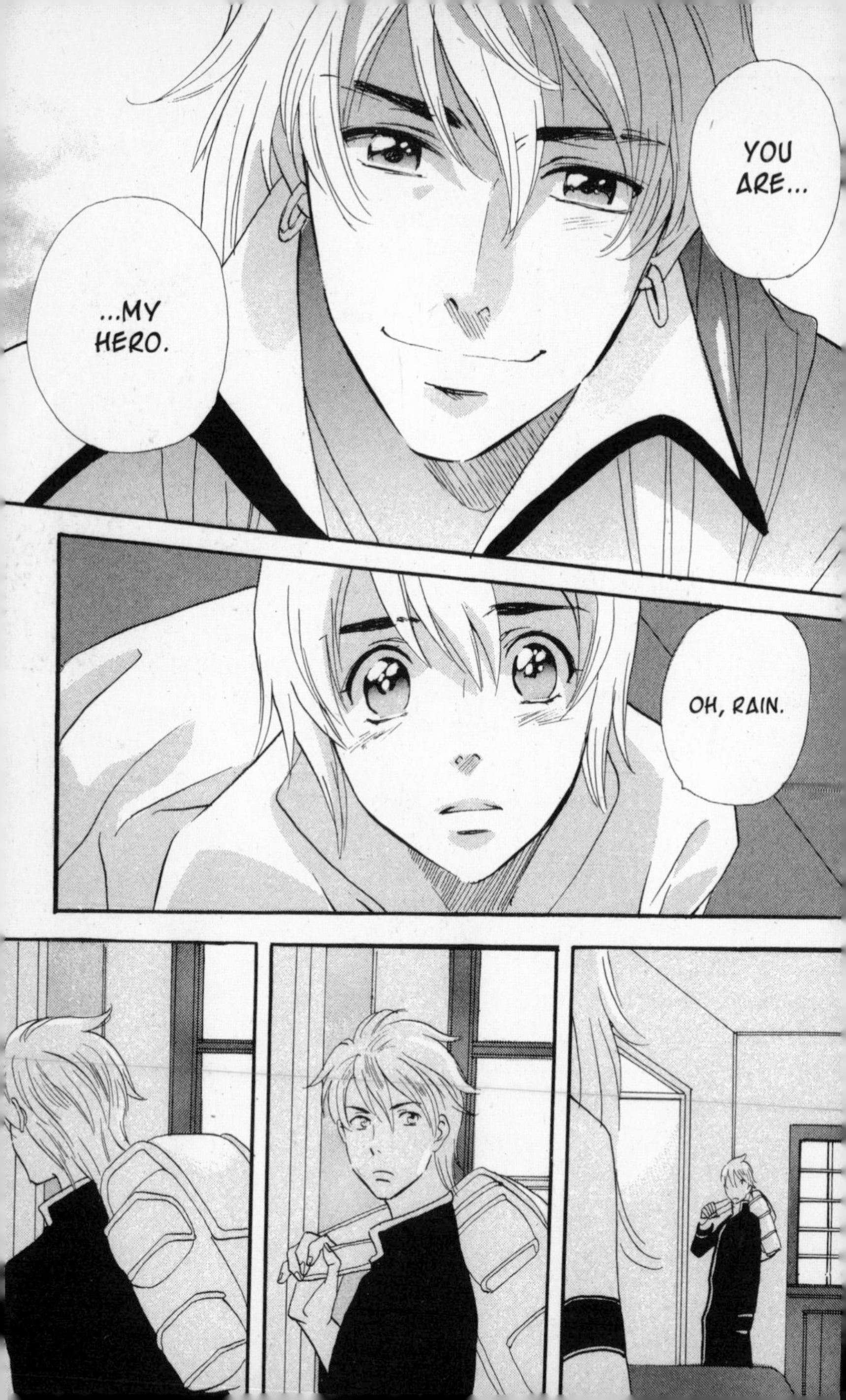
YOU ARE...
...MY HERO.
OH, RAIN.

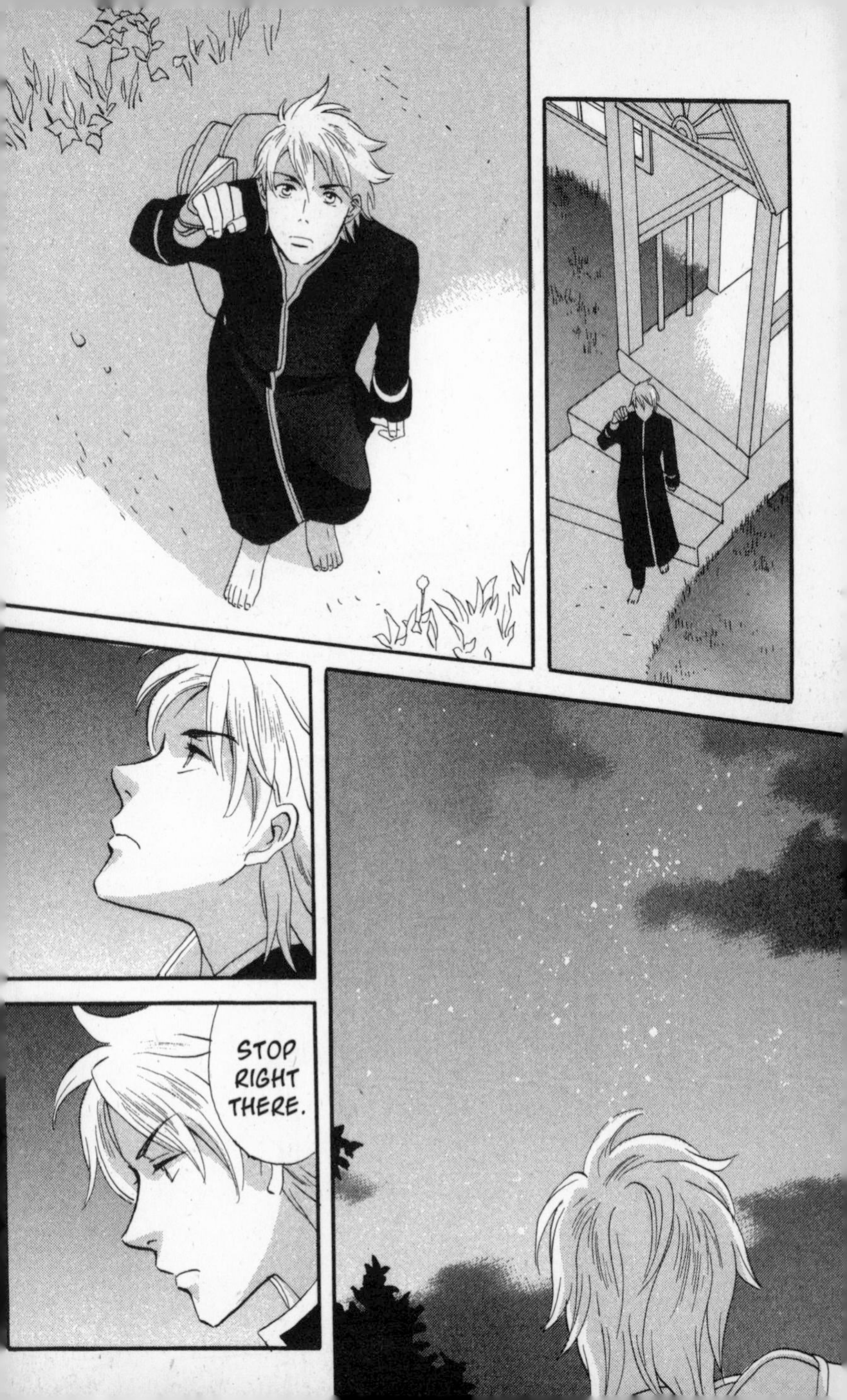
STOP RIGHT THERE.

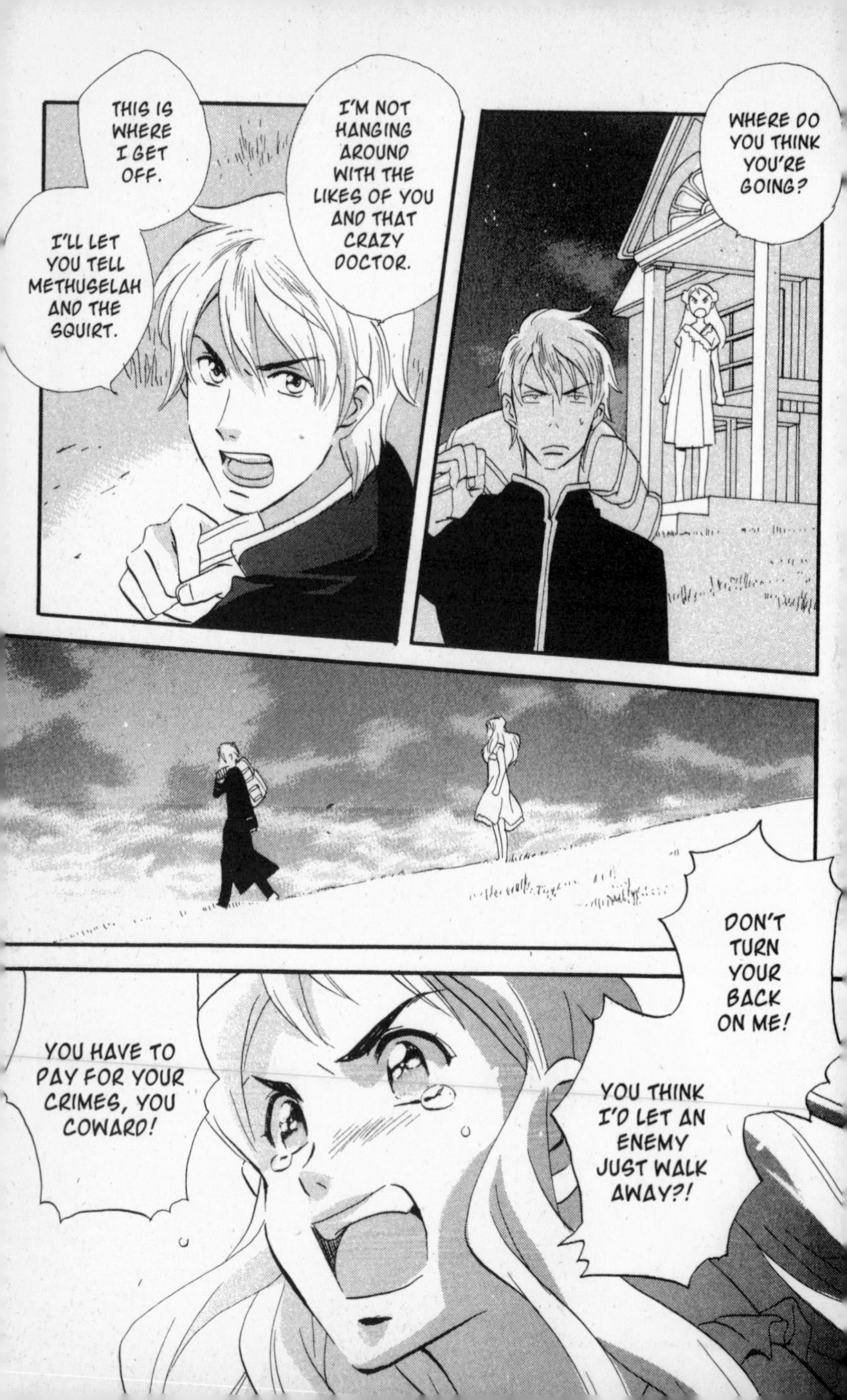
WHERE DO YOU THINK YOU'RE GOING?
THIS IS WHERE I GET OFF.
I'M NOT HANGING AROUND WITH THE LIKES OF YOU AND THAT CRAZY DOCTOR.
I'LL LET YOU TELL METHUSELAH AND THE SQUIRT.
DON'T TURN YOUR BACK ON ME!
YOU THINK I'D LET AN ENEMY JUST WALK AWAY?!
YOU HAVE TO PAY FOR YOUR CRIMES, YOU COWARD!

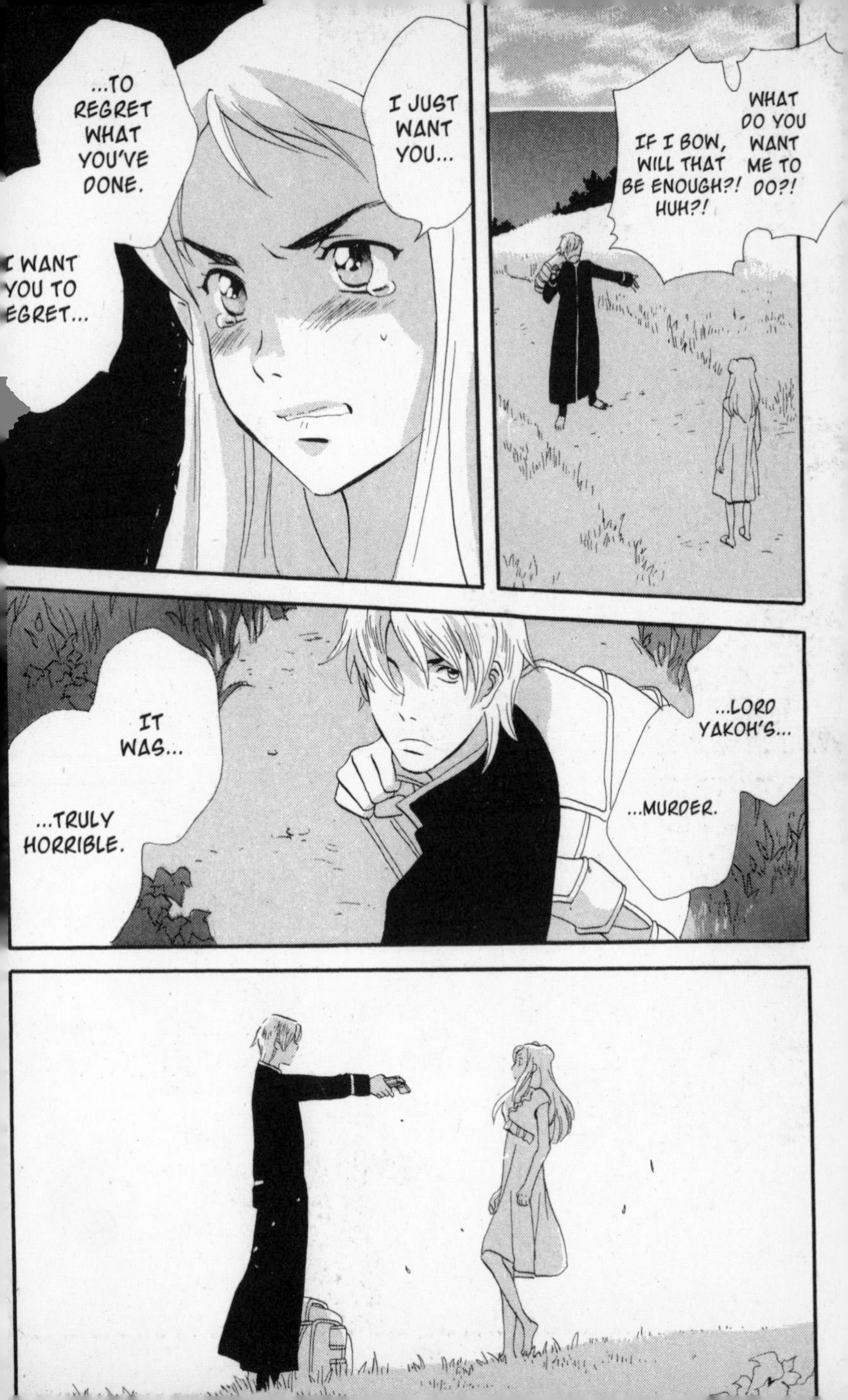
WHAT DO YOU WANT ME TO DO?!
IF I BOW, WILL THAT BE ENOUGH?! HUH?!
I JUST WANT YOU...
...TO REGRET WHAT YOU'VE DONE.
I WANT YOU TO EGRET...
...LORD YAKOH'S...
...MURDER.
IT WAS...
...TRULY HORRIBLE.

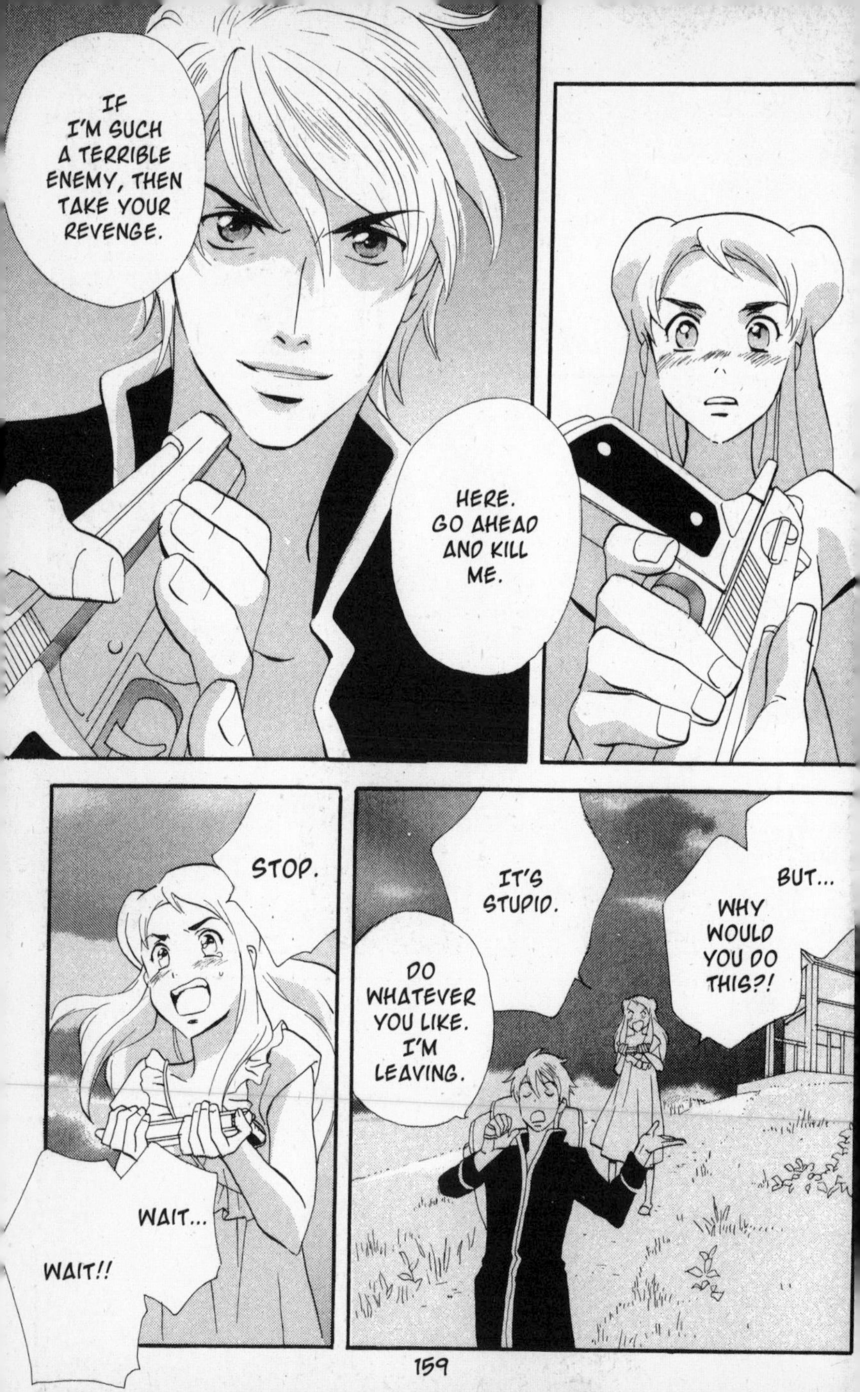
IF I'M SUCH A TERRIBLE ENEMY, THEN TAKE YOUR REVENGE.
HERE. GO AHEAD AND KILL ME.
BUT... WHY WOULD YOU DO THIS?!
IT'S STUPID.
DO WHATEVER YOU LIKE. I'M LEAVING.
STOP.
WAIT...
WAIT!!

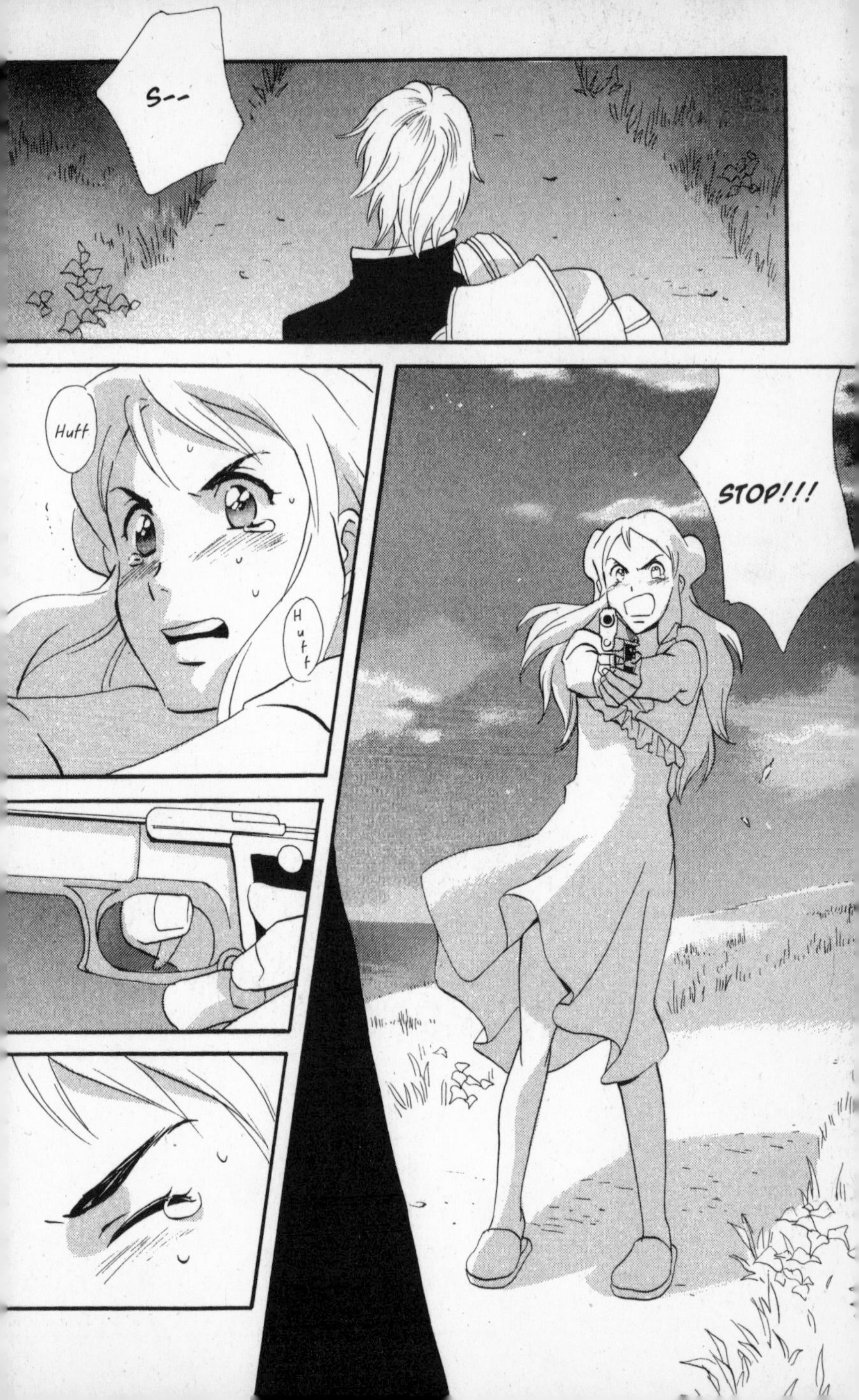
S--
STOP!!!
Huff
Huff

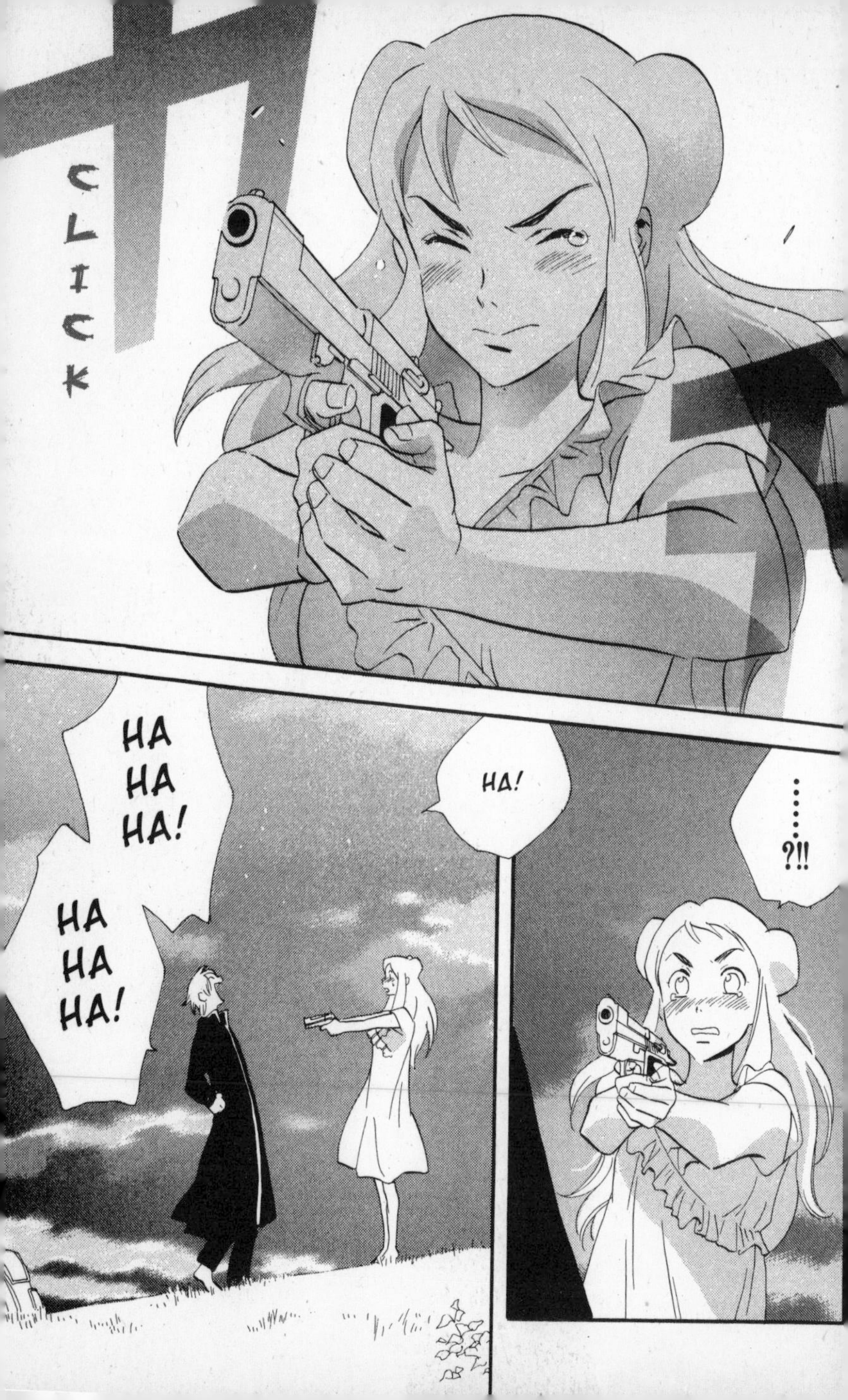
CLICK
......?!!
HA!
HA HA HA!
HA HA HA!

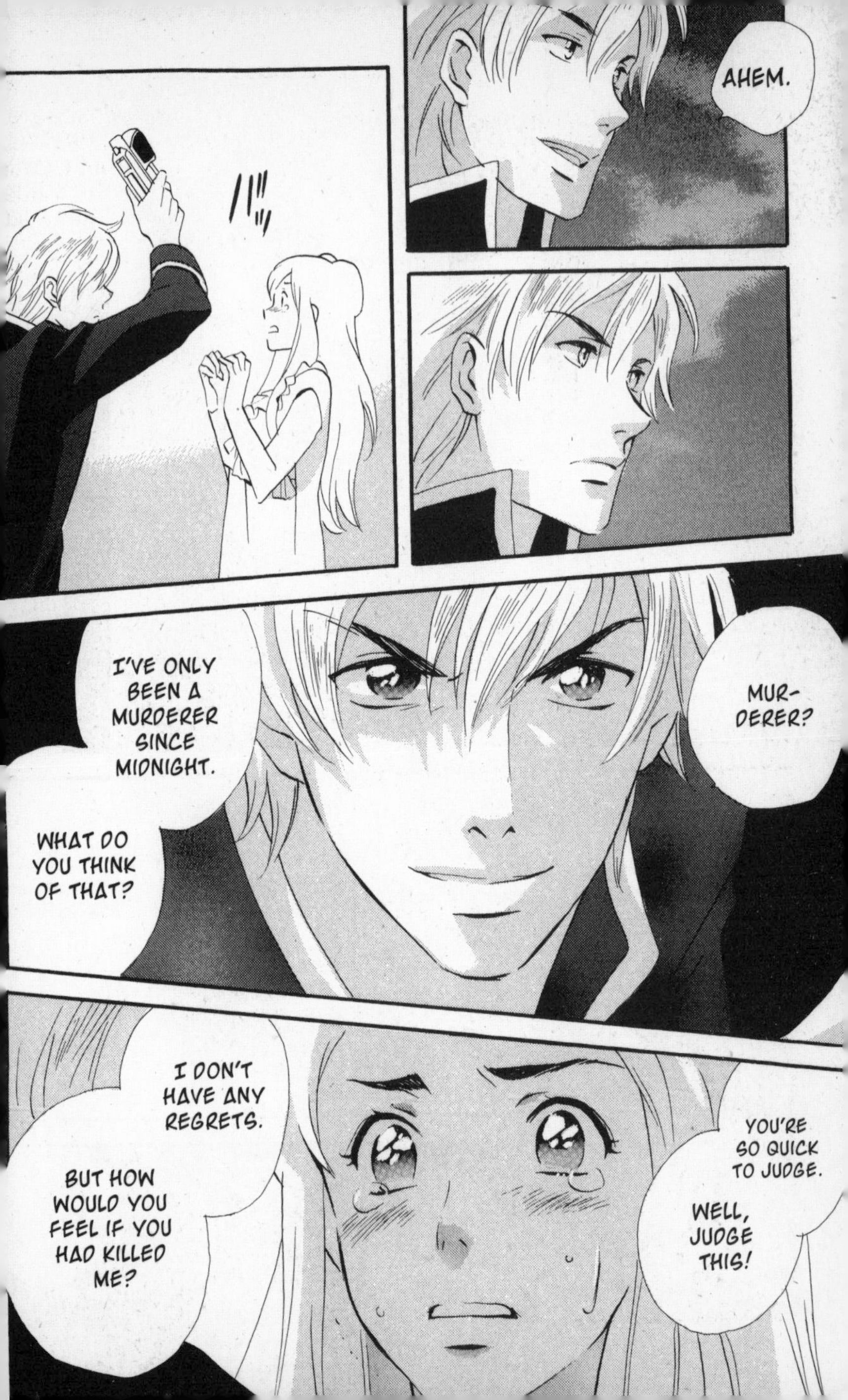
AHEM.
MUR-DERER?
I'VE ONLY BEEN A MURDERER SINCE MIDNIGHT.
WHAT DO YOU THINK OF THAT?
YOU'RE SO QUICK TO JUDGE.
WELL, JUDGE THIS!
I DON'T HAVE ANY REGRETS.
BUT HOW WOULD YOU FEEL IF YOU HAD KILLED ME?

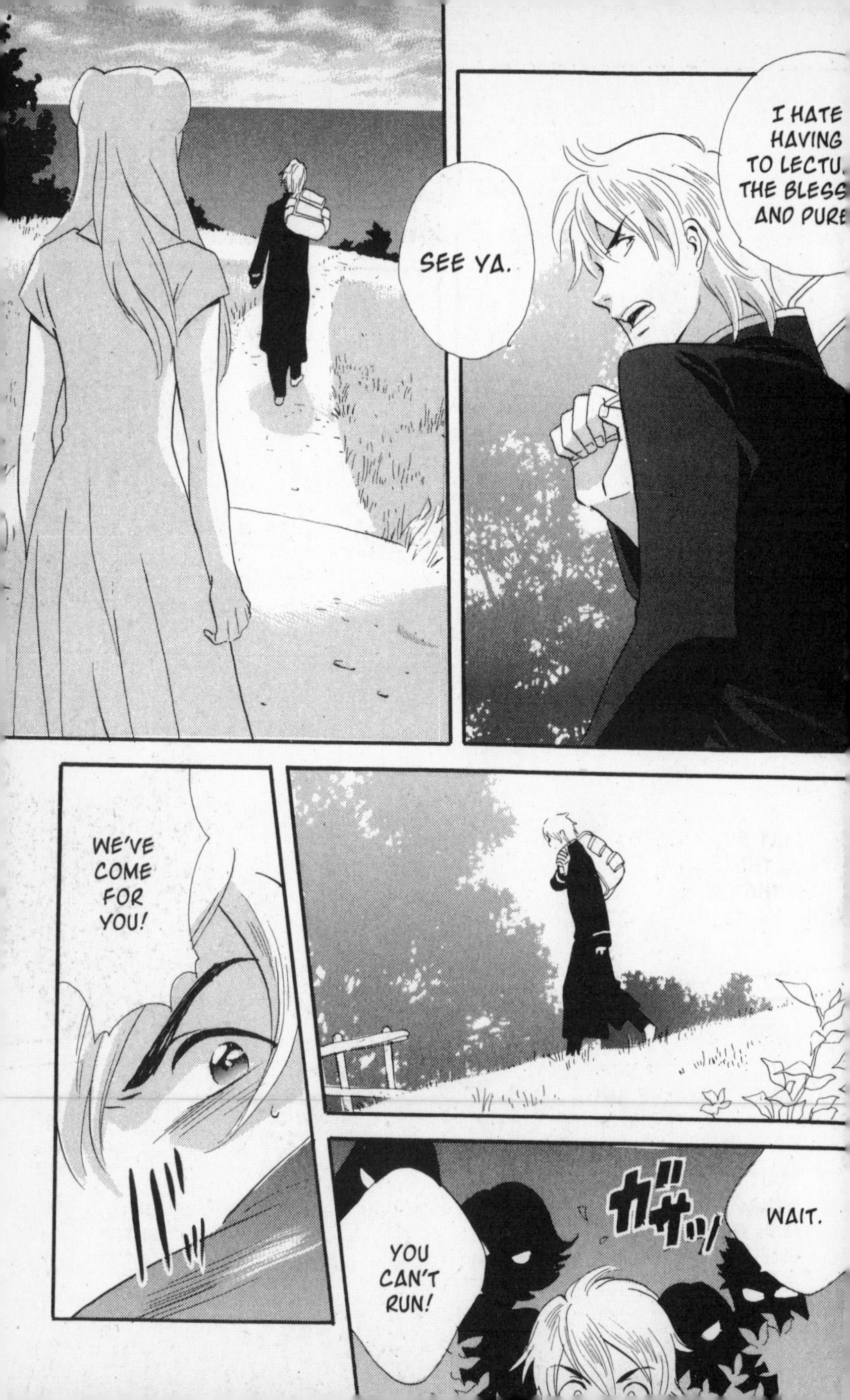
I HATE HAVING TO LECTU THE BLESS AND PURE
SEE YA.
WAIT.
ガサッ
YOU CAN'T RUN!
WE'VE COME FOR YOU!

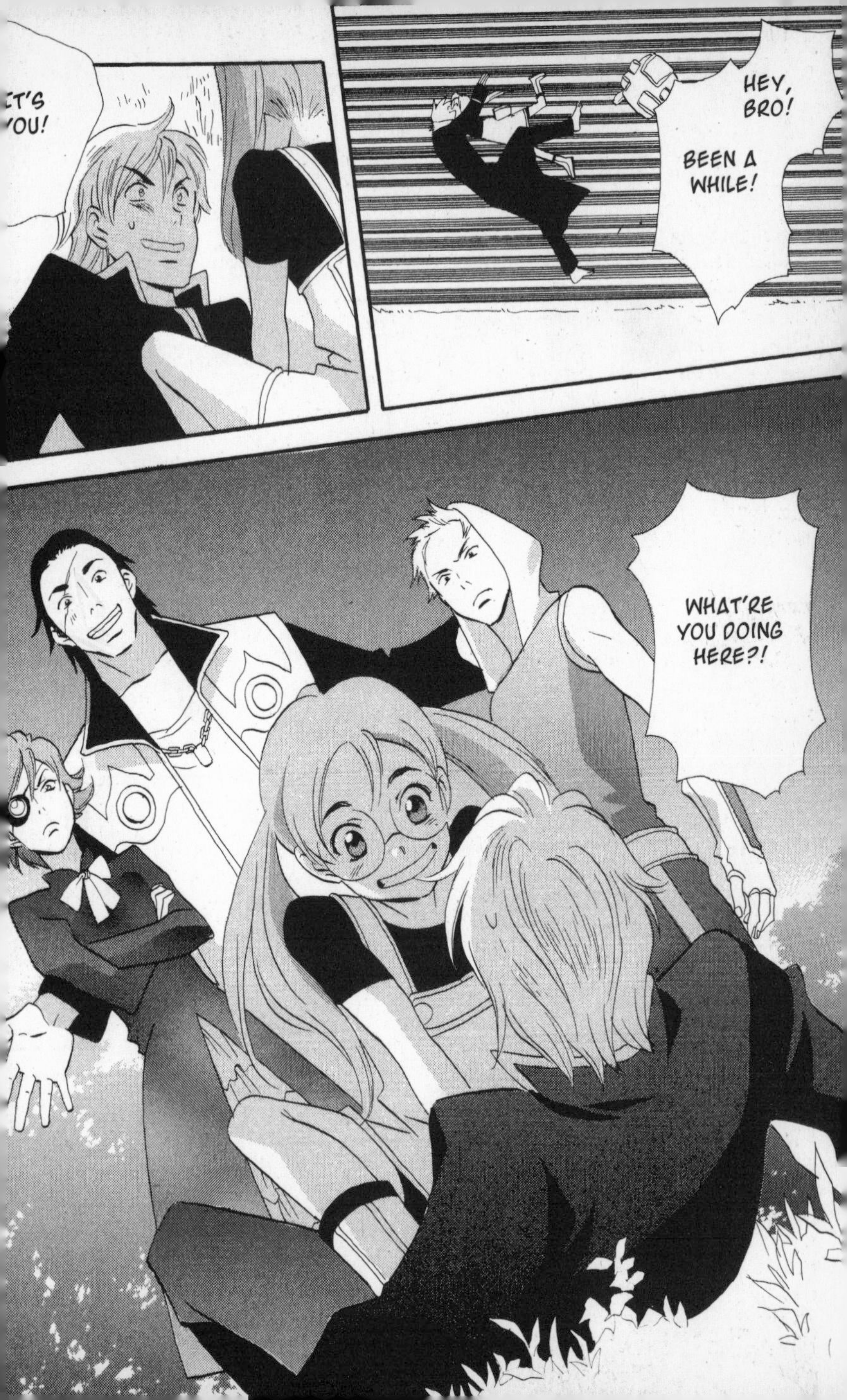
HEY, BRO!
BEEN A WHILE!
T'S YOU!
WHAT'RE YOU DOING HERE?!

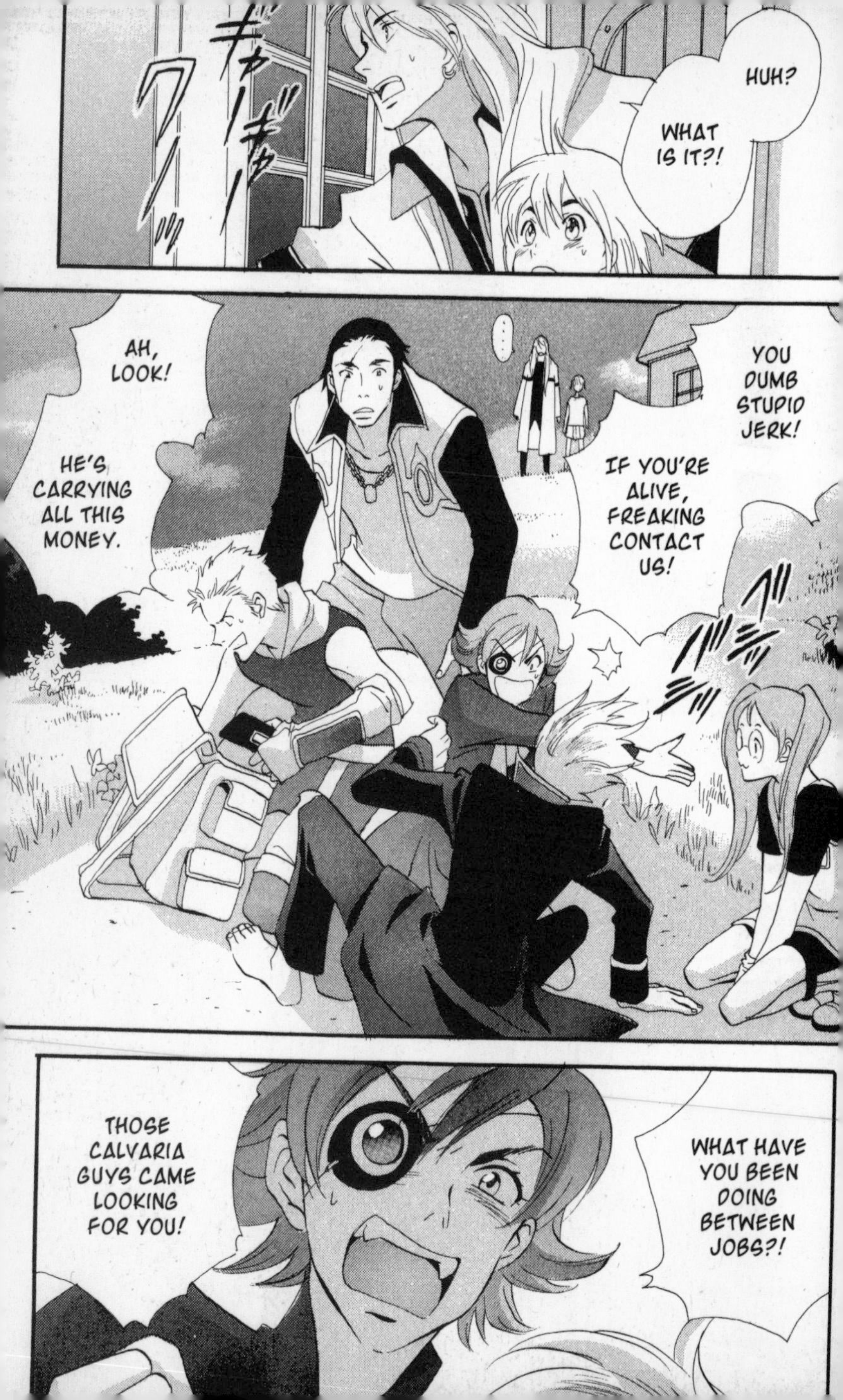
HUH?
WHAT IS IT?!
...
YOU DUMB STUPID JERK!
IF YOU'RE ALIVE, FREAKING CONTACT US!
AH, LOOK!
HE'S CARRYING ALL THIS MONEY.
WHAT HAVE YOU BEEN DOING BETWEEN JOBS?!
THOSE CALVARIA GUYS CAME LOOKING FOR YOU!

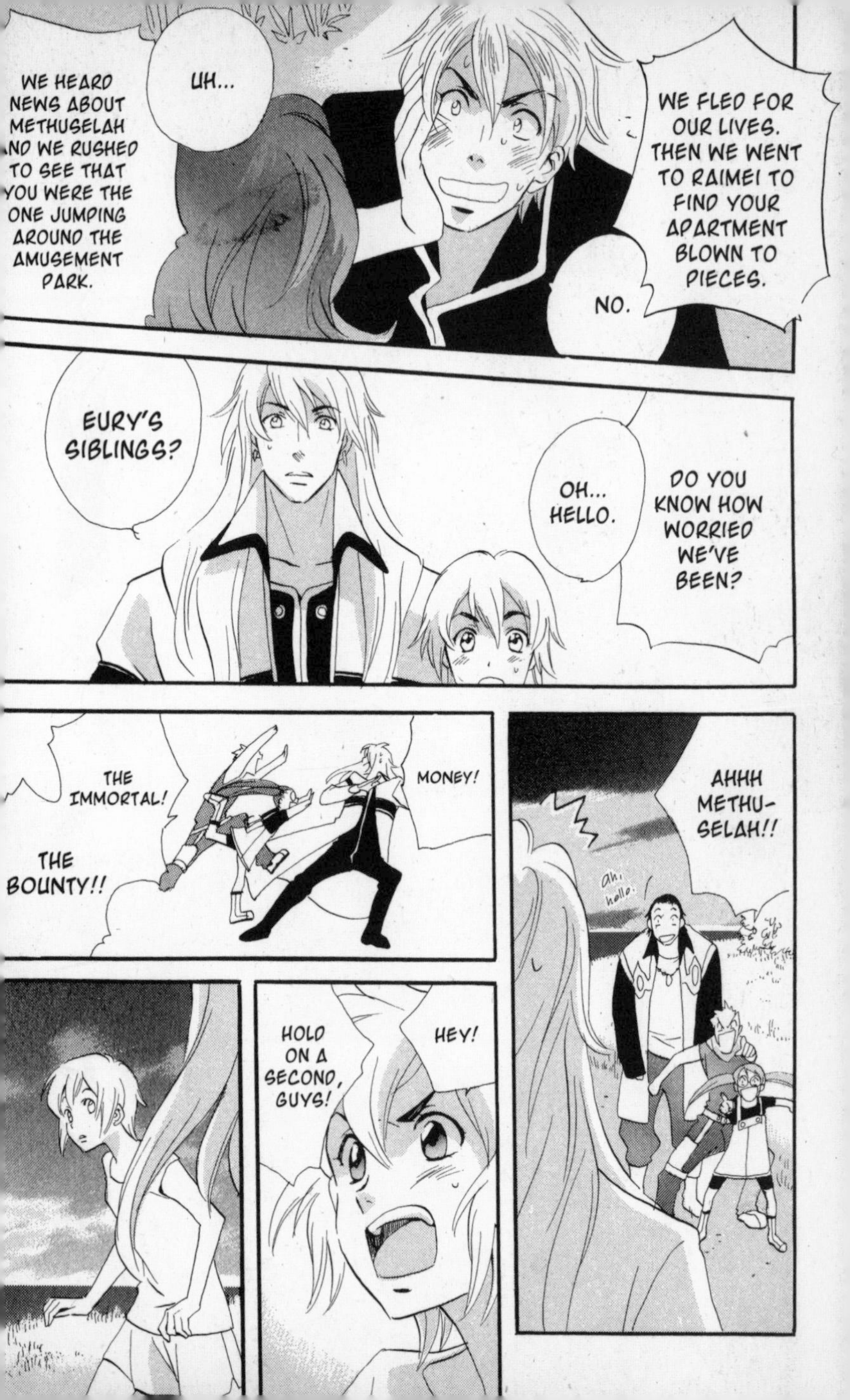
WE FLED FOR OUR LIVES. THEN WE WENT TO RAIMEI TO FIND YOUR APARTMENT BLOWN TO PIECES.
NO.
UH...
WE HEARD NEWS ABOUT METHUSELAH ND WE RUSHED TO SEE THAT YOU WERE THE ONE JUMPING AROUND THE AMUSEMENT PARK.
DO YOU KNOW HOW WORRIED WE'VE BEEN?
OH... HELLO.
EURY'S SIBLINGS?
AHHH METHU-SELAH!!
ah, hello.
MONEY!
THE IMMORTAL!
THE BOUNTY!!
HEY!
HOLD ON A SECOND, GUYS!

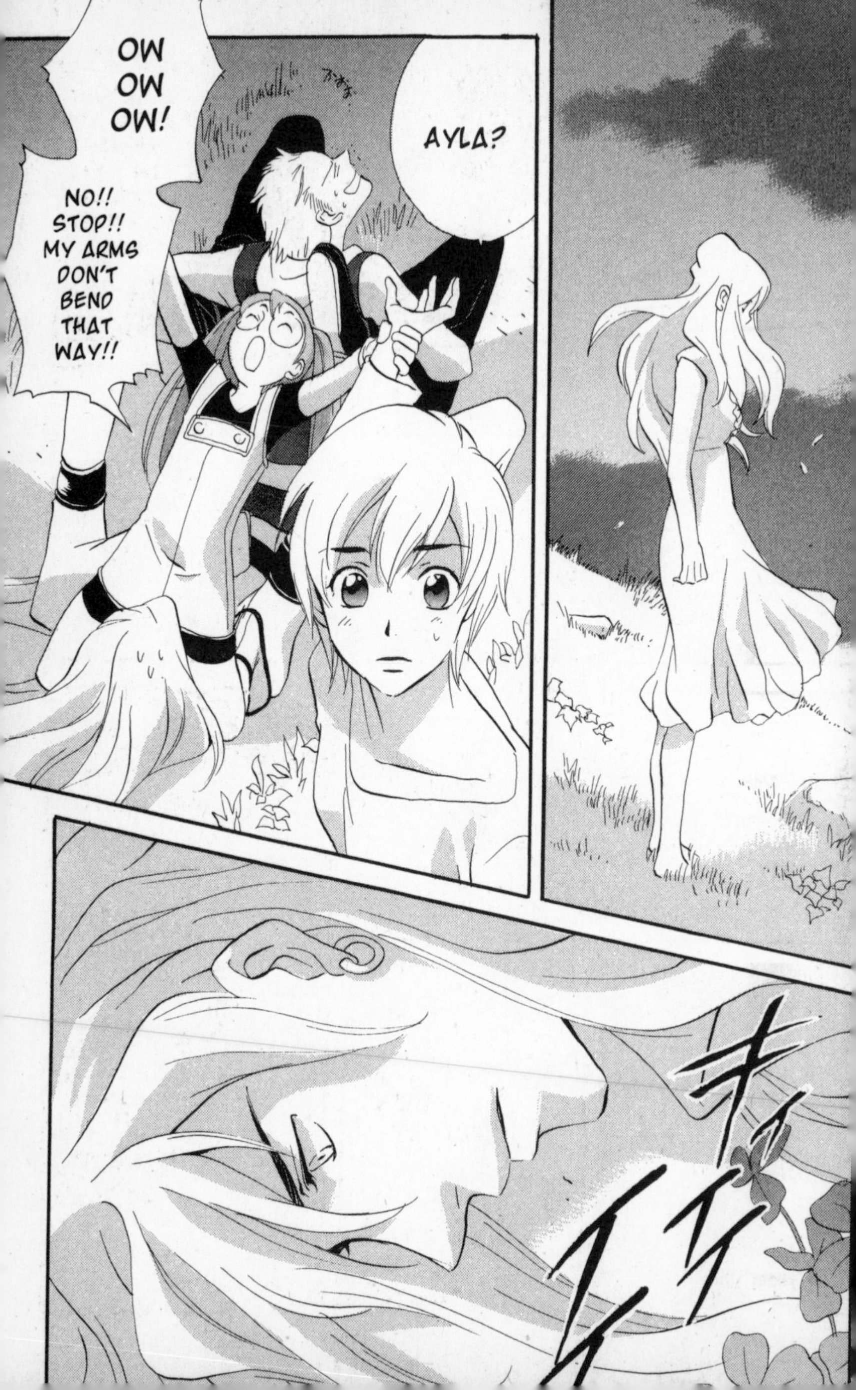
AYLA?
OW OW OW!
NO!! STOP!! MY ARMS DON'T BEND THAT WAY!!

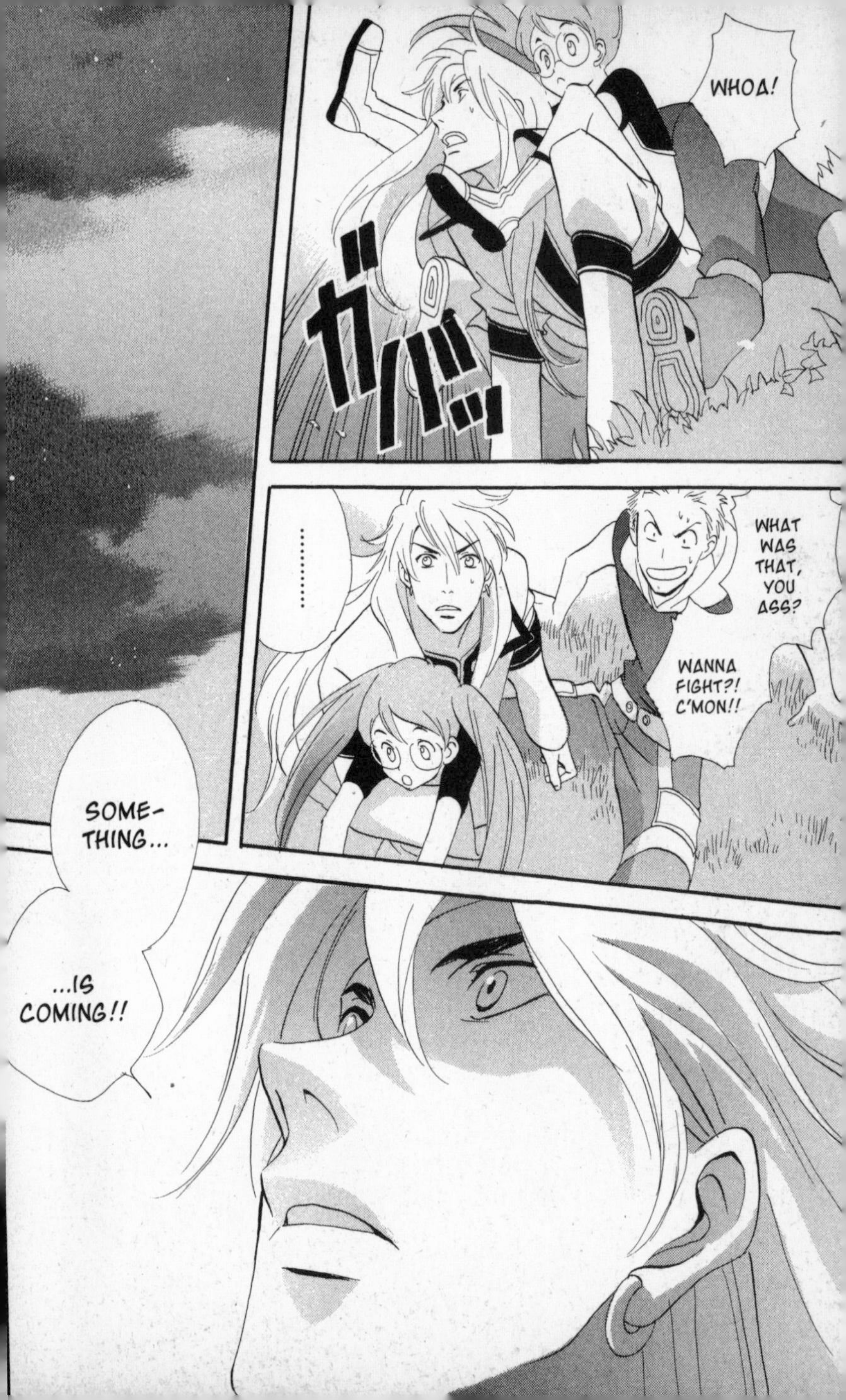
WHOA!
ガバッ
WHAT WAS THAT, YOU ASS?
WANNA FIGHT?! C'MON!!
....
SOME-THING...
...IS COMING!!

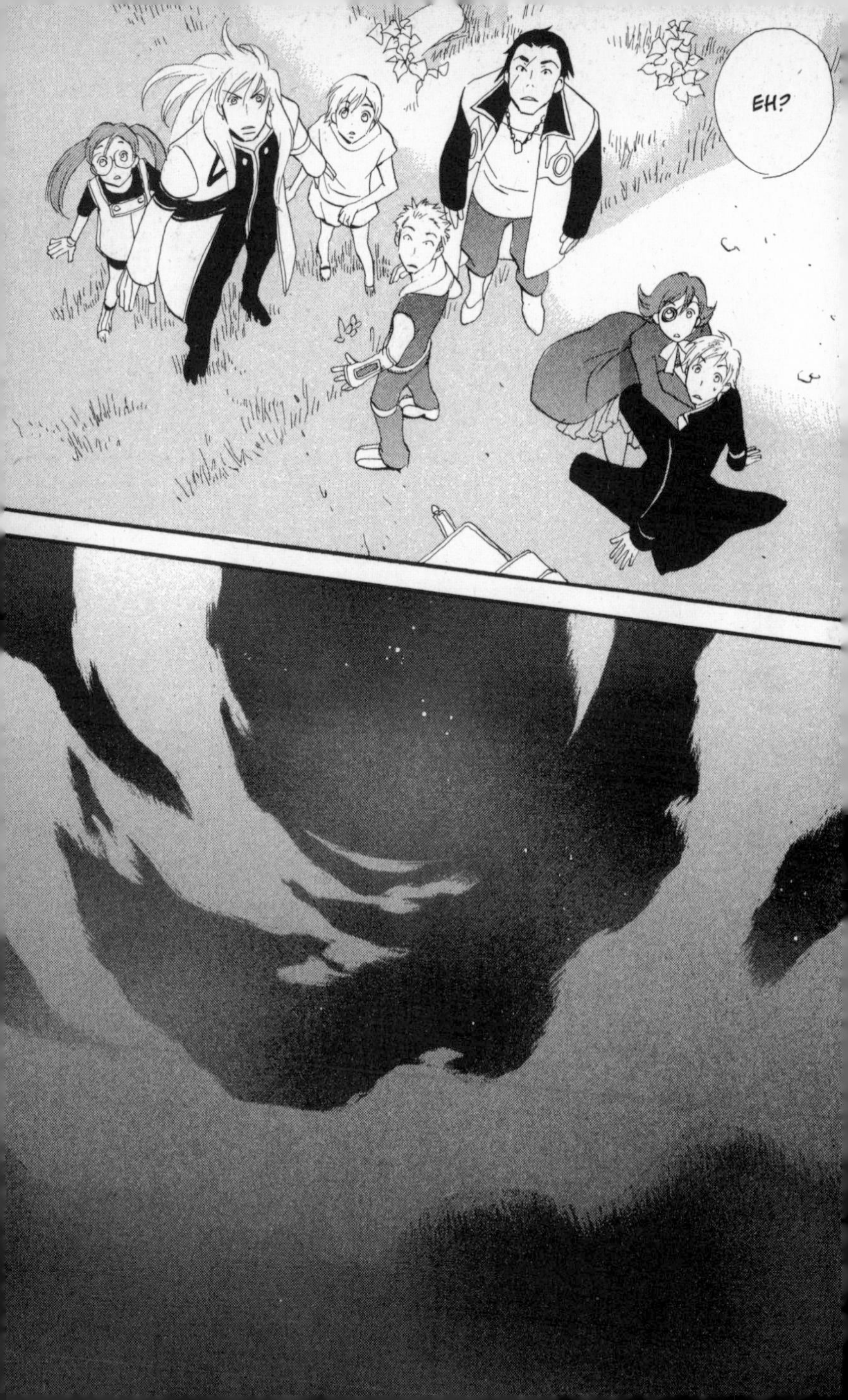
EH?

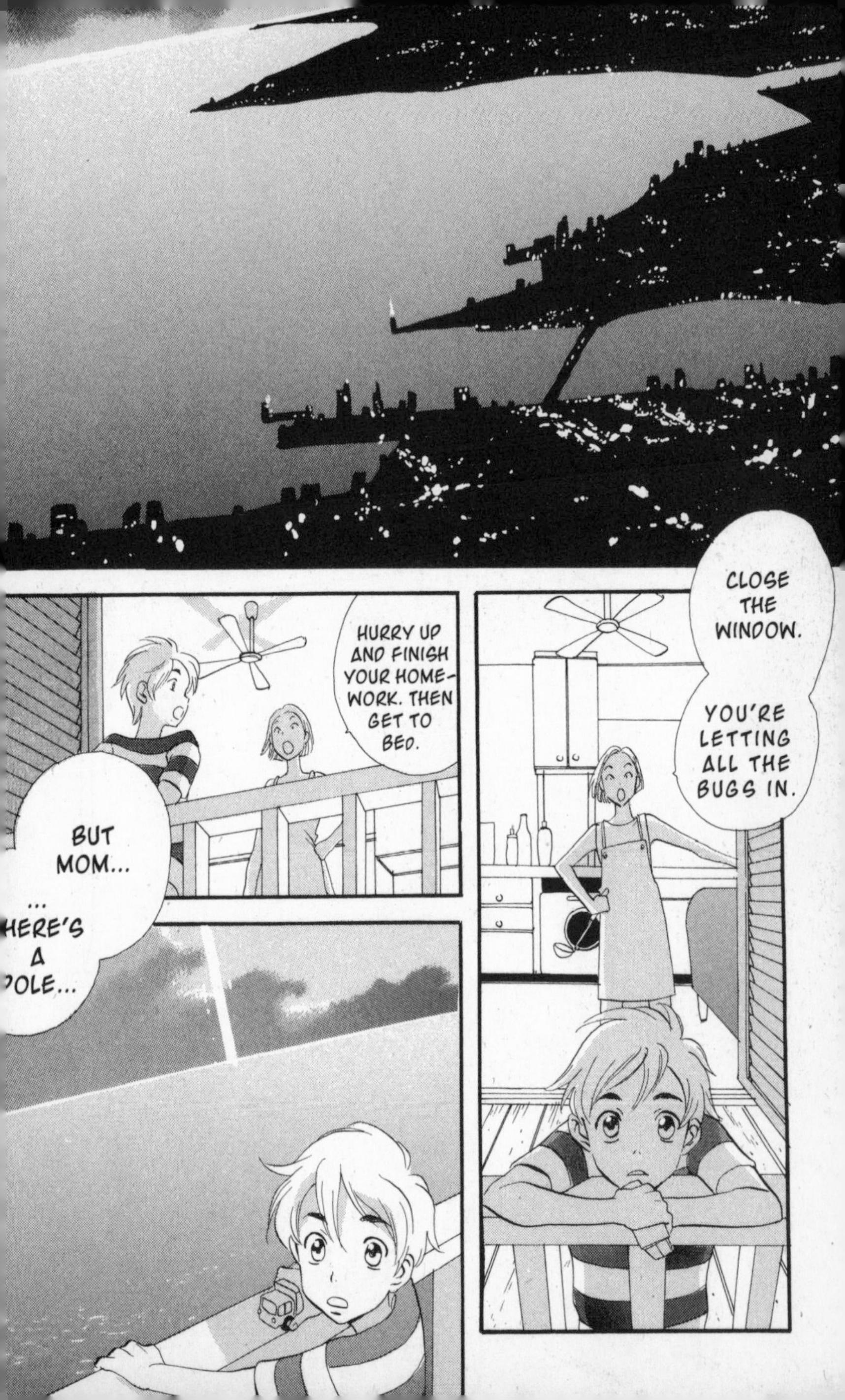
CLOSE THE WINDOW.
YOU'RE LETTING ALL THE BUGS IN.
HURRY UP AND FINISH YOUR HOME-WORK. THEN GET TO BED.
BUT MOM...
... HERE'S A POLE...

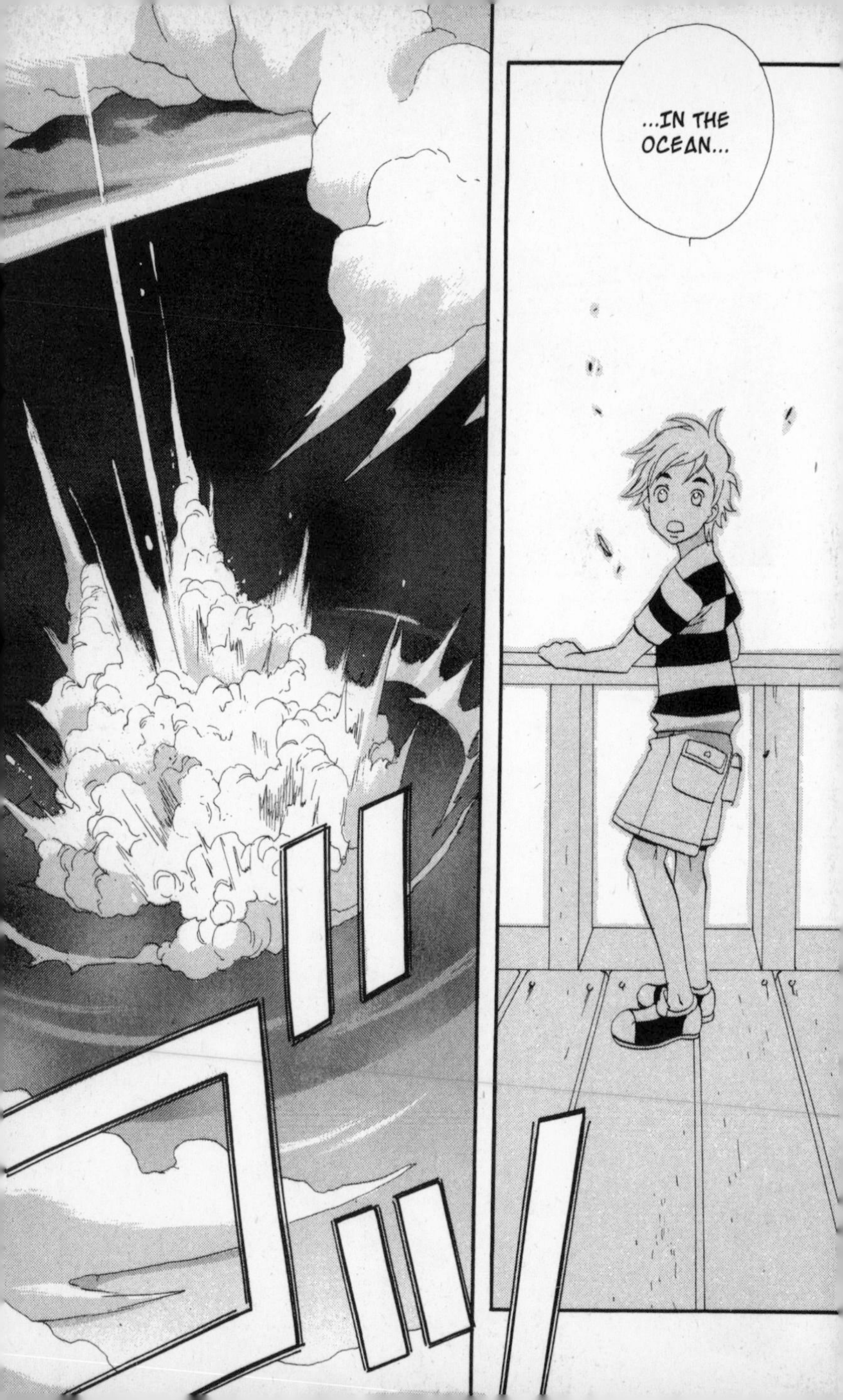
...IN THE OCEAN...

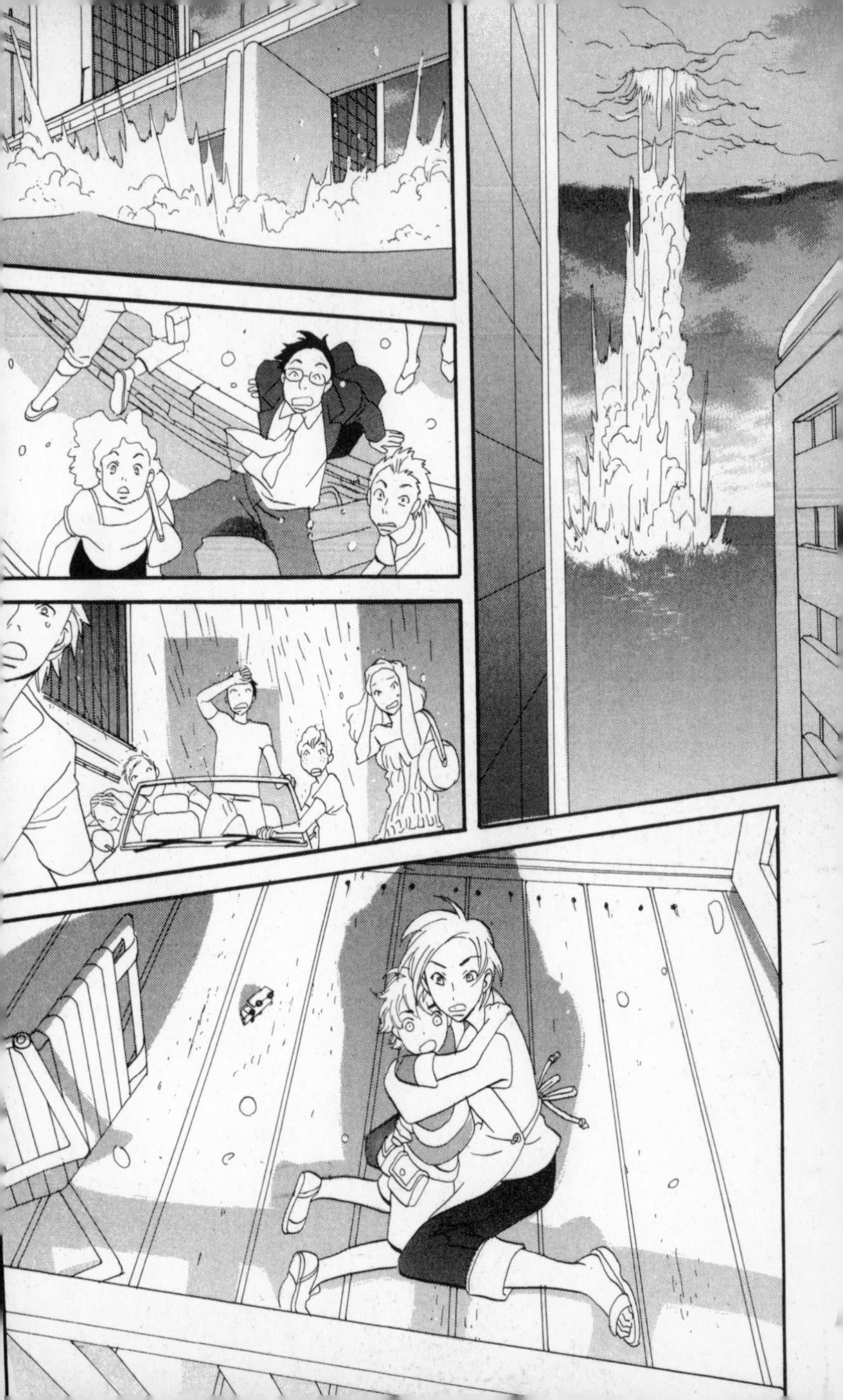

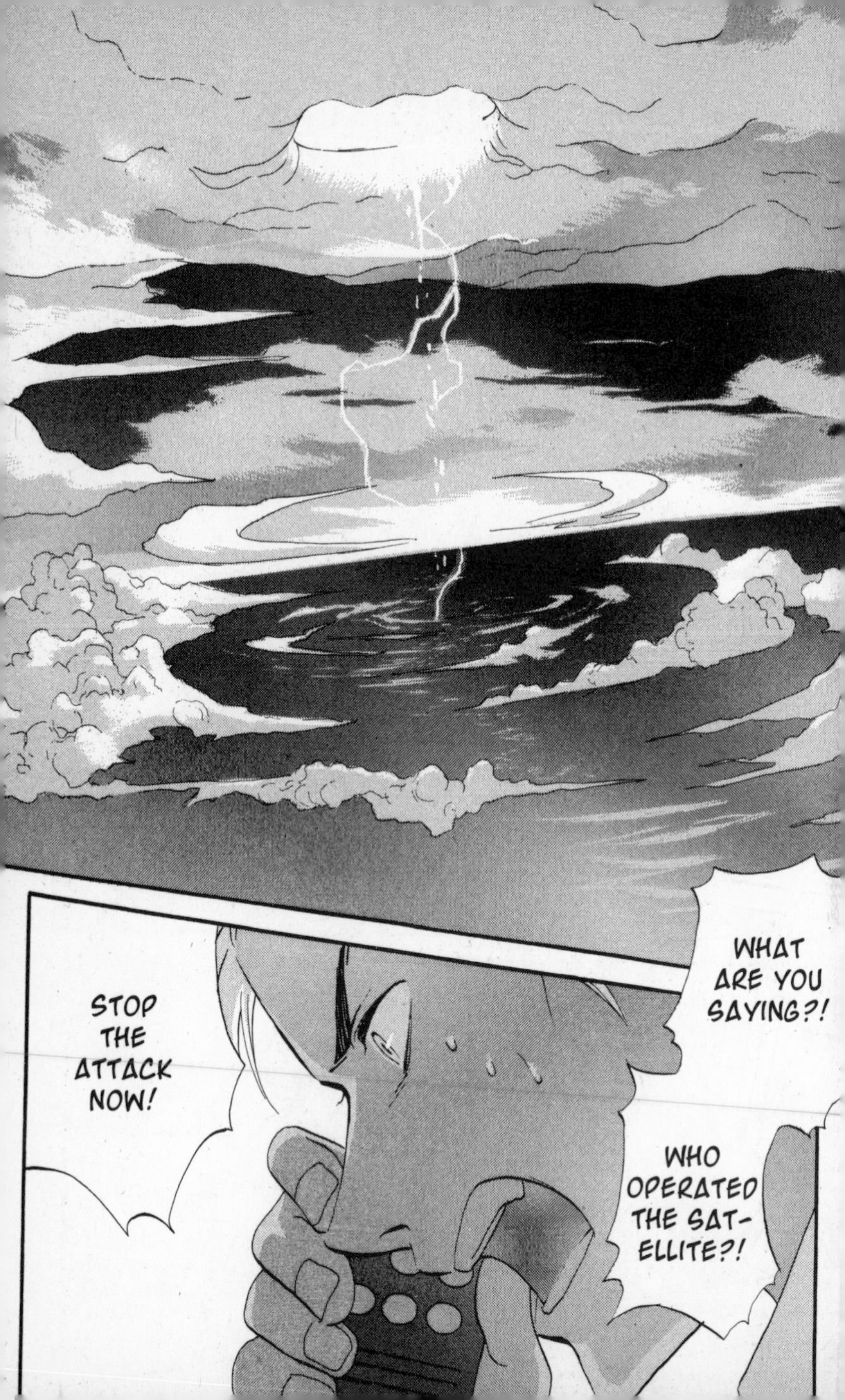
WHAT ARE YOU SAYING?!
STOP THE ATTACK NOW!
WHO OPERATED THE SAT-ELLITE?!

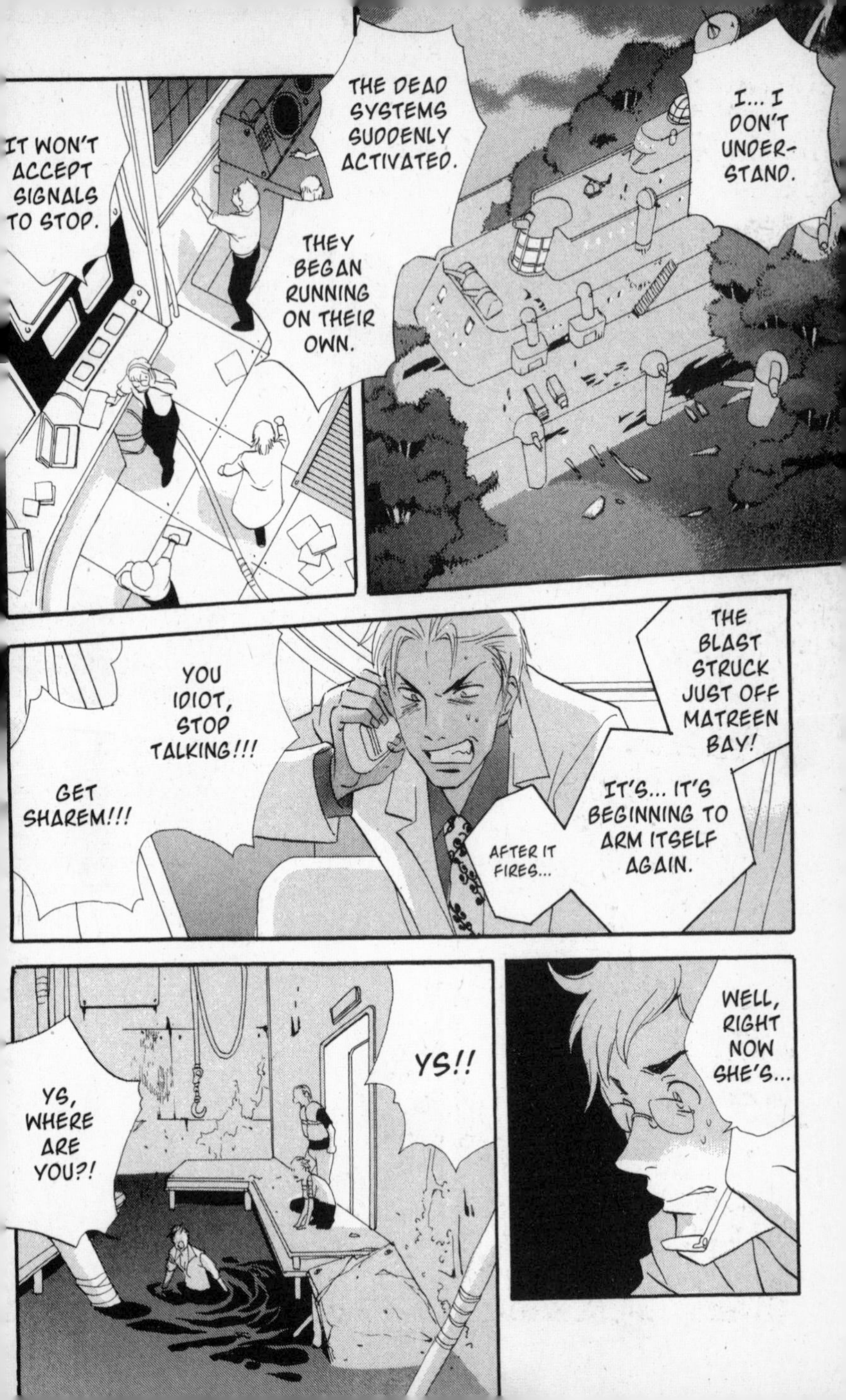
I... I DON'T UNDER-STAND.
THE DEAD SYSTEMS SUDDENLY ACTIVATED.
THEY BEGAN RUNNING ON THEIR OWN.
IT WON'T ACCEPT SIGNALS TO STOP.
THE BLAST STRUCK JUST OFF MATREEN BAY!
IT'S... IT'S BEGINNING TO ARM ITSELF AGAIN.
AFTER IT FIRES...
YOU IDIOT, STOP TALKING!!!
GET SHAREM!!!
WELL, RIGHT NOW SHE'S...
YS!!
YS, WHERE ARE YOU?!

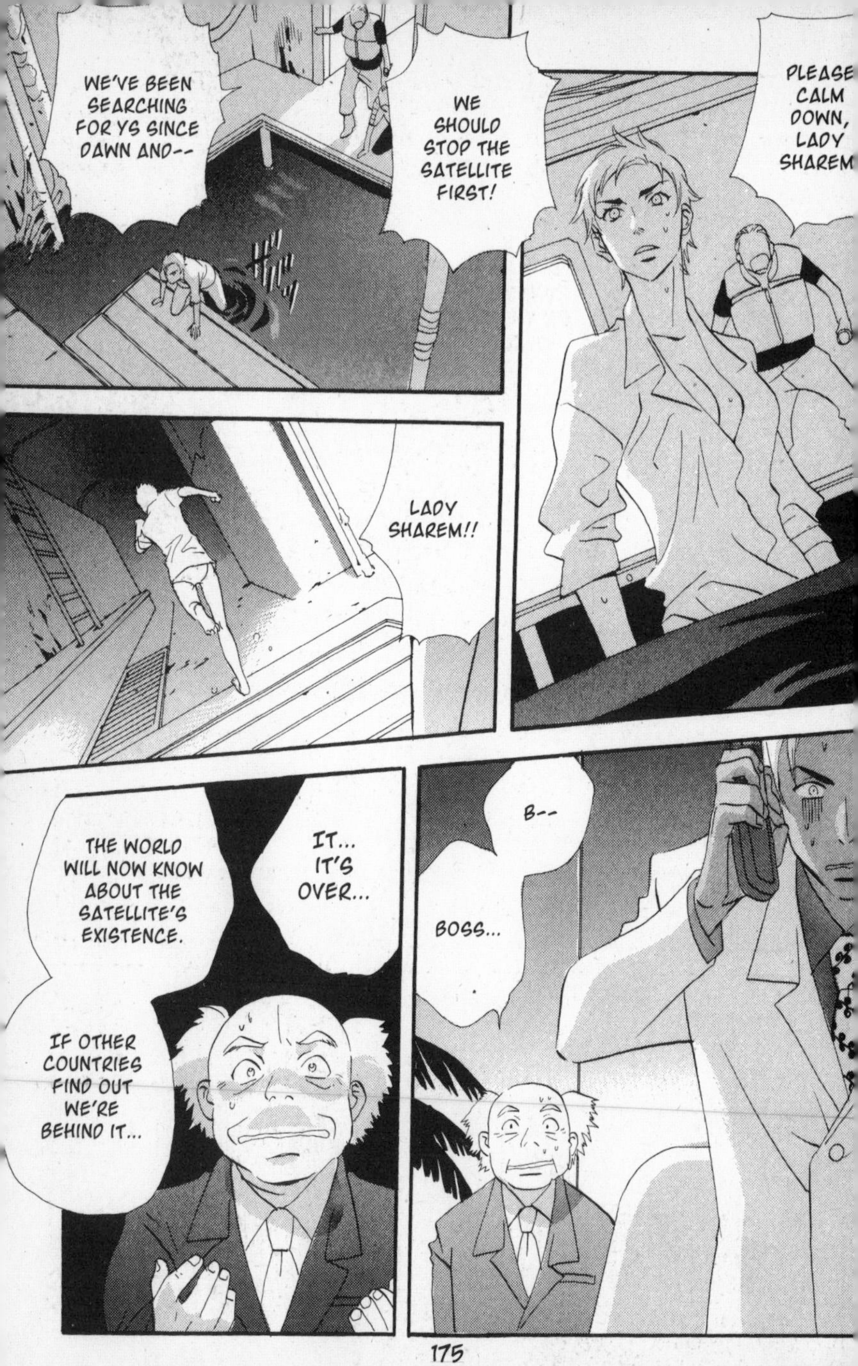
PLEASE CALM DOWN, LADY SHAREM
WE SHOULD STOP THE SATELLITE FIRST!
WE'VE BEEN SEARCHING FOR YS SINCE DAWN AND--
LADY SHAREM!!
B--
BOSS...
IT... IT'S OVER...
THE WORLD WILL NOW KNOW ABOUT THE SATELLITE'S EXISTENCE.
IF OTHER COUNTRIES FIND OUT WE'RE BEHIND IT...

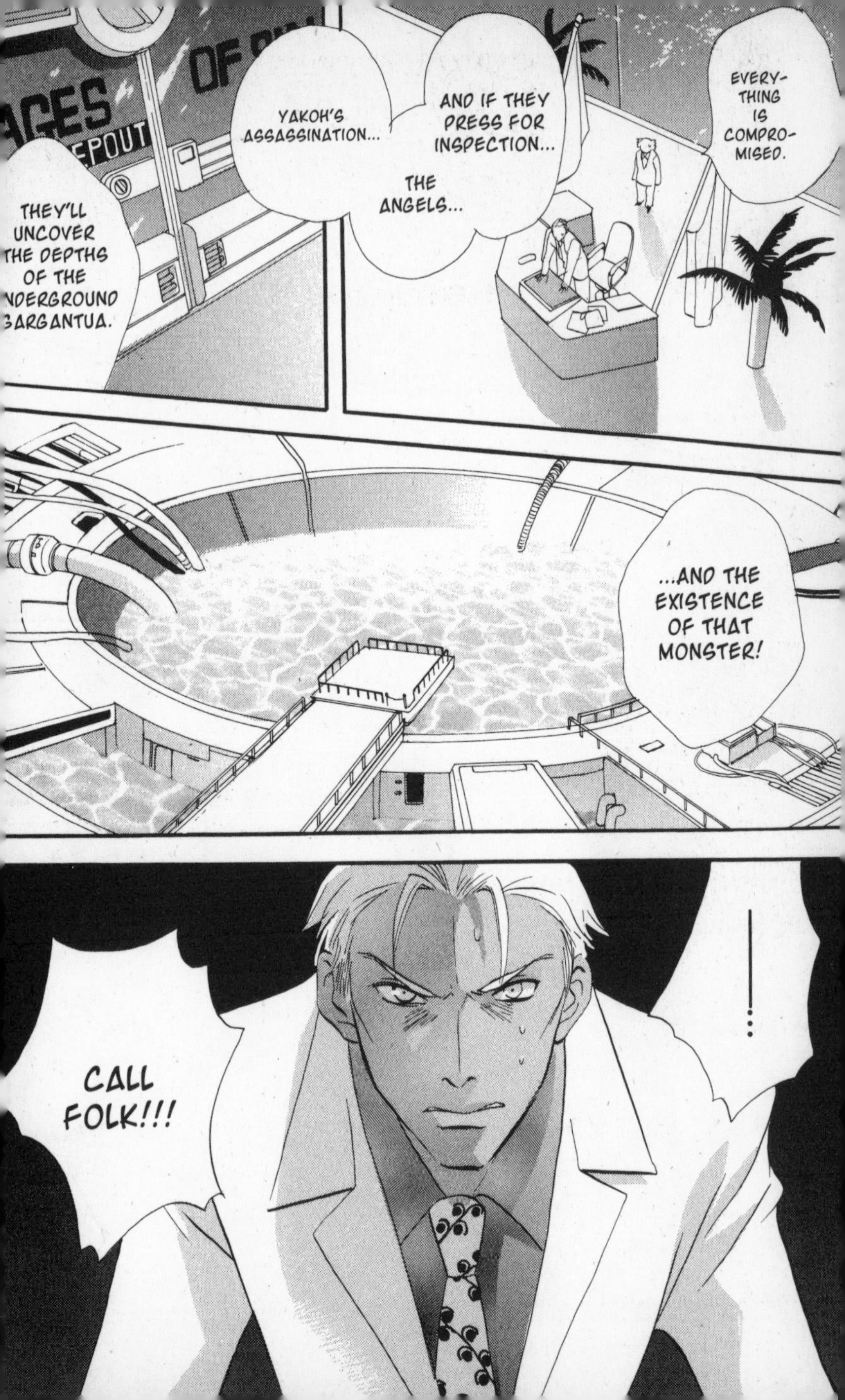
EVERYTHING IS COMPROMISED.
YAKOH'S ASSASSINATION...
THE ANGELS...
AND IF THEY PRESS FOR INSPECTION...
THEY'LL UNCOVER THE DEPTHS OF THE UNDERGROUND GARGANTUA.
...AND THE EXISTENCE OF THAT MONSTER!
......
CALL FOLK!!!

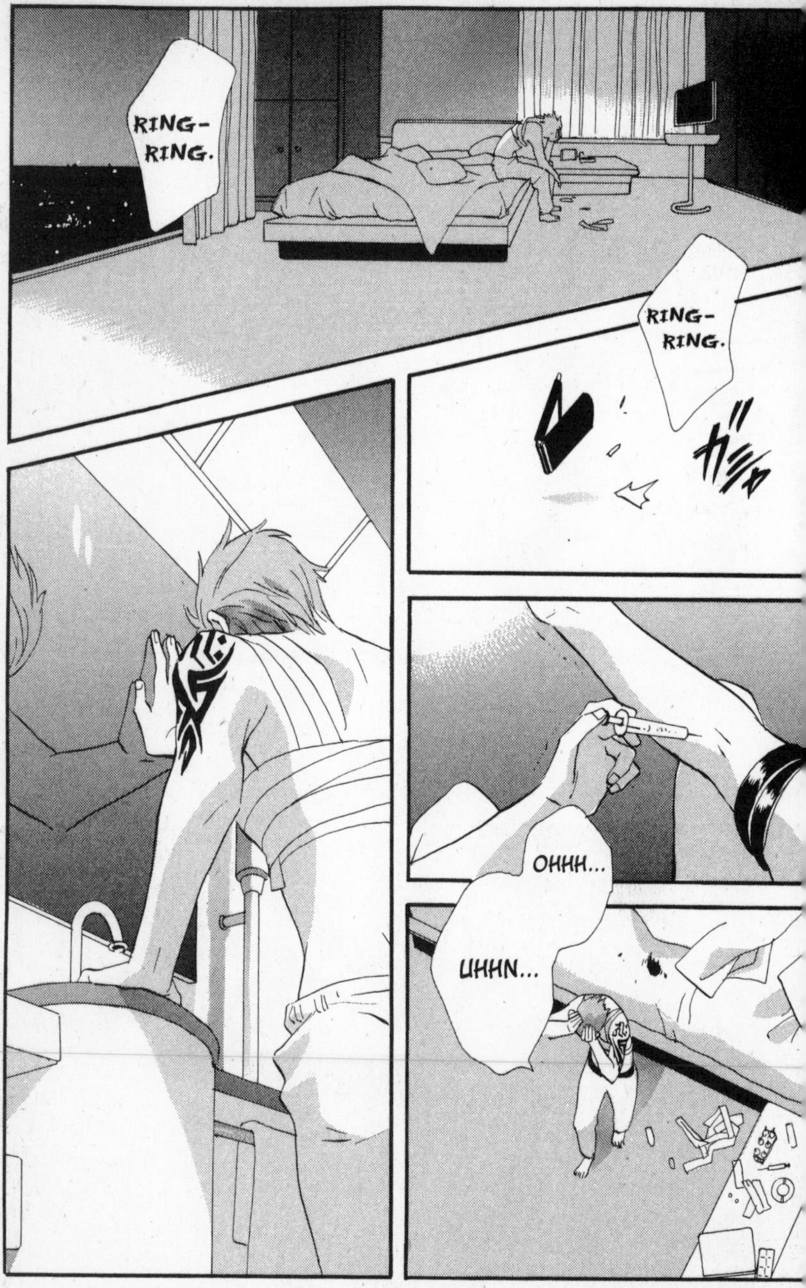
RING-
RING.
RING-
RING.
ガシャ
OHHH...
UHHN...

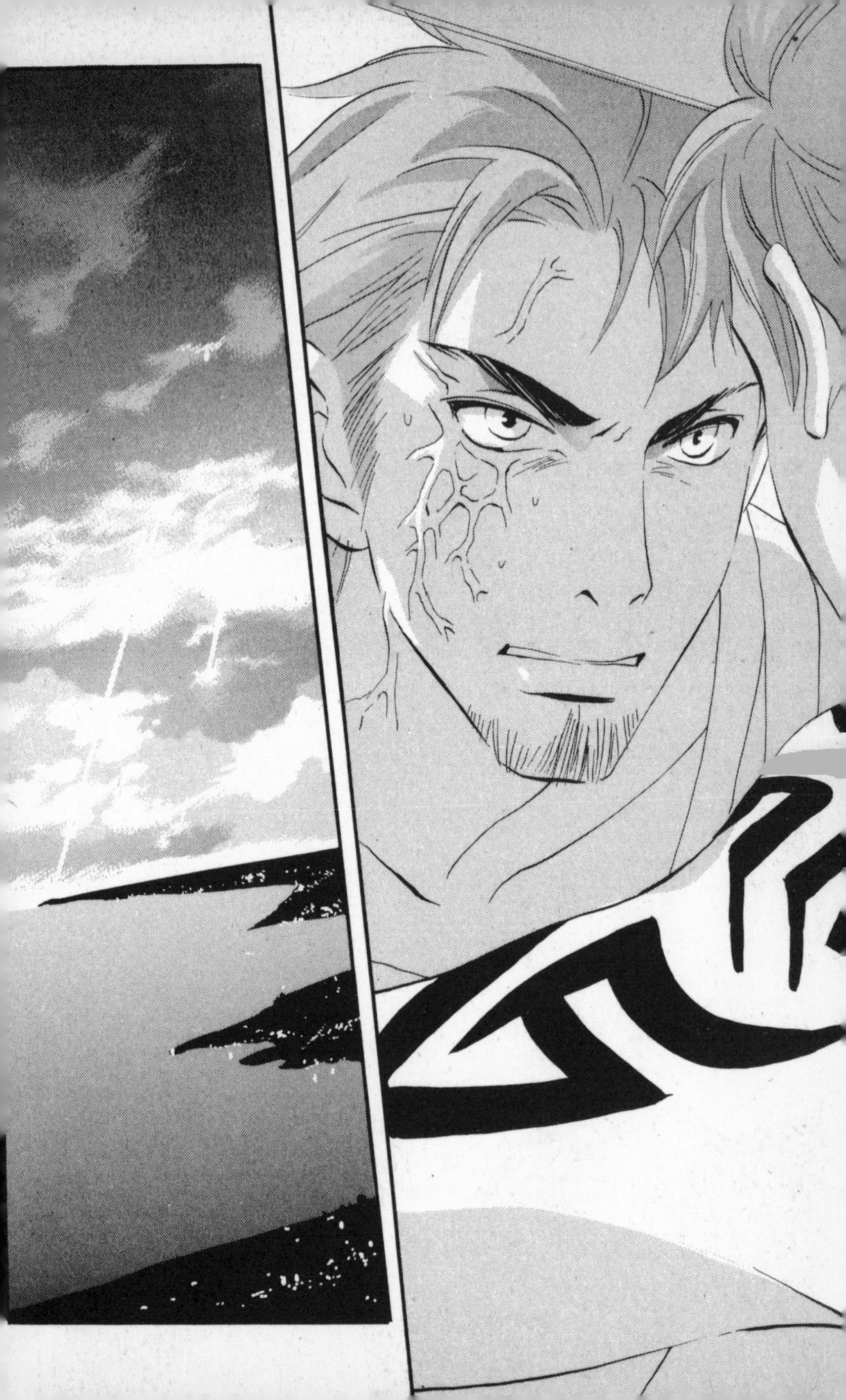

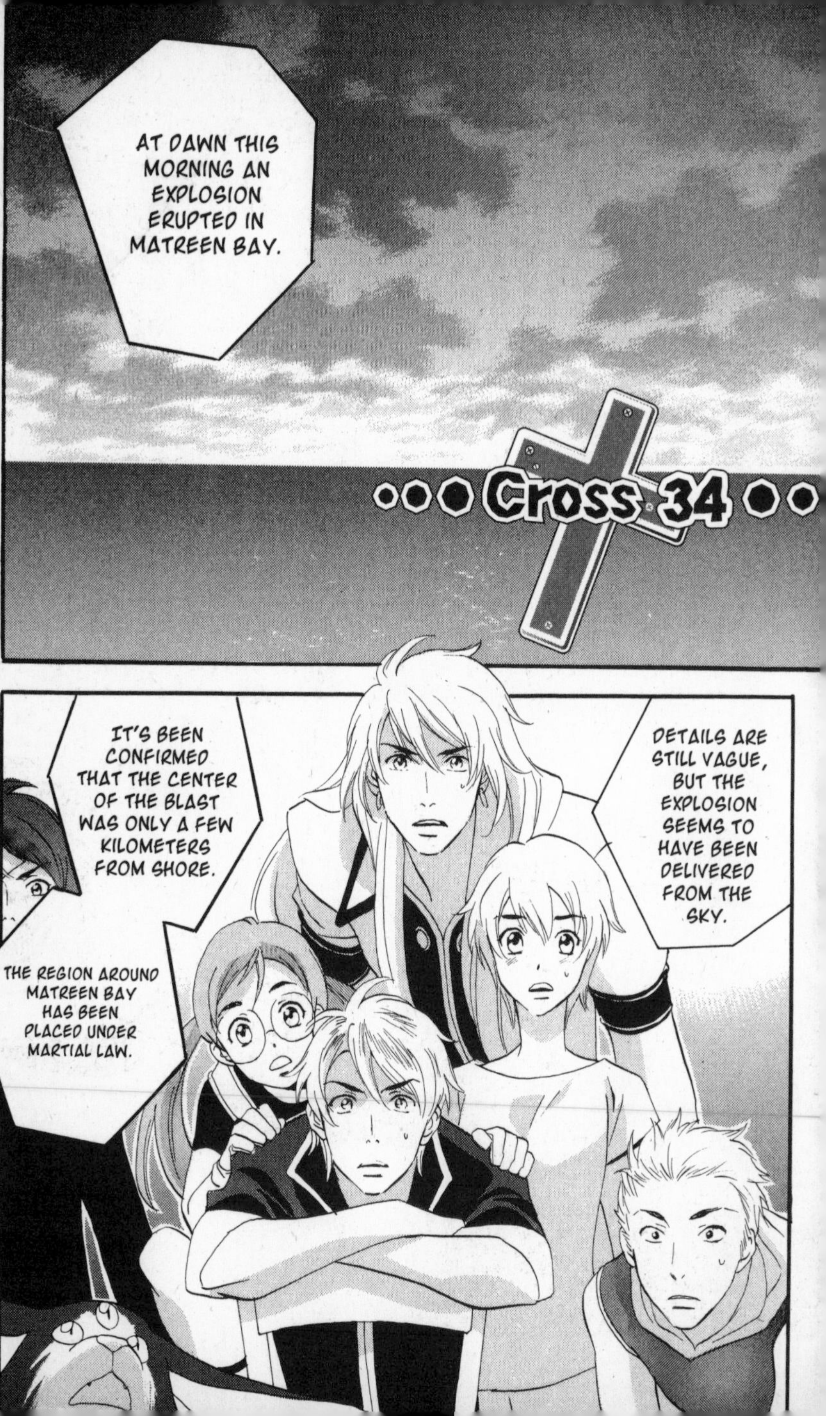
AT DAWN THIS MORNING AN EXPLOSION ERUPTED IN MATREEN BAY.
Cross 34
DETAILS ARE STILL VAGUE, BUT THE EXPLOSION SEEMS TO HAVE BEEN DELIVERED FROM THE SKY.
IT'S BEEN CONFIRMED THAT THE CENTER OF THE BLAST WAS ONLY A FEW KILOMETERS FROM SHORE.
THE REGION AROUND MATREEN BAY HAS BEEN PLACED UNDER MARTIAL LAW.

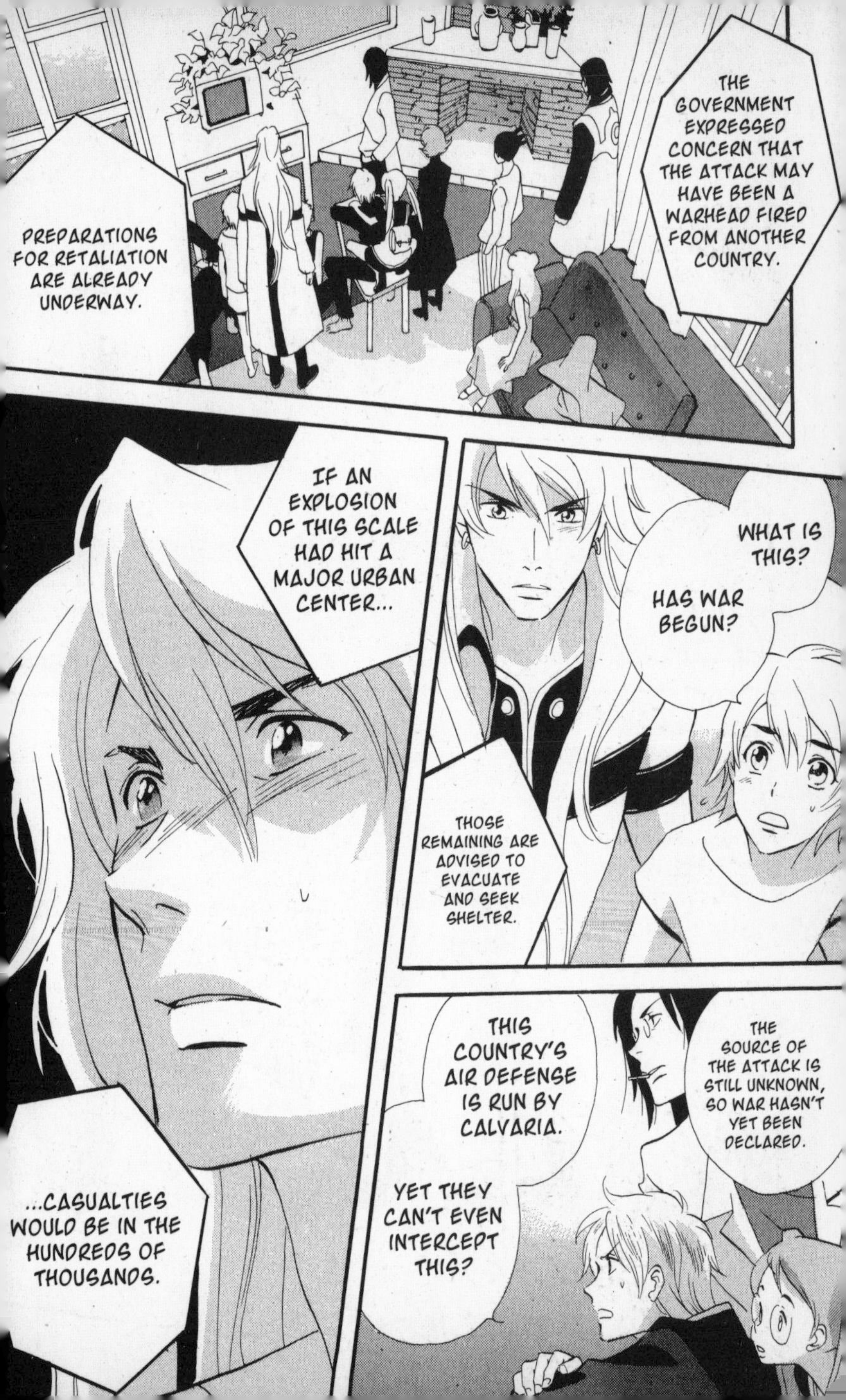
THE GOVERNMENT EXPRESSED CONCERN THAT THE ATTACK MAY HAVE BEEN A WARHEAD FIRED FROM ANOTHER COUNTRY.
PREPARATIONS FOR RETALIATION ARE ALREADY UNDERWAY.
WHAT IS THIS? HAS WAR BEGUN?
THOSE REMAINING ARE ADVISED TO EVACUATE AND SEEK SHELTER.
THE SOURCE OF THE ATTACK IS STILL UNKNOWN, SO WAR HASN'T YET BEEN DECLARED.
THIS COUNTRY'S AIR DEFENSE IS RUN BY CALVARIA.
YET THEY CAN'T EVEN INTERCEPT THIS?
IF AN EXPLOSION OF THIS SCALE HAD HIT A MAJOR URBAN CENTER...
...CASUALTIES WOULD BE IN THE HUNDREDS OF THOUSANDS.

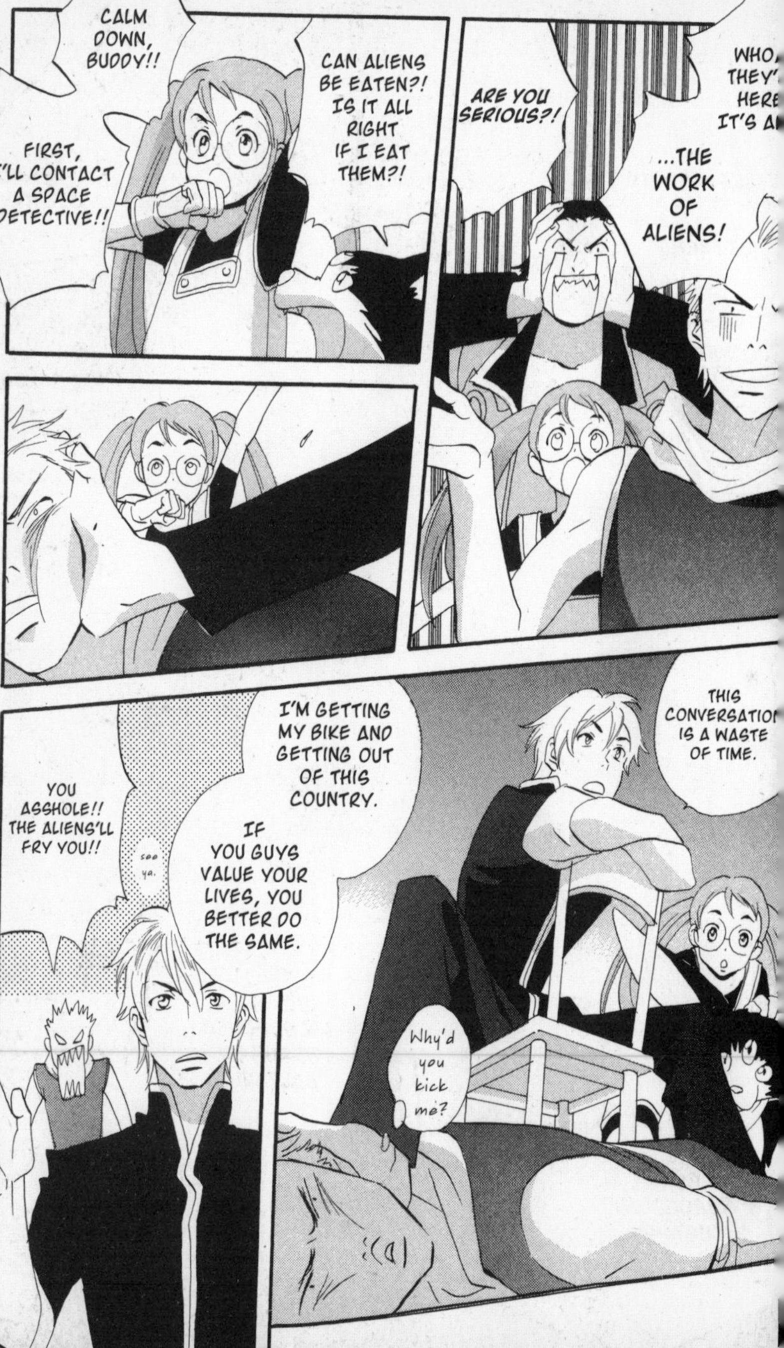
...THE WORK OF ALIENS!
ARE YOU SERIOUS?!
CAN ALIENS BE EATEN?! IS IT ALL RIGHT IF I EAT THEM?!
CALM DOWN, BUDDY!!
FIRST, I'LL CONTACT A SPACE DETECTIVE!!
THIS CONVERSATION IS A WASTE OF TIME.
Why'd you kick me?
I'M GETTING MY BIKE AND GETTING OUT OF THIS COUNTRY.
IF YOU GUYS VALUE YOUR LIVES, YOU BETTER DO THE SAME.
see ya.
YOU ASSHOLE!! THE ALIENS'LL FRY YOU!!

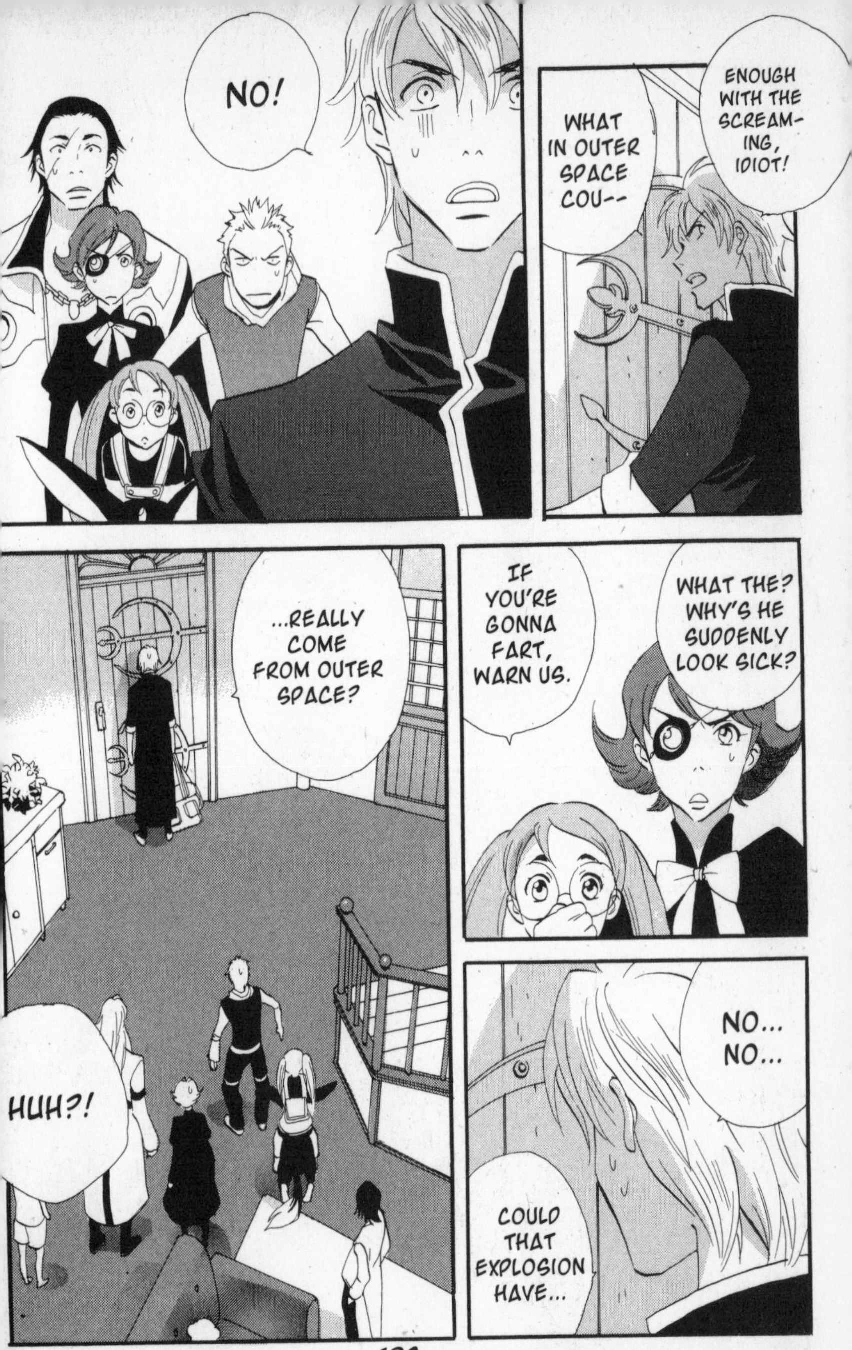
ENOUGH WITH THE SCREAMING, IDIOT!
WHAT IN OUTER SPACE COU--
NO!
WHAT THE? WHY'S HE SUDDENLY LOOK SICK?
IF YOU'RE GONNA FART, WARN US.
NO... NO...
COULD THAT EXPLOSION HAVE...
...REALLY COME FROM OUTER SPACE?
HUH?!

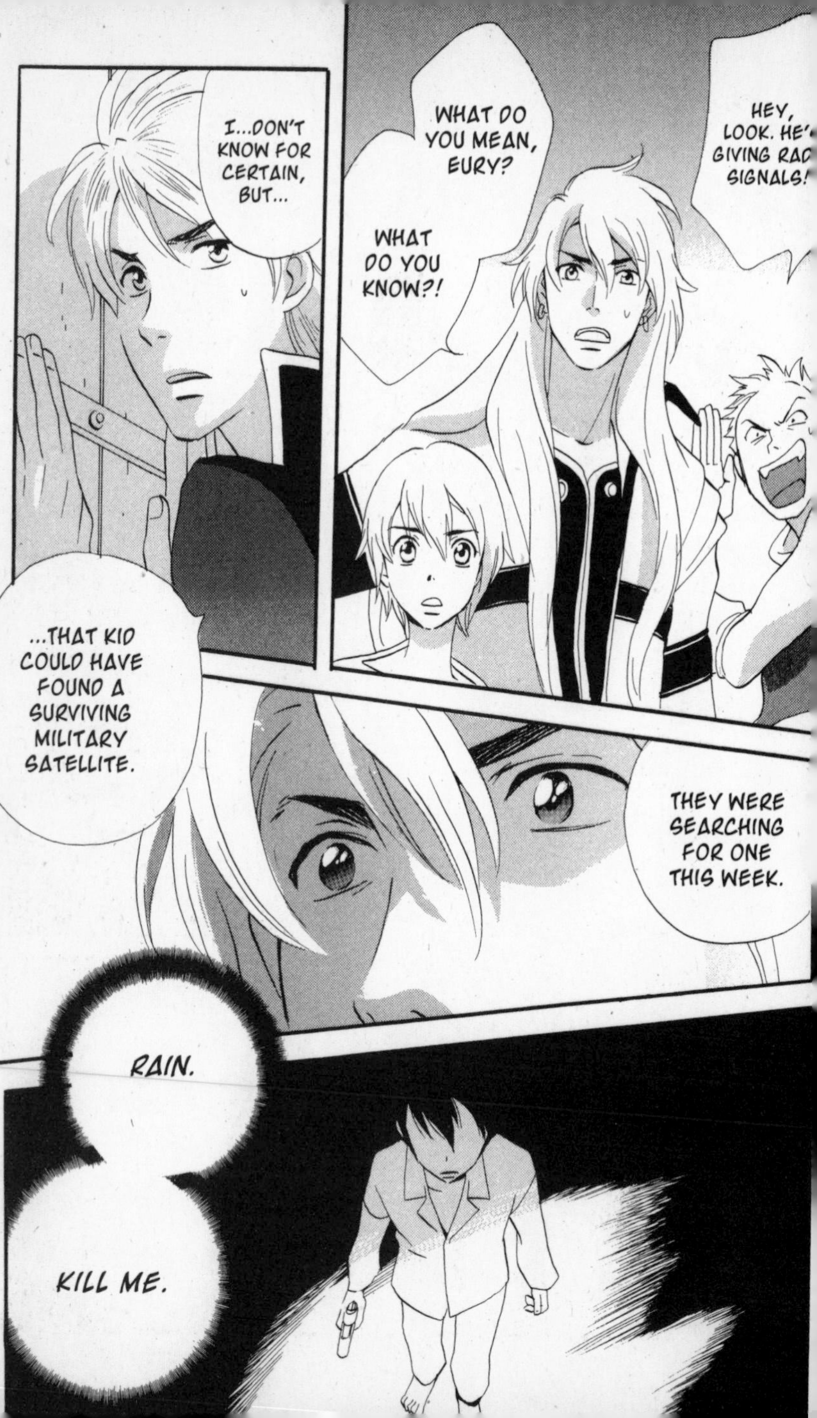
HEY, LOOK. HE' GIVING RAD SIGNALS!
WHAT DO YOU MEAN, EURY?
WHAT DO YOU KNOW?!
I...DON'T KNOW FOR CERTAIN, BUT...
...THAT KID COULD HAVE FOUND A SURVIVING MILITARY SATELLITE.
THEY WERE SEARCHING FOR ONE THIS WEEK.
RAIN.
KILL ME.

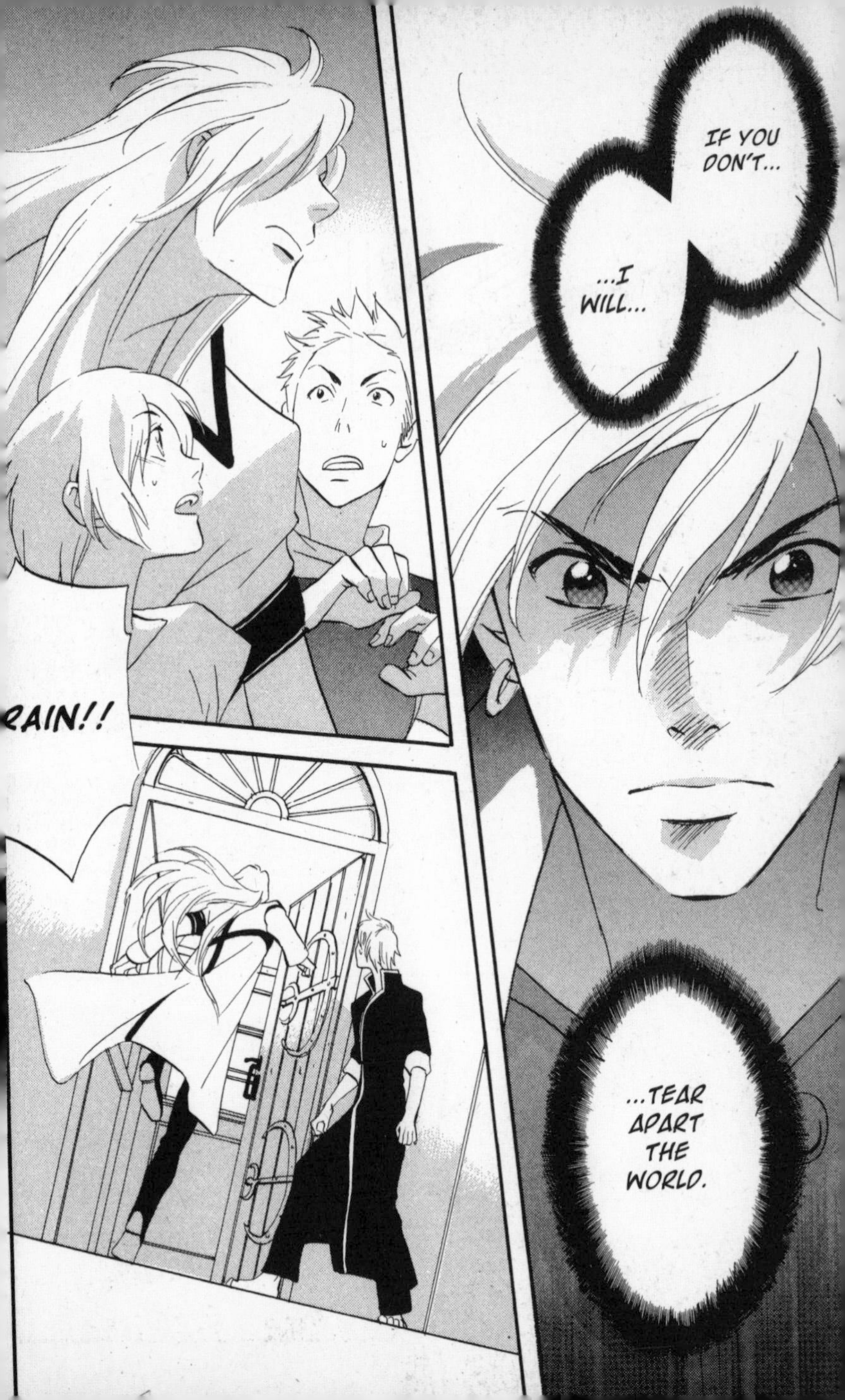
IF YOU DON'T...
...I WILL...
...TEAR APART THE WORLD.
RAIN!!

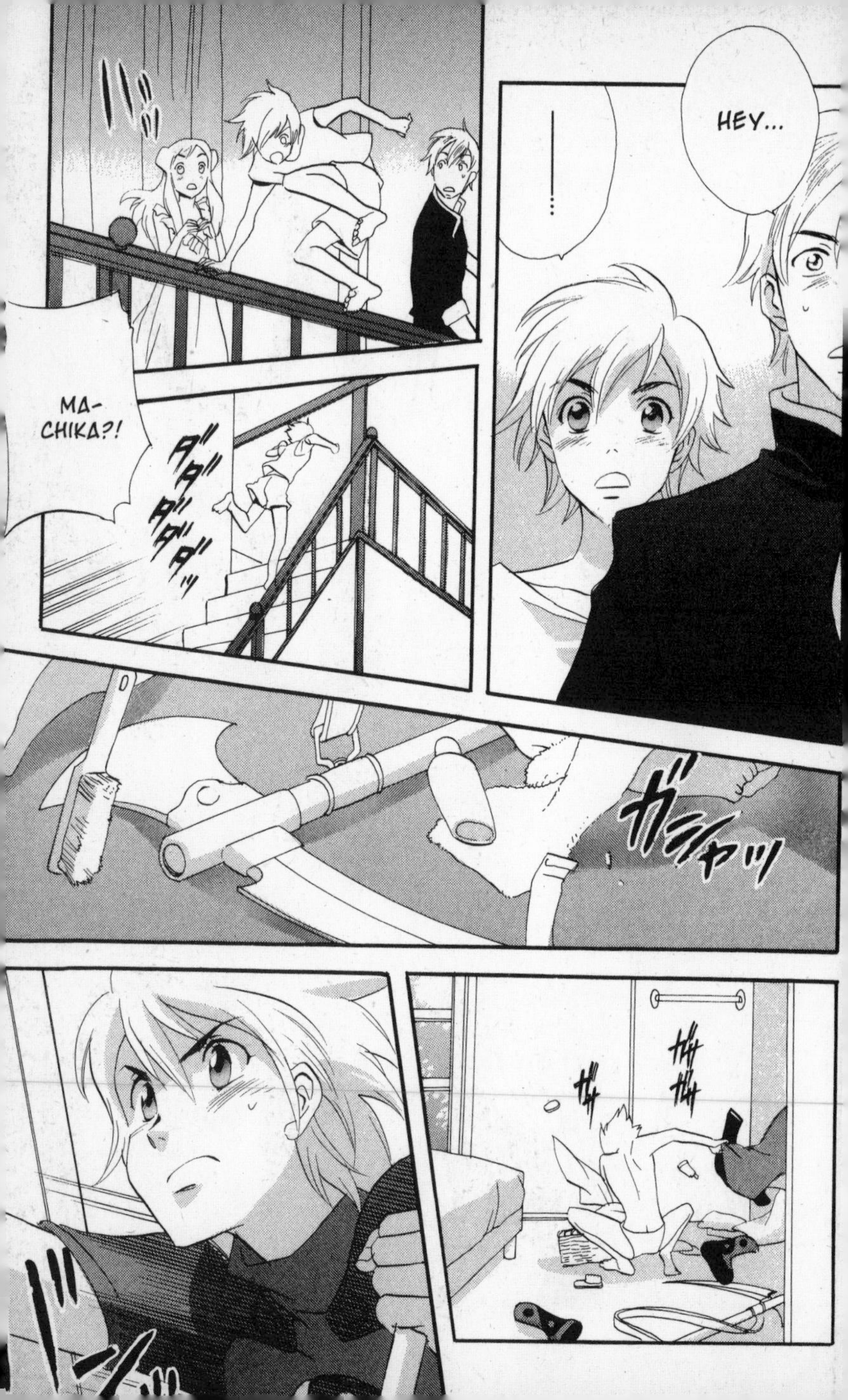

HEY...
......
MA-CHIKA?!
ガシャッ

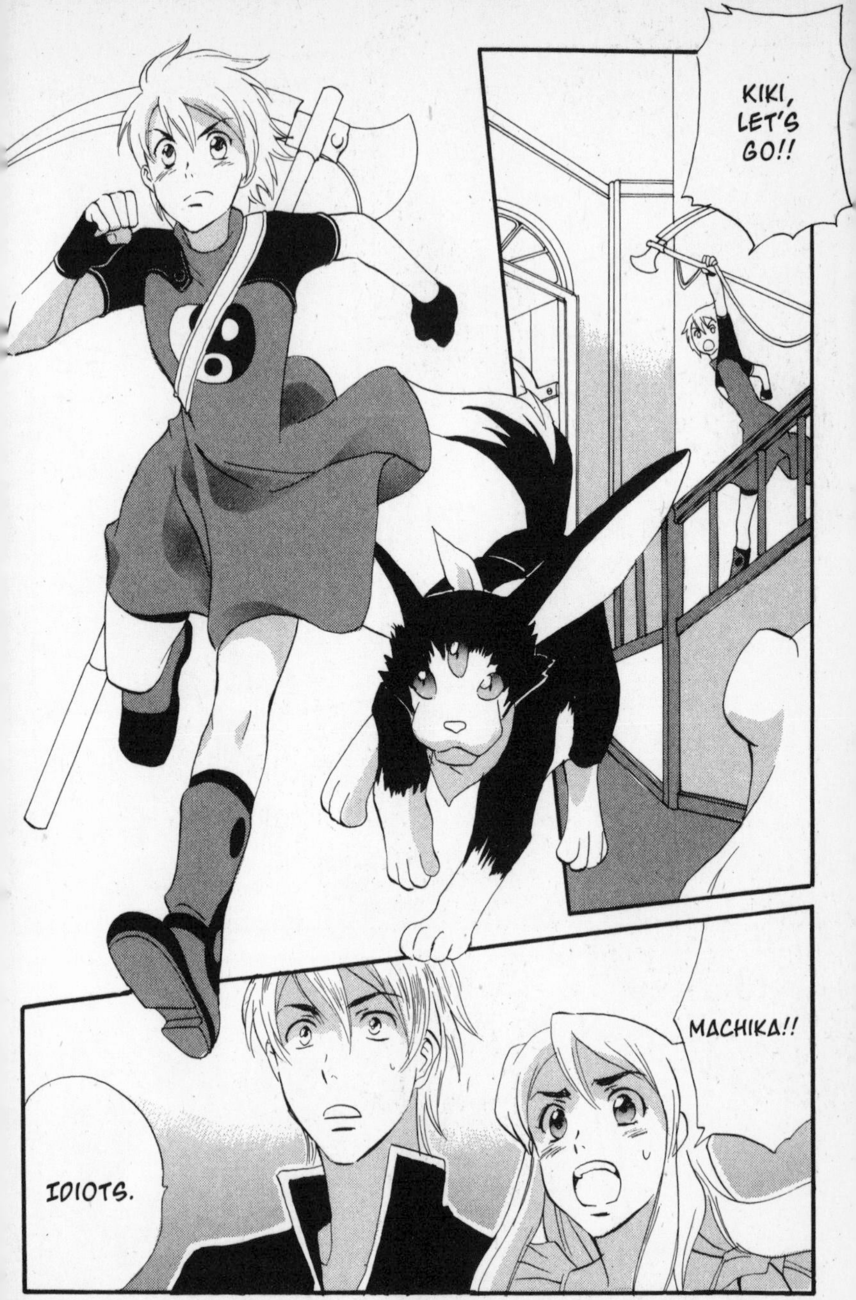
KIKI, LET'S GO!!
MACHIKA!!
IDIOTS.

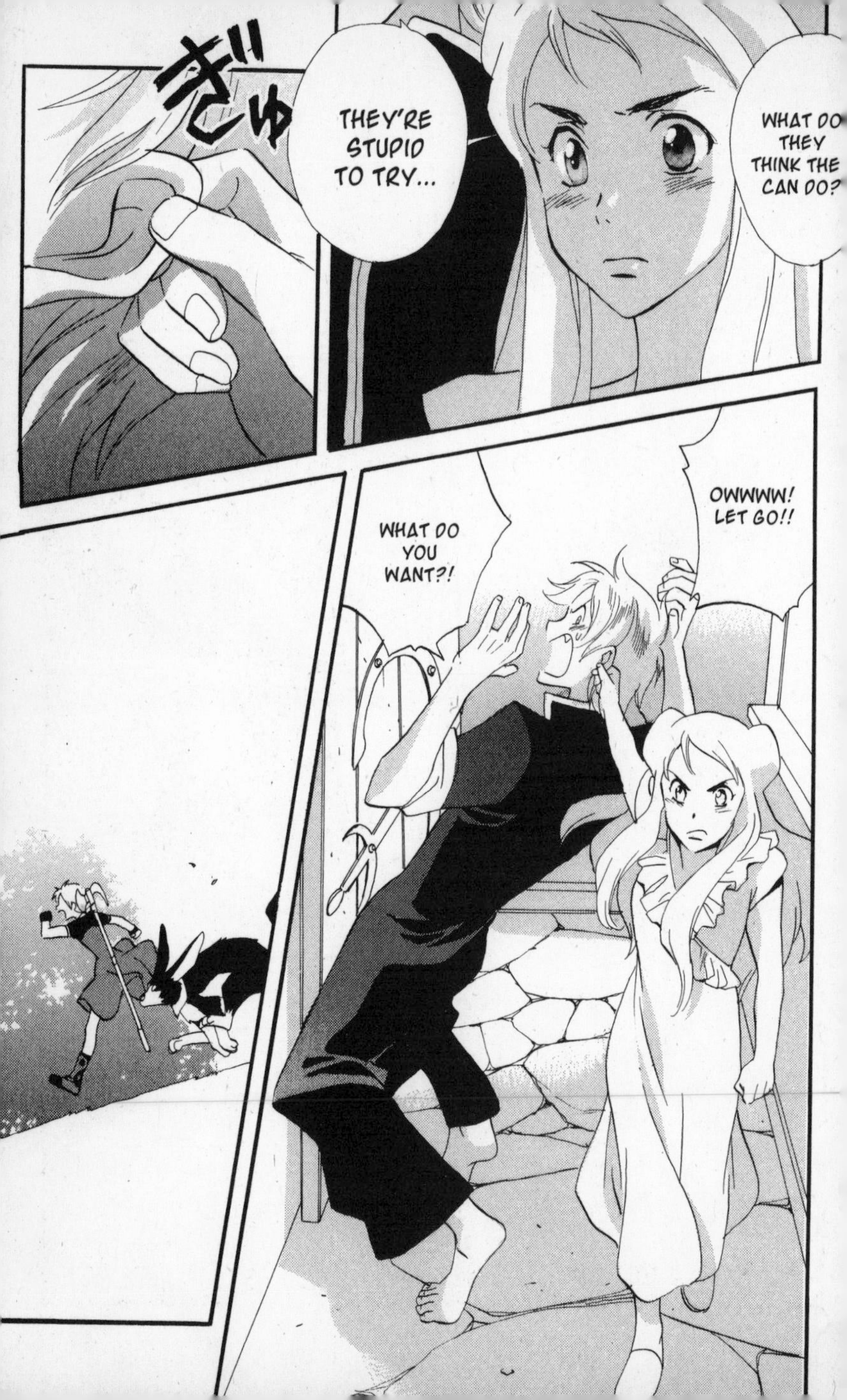
WHAT DO THEY THINK THE CAN DO?
THEY'RE STUPID TO TRY...
ぎゅ
OWWWW! LET GO!!
WHAT DO YOU WANT?!

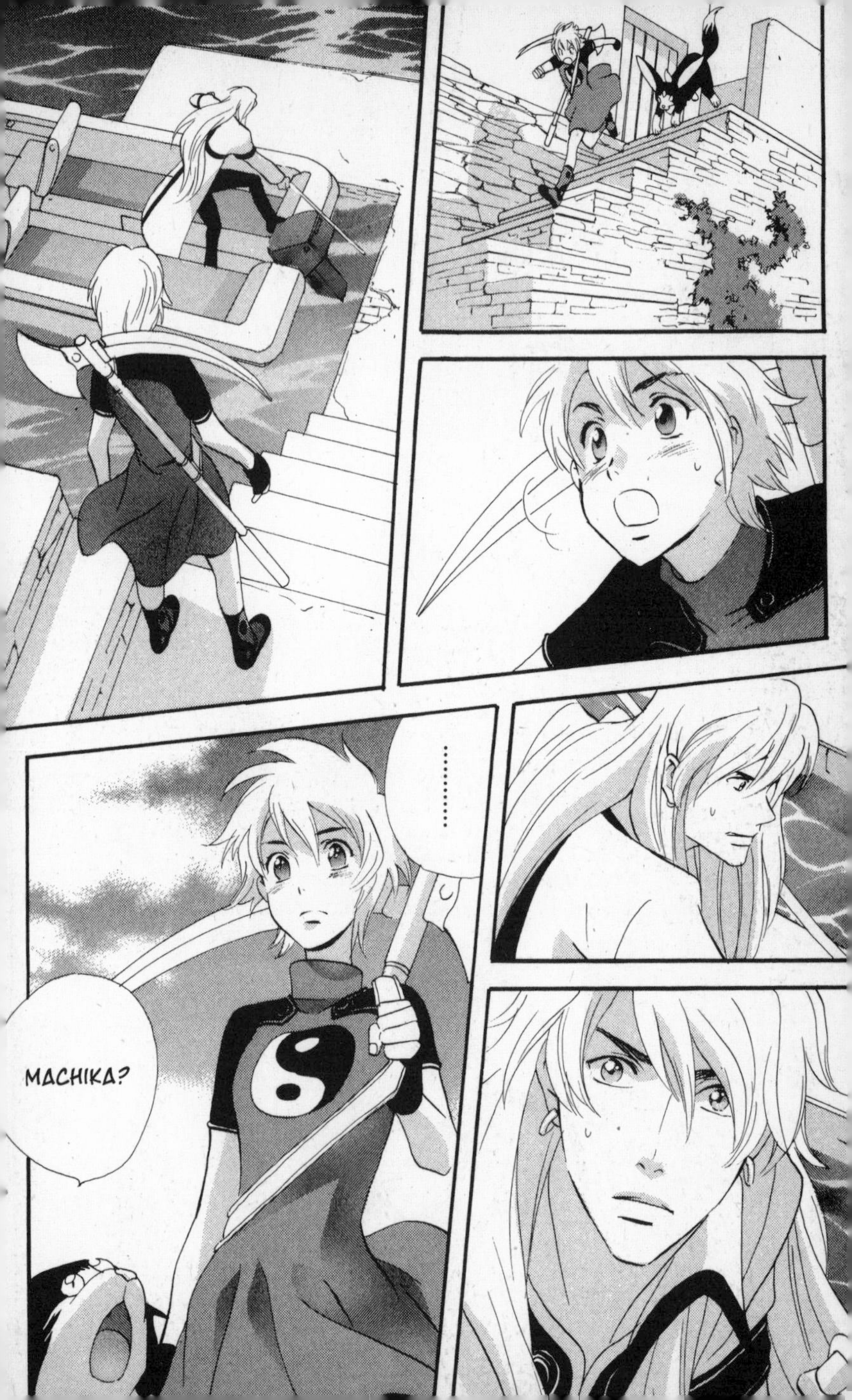
....
MACHIKA?

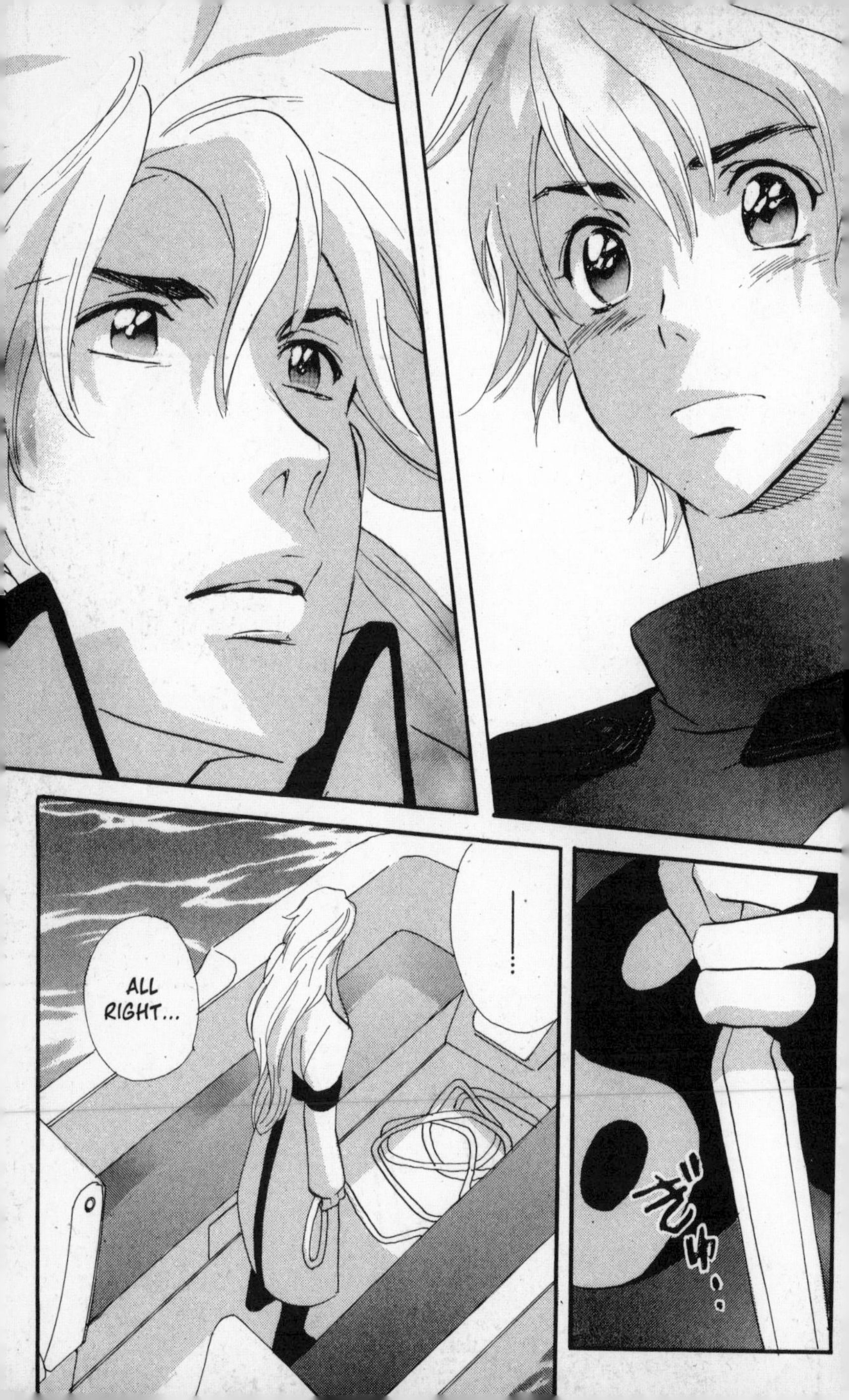
ぎゅ。。
—...
ALL RIGHT...

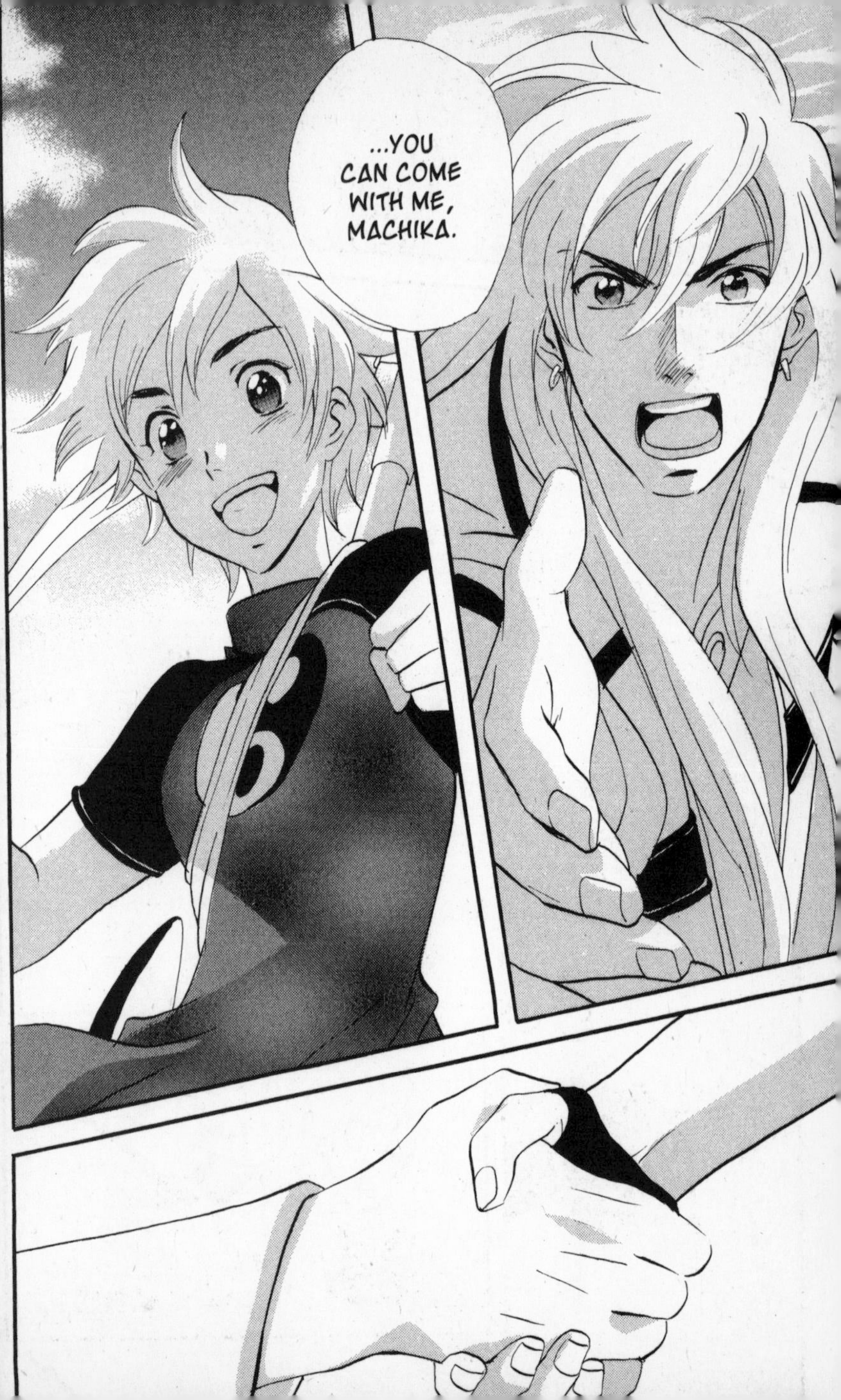
...YOU CAN COME WITH ME, MACHIKA.

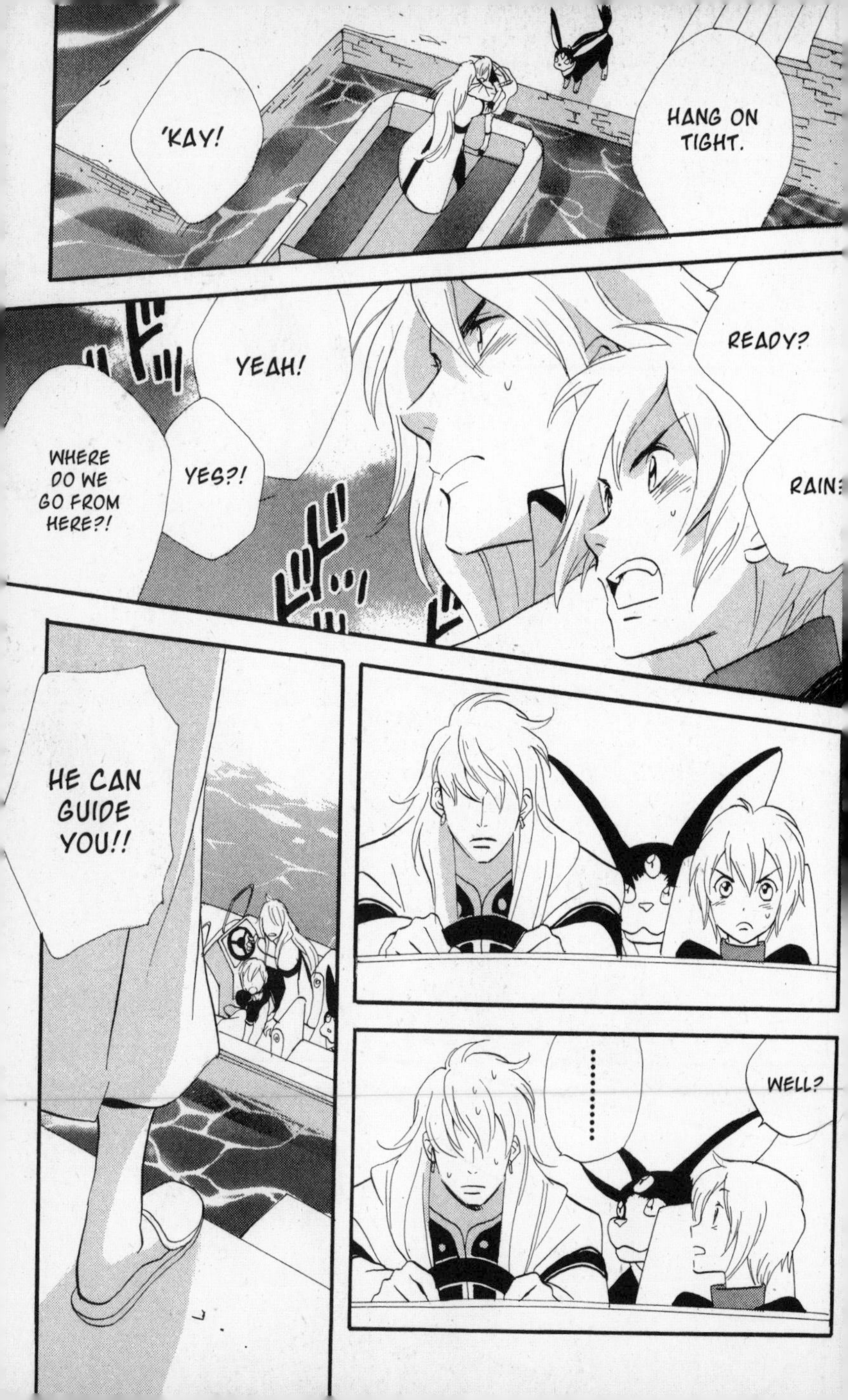
HANG ON TIGHT.
'KAY!
READY?
RAIN
YEAH!
YES?!
WHERE DO WE GO FROM HERE?!
WELL?
....
HE CAN GUIDE YOU!!

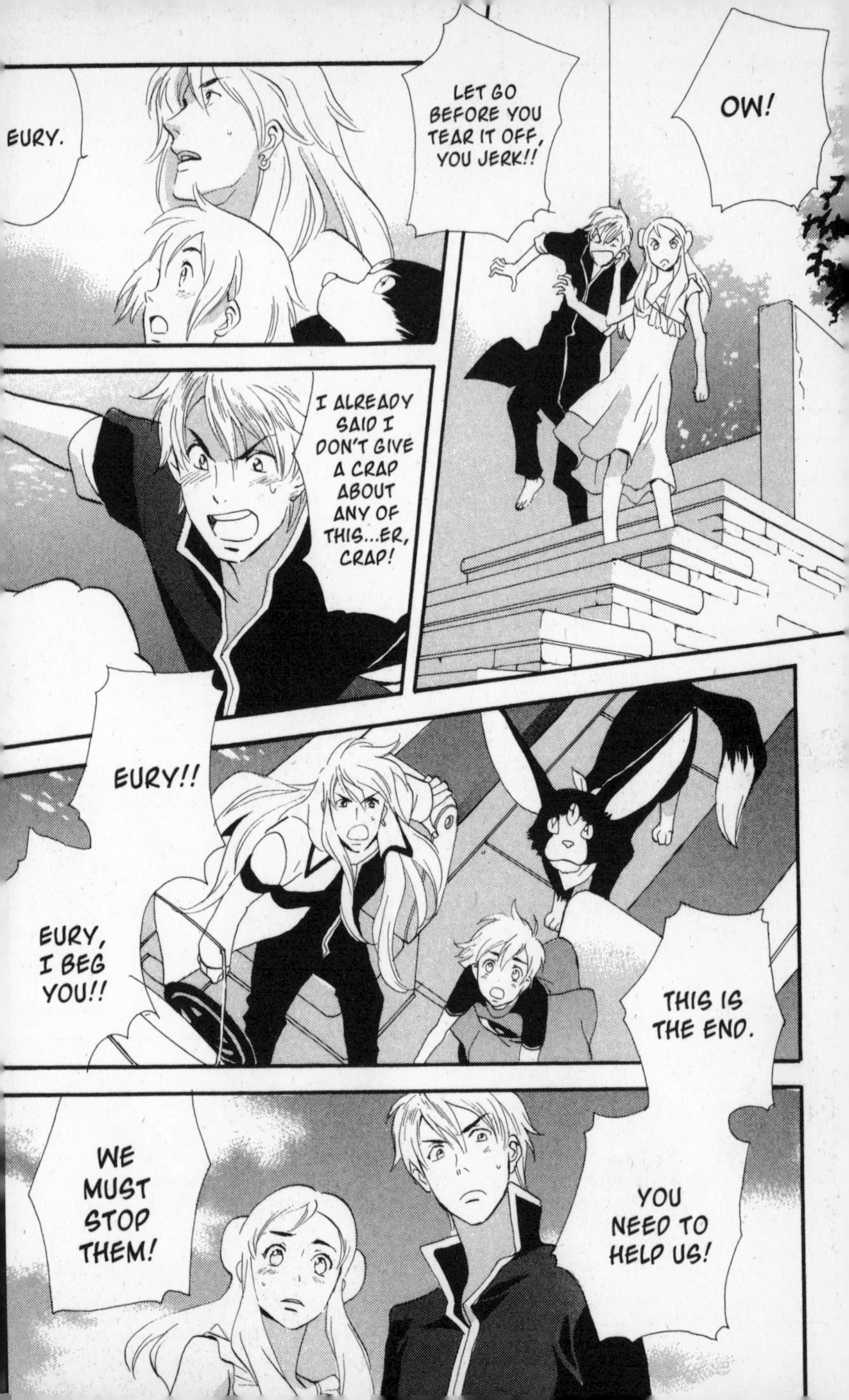
OW!
LET GO BEFORE YOU TEAR IT OFF, YOU JERK!!
EURY.
I ALREADY SAID I DON'T GIVE A CRAP ABOUT ANY OF THIS...ER, CRAP!
EURY!!
EURY, I BEG YOU!!
THIS IS THE END.
YOU NEED TO HELP US!
WE MUST STOP THEM!

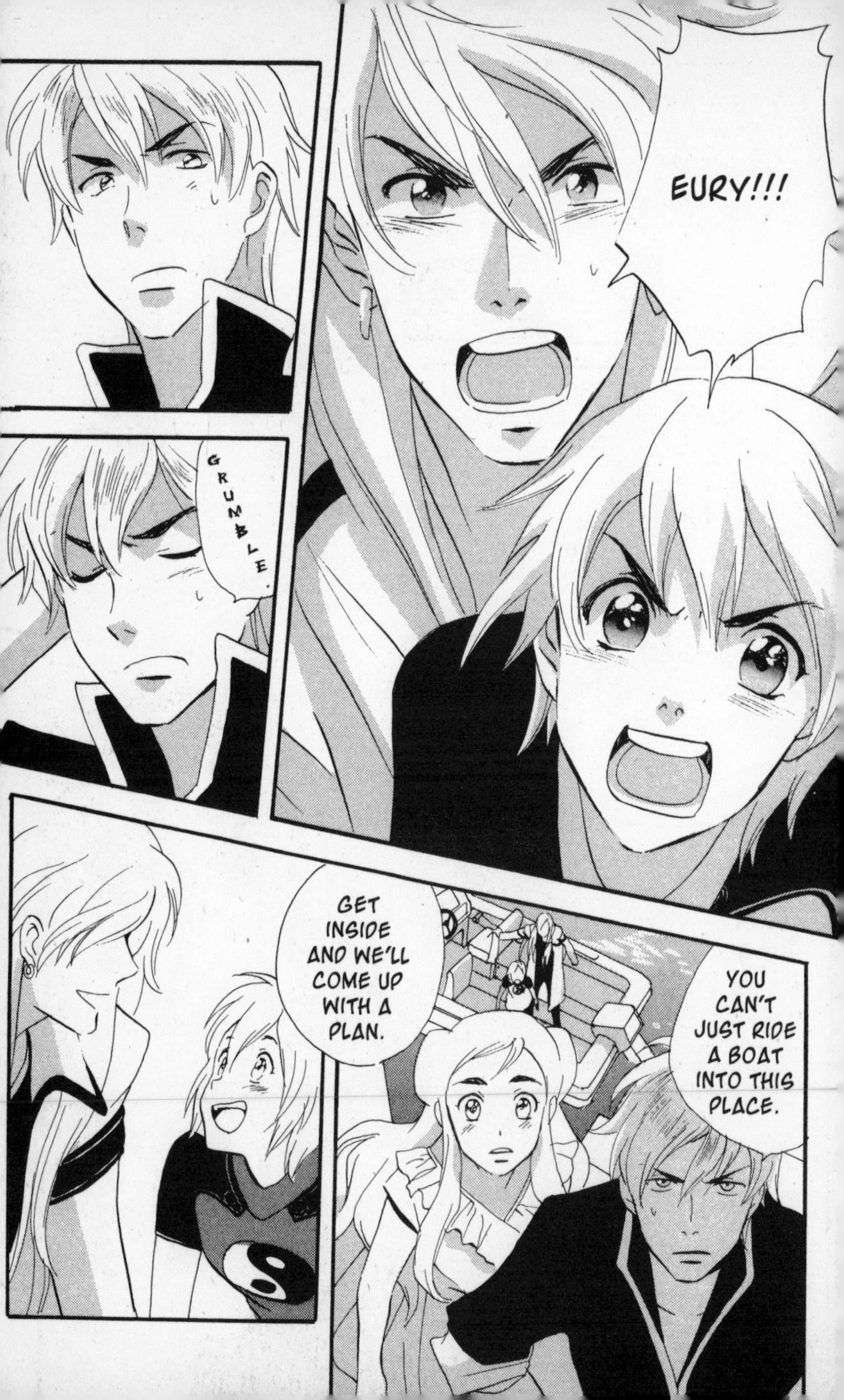
EURY!!!
GRUMBLE.
YOU CAN'T JUST RIDE A BOAT INTO THIS PLACE.
GET INSIDE AND WE'LL COME UP WITH A PLAN.

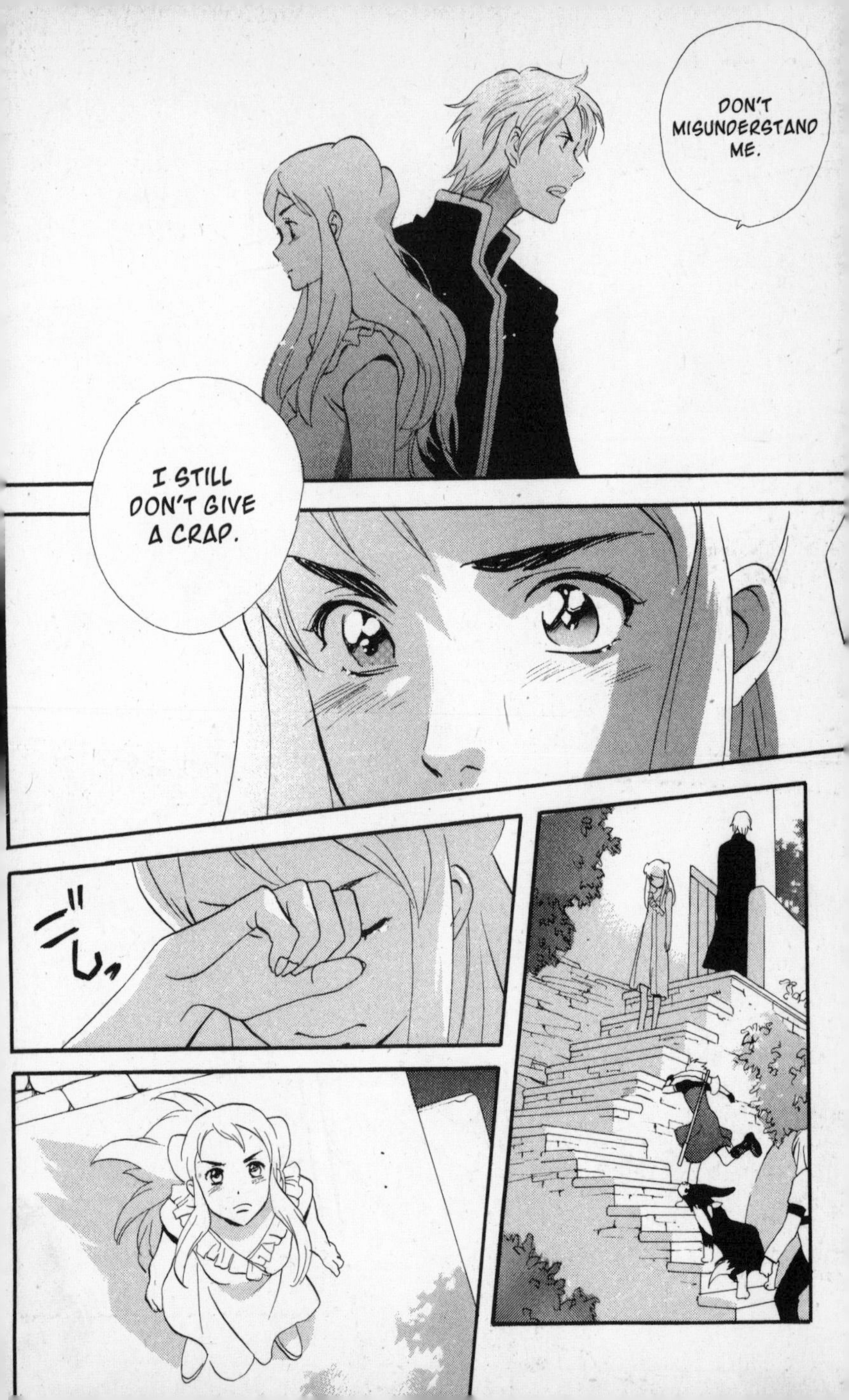
DON'T MISUNDERSTAND ME.
I STILL DON'T GIVE A CRAP.
ごしっ

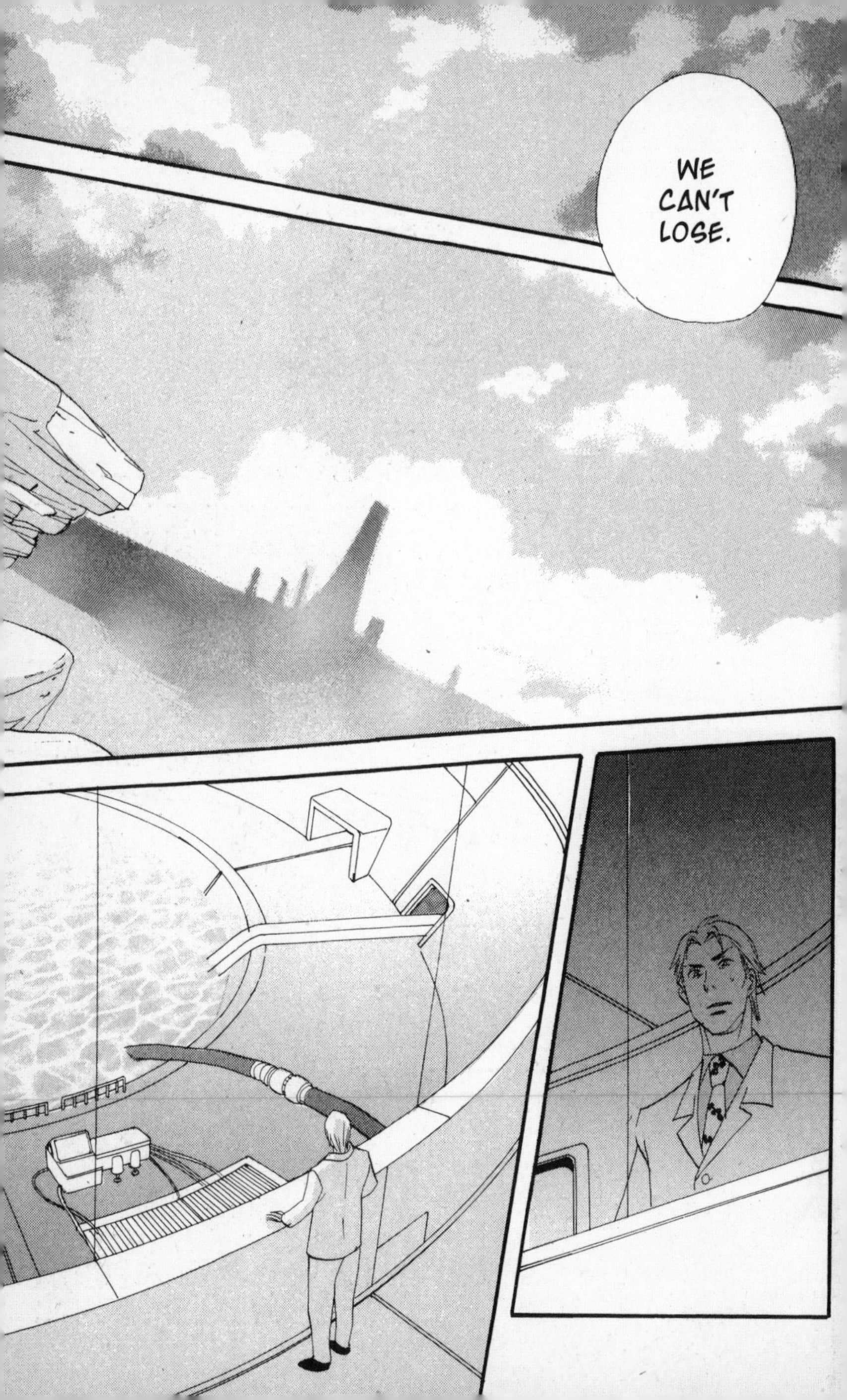
WE CAN'T LOSE.

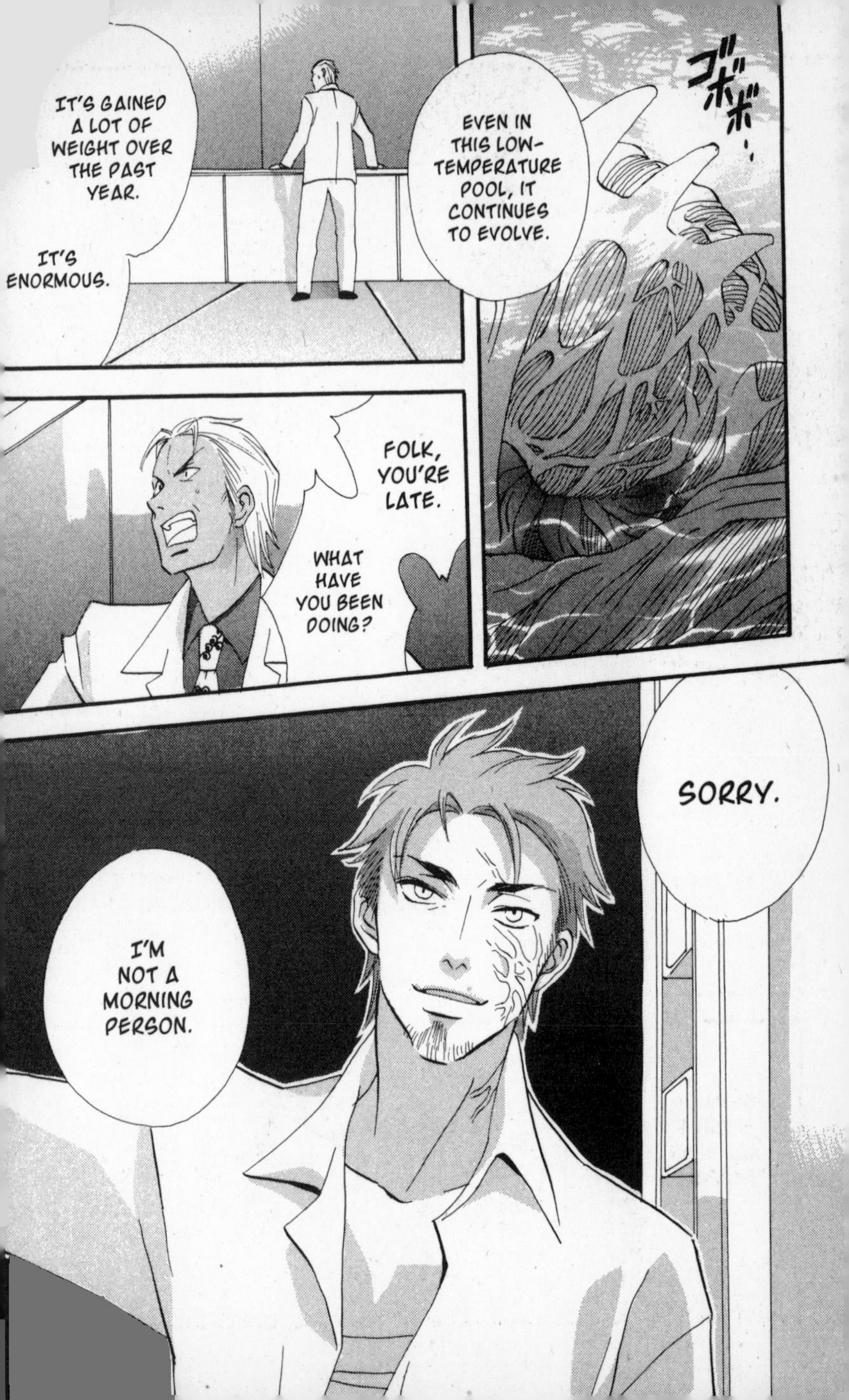
ゴボボ…
EVEN IN THIS LOW-TEMPERATURE POOL, IT CONTINUES TO EVOLVE.
IT'S GAINED A LOT OF WEIGHT OVER THE PAST YEAR.
IT'S ENORMOUS.
FOLK, YOU'RE LATE.
WHAT HAVE YOU BEEN DOING?
SORRY.
I'M NOT A MORNING PERSON.

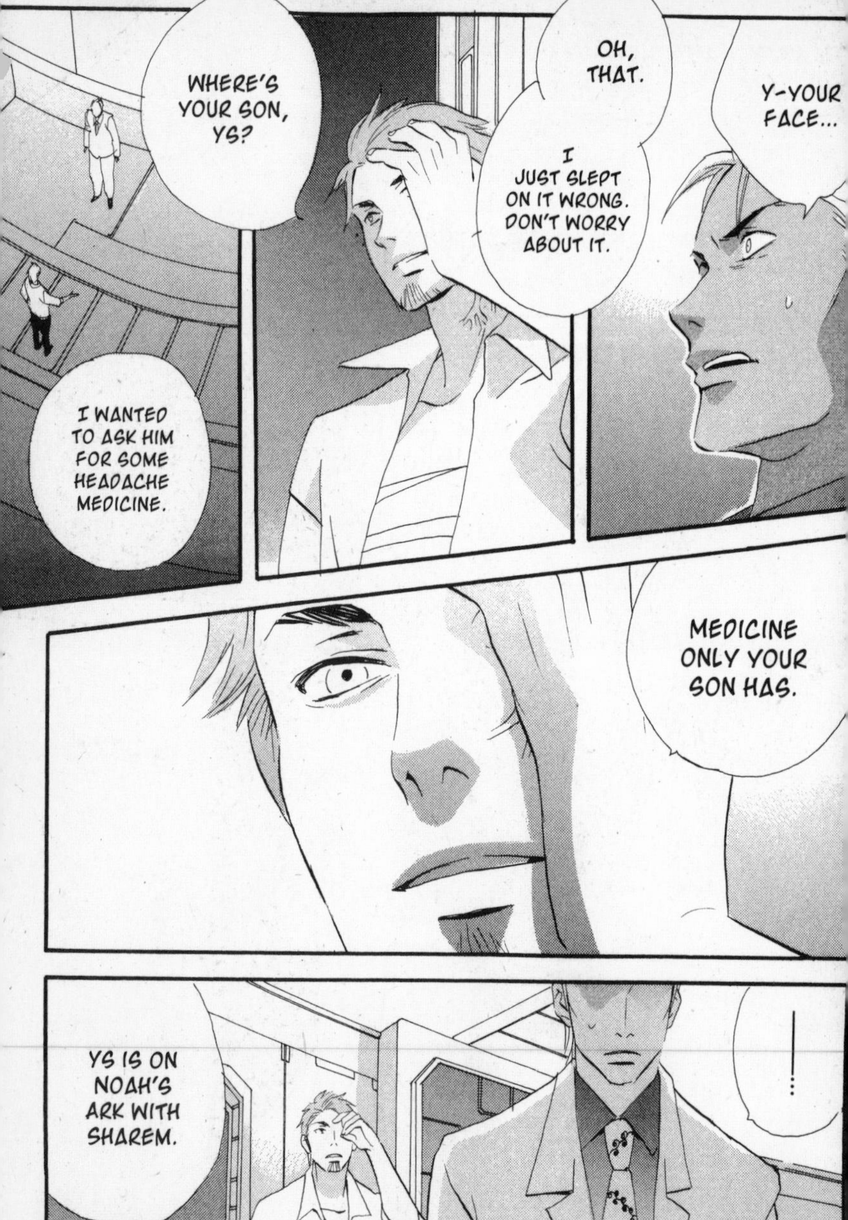
Y-YOUR FACE...
OH, THAT.
I JUST SLEPT ON IT WRONG. DON'T WORRY ABOUT IT.
WHERE'S YOUR SON, YS?
I WANTED TO ASK HIM FOR SOME HEADACHE MEDICINE.
MEDICINE ONLY YOUR SON HAS.
!...
YS IS ON NOAH'S ARK WITH SHAREM.

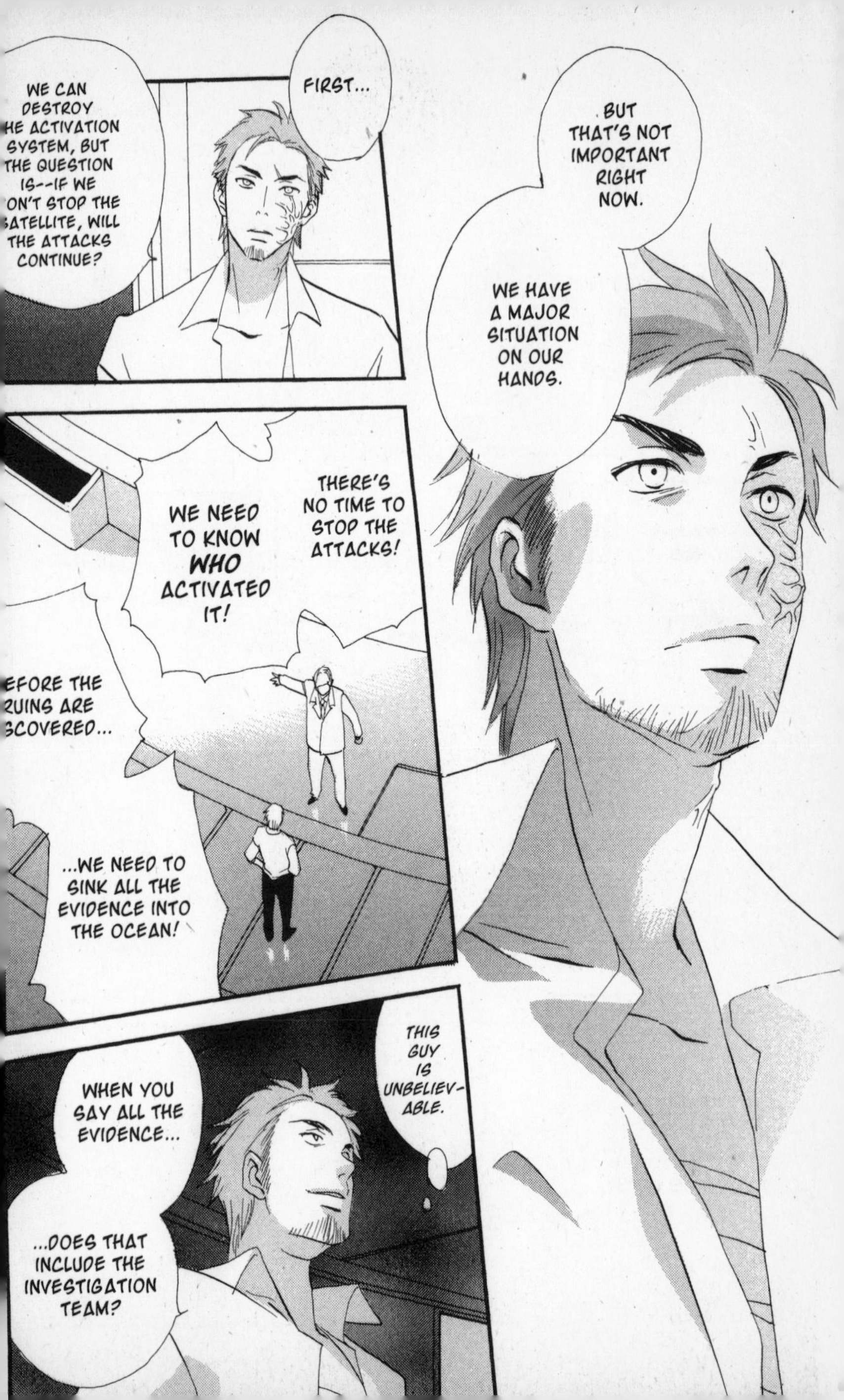
BUT THAT'S NOT IMPORTANT RIGHT NOW.
WE HAVE A MAJOR SITUATION ON OUR HANDS.
FIRST...
WE CAN DESTROY HE ACTIVATION SYSTEM, BUT THE QUESTION IS--IF WE ON'T STOP THE ATELLITE, WILL THE ATTACKS CONTINUE?
THERE'S NO TIME TO STOP THE ATTACKS!
WE NEED TO KNOW **WHO** ACTIVATED IT!
EFORE THE RUINS ARE SCOVERED...
...WE NEED TO SINK ALL THE EVIDENCE INTO THE OCEAN!
THIS GUY IS UNBELIEV-ABLE.
WHEN YOU SAY ALL THE EVIDENCE...
...DOES THAT INCLUDE THE INVESTIGATION TEAM?

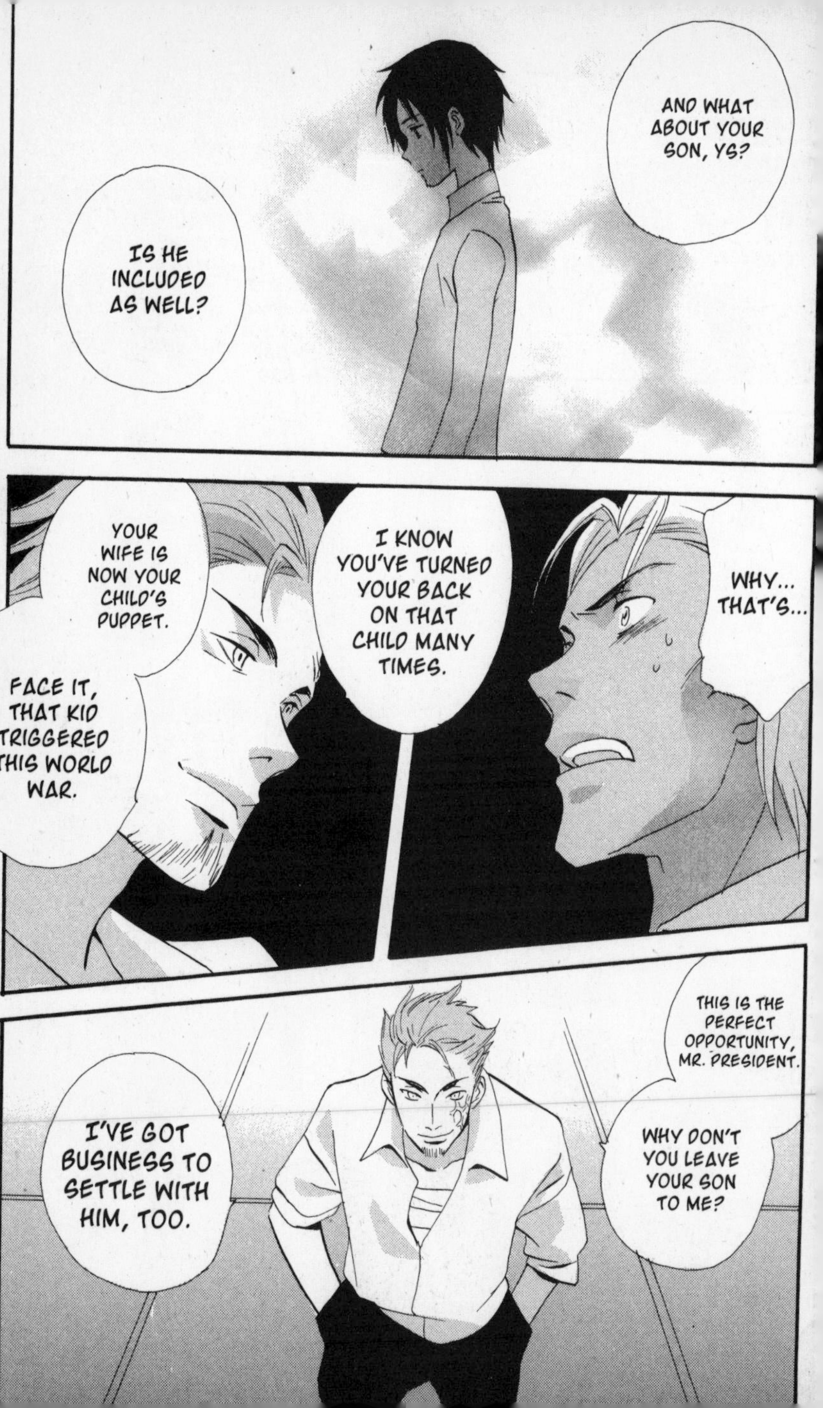
AND WHAT ABOUT YOUR SON, YS?
IS HE INCLUDED AS WELL?
WHY... THAT'S...
I KNOW YOU'VE TURNED YOUR BACK ON THAT CHILD MANY TIMES.
YOUR WIFE IS NOW YOUR CHILD'S PUPPET.
FACE IT, THAT KID TRIGGERED THIS WORLD WAR.
THIS IS THE PERFECT OPPORTUNITY, MR. PRESIDENT.
WHY DON'T YOU LEAVE YOUR SON TO ME?
I'VE GOT BUSINESS TO SETTLE WITH HIM, TOO.

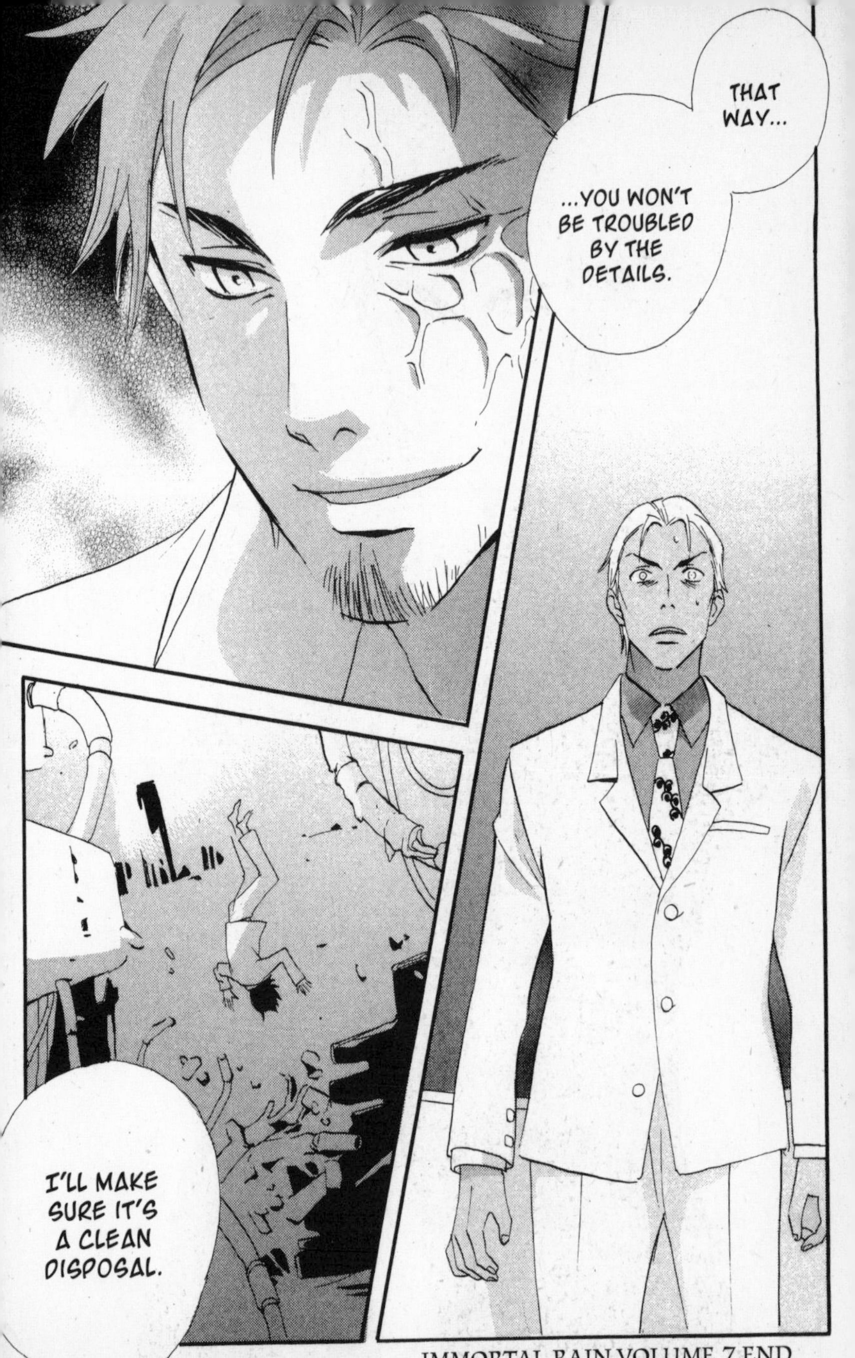
THAT WAY...
...YOU WON'T BE TROUBLED BY THE DETAILS.
I'LL MAKE SURE IT'S A CLEAN DISPOSAL.

IMMORTAL RAIN VOLUME 7 END

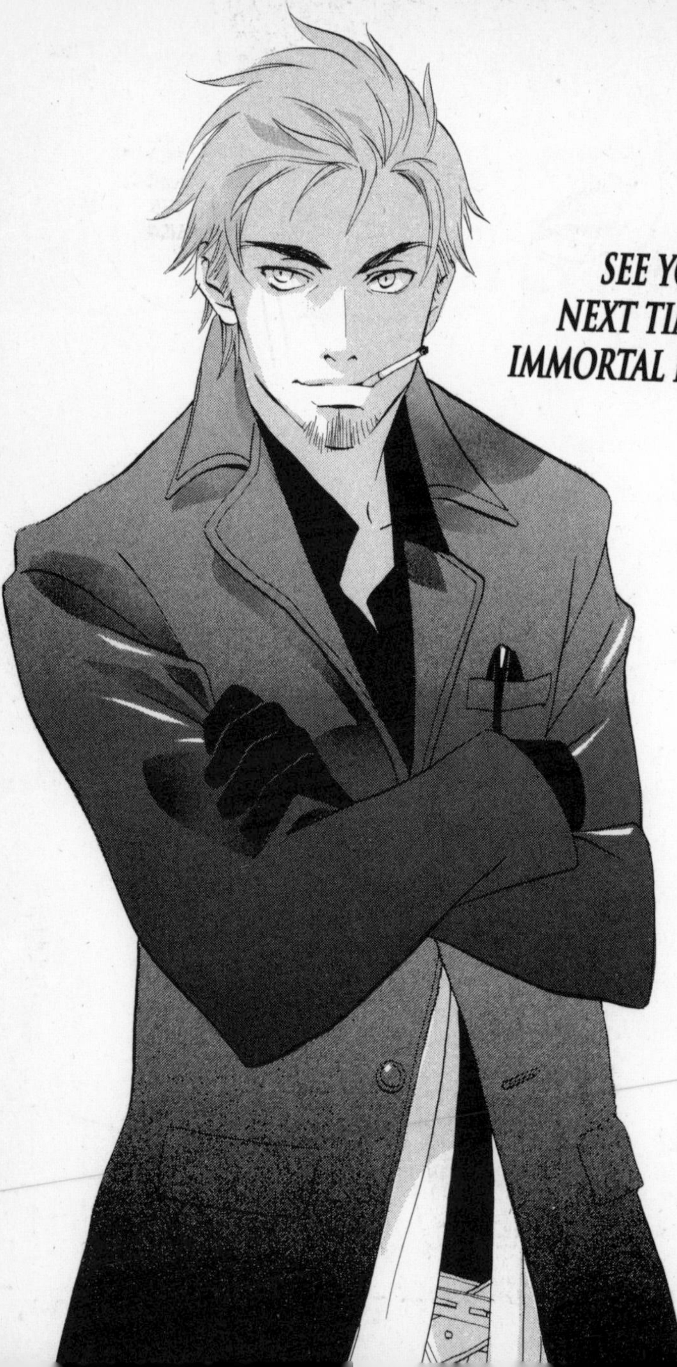

SEE YOU
NEXT TIME IN
IMMORTAL RAIN VIII

IN THE NEXT VOLUME OF

IMMORTAL RAIN

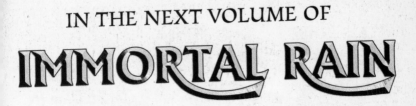

The duplicitous Dora Folk continues to plot and scheme, playing all sides against each other. Could he possibly succeed in the seemingly impossible—the death of Ys, the reborn Yuca Collabell? And what is that horrible creature inside the tank? How will Rain, Machika, Eury and the crew stop this madness once and for all?

Find out in the next installment of Immortal Rain!

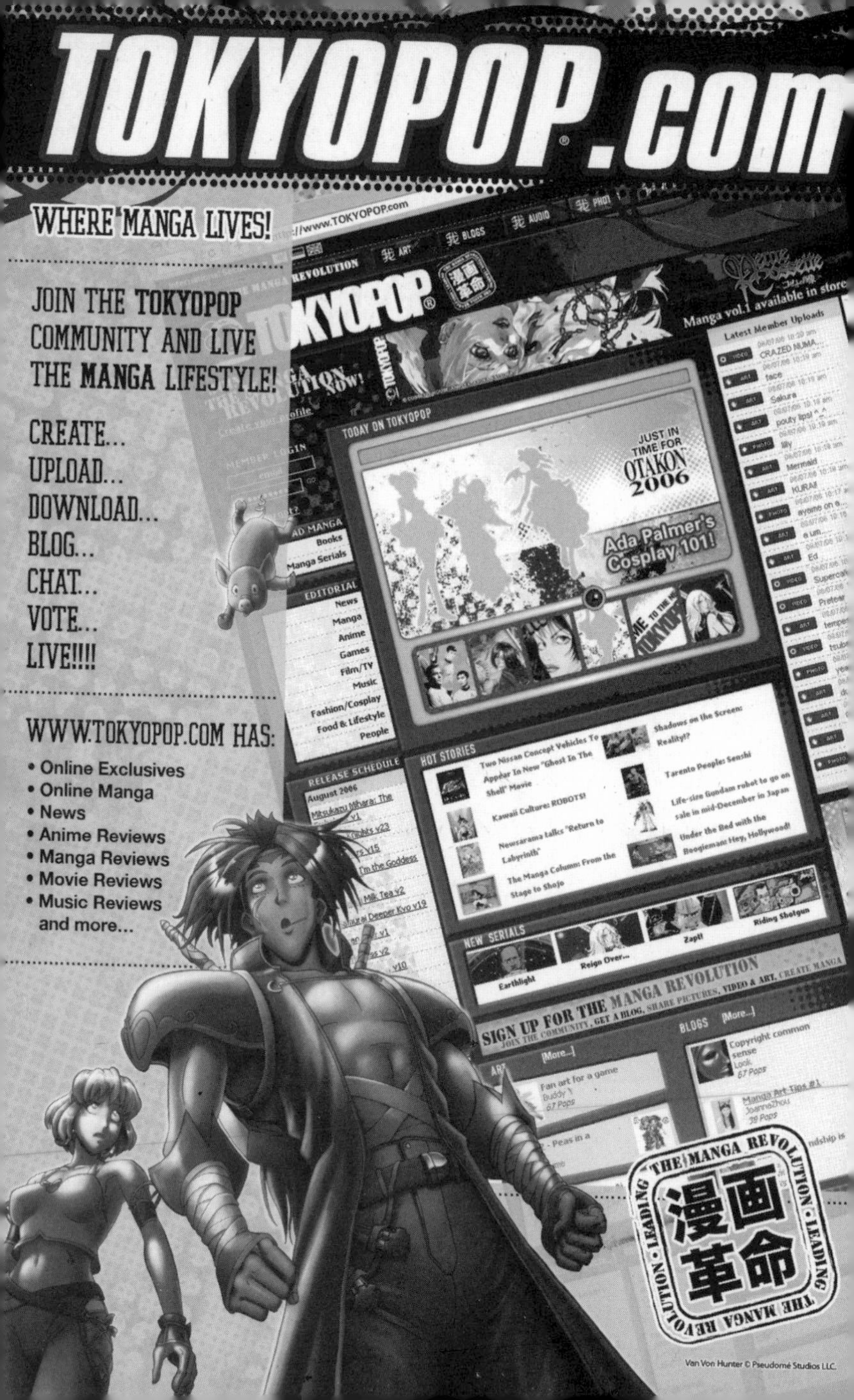
TOKYOPOP.com
WHERE MANGA LIVES!
JOIN THE TOKYOPOP COMMUNITY AND LIVE THE MANGA LIFESTYLE!
CREATE...
UPLOAD...
DOWNLOAD...
BLOG...
CHAT...
VOTE...
LIVE!!!!
WWW.TOKYOPOP.COM HAS:
• Online Exclusives
• Online Manga
• News
• Anime Reviews
• Manga Reviews
• Movie Reviews
• Music Reviews
and more...
THE MANGA REVOLUTION · LEADING
漫画革命
Van Von Hunter © Pseudomé Studios LLC.

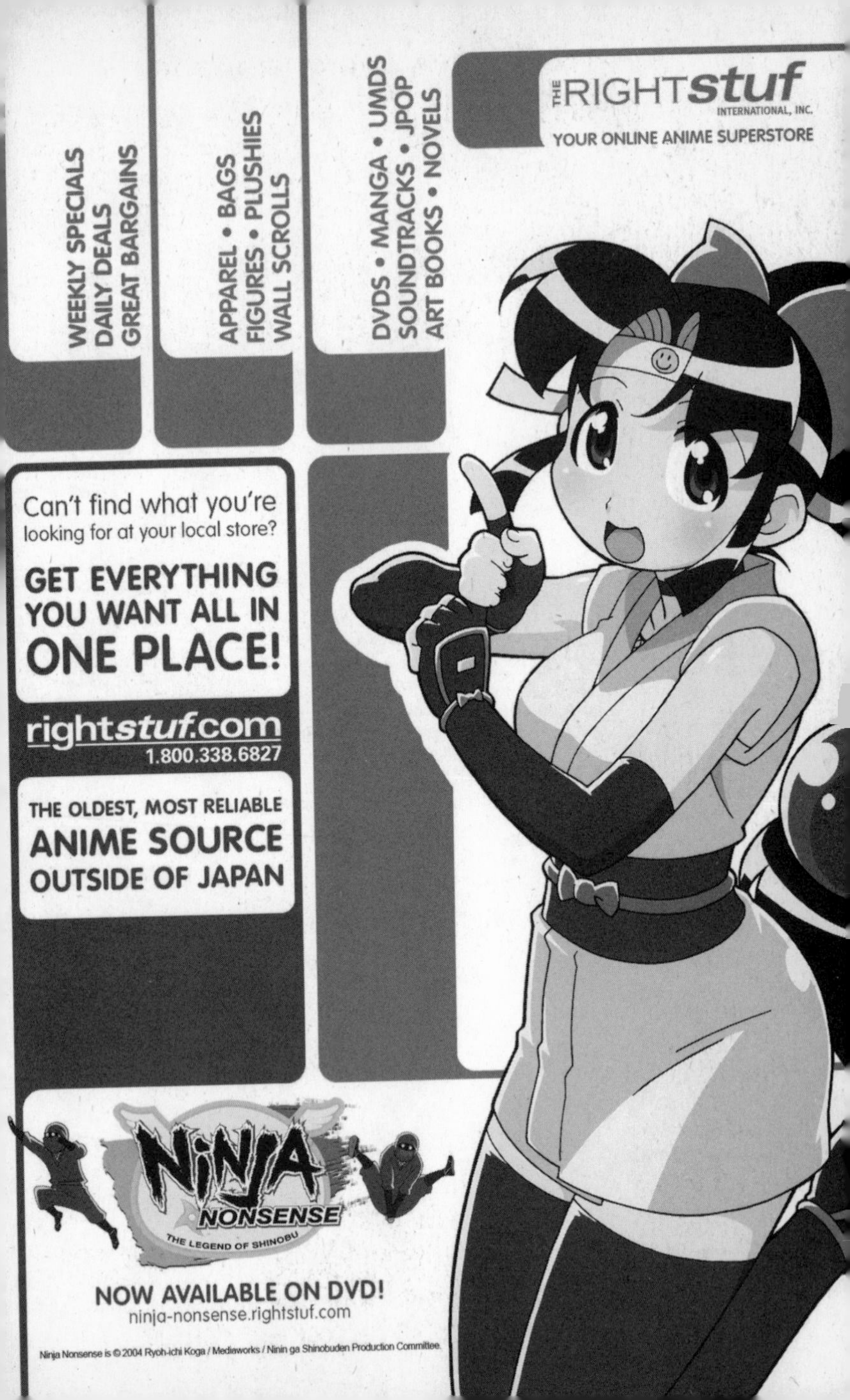
THE RIGHTstuf INTERNATIONAL, INC.
YOUR ONLINE ANIME SUPERSTORE
WEEKLY SPECIALS
DAILY DEALS
GREAT BARGAINS
APPAREL • BAGS
FIGURES • PLUSHIES
WALL SCROLLS
DVDS • MANGA • UMDS
SOUNDTRACKS • JPOP
ART BOOKS • NOVELS
Can't find what you're looking for at your local store?
GET EVERYTHING YOU WANT ALL IN ONE PLACE!
rightstuf.com
1.800.338.6827
THE OLDEST, MOST RELIABLE ANIME SOURCE OUTSIDE OF JAPAN
NINJA NONSENSE
THE LEGEND OF SHINOBU
NOW AVAILABLE ON DVD!
ninja-nonsense.rightstuf.com
Ninja Nonsense is © 2004 Ryoh-ichi Koga / Mediaworks / Ninin ga Shinobuden Production Committee.

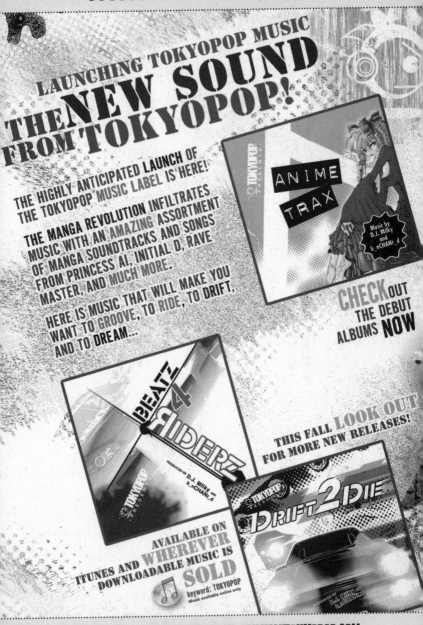